Children's Literature
Volume 29

Founder and Senior Editor: Francelia Butler (1913–98)

Editor-in-Chief: R. H. W. Dillard

Editors: Elizabeth Lennox Keyser and Julie Pfeiffer

Editorial Assistant: Jennifer Bolton

Book Review Editor: Christine Doyle

Advisory Board: Janice M. Alberghene, Ruth B. Bottigheimer, Beverly Lyon Clark, Margaret Higonnet, U. C. Knoepflmacher, Alison Lurie, Roderick McGillis, Mitzi Myers, Kathy Piehl (representing the ChLA), Albert J. Solnit, M.D.

Consultants for Volume 29: Gillian Adams, T. J. Anderson, Brian Attebery, Sandra Beckett, Phyllis Bixler, George Bodmer, Ruth B. Bottigheimer, Stephen Canham, Ben Clark, Beverly Lyon Clark, Paula Connolly, Christine Doyle, Greg Eiselein, Elizabeth Epperly, Richard Flynn, Elizabeth Rose Gruner, Nancy Huse, Kenneth Kidd, Lois Kuznets, Valerie Lastinger, Claire Malarte-Feldman, Jean I. Marsden, Perry Nodelman, Lissa Paul, Anne Phillips, Jerry Phillips, Mary S. Pollock, Suzanne Rahn, Mavis Reimer, David Russell, Donelle Ruwe, Sharon Scrapple, Carolyn Sigler, Katherine Capshaw Smith, Sharon Smulders, Joe Stanton, Morag Styles, Jan Susina, Tom Travisano, Roberta Seelinger Trites, Ian Wojcik-Andrews

The editors gratefully acknowledge support from Hollins University.

Volume 29

Annual of
The Modern Language Association
Division on Children's Literature
and The Children's Literature
Association

Yale University Press

New Haven and London

2001

Children's Literature

Published with assistance from the Louis Stern Memorial Fund.

Manuscripts submitted should conform to the style in this issue. An original on non-erasable bond with a self-addressed envelope, and return postage, or submission as an e-mail attachment (MS Word) is requested. Yale University Press requires double-spacing throughout text and notes as well as unjustified margins. Writers of accepted manuscripts should be prepared to submit final versions of their essays on computer disk in Word 97 or Rich Text Format.

Editorial correspondence should be addressed to The Editors, *Children's Literature,* Hollins University, P.O. Box 9677, Roanoke, VA 24020 or to child.lit@hollins.edu

Volumes 1–7 of *Children's Literature* can be obtained directly from Susan Wandell, The Children's Literature Foundation, P.O. Box 94, Windham Center, CT 06280. Volumes 8–28 can be obtained from Yale University Press, P.O. Box 209040, New Haven, CT 06520–9040, or from Yale University Press, 23 Pond Street, Hampstead, London NW3 2PN, England.

Set in Baskerville type by Tseng Information Systems, Inc., Durham, N.C.
Printed in the United States of America by Vail-Ballou Press, Binghamton, N.Y.

Library of Congress catalog card number: 79-66588
ISBN: 0-300-08891-4 (cloth); 0-300-08892-2 (pbk.); ISSN 0092-8208

A catalogue record for this book is available from the British Library.

The paper in this book meets the guidelines for permanence and durability of the Committee on Production Guidelines for Book Longevity of the Council on Library Resources.

10   9   8   7   6   5   4   3   2   1

Contents

From the Editors

Volume 29 of *Children's Literature* brings together essays on literature spanning two centuries. What these essays suggest is that ideology—its creation, its reinforcement, its critique—remains as central to children's literary studies as ever.

The ideological focuses that appear in this volume, however, are tremendously varied. Donelle Ruwe challenges twentieth-century understandings of "the romantic ideology" with her analysis of Sarah Trimmer's work. Ruwe claims that Trimmer embodies a self-confidence and rejection of the imagination that conflict with our assumptions about romanticism and the nineteenth-century female artist. In her essay on nineteenth-century France, Ruth Carver Capasso uses *La Bibliothèque Rose* as an example of how philanthropy literature was used to shape class and gender identity for children. Both of these essays focus on the significance that educating children, and thus the formation of ideology, holds in the nineteenth century.

In another essay on a nineteenth-century text, Alcott's *Little Women*, Ken Parille argues, like Ruwe, that twentieth-century feminist ideologies may lead to misreadings of nineteenth-century ideologies. In particular, Parille claims that the "ethic of submission" determines Laurie's roles as much as it does those of the little women.

Claudia Nelson's essay on shifting representations of the orphan in American literature published between 1870 and 1930 places changing ideologies in the context of a changing culture. Nelson traces the evolution of the orphan from a source of labor to an individual with his or her own needs. The texts Nelson examines, however, often critique the social structure they reflect by emphasizing the orphan's transformative function. Though the adults in orphan fiction may see the children they take on in terms of the physical labor they will contribute to the household, the orphan's real task turns out to be the emotional one of healing the adult world (think, for example, of *Anne of Green Gables*). Kate Lawson's essay on the *Emily* trilogy looks more closely at Montgomery's depiction of the orphan as artist. Lawson uses conflated images of home and loss to reveal the anxiety that lurks in Emily's moments of epiphany. In contrast to the Wordsworthian notion of art as "abundant recompense" for the loss of childhood, Lawson sees artistic revelation as linked to trauma in Montgomery's depiction of the child's experience of the uncanny.

The next essays in this volume focus explicitly on the ways that language and pictures shape ideology. Fern Kory's essay on the *Brownies' Book* considers the "peculiar" situation of early twentieth-century African Americans from the perspective of the rhetorical strategy of "signifying." Kory uses the fairy tales published in this children's magazine as examples of the refashioning of children's literature, as Henry Louis Gates says, " 'authentically,' with a Black difference." Her work suggests that these tales required African American children to see themselves both as outside of Eurocentric fairy tales and as participants in a tradition of childhood culture.

Laura B. Comoletti and Michael D. C. Drout ask similar questions based on a very different set of texts. Their analysis of Ursula K. Le Guin's Earthsea tetralogy asks how it is that knowledge and self-knowledge lead to power and wisdom. They, like Kory, claim that it is language, "doing things with words," that allows Le Guin to assert female power in *Tehanu* without overturning the social structure she constructed in the earlier Earthsea books.

In an increasingly video-driven culture, it seems essential to look at the roles visual images play in constructing and critiquing ideology. The next two essays do just that by using illustration to critique dominant ideologies. Philip Nel, with his analysis of Crockett Johnson, returns to the link between ideology and imagination that Ruwe identifies in the nineteenth century. Instead of focusing on self-knowledge, as Kory, Comoletti, and Drout do, Nel asks the question: "how do you know what's real?" He suggests that Crockett's apparently simple work provokes larger questions about U.S. policy and society. Nel's essay makes explicit ideological issues that are implicit in most of the essays in this volume: the concern that what appears to be natural may instead be social and the belief that the artist can create (rather than simply reflect) reality. Sandra Beckett extends Nel's work on parody to an analysis of contemporary picture books. She, like Ruwe and Capasso, suggests that children are particularly receptive to parody because their ideological framework is still only partially formed. Unlike nineteenth-century children, "the Simpsons generation" has the advantage of their experience of TV parody.

The last of the essays in this volume, Clare Bradford's witty discussion of postcolonialism, asks that we remain conscious of the ways that old ideologies hang on even as we see ourselves moving beyond them. Though recognizing that what we once held as "truth" is in fact ideology is the first step away from hegemony, ideology persists because it feels inevitable, necessary, natural. The temptation to divide the world into binary oppositions, to retain conceptual notions of imperialism even as we decry literal imperialism, is both reflected and parodied in the books Bradford examines. Bradford's emphasis on the persistence of colonial ideologies is balanced by her examples of resistant voices; the voices of the supposedly "muted" people who have lost their cultures ring loud and clear in her essay.

As a whole, this volume of *Children's Literature* attempts to add new voices, new perspectives, to the conversation about literature, art, and children. These voices are, of course, engaged with many others: the scholars whose work directly or indirectly provides a foundation for new interpretations and the readers whose responses to these essays often shaped dramatically the versions you see here. Thanks to all who contributed to another fine volume!

Julie Pfeiffer and Elizabeth Lennox Keyser

Articles

Guarding the British Bible from Rousseau: Sarah Trimmer, William Godwin, and the Pedagogical Periodical

Donelle Ruwe

Sarah Kirby Trimmer produced biblical and historical prints, educational tracts, children's books, textbooks, religious commentaries, numerous best-selling editions of the Bible, a spiritual autobiography, and two magazines.[1] She founded Sunday schools and an industrial school. Her still-popular fable of Robin Redbreast defined the genre of the children's animal allegory and became the text with which all other animal fables contended. She knew Johnson, Hogarth, and Gainsborough[2] and was among the privileged few to be mocked by Byron and damned by Charles Lamb. Always she wrote with an extraordinary self-confidence and even, at times, with what appears to be overconfidence. For example, included in the two-volume memoirs of her life is the following letter to "Mrs. S—":

> During my early years I relied upon the judgment, and took up the opinions of a parent, who had made Polemic Divinity his particular study, and who cautioned me against following his example in that particular, as he said it had at times greatly disturbed and perplexed his mind, though it ended at last in a firm belief of the doctrines of the Established Church. . . . Convinced that he had chosen the right way, [I] resolved to obey his injunctions, by avoiding those publications which he warned me against; and when I came to years of maturity, instead of giving up my mind to researches into the various opinions of human beings, [I] set myself seriously to examine the principles in which I had been edu-

Children's Literature 29, ed. Elizabeth Lennox Keyser and Julie Pfeiffer (Yale University Press, © 2001 Hollins University).

cated, by the Word of God. This I have repeatedly done with the
most perfect satisfaction; and having no doubts, why should I seek
to raise them? I have, it is true, read many books of divinity; but
very few, that I can recollect, of a controversial nature. If I found
it necessary to read one side of the argument, I should think it in-
cumbent upon me to read the other; but surely what is requisite
in merely worldly affairs, ought not to be extended to a subject
in which we have an infallible guide—the word of God; on that
word then, I choose to build my faith, in preference to any human
authority whatever. (*Some Account* 1.91–92)

This letter is indeed uncomfortable reading. Perhaps it, and countless
other similar examples from Trimmer's writings, explains why scholars of British romanticism as well as feminists working to recuperate
women writers have, in large measure, avoided Trimmer. It is difficult
to praise Trimmer's scholarship and the theological rigor of her writings when she publicly professes never to have questioned her own beliefs. For feminists who dedicate limited time, energy, and other resources to the ongoing project of recovering women authors, there
are more appealing women writers to recuperate. Indeed, in terms of
our project of creating women's literary history, Trimmer can be read
as a useful figure who allows us to examine the limits of our recovery
efforts. As Margaret Ezell reminds us, Anglo-American feminism cele-
brates the authors who represent contemporary feminist values and
overlooks others who are difficult to fit into our paradigms for reading
women's texts.[3]

At the same time, Trimmer has fared little better in the historiog-
raphy of children's literature: as Mitzi Myers and William McCarthy
have compellingly documented, the story of how children's literature
developed has been a "story almost Manichaean in its need to dichoto-
mize, and then to extol or damn its dichotomized terms" (McCarthy
198). Authors who "instruct" children are aligned with an oppressive
hegemony in contrast to an ongoing celebration of texts considered
imaginative, pleasurable, delightful, or playful. In other words, fairy
tales and nonsense rhymes are superior to textbooks no matter how
innovative the textbook and how derivative the tale. Myers argues that
this genre dichotomizing is also explicitly gendered. She traces the ongoing excoriation of pedagogical writings (and women pedagogues)
to a reinscription of the romantic myth of the child of nature into
our constructions of children's literature. The child, "trailing clouds

of glory," comes from God into nature but is gradually corrupted by a feminized and feminizing culture. Subsequently, when the history of romanticism or of children's literature is constructed, authors such as Trimmer (I could add Hannah More, Anna Barbauld, and Maria Edgeworth) who openly educate children into this feminizing culture are criticized, demonized, belittled, or ignored.

My project here, however, is not to explore why Trimmer has been neglected within women's literary histories or within histories of children's literature. Rather, my aim is to examine what happens to our constructions of British romanticism when we consider Trimmer as a participant in its formal practices, thematic content, and ideological positions. Rather than challenge the limitations of our received understandings of what constitutes romanticism—what we might call the romantic ideology—I find it a useful aesthetic category for which we have a history of literary criticism and by which we can read texts such as Trimmer's as engaged in a shared body of concerns: an engagement with political, social, and poetic revolutions; a questioning into the nature of genius and the creative imagination; an increased attention to the specific and local as opposed to the general; the use of nature imagery; a renewed focus on the growth of the poet's own mind; an intense subjectivity; and a masculine colonization of feminine genres, sensibilities, and subject matter. In order to place Trimmer within British romanticism, I scrutinize a group of texts from the conservative Trimmer and the radical Godwin (writing under the pseudonym of William Scolfield), untangling the complicated intertextuality of Trimmer's and Godwin's debates about the nature of the imagination and its place within pedagogy and the growth of a child into an adult.

By the confluence of political, historical, and pedagogical events at the turn of the century, a woman such as Trimmer was able to gain a greater visibility in the realm of public letters than was perhaps typical before or after.[4] Oxford and Cambridge Universities had reacted to the French Revolution by shutting down dialogue on all controversial subjects—even replacing oral exams with written exams. In the absence of academic dialogue, intellectuals developed and disseminated ideas through journals, political clubs, and professional organizations. Coleridge, for example, created *The Friend* in 1800. Trimmer created *The Guardian of Education* in 1802.[5] In the first volume of this work, Trimmer lambastes a children's text that contemporary scholars have only recently attributed to William Godwin.[6]

For two authors who write from opposing ends of the political spec-
trum, the radical Godwin and the conservative Trimmer share a surprisingly extensive intertextual history. Godwin's two-volume *Fables,
Ancient and Modern. Adapted for the Use of Children* (1805, under the pseudonym of Edward Baldwin, Esq.) was modeled after Trimmer's popular *Ladder to Learning. A Collection of Fables Consisting of Words of One,
Two, and Three Syllables, with Original Morals* and would have been in
direct competition with this text and her popular *Fabulous Histories*
(1786). Certainly Godwin's reputation as a radical ensured that he
would run afoul of influential critical organs such as Trimmer's *Guardian of Education*. Forced to write under a variety of pseudonyms and
struggling financially, Godwin enhanced the marketability of his own
texts through a gendered form of criticism that attacked the feminine
status of his competitors, treating their works as obviously of lesser
value. In particular, the preface to his 1802 *Bible Stories,* written under
the pseudonym William Scolfield, is a polemic against other moral im-
provers who are overwhelmingly female or, if male, feminized.

Godwin's preface to *Bible Stories* is a useful place for my analysis
to begin, for it contains much that we, as contemporary critics, have
come to associate with British romanticism: an intermixing of Rousseau's *Emile,* associationist philosophy, and Adam Smith's version of
the sympathetic imagination:

> these modern improvers have left out of their system that most
> essential branch of human nature the imagination. . . . Every
> thing is studied and attended to, except those things which open
> the heart, which insensibly initiate the learner in the relations
> and generous offices of society, and enable him to put himself in
> imagination into the place of his neighbour, to feel his feelings
> and to wish his wishes.
>
> Imagination is the ground-plot upon which the edifice of a
> sound morality must be erected. Without imagination we may
> have a certain cold and arid circle of principles, but we cannot
> have sentiments: . . . we can neither ourselves love, nor be fitted
> to excite the love of others.
>
> Imagination is the characteristic of man. (ii–iii)

Godwin/Scolfield presents the familiar ideal of the sympathetic imagination and connects this imagination to charitable emotion. As in
Rousseau's *Emile,* Godwin emphasizes age-appropriate learning and is
concerned that children are too frequently given Bibles that contain

moralizing commentary beyond their comprehension level. Godwin's *Bible Stories* does not provide commentary and prints only narratives that had "most forcibly seized upon his youthful imagination . . . before he was but seven years of age" (vii). Godwin's introduction also builds on associationist philosophy—he suggests that his text presents the Bible as a "posy of sweet-smelling flowers, without one shrub of evil scent," and thus the child will have "none but pleasing recollections associated with the sacred volume" (v). Such early recollections, Godwin insists, are the foundation of a "sincere and manly sentiment of religion" (vi). For the same associationist reasons, *Bible Stories* follows the original King James translation (with one exception that I discuss later). Godwin contends that to alter the original phrasings for the child's understanding will eventually cause pain to the child-as-adult: these alterations will be unpleasantly jarring to the reader's positive associations with the original language and will cause a "painful and injurious sensation" in the mind (vi).

Trimmer's review of Godwin's *Bible Stories* accurately outlines her crucial objections to his text—that this edition is the product of Rousseau-influenced and Deist-based modern philosophy and leads children away from religion. This twenty-page review of *Bible Stories* is by far the longest of all of her *Guardian* reviews in the running feature "Examination of Books for Children"; the typical length of these reviews runs from a third of a page to four pages. Clearly, she uses this review to establish the principles by which children's books should be evaluated, principles she has delineated in her periodical's opening essay: "Introduction: Containing Observations on the Instruction of Children and Youth from the Time of the Reformation; and a Short Account of the Present Work." Found in the first installment of her journal, this lead article is a political-historical discussion in which Trimmer spells out her version of the history of religious education and religious writers.

In her discussion of Christian education, Trimmer carefully defines her moment in history as a moment of crisis in which Christianity is under siege: a "CONSPIRACY *against the* CHRISTIAN RELIGION (to which we shall have frequent occasion to allude) was first organized by three persons: namely, VOLTAIRE, the chief; FREDERICK *the second, King of Prussia,* the protector; D'ALEMBERT, the agent; to whom was afterwards added Diderot" (9). These writers, in combination with earlier British writers who had attempted to establish Deism on the ruins of true religion, had developed a "concerted plan to propagate their abominable principles, the French ENCYCLOPEDIA, which mixed their abominable principles with doctrines of truth and caused a general taste for metaphysical studies" (10). Although this abominable philosophy is fed by the "seducing pen of *Voltaire*," the greatest injury of all is "*Rousseau*'s system given to us by *Emilius,* an imaginary pupil educated in a new principle from which Christianity [is] banished" (11). Rousseau's *Emile*, Trimmer contends, works in concert with Diderot's *Encyclopedia* to weaken religion, propagate modern philosophy, and undermine British morality.

In *Bible Stories,* Trimmer discovers a clear example of French-inspired modern philosophy and shows her readers how to discover for themselves the Deism that permeates his biblical text. She reprints all of Godwin's preface and, in a smart pedagogical strategy for emphasizing her key points, italicizes or capitalizes every word that comes from the "language of *modern philosophy.*" Trimmer's typographical aggression and her insistence that Godwin has mutilated the Bible indicate a sophisticated aesthetic maneuvering. She understands what is at stake in Godwin's text: children's first introduction to the foundational text of Christianity and Western society. Her review lists the dangerous gaps in Godwin's good-parts version while simultaneously engaging in a romantic gesture of doing violence to Godwin's words.

What Trimmer excoriates in Godwin's *Bible Stories* is precisely what Godwin suggests is the positive effect of his book: that, by inspiring young children's passions and imaginations, he would be encouraging them to read, remember, and be inspired by the Bible. By contrast, Trimmer suggests that his good-parts version of the Bible fosters the false sympathy of the imagination that gives rise "to the *fictitious virtues philanthropy, mental energy,* and *sensibility*" while destroying habits of "charity, reverence and attachment. *Liberty* and *equality* [are] the ultimatum of modern philosophy" (249). In short, Godwin's Bible foments antigovernment sentiment and espouses liberty and equality for all. Because she condemns the sympathetic imagination and sensibility, Trimmer raises questions for contemporary critics who have associated the rise of sensibility with the rise of the domestic novel and women's literary authority. Trimmer argues against sensibility—the creation of sympathetic bonds between humans through human interaction—by revealing its solipsistic nature. Trimmer argues that all forms of morality based on human faculties such as the imagination are wrongly hubristic: to rely on empathy and fellow feeling for morality is ultimately human and not God-centered. One must care for other humans whether or not one is able to sympathize with them. In her opposition to the sympathetic imagination, Trimmer diverges from the paradigm of a female romanticism established by critics such as Anne Mellor. In identifying the markers of a feminine romanticism, Mellor links women writers to the sympathetic imagination, which, she notes, is strikingly similar to Carol Gilligan's ethic of care. Trimmer, however, finds such human-centered concepts of morality dangerously hubristic. In fact, Trimmer's stance ultimately implies that all secular theories of morality including Adam Smith's theory of moral sentiments are implicitly flawed.[7] The great humanitarian strength of Trimmer's Christianity is its inflexibility: one must be moral whether one feels like it or not.

Trimmer locates irrefutable proof of Godwin's anti-God, antigovernment stance in his one alteration of the language of the King James translation: he replaces "The Lord" with "Jehovah." Godwin's explanation for this substitution is that he is giving parents the freedom to present Jehovah as just another mythic character like Zeus or Diana. If they wish to insist on God's supreme authority, Godwin suggests that parents may tell their child that Jehovah means the all-powerful Lord. Trimmer insists that this removal of "The Lord" is openly subversive, for it places "the SUPREME BEING on a level with the idols of heathen nations" and denies the presence of God as the sole instigator of the text. Trimmer then notes that Godwin's *Bible Stories* does not begin with the creation story, in which God acts as an omnipotent progenitor, but instead begins with the human stories of Abraham and Sara. She next responds, point by point, to Godwin's premises, explaining how his apparently moral ideas are in fact seductively immoral. Ultimately, her review teaches parents to read between the lines, to detect French-inspired "modern philosophy," even when disguised within the Bible. In an interesting sidenote to the story of Trimmer and Godwin, ten years after Trimmer's attack on Godwin's pedagogy, Godwin's subversive writings for children became the focus of a special investigation by the Privy Council in 1813. They, though ambivalent, chose not to take action.

To read Trimmer's twenty-page review of *Bible Stories* as merely a reactionary rejection of the sympathetic imagination or religious dogmatism is to misread Trimmer's complicated argument. Trimmer herself produced numerous imaginative works such as *Fabulous Histories, Designed for the Instruction of Children, Respecting Their Treatment of Animals* (which was later known and loved as "The History of the Robins"

—Dicky, Flapsy, Pecksy, and Robin Redbreast). Trimmer refused to refer to this wildly popular tale by any other name than "fabulous history," for she wished to be clear that she was not writing history but rather was writing an imaginative fabrication. In other words, she does not deny imagination but merely refuses to mislead audiences by mixing genres. As she insists, both works of "accurate fact" and works of "acknowledged fiction" are worthwhile so long as "truth and fable may ever be kept separate and distinct in the mind." Trimmer's insistence that "The History of the Robins" be referred to under its original title, *Fabulous Histories,* illuminates an additional motivation behind her response to Godwin's text—the full title of Godwin's book is *Bible Stories, Memorable Acts of the Ancient Patriarchs, Judges, and Kings, Extracted from Their Original Historians for the Use of Children.*

It is not the imagination per se to which Trimmer objects in *Bible Stories* but the extraction of the story from the sacred text, the intermixing of human imagination with the word of God. Trimmer wishes to keep distinct the different types of inspired works—those inspired by God and those inspired by human fancy. To reconstruct the Bible imaginatively is a sacrilege of a particularly insidious order, and, further, Godwin claims the authority not of divine inspiration but of a secular, human-centered imagination. Trimmer discovers that

> the *ingenuity* and *contrivance* [of *Bible Stories*] consisted, not in *connection* and *uniformity,* but in *detachment* and *incoherence;* in an *outline,* (if such it may be called) *irregular, twisted,* and *broken,* as might best answer the purpose of the compiler, by destroying the effect of that SACRED VOLUME, in which there is such perfect harmony and agreement in all its parts, though written by different hands, and at different periods of time as prove its Divine origin beyond a doubt, to the unprejudiced mind. (254)

Godwin's "extractions" not only break the narrative coherence of the Bible but also leave gaps in the text that the imagination rushes to fill. Trimmer fears that visionary imaginations mislead rather than lead the individual. Those in need of spiritual guidance, who seek a way of grounding their "warm imaginations," will be led, all unconsciously, back into the dangerous realm of the imagination and, even worse, into the realm of modern metaphysical speculation. In short, the "impressionable minds" of children will fabulate false stories. For Trimmer, human passions and human imaginations are not a sufficient foundation for a system of morality or a rewriting of religious history, and there are substantive differences between fabulous (secular) histories and the divinely inspired Bible.

Trimmer's critique of Godwin's project anticipates contemporary readings of Godwin's use of historical writing to transform political culture. In his recent examination of Godwin's *Enquirer* from 1797, Jon Klancher reminds us that Godwin contrasts two versions of history—Enlightenment universal history (which depends on abstract generalizations about periods and movements to create a patriotic version of British nationhood) versus a history that follows the "arduous, the enthusiastic, and the sublime license of imagination" (Godwin, in Klancher 147). Godwin, of course, desired a history that was imaginative. In a particularly telling phrase, Godwin, who turns to the writers of ancient history for inspiration and a prototype of intellectual agency, writes that ancient history is not "a species of fable" but a "genuine praxis upon the nature of man," for "all history bears too near a resemblance to fable" (Klancher 158). Godwin's *Bible Stories*, "extracted from the original historians" and introduced by a preface in praise of the imagination, is (to use Godwin's own terminology) a type of fabulous rather than enlightenment history.

In reviewing Bibles, Trimmer was speaking not just as a devoutly religious woman but as her era's greatest living expert on children's Bibles. She was a published pedagogue, a mother, a Sunday school administrator, education advisor to Princess Sophia, and a woman who had spent much of her life in the center of literary and cultural activity. When Trimmer refuses to accept that the creative imagination is an adequate source of Christian sentiment and social morality, she is making a carefully considered aesthetic and epistemological choice. She acts not as a reactionary but as a leading authority responding to a dangerously misleading text. Long before Godwin's *Bible Stories* was published, Trimmer had suggested that most exemplary histories and improving books were too difficult for young children and argued for a developmental approach to religious education. Like the rationalists (and even Rousseau), she suggested that a Christian education begins with the child's own curiosities about the natural world. Wrongly grouped with the catechists, Trimmer in fact worried that children might learn Scripture by rote. For example, in *An Easy Introduction to the Knowledge of Nature, and Reading the Holy Scriptures (Adapted to the capacities of children)* (1780), she writes that children should first be introduced to nature and only then to "scientific accounts" and religious study.[8] Trimmer advocates an interactive approach to the reading of the Bible in which a mother reads the Bible along with her children and interprets and explains the text after several chapters have been read. Children, writes Trimmer in the preface to *An Easy Introduction,* must learn to read "the Volume of Nature, in order to discover [God's] *Wisdom* and *Goodness,* a desire of doing his Will might from thence be excited in their minds, before they were permitted to read the *Holy Scriptures,* which they should not begin till they had been previously taught, that they contain the Revelation which he has vouchsafed to make" (viii).

One of Trimmer's most popular books, *An Easy Introduction* reveals her concern with women's roles as active spiritual leaders by dramatizing women and girls as teachers and students of biblical knowledge. The first two-thirds of the text presents long monologues in which a mother talks to her children during daily nature walks, teaching them how to marvel at God's manifold creations. Significantly, the two children taught by Trimmer's mother-figure are of different genders: Henry, a young boy who has just gone into breeches but has "a great many Things . . . to learn yet, [that the mother] shall be happy to teach" (3), and Charlotte, an older daughter who is the primary focus of the mother's biblical instruction. By contrast, Rousseau's contention in *Emile* is that little girls must memorize by rote scriptural and religious knowledge as soon as possible, for, as adult women, they would be incapable of mature theological reasoning. For Emile (unlike Rousseau's Sophy) formal religious training is the capstone of his education. Not unlike Trimmer's Henry and Charlotte, Emile learns first from nature through his tutor's manipulations of his natural curiosity. Unlike the tutor, however, who has an almost sinister ability to educate Emile through anticipating his questions and controlling his environment, Trimmer's mother is direct in her instructions, and her interpretations are explicit rather than manipulative. It is a marvelous corrective to Rousseau's explicit misogyny that, in Trimmer's woman-centered narrative, little Henry is the one incapable of comprehending the Bible. He can participate in the nature walks, but only his sister is mature enough for theological and biblical lessons: "I suppose Henry thinks himself slighted by being excluded from our party, but we will take him a walking this Afternoon to make him amends.—I despair'd of fixing his attention, and besides the Subject was above his Years" (262). Admittedly, what Charlotte learns is not particularly enlightened by today's standards: Satan tempts Eve and not Adam because Eve "was inferior to her husband in point of reason" (247). But that a mother (rather than a father, a tutor, or an established church authority) imparts to her children the proper interpretation of the Bible is a significant and empowering act for all mothers who purchased her popular and continually reprinted text.[9]

Arguably, Trimmer's most powerful political act is in her editing of annotated editions of the Bible and study guides for specialized audiences of Bible readers such as working-class readers or children as in *Easy Introduction*. She was one of the forerunners in the production of British children's Bibles, and, as her private letters indicate, was fully aware that she was breaking into a patriarchy—the holy text of the supreme patriarch. Always a smart marketer, she skillfully rode a wave of anti-Jacobin sentiment (the French had had, for some time, state-of-the-art vernacular Bibles) and anti-Catholic sentiment (the only eighteenth-century British Bibles for children were from Catholic presses)—and became one of the most famous and widely published women in England. Trimmer's *Easy Introduction to the Knowledge of Nature, And Reading the Holy Scriptures* (1780) was later enlarged to the six-volume *Sacred History* (1782–84). The six volumes were edited down to two and renamed *Abridgement of Old Testament History* and *Abridgement of New Testament History*, which the Society for the Propagation of Christian Knowledge put on its list in 1793. And there they remained for seventy-seven years, selling more than 750,000 copies.[10]

Ruth Bottigheimer's award-winning history of children's Bibles acknowledges the crucial role played by Trimmer in the eighteenth and nineteenth centuries and examines the social, historical, and hegemonic force wielded by these editions. Children's Bibles consist of the story sections of the Bible to which commentary, verses, summaries, questions and answers, and history are sometimes added. All children's Bibles were produced by men until the late eighteenth century and tended to emphasize stories in which girls die (not boys), and in which fathers retain full power over their children's lives. Children's Bibles are neither merely simplified retellings of Bible stories nor the "good parts" versions. Rather, the extensive editing and redaction of the Bible necessary to fit the Bible to an audience of children allows editors to shape Scripture for their own ideological agendas. As Bottigheimer notes, these texts therefore are gender- and class-specific social commentary rendered in a godly context that makes the author's espoused ideology virtually unassailable. Bottigheimer reminds us that children's Bibles frequently delete sexually graphic material (Amnon's incest, Dinah's rape in Genesis, the entire Song of Solomon) while simultaneously adding socially slanted commentary. For example, Trimmer's *Help to the Unlearned in the Study of the Holy Scriptures Adapted According to the Opinion of Approved Commentators* (1805) was intended to teach poor children an ethic of work through the study of the Bible—Sodom and Gomorrah fell because people weren't working, and David coveted Bathsheba because he had too much time on his hands. Class-specific children's Bibles became so popular in this era, notes Bottigheimer, that in practical terms it was a two-tiered genre—Bibles for the poor and Bibles for the upper and middle classes.[11]

Thus, when Trimmer attacks Godwin's excerpted and simplified Bible story selections, her attack is the result of 150 years of debates about which Bible stories belong in the hands of the poor and the hands of children. It is also the result of twenty-five years of creating her own and commenting on others' Bible editions. When Trimmer's review of Godwin lists, for four pages, the passages, stories, and details that Godwin omits in his *Bible Stories,* and when she describes these omissions, over and over, as "mutilations,"[12] she does so not out of reactionary fervor but out of scholarly energy. Nothing enrages a scholar more than someone else's slipshod editions: Trimmer is all too aware that children's Bibles allow authors to control and transform stories—and that Bible stories express social values and transmit cultural norms from generation to generation.

Although I would never argue that Trimmer is a radical, on the other hand, the social values that Trimmer transmits are not always strictly conservative—particularly in her portrayal of women figures from the Old Testament. It is true that Trimmer's children's Bibles contained commentary that supported the hierarchical relations between the classes, but as Bottigheimer also notes, her Bibles did retain strong women figures that other editors belittled or simply excised from their texts: for example, the story of Jael and Sisera from the Song of Deborah (5 Judges). Deborah is a Hebrew judge who led the host to defeat Canaan—Sisera, the Canaanite leader, was murdered by Jael after she invited him to her tent and drove a tent peg through his temple. In Bottigheimer's research into the history of Jael's story, she learned that this passage had always been a site of contention—early German Lutherans were upset that the King James translation had Jael cut off Sisera's head, but they were even more upset that when Sisera requests milk, Jael brings water. Eventually, both Deborah and Jael are erased from children's Bibles and their victory over the Canaanites becomes part of Gideon's story—this erasure is still the standard practice in contemporary children's Bibles. Late eighteenth- and early nineteenth-century English male authors had only reproach for Jael, but Trimmer justified Jael's act by taking into consideration the circumstances of the Israelites. Although Trimmer admits that women are the weaker instruments, Jael's success proves that women and men are equally indebted to God for strength.

Perhaps the woman-centered version of the Bible that appears within Trimmer's otherwise strict hegemonic text can help explain several other anomalies in what would appear to be Trimmer's seamlessly conservative career. On the political front, Trimmer had already digressed from the conservative party line in unexpected ways. For example, she supported Hannah More in *The Guardian of Education* even at the height of the Blagdon Controversy, praising More as a "pious and justly celebrated author," refusing to be "guilty of blameable omission" by not acknowledging More's pedagogical authority. After reading *The Rights of Woman,* Trimmer confessed that "Miss Woolstonecroft [*sic*] is a woman of extraordinary abilities" (*Some Account* 1.355).[13]

I'd like to reread the Trimmer letter that I quoted at the opening of this essay—not as a sample of Trimmer's conservative closed-mindedness but as an example of a surprisingly familiar romantic narrative. In this letter, Trimmer explores the growth of her own mind and refuses to bow to "any human authority whatever" but only to the authority of sublime words. She was passionately engaged with the theories and practices of pedagogy, of one's coming into a subjectivity. Like Coleridge, Godwin, Kant, Wollstonecraft, and Rousseau, she was preoccupied with the nature of the creative imagination and its political and emotional effects. She wrote a mixed-genre autobiography of original letters, meditations, prayers, and memories not unlike Coleridge's *Biographia Literaria.* She likewise published essays on theology and education, many of which appeared posthumously. Although considered conservative, she was, taken from a different perspective, more leveling than Wordsworth. He spoke to the educated about writing in the language of ordinary men—she, however, wrote for the ordinary, for the uneducated, and for those who sought self-education.[14] She specialized in easy-to-read Bible editions and easy-to-follow learning guides to the Bible as well as children's books that are arranged developmentally into age-appropriate language. She created and sponsored whole new genres of literature: the teacher's guide and nursery room educational prints and engravings.

Perhaps one clue as to why Trimmer has been neglected in the history of romanticism is that although her content is frequently identifiably romantic, her attitude rarely is. Trimmer, as in my opening letter, appeared to be without doubt or anxieties about her project, her writing, her understanding, or her place in the world. She registered no Bloomian anxiety of influence; she showed no desire to project the supernatural onto the natural. She did not evidence, as Margaret Homans, Sandra Gilbert, and Susan Gubar once argued of nineteenth-century women writers, any anxiety of authorship or any aesthetic of self-renunciation. She did not embrace the sympathetic imagination or engage in a politics of the beautiful or the sentimental, as Anne Mellor, Isobel Armstrong, and Jerome McGann have argued, respectively, in recent discussions of women romantic poets. She was not outside the "contours of masculine desire," but neither did she fit comfortably within its parameters. She successfully broke into the patriarchal field of Bible scholarship, but she rarely advocated that other women do so. Even so, she served as a role model for other women authors of the romantic and Victorian periods who followed in her footsteps, who published children's books and primers such as *The Footsteps to Mrs. Trimmer's Sacred History* that refer to and capitalize on her successes.

Notes

I would like to thank the Boston Public Library and the University of California, Los Angeles Department of Special Collections (Children's Book Collection) for the use of their rare book collections in preparing this research. I would also like to thank the UCLA Special Collections for an Ahmanson Short Term Research Fellowship in the summer of 1999.

1. Trimmer initiated and edited *The Family Magazine* (1778–89) for the serving class and *The Guardian of Education* (1802–6) for the affluent, intending to combat Jacobin influences. Trimmer's *Guardian* "was as much a manual for prospective writers as a guide for parents' selections" and inspired a flood of imitators (Jackson 183). In 1990, Andrea Immel published an excellent index of the book reviews, essays, extracts, and correspondence published in the *Guardian of Education*.

2. Her father was an architect who was a friend of Hogarth, Reynolds, and Gainsborough (who asked to be buried beside her father and was).

3. Though not in constructions of women's literary history and romanticism, Trimmer is present in a limited fashion in the histories of children's literature and education. See, for example, Mary Jackson's history of children's literature in England or Gillian Avery's history of American children and their books. For discussions of Trimmer as an author of religious books for children, see Patricia Demers's *Heaven upon Earth;* see also Ruth Bottigheimer's study of the history of children's Bibles. Winner of the 1996 Children's Literature Association Book Award, Bottigheimer's *The Bible for Children* contains an extensive discussion of Trimmer's innovations in the field of children's and working-

class Bibles. My comments on the history of children's Bibles are drawn largely from her work. Richardson's study of pedagogy and literature, *Literature, Education, and Romanticism,* is unusual in that he addresses Trimmer's writings as a romantic-era literary critic of books for children. He primarily uses Trimmer as a representative figure of the conservative politics of children's literature, however.

4. As Christine Krueger and Anne Mellor have discussed at some length, conservative women such as Hannah More were particularly influential during the latter half of the seventeenth century and not only created new literary genres but, in so doing, also amassed personal fortunes and an international reputation as leading educators and moralists. See Krueger's *Reader's Repentance* and Mellor's presentation, "Hannah More: *Agent Provocateur.*" The classic discussion of the power of the Georgian-era rational woman and teacher is Mitzi Myers's "Impeccable Governesses."

5. I have drawn much of my information on the political situation of journal publishing during the early 1800s from Hewitt's discussion of *The Friend* and the early stages of sociology.

6. For a full discussion of why the pseudonym "Scolfield" is attributed to William Godwin, see William St. Clair's article, "William Godwin as Children's Bookseller." That it was not until 1989 that this book was identified as Godwin's suggests that the dichotomous schema that one is either a good radical and celebrant of the imagination or a bad didacticist and defender of the hegemony is a very compelling paradigm indeed.

7. Adam Smith's *Theory of Moral Sentiments* was denounced by many Christian philosophers in the eighteenth century for its secularization of human morality. Smith proposes, in effect, that human morality arises from empirical experience. As humans interact with others they learn that certain behaviors are harmful or hurtful. Through the sympathetic imagination, each person can imagine how his or her behavior will affect others and attempts to behave in ways that are socially acceptable.

8. Trimmer's *Easy Introduction,* as her preface explains, is intended to blend Isaac Watts's *Treatise on Education* with Barbauld's *Lessons for Children* (a book that she recommends to her readers, even including the exact address at which the book can be purchased: No. 72, St. Paul's Church Yard). Trimmer quotes Watts's advice to parents: "Teach [children] to observe the various occurrences of Nature and Providence . . . that the GREAT God made all these," and praises Barbauld's use of an approachable "stile of familiar conversation, and free from all formality" (vii, xii). For an excellent discussion of Barbauld's influential *Lessons,* see William McCarthy, "Mother of All Discourses." *An Easy Introduction* was first published in 1780, although the Dictionary of National Biography inaccurately dates its first publication in 1782.

9. Trimmer, like other women pedagogical writers from the Georgian period, created mother-teacher figures who are powerful authority figures. For discussions of Wollstonecraft's Mrs. Mason from *Original Stories,* see Myers's "Impeccable Governesses"; of Smith's Mrs. Talbot from *Conversations Introducing Poetry,* see Ruwe's "Benevolent Brothers"; of Barbauld's mother-pedagogue figure, see Myers's " 'Of Mice and Mothers' " and Sarah Robbins's "*Lessons for Children.*"

10. The French had had vernacular children's Bibles for some time (numerous editions copied Nicolas Fontaine's 1670 text, *The History of the Old and the New Testament*). In 1726, the first complete Bible was rewritten for children in English, *A Compendius History of the Old and New Testament* (which borrowed heavily from Fontaine's *History* and its illustrations by Merian). In the 1780s, two British firms produced Bible stories for Catholic children, setting off a sudden proliferation of Protestant children's Bibles. See Bottigheimer for a full discussion of children's Bibles during the eighteenth century. The *Dictionary of Literary Biography* lists the publication and circulation figures for Trimmer's Bible editions (1159).

11. In her otherwise complimentary review of Bottigheimer's *Bible for Children,* Andrea Immel remarks that, in the interest of creating a survey of children's Bibles, Bottig-

heimer oversimplifies her representations of class: the two-part model of the affluent and the poor is "no longer viable in the light of recent researches on the history of the book, book trade economics, the sociology of readers or the formation of the middle class" (Immel 30).

12. "SOLOMON's history is dispatched in a few short mutilated lessons," and "the account of David killing Goliath is mutilated" (260).

13. The full quotation discussing Wollstonecraft is as follows: "Of the *Rights of Women*, I can now say nothing more than that I found so much happiness in having a husband to assist me in forming a proper judgment, and in taking upon him the chief labour of providing for a family, that I never wished for a further degree of liberty or consequence than I enjoyed. Miss Woolstonecroft [*sic*] is a woman of extraordinary abilities, I confess; I cannot help thinking they might be employed to more advantage to society. — But my recent misfortune [the death of her husband of twenty-nine years] has almost obliterated the remembrance of the contents of her book" (*Some Account* 1.355).

14. She was attentive to the lower classes though, as Alan Richardson and Wilfred Keutsch note, Trimmer's educational texts are intended to re-educate the lower classes into passivity and to maintain hierarchical power relations (Richardson 65).

Works Cited

Armstrong, Isobel. "The Gush of the Feminine: How Can We Read Women's Poetry of the Romantic Period?" In *Romantic Women Writers: Voices and Countervoices*. Ed. Paula R. Feldman and Theresa M. Kelley. Hanover: University Press of New England, 1995. Pp. 13–32.

Avery, Gillian. *Behold the Child: American Children and Their Books 1621–1922*. Baltimore: Johns Hopkins University Press, 1994.

Bottigheimer, Ruth. *The Bible for Children: From the Age of Gutenberg to the Present*. New Haven: Yale University Press, 1996.

Demers, Patricia. *Heaven upon Earth: The Form of Moral and Religious Children's Literature, to 1850*. Knoxville: University of Tennessee Press, 1993.

Ezell, Margaret J. M. *Writing Women's Literary History*. Baltimore: Johns Hopkins University Press, 1993.

The Footsteps to Mrs. Trimmer's Sacred History: For the Instruction, and Amusement of Little Children. London: John Marshall, [1790].

Gilbert, Sandra, and Susan Gubar. *The Madwoman in the Attic: The Woman Writer and the Nineteenth-Century Literary Imagination*. New Haven: Yale University Press, 1979.

Gilligan, Carol. *In a Different Voice: Psychological Theory and Women's Development*. Cambridge: Harvard University Press, 1982.

Godwin, William. *Bible Stories. Memorable Acts of the Ancient Patriarchs, Judges, and Kings, Extracted from Their Original Historians for the Use of Children*. 1802. Philadelphia: Thomas and William Bradford, 1803.

———. *The Enquirer: Reflections on Education, Manners, and Literature*. London: G.G. & Robinson, 1797.

———. *Fables, Ancient and Modern. Adapted for the Use of Children*. 1805. New York: Garland, 1976.

Hewitt, Regina. "*Friendly* Instruction: Coleridge and the Discipline of Sociology." In *Lessons of Romanticism: A Critical Companion*. Ed. Thomas Pfau and Robert F. Gleckner. Durham: Duke University Press, 1998. Pp. 98–102.

Homans, Margaret. *Bearing the Word: Language and Female Experience in Nineteenth-Century Women's Writing*. Chicago: University of Chicago Press, 1986.

Immel, Andrea. Review of *The Bible for Children: From the Age of Gutenberg to the Present*, by Ruth Bottigheimer. *Children's Books History Society Newsletter* 59 (19 Nov. 1999): 30–31.

————. *Revolutionary Reviewing: Sarah Trimmer's* Guardian of Education. Occasional Papers 4. Los Angeles: Department of Special Collections, University of California, Los Angeles, 1990.

Jackson, Mary V. *Engines of Instruction, Mischief, and Magic: Children's Literature in England from Its Beginnings to 1839.* Lincoln: University of Nebraska Press, 1989.

Keutsch, Wilfred. "Teaching the Poor: Sarah Trimmer, God's Own Handmaid." *Bulletin of the John Rylands University Library* 76, no. 3 (1994): 43–57.

Klancher, Jon. "Godwin and the Republican Romance: Genre, Politics, and Contingency in Cultural History." *MLQ* 56, no. 2 (June 1995): 145–65.

Krueger, Christine. *The Reader's Repentance: Women Preachers, Women Writers, and Nineteenth-Century Social Discourse.* Chicago: University of Chicago Press, 1992.

McCarthy, William. "Mother of All Discourses: Anna Barbauld's *Lessons for Children.*" *Princeton University Library Chronicle* 60, no. 2 (winter 1999): 196–219.

McGann, Jerome. *The Romantic Ideology: A Critical Investigation.* Chicago: University of Chicago Press, 1983.

Mellor, Anne K. "Hannah More: *Agent Provocateur.*" American Conference in Romanticism: Cross-Currents in Romanticism. University of California, Santa Barbara, 15 Oct. 1998.

————. *Romanticism and Gender.* New York: Routledge, 1992.

Myers, Mitzi. "Impeccable Governesses, Rational Dames, and Moral Mothers: Mary Wollstonecraft and the Female Tradition in Georgian Children's Books." *Children's Literature* 14 (1986): 31–59.

————. "Of Mice and Mothers: Mrs. Barbauld's 'New Walk' and Gendered Codes in Children's Literature." In *Feminine Principles and Women's Experience in American Composition and Rhetoric.* Ed. Louise Wetherbee Phelps and Janet Emig. Pittsburgh: University of Pittsburgh Press, 1995. Pp. 225–88.

Richardson, Alan. *Literature, Education, and Romanticism: Reading as Social Practice, 1780–1832.* New York: Cambridge University Press, 1994.

Robbins, Sarah. "*Lessons for Children* and Teaching Mothers: Mrs. Barbauld's Primer for the Textual Construction of Middle-Class Domestic Pedagogy." *The Lion and the Unicorn* 17 (1993): 195–51.

Ruwe, Donelle R. "Benevolent Brothers and Supervising Mothers: Ideology in the Children's Verses of Mary and Charles Lamb and Charlotte Smith." *Children's Literature.* Ed. U. C. Knoepflmacher and Mitzi Myers. New Haven: Yale University Press, 1997. Pp. 161–80.

St. Clair, William. "William Godwin as Children's Bookseller." In *Children and Their Books: A Celebration of the Work of Iona and Peter Opie.* Ed. Gillian Avery and Julia Briggs. Oxford: Clarendon, 1989. Pp. 165–79.

Trimmer, Sarah. *An Easy Introduction to the Knowledge of Nature, and Reading the Holy Scriptures.* London: J. Dodsley, 1780.

————. *An Essay on Christian Education.* London: 1812.

————. *Fabulous Histories, Designed for the Instruction of Children, Respecting Their Treatment of Animals.* 1786. 11th ed. London: N. Hailes, 1817.

————. "Introduction: Containing Some Observations on the Instruction of Children and Youth from the Time of the Reformation; and a Short Account of the Present Work." *Guardian of Education* 1 (1802): 1–16.

————. *Ladder to Learning: A Select Collection of Fables.* J. Harris: London, 1805.

————. Review of *Bible Stories, Memorable Acts of the Ancient Patriarchs, Judges, and Kings, Extracted from Their Original Historians, for the Use of Children,* by William Scolfield. [William Godwin] *Guardian of Education* 1 (1802): 244–64.

————. *Some Account of the Life of Mrs. Trimmer with Original Letters and Meditations and Prayers, Selected from Her Journal.* 2 vols. London, 1814.

Philanthropy in Nineteenth-Century French Children's Literature: The Example of La Bibliothèque Rose

Ruth Carver Capasso

In a memorable scene from the Countess de Ségur's popular children's novel *Les Petites Filles Modèles* [*The Model Little Girls*] (1858), the young protagonists enthusiastically gather furniture and a wagonload of food to help an impoverished mother and child. Their sensitivity and generosity model sentimental values that the author clearly wishes to promote in child readers. But the technique of doing good remains to be taught; when a laughing servant tells them to take back most of the food, because it would only spoil, she demonstrates the need to do charity in a rational and pragmatic manner. Such lessons of philanthropy, with their dual appeal to emotion and reason, figured prominently in children's literature of the nineteenth century in France. This study of the *Bibliothèque Rose Illustrée* [*Illustrated Pink Library*] examines how an audience of predominantly middle- and upper-class children was taught to see and to respond to the poor and through this to understand their own identity in terms of class and gender roles.

Acts of private charity were common and important in nineteenth-century France. Socialist and utopian thinkers of the 1830s and 1840s had advocated radical restructurings of society to erase inequalities and to provide justice, not charity. Yet government officials, moral economists, and Catholic leaders countered the call for political and economic reform with arguments that the patterns of private life were the root causes of poverty and its accompanying social disorder (Lynch 11–12). Social Catholicism, as typified by the foundation of the Society of Saint Vincent de Paul in the 1830s, preached the application of Christian benevolence in the form of material and moral assistance to the marginalized through private intervention in personal lives. Such outreach was promoted not only to relieve the poor for humanitarian and egalitarian reasons but in hopes that demonstrations of solidarity might ensure stability in a country that had seen violent class warfare and continued interclass tensions. The ideal of society as "the harmonious integration of various social groups into

Children's Literature 29, ed. Elizabeth Lennox Keyser and Julie Pfeiffer (Yale University Press, © 2001 Hollins University).

a transcendent whole" (Maza 228–29) formed an essential base of
French thought and influenced the education of children, as recognition of moral responsibility and commitment to others were articulated as important goals for their development. Catholicism in particular stressed the role of mothers in the formation of benevolent
children, for women were seen to possess sensitive and suffering na-
tures that could empathize with those in need, and their centrality in
the domestic realm enabled them to actively do charitable work and
to model it to the next generation. One unidentified mother left a
memorandum detailing how she would accomplish the goal of teaching charity to her children through discussion and action: "A coffer
will be placed in the children's chapel, so that they can dispose of
their own alms of their own free will, alone without witnesses. The
small sums collected in this coffer will be given to a poor person in the
neighborhood, possibly in the form of bread or clothing" (Hellerstein
et al. 249).[1]

But not all observers were confident in the adequacy of parents to
raise children with appropriate values; in an "approbation" prefatory
to Ségur's *Evangile d'une Grand'mère* [*A Grandmother's Gospel*] (1866),
Cardinal Donnet wrote: "well-intentioned parents don't know the path
to follow to form Christians in the home and see themselves condemned to trust to others" (v).[2] Writers for children (the vast majority
of them women) were among the "others" entrusted to teach children
private values and public actions appropriate to their age, gender, and
class. From their stories and novels for children, it seems clear that
upper-class women, perhaps to emphasize their own significance, embraced the mission to counter the competitive market values of indus-
trialization with a view of society as a "collection of families" where
women and children were central (Smith 160).[3]

The middle-class and aristocratic writers analyzed in this study
painted visions of social reconciliation based on the mutual dependence of the social orders, what the historian Roger Price called "inte-
grative ideologies, which affirmed the community of interests between
rich and poor" (193–94). As their tales model interpersonal and corporate approaches to social action, they focus on a direct solution to
individual cases of need. But the utilitarian, didactic voice is nuanced
when the child protagonist, trying to identify with the marginalized,
wonders at the source or consequences of poverty. The decision to dramatize misery is in itself a hint of protest, for, Pessin argues, any depiction of poverty is an implicit criticism of society (240). More than

one writer of the Bibliothèque is openly critical of the materialism, indifference, and economic speculation of the upper classes in late nineteenth-century France. The interests of the lower class and its resentment are voiced in works by Ségur and others, even if the writers quickly work to defuse its potential violence. It is somewhat surprising that publishers, parental purchasers, and even contemporary critics find it easy to dismiss any social criticism implied by these children's novels.

An explanation may lie in their packaging. The *Bibliothèque Rose Illustrée* was a collection of more than 175 books published from the 1850s to World War I, with an intended audience of children ages eight to fourteen.[4] The candy-colored collection was declared to be apolitical: the publisher Louis Hachette wrote in 1852: "a sincere respect for morals and religion, a scrupulous care to avoid all political declamation should govern our publication" (quoted in Mistler 129). Questions about the social order were further masked by the patterns of sentimental writing and by the nature of the readership: the novels addressed the tender and (for the time being) powerless audience of children. This study examines tales of charity not as endearing or indulgent sentimental episodes but as conscious efforts to educate children as developing members of society, efforts that convey messages about class, community, age, and gender.

Philanthropy was important in children's literature as early as Berquin in the eighteenth century, but in order to maintain a clear focus and relate my discussion to a specific historical period I have chosen to limit my study to a cluster of writers who span the Second Empire and the Third Republic. The Countess de Ségur (1799–1874) was the most widely published children's author of the collection, publishing twenty works in this group along with religious texts for children and a volume on children's health. She helped establish the popularity of the collection and is the only writer to remain steadily in print to this day. Henriette de Ségur (1829–1905), one of Ségur's daughters, published four novels under her married name of Mme Armand Fresneau and continued to draw from the aristocratic and Catholic milieu of her family. Zulma Carraud (1796–1889), a close friend of Balzac, wrote works for children to practice reading in school; her novel *La Petite Jeanne* [*Little Jeanne*] won a prize for "utility" from the Académie Française. Along with Ségur, she wrote for *La Semaine des Enfants* [*The Children's Week*]. Julie Gouraud (1810–1891) was a successful writer under the pseudonym of Louise d'Aulnay and under her own name. She founded and directed two journals, *Le Journal des Jeunes* [*The Young People's Journal*] and *La Femme et la Famille* [*Woman and the Family.*] She wrote eighteen novels for *La Bibliothèque Rose Illustrée,* many of which went through multiple editions. Little is known of Mme de Stolz, although the particle indicates nobility. She published sixteen volumes for *La Bibliothèque Rose Illustrée* and also wrote for the Catholic publishing house, Périsse frères. Although political regimes may have changed during the writing lives of some of these authors, a conception of the family as building block of the nation continued, and the novels reveal a common set of values and approaches, indicating that children's fiction, at least, may often owe more to the formation of the writers and their general milieu than to the impact of specific political changes.

In *Emile* Rousseau had advocated the careful selection of an individual as exemplar, as representative of poverty incarnate: "One single object, chosen well and shown in an appropriate light, will give [the child] a month of *compassion* and *reflection*" (517, emphasis added). Through the *Bibliothèque Rose,* Rousseauist patterns of education that appealed both to sentiment and to rational analysis are maintained as a remarkable number of novels lead the protagonist and the child reader through an encounter with a poor person. In Stolz's *Le Vieux de la Forêt* [*The Old Man of the Forest*] (1883) the narrator explains: "What is necessary is to see misfortune up close, then to return to one's happy home. The comparison brings a desire to do good" (238).

Private values and public roles immediately collide in the encounter between protagonist and the Other, the poor individual. Such meetings occur in so many novels and so centrally that, morphologically, the encounter is much like a love story; the sudden experience transforms the character's emotional being. The meeting generally occurs by chance as the privileged child leaves his or her comfortable home and comes upon a poor person, almost never a beggar, but rather someone seen exhausted by the side of the road or in the woods, physically as well as socially marginalized. Reader identification and engagement with the moment are encouraged through narratorial comments that invite or assume a sympathetic reader reaction: in the many novels by Gouraud, the narrator frequently enters the text with comments such as "We who have a good heart, we are happy to see the milkmaid prosper" (*Les Enfants de la Ferme* [*The Farm Children*], 1869, 60). Children's literature of the sentimental tradition clearly works to build a dialogic exchange, creating a sense of emotional community across classes and across ages, from adult narrator to child reader (Basch 13).

Emotion is the private, immediate response to the sight of poverty, but the challenge of the encounter is to educate the child in the appropriate public action. A classic example, doubtlessly influenced by the biblical story of Ruth and Boaz, is the meeting with the little reaper. The story presents an impoverished individual, forced to live on the gleanings left behind by harvesters on a productive farm. Because the poor person comes onto the property of the wealthy to take part of the harvest, issues of rights and of worth immediately come into question. The story can be used to teach boundaries (where the poor may and may not approach) and the protocol of philanthropy, as the child learns the responsibilities of wealth and the procedures for giving. As the child follows a catechism of charity, learning from the parent how to distinguish the worthy poor from the thief and to chart the limits of generosity, the charitable impulse is turned into a rational choice. In her memorandum on raising her children, the anonymous woman quoted above alludes to the hierarchy of worthy and unworthy poor, suggesting that the ability to distinguish between them will be part of her children's education: "When I am with the little ones, who cannot understand my motives, I will not refuse the requests for alms of those poor souls who are not respectable" (Hellerstein 249). The novels attempt to give case studies so that these distinctions of merit can be taught in a sympathetic yet clear method. In Stolz's *Les Protégés d'Isabelle* [*Isabelle's Protégés*] (1890) a benefactress faced with two poor children declares: "one must do charity in a prudent and reasonable manner; we must start out by learning if the woman with whom these children live and if the children themselves are worthy of interest" (30). In Zulma Carraud's novel *La Petite Jeanne* [*Little Jeanne*] (1852) a wealthy child, Isaure, offers to give her own clothing to an impoverished child whom she has just met: "I have so many dresses that are of no more use to me! Couldn't I give one of them to the little Jeanne?" Her mother quickly establishes a distinction in classes and roles when she replies practically: "My daughter, your dresses would be of poor use for this child; they would stay caught on the thorns of bushes near which she must pass, and the mud from the bad paths where Jeanne has to walk would tear the material when she tried to rub it off" (35). The child is taught to buy coarse, durable material and to sew simple garments for the other girl. Although encounters with the poor may result in what Denby has called a kind of "sentimental and moral epiphany" (78), this moment, which seems to transcend social differences, does not erase them (9).

Little Jeanne has to walk along muddy paths to beg door to door. The reaper, who comes onto the property of the wealthy, brings an even greater challenge to the possessing classes. In Gouraud's *Les Enfants de la Ferme,* a servant girl takes pity on a poor woman and attempts to gather wheat for her in a neighbor's field that has not been fully harvested. She is attacked by several farm workers and arrested by a gendarme. The support of her employers and neighboring farmers and, most essentially, the influence of the local chatelaine, keep her out of jail. The text upholds the law in the sense that the child is admonished to observe carefully the regulations about gleaning. The chatelaine, "all the while appreciating the injustice which Manette had suffered, gave her a little lesson that the poor child understood quite well" (93). Compassion for the poor cannot lead to an abandonment of principles of law and property or to an imprudent emotional response.

Yet the sentimental weight of the text is clearly on the child's side: the chapter is titled "Where the author cried," preparing the reader to be moved with pity or admiration. Her female attackers are called "bad" (86), and the male "dared to strike the poor girl" (87). In an interesting use of *style indirect libre* (which here puts the statement somewhere between the common farmer's and the educated narrator's views) the gendarme is criticized: "the gendarme would have done better if he'd run after the man who had beaten Manette" (91). An accompanying engraving gives a sympathetic rendering of the young and vulnerable girl bent in shame, using her hands and an apron to hide her face (visual signs of purity and vulnerability, according to Andew S. Winston's study of sentimental art [125]). The contrasting brutality and smug assurance of the authority figure who towers above her on a frightening horse seem to invoke reader identification with the child and condemnation of the domination of the authority figure. Not only is the gendarme armed, but his uniform, elaborate in contrast with his limited authority, suggests an exaggerated pride in his power, making him a ludicrous figure. The novel seems to confirm negative rural perceptions of the justice system as described by Weber, who titled one chapter of his book on peasant France: "From Justice, Lord, Deliver Us!"

Gouraud and the illustrator Bayard denigrate the officer of the law because he appears to judge the poor as a class, routinely applying abstract laws without taking the trouble to judge the merits of each case. Significantly, it is people endowed with a small amount of power and authority who are portrayed as abusing it through such careless and dismissive attitudes. The novel is not antiauthoritarian, but rather suggests that the gendarme is a minor and imperfect representative of a power wielded much more effectively by the commune's wealthy and prominent citizens. In certain of the *Bibliothèque Rose* texts the aristocratic writers seem to elide the agent of the state and the bourgeois, hinting that judgment is both a privilege and a responsibility of the highest class, here most clearly defined as the old landed aristocracy. One child who has absorbed this lesson declares: "Mama says that giving is the most beautiful privilege of those who are above the crowd because of their fortune" (182). To underscore the idea that "fortune" here applies as much to fate as to wealth, the child immediately compares herself to a poor village girl, her friend, and explains: "Madeleine is like me in age and size; the difference is that she has always been good and that God, when He sent her into this world, didn't put *a big purse* next to her like He did for me" (Stolz, *Le Trésor de Nanette* [*Nanette's Treasure*] 182, emphasis added). The wealthy, if grateful for their benefits, are portrayed as those better capable of helping the poor than those whose moderate means lead them to greed or to a sense of merit and self-determination.

This literature is not rich in images of a middle class of employers, teachers, or lawyers who effect public or domestic change. This may be a result of distrust of industrial development and secular change throughout the century and a sense that the dangers of the revolution require a reconciliation of the two most distant social orders, a union of them against the upstart bourgeoisie that threatened aristocratic domination. It may also reflect some resistance on the part of women to bourgeois associations, predominantly male, who pursued "scientific charity" and were generally separate from confessional efforts and critical of the unorganized almsgiving most frequently associated with women (Harrison 159–64). The familial image of maternal charity by the rich and filial gratitude from the childlike poor is not only a concept understandable to children; it emphasized a hierarchical thinking that placed everyone, including the rich, in a pattern of mutual dependency and, ultimately, subordination to the higher power of God.

The novels do not gloss over class tensions, however. In *Le Trésor de Nanette*, an old woman, reminiscent of the revolutionary *tricoteuses*, speaks scornfully of the hardness of heart seen in the rich (93). And the poor are not always shown as endearing. In *Les Enfants de la Ferme,* a series of bad harvests leads to widespread hunger and to the fear of marauading bands of the impoverished "who cried with arrogance: 'Bread! Bread!' " (181). Sympathy with the poor is moderated by the fear of violence and an implied scorn for idleness; the generally tender heroine Renotte speaks of the beggars as "good-for-nothings." A vignette shows the beggars besieging a house, perhaps inhabited by the protagonists, a family of children whose hard work to support themselves on the farm after the deaths of their parents has left them with some reserves of food. Significantly, the vignette sends a mixed message; the band includes grown men, one of whom encroaches on the private space of the window behind which a young woman cowers, while another carries a stick or club. Yet the group also includes an emaciated woman who holds a child up for pity. Crutches lie on the ground; all of the figures are barefoot and ragged. The image combines the fear of the poor who threaten violent revolution and the call to sympathy and charity. In this novel of reconciliation, every level of society is drawn in to ease the situation, as the poor Renotte struggles to feed her worthy neighbors, the doctor gives free care, and those "neither rich nor poor" contribute (186). Final order replaces chaos when the wealthy baroness, traveling in Rome, receives word of the disaster and writes back to order sustained assistance.

The encounter with the poor stretches the child's capacities for identification and feelings of fraternity, but it also stretches her toward the adult world and to a position of power. Although the overt messages of these texts stress charity as building community by restoring the outcast and marginalized to productive roles in society, one may also see this evocation of order as repressive and exploitative. Vinson speaks of "strategies of condescension" (100) in the novels of Ségur and declares: "Charity, a dynamic process, functions to substitute for the marginality of the indigent the normality of the worker, who is unconditionally won over to the moral code of the privileged" (93). Smith confirms this, arguing that women of the period acted out of a desire to maintain social order as a "static and hierarchical construct" (9). Although Vinson admits that the individual writers may have written from an altruistic perspective, she insists that they serve to further the domination of the ruling class: "While personal motivations are rather of the order of touched emotion, of consoling morale, the duty of charity obeys, in the final analysis, a political end" (23). In this critical (and modern) perspective, the writers appear to have little more sophistication or awareness than their young audience.

Vinson's arguments treat primarily Ségur's novels for a very young readership, such as *Les Petites Filles Modèles,* which have a domestic focus and, through the depiction of material assistance, may underscore the dependency of the poor on the patronage of the rich. These novels do not develop the broader vision presented in later works by Ségur and others in the collection. Marie-France Doray, analyzing a wider range of novels by Ségur, sees a pattern in which philanthropy addresses, in this order, material needs such as food and clothing, health care, support of churches, and the building of schools (161). It is true that such projects may not seem politically significant in that they are on a local scale; Doray rightly observes that "their harmony only seems possible through relations of proximity, within microcosms juxtaposed in space" (163). The relationships established through acts of benevolence were, ultimately, of more value than the material benefits and functioned to help the hearts of the rich as much as the bodies of the poor. The young heroine of *Le trésor de Nanette,* who spoke of her resemblance to the poor Madeleine, was transformed through this friendship from an egotistical and lazy child to a caring young woman. Although the sentimental language of the texts may strike the modern ear as patronizing, it is anachronistic to seek a conceptualization of political action and egalitarianism not yet part of the French social imagination (Harrison 4). There is no reason to doubt the sincerity of Stolz as she writes of "the bonds of charity that should unite all men" (*Le Vieux* 243). She goes so far as to claim that the poor also must make an effort at forming community: "We don't know one another well enough. If people came together more, some through trust, others through charity, there wouldn't be so many incurable evils" (93). The writers of this collection did not present society as consisting of horizontal layers, made up of classes, but as vertical, through religious appeals to a higher power or through familial images of dependency and trust. Charitable impulses were complex and often combined idealism with realism, sincere religious beliefs with a pragmatic desire not to be cheated. As Harrison concludes: "The charitable imperative that all bourgeois Frenchmen recognized in fact pulled them in a variety of different directions" (160). The same can be argued for French women and even the children they taught.

Most writers attempt to resolve the distress evoked by the sight of poverty through modeling a material response that leads to a happy ending; as Doray wrote of Ségur: "Doubtless the most important thing for the countess is that her heros find a way to do good . . . agreeably, associating activity and calm happiness" (164). But in some significant texts, impatience with the inadequacy of social reform leads to a depiction of poverty and philanthropy on a broader scale.

Although many authors encourage a sentimental identification with the sufferings of the marginalized or the powerless, the Countess de Ségur gives voice to their anger and impatience. In *Un Bon Petit Diable* [*A Good Little Devil*] (1865) the protagonist, Charles, suffers mental and physical attacks at the hands of a miserly aunt and a cruel schoolmaster. His sense of injustice leads to acts of purposeful revolt (he leads an uprising in the brutal school) as well as misplaced aggression (he repeatedly torments a cat). Critics have been troubled by the sometimes gratuitous nature of the violence in Ségur's novels, yet here it seems clear that it provides an undercurrent of unease, a sense that if conditions are not righted, violence will break out, in rational or irrational manners. Charles embodies a young and poorly directed sense of revolution; that he is a "good little devil" suggests both that he has justification for his anger and that he is a menace to his community. Throughout the novel there is a sense of apprehension; what will Charles become when he is no longer little? Ségur, a firm believer in the need for a strong but benevolent social order, provides for the reformation of Charles through the loving example of a young blind girl, Juliette, who inspires Charles to use the wealth he providentially acquires in order to help others in need. Society is saved from Charles's anger as he, loved and accepted, learns to take a responsible role. The novel presents his moral growth from a selfish and angry child to a mature and giving adult; it also indirectly models the reformation of society through the condemnation of materialism in the person of the miserly aunt, a plea for the protection of children through the scenes of the Dickensian school,[5] and the role of the wealthy in the establishment of institutions to help the poor. The domestic peace shown at the end of the novel is a symbol of the social peace possible if the anger and violence brewing in society are transformed through positive interpersonal relations.

Charles shows a certain impatience with the inadequacies of temporary assistance efforts; he plans for the use of his resources in order to repair a church and build a school and hospital for the poor: "You will help me to help, not as up to now, poorly and imperfectly, the poor of our parish, but very completely by giving them and assuring to them the means of work and of existence" (Laffont ed. 2:1267). Endowed with a broad vision, he sees poverty as more than a matter of temporary misfortune and need; he looks for its roots in unemployment, poor health care, and limited educational opportunities. This novel highlights gender roles; in the tender Juliette we see the modest domestic model of women's charity: gifts of alms, clothing, and words of encouragement. The Catholic education of women stressed their special aptitude and duty to relieve suffering: "Gifted with heart, woman exercises charity first by a natural penchant, then by duty" (Levy 200). The majority of children's texts equate children's philanthropy with the female model. Charles, as he grows into manhood, shows the possibilities that greater resources and opportunities afford charitable men.

One example of a woman who steps out from the limited role of almsgiver suggests, however, that children's books did not entirely adopt the gender stereotypes of their time. In Ségur's *Pauvre Blaise* [*Poor Blaise*] (1861) we see a widow who "having no children . . . resolved to consecrate herself entirely to the service of the poor by founding charitable works. She established a daycare [facility] and a school directed by nuns. She often visited them and spent entire hours there" (807). This charity, clearly a substitute for maternal activities and, since she is accompanied by her parents, an extension of childish "good works," underscores the expectation that even a strong and independent woman will be defined by a domestic role. It highlights the complexity of these texts, which are both liberal in their desire to integrate the outcast into society and conservative in their interpretation of what form that society should preserve. By portraying "angels" of charity, women writers emphasized their own importance, but in a carefully restricted arena.

In contrast, a male who seems to adopt the female pattern of giving through close personal contact and long-term relationships is Ségur's famous creation General Dourakine. In the two novels involving him, *L'Auberge de l'Ange Gardien* [*The Guardian Angel Inn*] (1863) and *Le Général Dourakine* (1863), he lavishly gives money to help individuals who have captured his heart and adopts charming and hard-working poor people into his family. Significantly, however, he lacks the discipline generally demonstrated by female characters, and his actions are capricious and uneven. Abel, the aristocrat of Ségur's *Jean qui grogne et Jean qui rit* [*Jean Who Groans and Jean Who Laughs*] (1865) is another avatar of this generous but judgmental figure, who is capable of giving on a grand scale but whose gestures express his emotional preferences rather than a concerted effort to change society.

Despite these exceptions, charity is generally clearly gendered, and the organized and rationalized giving on a larger scale that we often associate with the term *philanthropy* is a pattern displayed by male characters. Instead of a poor reaper, male philanthropists in these novels tend to help "the poor" in the nameless plural. The figure of the modern philanthropist as we know it, a wealthy industrialist who uses his wealth to benefit society, appears in another Ségur novel, *La Fortune de Gaspard* [*Gaspard's Fortune*] (1866). Significantly, Gaspard begins as the son of a farmer. Intelligent and repulsed by the work of the farm, Gaspard devotes himself to academic success and lands a job as an accountant for a successful manufacturer. Using guile, he denigrates fellow workers and flatters his way into the old man's heart. He eventually becomes legally adopted by the wealthy man, renouncing his membership in the fully intact and functioning farm family. Here the theme of "adoption," so positive in other novels in which the rich reached out to the truly needy, becomes a sign of Gaspard's greed and ambition. Interestingly, he comes truly to care for the old man, and a slow moral and emotional transformation begins. This reformation is culminated by his marriage to an angelic woman who through example teaches him the joys of charity. In the end he uses his significant wealth to transform the region through labor reform, education, the building of a hospital, and the reparation of a church. The female role of performing humble good works and exerting sentimental influence is played by the wife, Mina, and in fact it is crucial to the moral transformation of the man. But the male character is central. He shows the underside of the class divisions—the farm boy's resentment and desire to scramble up from his powerless position by any means. A kind of children's Julien Sorel, Gaspard burns to leave his home and exploits his education to manipulate society and find a path to success.[6] His rejection of his parentage flies in the face of the family-centered values propounded by Ségur and by the majority of other contemporary children's writers and makes him appear selfish, even a villain for much of the novel. In a sense, he is a model of another form of revolutionary threat, the "self-made man" who pursues wealth and power at the expense of community and family. Until he meets Mina, Gaspard threatens to be a "devil" in a much less amusing way than Charles in the novel discussed above. His anger and resentment, like the demands of the poor in *Les Enfants de la Ferme* and the fury of Charles in *Un Bon*

Petit Diable, are not entirely unjustified, and his grievances, like his manipulations, are realistic reproaches to a false image of the family and
of a competitive society. Through Mina, who is the daughter of a rich
industrialist but who because of her limited personal resources and
restricted life as a woman seems more materially impoverished than
Gaspard, he has his own kind of encounter with poverty and learns of
love from a lower order, from a powerless being. When he uses his vast
resources to put her wishes into effect, at once drawing on his understanding of society to work through the system and transform it, the
sentimental, exemplary woman and the efficient man combine heart
and head, sentiment and reason, to transform an entire community.

The public reform initiated by Gaspard follows an inner spiritual
and moral transformation, achieved through the power of emotion
and example, through humble actions that address individuals in a
personal and committed relationship. All of the local economic and
societal transformations come through the family, that model of stability and hope for the society at large. This model remains that of
women and children's charity, now given extension through male
power and resources until Gaspard becomes not only father of his
household but also father to his workers. Again, one could speak of
control and domination, of a placating of the poor through patronage. Or one could argue that writers such as Ségur looked beyond the
prejudices of their order to raise a generation that would strive to overcome class hostility. Although I argue for the latter, the complexity of
the seemingly innocuous texts allows for both interpretations.

What is obvious is the commitment of these writers to the child readers as thinking and feeling beings who must learn to ask and answer
questions when confronted with someone poorer or weaker than
themselves. Considering the social issues addresssed in Ségur's novel,
Marc Soriano argues that *Gaspard* is a book that slipped past readers
through "the surest of disguises, that of literature for youth" (cited in
Marcoin 19). Critics sometimes suggest that women chose to write for
children because they could, through these inoffensive volumes, express themselves as they dared not do in adult fiction. I would argue
that this denigrates their commitment to, and belief in, their readership. Children's writers of the second half of the nineteenth century
in France were not ready to postpone issues of private suffering and
social failings until readers reached adulthood. They seemed to write
from a sense of mission and dedicated themselves to the education
of children into social responsibility. This is a model that should not

be denigrated or lost. In her conclusion to a study of the Countess de Ségur, Marie-France Doray points to the aristocratic writer's continuing success among child readers as proof that one can bring to young children images of a world of conflict and need. Doray criticizes contemporary writers and teachers who are reluctant to speak of social problems to children and ends with a question: "Is it more difficult now than in the time of Napoleon III to help children understand violence, social inequalities or injustice?" (220).

Notes

1. For further information on the history of poverty and philanthropy in the nineteenth century, see Crubellier, *L'Enfance et la jeunesse;* Denby, *Sentimental Narrative;* Duprat, *Le Temps des philanthropes;* Fayet-Scribe, *Associations féminines et Catholicisme;* Forrest, *French Revolution and the Poor,* Harrison, *Bourgeois Citizen;* Heywood, *Childhood;* and Lehning, *Peasant and French.*

2. All translations are my own. Note that all of the novels cited come from a three-volume set published in the "Bouquins" series by Editions Robert Laffont, Paris, 1990. The list in Works Cited gives the original dates of publication by Hachette in Paris and the volume number for Laffont. The only exception is *L'Evangile,* not included in the collection.

3. Although this study concerned women in the north of France, Smith's comments on values seem to be supported by these authors, women living and publishing in the sophisticated Parisian area.

4. An important study of the *Bibliothèque Rose Illustrée* can be found in Mistler's *La Libraire Hachette.* Other helpful studies of French children's literature include Bleton, *La Vie Sociale;* Caradec, *Histoire;* Davis, *Happy Island; Fonds ancien de littérature;* Lhérété, "Morale du peuple"; and Trigon, *Histoire de la littérature.*

5. In the novel Charles reads aloud to his aunt from a French translation of *Nicholas Nickleby,* and the choice of novel is an *hommage* to Dickens, who published with Hachette.

6. The similarity to Julien Sorel has been noted by Cabanis and Marcoin; Cabanis equates Gaspard with Balzac's Rastignac (Marcoin, 19).

Works Cited

Basch, Françoise. "Réflexion sur le sentimental et le 'genre' dans deux romans victoriens: Charles Dickens, *David Copperfield* et George Eliot, *Le Moulin sur la Floss.*" In *Le Roman Sentimental.* Limoges, France: Université de Limoges, 1990. Pp. 131–42.

Bleton, Pierre. *La Vie sociale sous le Second Empire: Un étonnant témoignage de la comtesse de Ségur.* Paris: Editions Ouvrières, 1963.

Caradec, François. *Histoire de la littérature enfantine en France.* Paris: Albin Michel, 1977.

Carraud, Jeanne. *La Petite Jeanne [Little Jeanne].* 1852. Paris: Hachette, 1893.

Crubellier, Maurice. *L'Enfance et la jeunesse dans la société française 1800–1950.* Paris: Armand Colin, 1979.

Davis, James Herbert. *The Happy Island: Images of Childhood in the Eighteenth-Century French Théâtre d'éducation.* New York: Lang, 1987.

Denby, David J. *Sentimental Narrative and the Social Order in France, 1760–1820.* Cambridge: Cambridge University Press, 1994.

Doray, Marie-France. *Une Etrange paroissienne, la Comtesse de Ségur.* Paris: Rivages, 1990.

Duprat, Catherine. *Le Temps des philanthropes: La philanthropie des Lumières à la monarchie de Juillet.* Vol. 1. Paris: Editions C. T. H. S., 1993.

Fayet-Scribe, Sylvie. *Associations féminines et Catholicisme. De la Charité à l'action sociale XIXe–XXe siècle.* Paris: Editions Ouvrières, 1990.

Forrest, Alan. *The French Revolution and the Poor.* New York: St. Martin's, 1981.

Fonds ancien de littérature pour la jeunesse: Catalogue des livres imprimés avant 1914. Paris: Bibliothèque de l'Heure Joyeuse, 1987.

Fresneau, Mme Armand. *Les Protégés d'Isabelle.* [*Isabelle's Protégés*] Paris: Hachette, 1890.

Gouraud, Julie. *Les Enfants de la Ferme* [*The Farm Children*] 1869. Paris: Hachette, 1904.

Harrison, Carol E. *The Bourgeois Citizen in Nineteenth-Century France: Gender, Sociability, and the Uses of Emulation.* Oxford: Oxford University Press, 1999.

Hellerstein, Erna Olafson, Leslie Parker Hume, and Karen M. Offen, eds. *Victorian Women: A Documentary Account of Women's Lives in Nineteenth-Century England, France, and the United States.* Palo Alto: Stanford University Press, 1981.

Heywood, Colin. *Childhood in Nineteenth-Century France: Work, Health, and Education Among the "classes populaires."* Cambridge: Cambridge University Press, 1988.

Lehning, James R. *Peasant and French: Cultural Content in Rural France During the Nineteenth Century.* Cambridge: Cambridge University Press, 1995.

Levy, Marie-Françoise. "Morale familiale et morale chrétienne dans l'éducation des filles de la bourgeoisie en France sous le second empire: L'enjeu du savoir." Ph.D. diss., University of Paris 1983.

Lhérété, Annie. "Morale du peuple et morale pour le peuple dans la littérature enfantine (18e–19e siècle)." In *Popular Traditions and Learned Culture in France from the Sixteenth to the Twentieth Century.* Ed. Marc Bertrand. Palo Alto: Anma Libri, 1985. Pp. 115–32.

Lynch, Katherine A. *Family, Class, and Ideology in Early Industrial France: Social Policy and the Working-Class Family, 1825–1848.* Madison: University of Wisconsin Press, 1988.

Marcoin, Francis. *La Comtesse de Ségur ou le Bonheur Immobile.* Arras: Artois Presses Université, 1999.

Maza, Sarah. "Luxury, Morality, and Social Change in Prerevolutionary France." *Journal of Modern History* 69 (1997): 199–229.

Mistler, Jean. *La Librairie Hachette de 1826 à nos jours.* Paris: Hachette, 1964.

Pessin, Alain. *Le Mythe du peuple et la société française au dix-neuvième siècle.* Paris: Presses Universitaires de France, 1992.

Price, Roger. *A Social History of Nineteenth-Century France.* New York: Holmes & Meier, 1987.

Rousseau, Jean-Jacques. *Oeuvres complètes.* Ed. B. Ganebin and M. Raymond. Vol. 4. Paris: Pléiade, 1959–69.

Ségur, Sophie de.

———. *L'Auberge de l'Ange Gardien.* [*The Guardian Angel Inn*] 1863. Vol. 1.

———. *Un Bon Petit Diable.* [*A Good Little Devil*] 1865. Vol. 2.

———. *L'Evangile d'une Grand'mère.* [*A Grandmother's Gospel*] Paris: Hachette, 1866. Paris: Société Liturgique, 1926.

———. *La Fortune de Gaspard.* [*Gaspard's Fortune*] 1866. Vol. 3.

———. *Le Général Dourakine.* 1863. Vol. 2.

———. *Jean qui grogne et Jean qui rit.* [*Jean Who Groans and Jean Who Laughs.*] 1865. Vol. 3.

———. *Pauvre Blaise* [*Poor Blaise*] 1862. Vol. 1.

———. *Les Petites Filles Modèles.* [*The Model Little Girls*]. 1858. Vol. 1.

Smith, Bonnie G. *Ladies of the Leisure Class: The Bourgeoises of Northern France in the Nineteenth Century.* Princeton: Princeton University Press, 1981.

Stolz, Mme de. *Les Protégés d'Isabelle.* [*Isabelle's Protégés*] Paris: Hachette, 1890.

———. *Le Trésor de Nanette.* [*Nanette's Treasure*] Paris: Hachette, 1900.

———. *Le Vieux de la Forêt.* [*The Old Man of the Forest*] Paris: Hachette, 1883.

Trigon, Jean de. *Histoire de la littérature enfantine de ma mère l'Oye au Roi Babar.* Paris: Hachette, 1950.

Vinson, Marie-Christine. *L'Education des petites filles chez la Comtesse de Ségur.* Lyon: Presses Universitaires de Lyon, 1987.

Weber, Eugen. *Peasants into Frenchmen: The Modernization of Rural France 1870–1914.* Palo Alto: Stanford University Press, 1976.

Winston, Andrew S. "Sweetness and Light: Psychological Aesthetics and Sentimental Art." In *Emerging Visions of the Aesthetic Process: Psychology, Semiology, and Philosophy.* Ed. Gerald C. Cupchick and Janos Laszlo. Cambridge: Cambridge University Press: 1992. Pp. 118–36.

"Wake up, and be a man": Little Women, Laurie, and the Ethic of Submission

Ken Parille

> *Justice has never been done to the sweetest and most attractive side of her nature—her real love for boys, which sprang from the boy nature that was hers in so marked a degree.*
>
> —Alfred Whitman

During the past twenty-five years, *Little Women* has been at the center of the feminist project of reading texts by nineteenth-century American women. A primary reason for the extensive interest in Alcott's novel is its discussion of the cultural spaces women occupied, or were excluded from, during the mid and late nineteenth century. Although critics have disagreed about whether the novel "seeks a new vision of women's subjectivity and space" or argues for a "repressive domesticity," it nevertheless offers us a complicated and compelling picture of Alcott and her culture's understanding of girls and women (Murphy 564). Yet an important story within *Little Women* remains largely untreated in recent criticism, one that will affect our understanding of the novel's exploration of gender: that of the male protagonist, Laurie. Although critics have done important work by drawing our attention to Alcott's exploration of patriarchal structures and their effect on girls and women, they have not looked in any detail at her concurrent examination of their effect on boys and men.

In many ways, Laurie's story is similar to that of many mid- and late-nineteenth-century middle-class young men. Like the struggles of the March girls, his struggle and ultimate submission to cultural expectations for young men narrate a typical confrontation with the limitations of gender roles. Throughout *Little Women,* Laurie is subjected to a version of what critics often describe as the "ethic of submission," an ethic usually deemed relevant only to girls' and women's lives because only they were expected to submit to patriarchal authority: "American women," Jane Tompkins argues, "simply could not . . . [rebel] against the conditions of their lives for they lacked the material means of es-

Children's Literature 29, ed. Elizabeth Lennox Keyser and Julie Pfeiffer (Yale University Press, © 2001 Hollins University).

cape or opposition. They had to stay put and submit" (*Designs* 161). For Tompkins and many critics after her, this ethic meant that girls and women were expected to conform to very narrow roles (dutiful daughter, caring mother, obedient wife), in contrast to boys and men, who were free from such limitations.[1]

In Alcott scholarship, the view of submission as a gendered phenomenon goes back to critics such as Nina Auerbach, Judith Fetterley, and Patricia Spacks, who, in her landmark work *The Female Imagination*, takes Jo at her word when she says "Boys always have a capital time," forgetting that the narrator and even Jo herself realize that this is often not the case (100).[2] Although critics have begun to question this gendered understanding of submission as it applies to men's and boys' lives, in Alcott studies it still remains a prevalent assumption; Jo's story is seen as a paradigmatic example of this ethic, while the ways in which Laurie's story parallels hers are neglected. Only Elizabeth Keyser and Anne Dalke have noted that *Little Women* dramatizes Laurie's struggle with patriarchal expectations. Keyser observes that Laurie "exemplifies . . . the masculine plight," yet she does not explore at any length what "the masculine plight" is, how Laurie represents this plight, and what cultural beliefs shape it (*Whispers* 66–67).[3] Dalke mentions that Laurie's narrative parallels the girls', but she does not examine this similarity or discuss its significance (573).[4] Critics need to see that Laurie's experience, like those of the March girls, is at every point conditioned by the kinds of patriarchal and materialist pressures that affected girls' lives. As Rita Felski has pointed out, the ideologies that animate culture should "be understood as a complex formation of beliefs, structures, and representations which shapes and permeates the subjective sense of self of both men and women" (27). The specific ideologies are, of course, historically contingent and differ based on factors such as race, class, and gender; Laurie, for example, is allowed and encouraged to attend college, but Jo is not. For boys, though, the pressure to live up to the standards and achievements of other males (especially the pressure to succeed in the market) has, in some sense, always circumscribed their field of possibilities, as it circumscribes Laurie's.

Using studies of masculinity in America during the nineteenth century by Michael Kimmel, Anthony Rotundo, Judy Hilkey, and Joe Dubbert, I will examine Laurie's capitulation to patriarchal and materialist pressures in the form of his grandfather's desire that he become a merchant and the way in which Amy March functions as the grand-

father's agent. By repeatedly questioning his masculinity, Amy shames
Laurie into acting in accord with his grandfather's wishes. Once we
understand Laurie's story in this way—as submission brought about by
shame—we can then revise the conventional critical position that the
"feminine quality of self-denial" is "the novel's . . . message" (Gaard 5).[5]
In order to understand more fully what Alcott and *Little Women* have
to say about gender, we must recover Alcott's narrative of masculine
self-denial.

Perhaps critics have not explored the parallels between Laurie's and
the March girls' narratives because in letters and journals Alcott often
idealized boyhood and set it in opposition to her life as a girl and
a woman, a life filled with disappointments and restrictions. The joy
and freedom she could not imagine for herself, she imagined as the
province of boys. In October 1860, for instance, Alcott saw the Prince
of Wales while he was on a tour through the United States. "Boys
are always jolly," she mused, "even princes" (*Journal* 100). Possibly in
part because of such idealizations, critics believe that Jo articulates a
truth about boyhood when she says that "boys always have a capital
time." But in *Little Women,* Laurie's story shows us that Alcott's ideas
about the lives of boys are much more complex; the text rarely makes
any idealizing claims about boyhood. Laurie is definitely not "always
jolly," and, puzzled that he could be wealthy and sad, Jo exclaims,
"Theodore Laurence, you ought to be the happiest boy in the world"
(52). Laurie's unhappiness results from his place in a world of men and
the concurrent pressure of proving himself a man to the novel's characters. According to Michael Kimmel, this pressure is a defining feature of American masculinity in the nineteenth century (ix), the era
that the historian Joe Dubbert calls "the masculine century" (13).

Gilded Age success manuals for young men published around the
time of *Little Women* often depict a boy's life as fraught with anxiety.
They present him as prone to worrying and suffering from "dissat-
isfaction with . . . [his] destiny" and "spells of melancholy" (cited in
Hilkey 76). Similarly, Alcott introduces us to Laurie as a lonely, frustrated young man. Unlike the nurturing domestic circle of the March
girls and their mother, Laurie's world is an isolated male enclave composed of his grandfather and his tutor, John Brooke, both of whom are
grooming him for a life he does not want; during a game called "rig-
marole," Brooke even relates a thinly veiled allegory of Laurie's submission and his role in it. As a knight, Brooke must "tame and train"

Laurie, "a fine, but unbroken colt" who is a "pet of the king's," Laurie's grandfather (127). Although Laurie eventually goes to work for his grandfather, he desperately wants "to enjoy myself in my own way": "I'm to be a famous musician myself, and all creation is to rush to hear me; and I'm never to be bothered about money or business, but just enjoy myself, and live for what I like" (29, 142). In spite of these fantasies, Laurie knows that his future involves a different kind of "capital time" than the one Jo thinks boys always have, namely, one devoted to "money and business." As Dubbert observes, men "were expected to cash in on . . . opportunities to maximize their gains and minimize their losses" and not, as Laurie says, "live for what [they] like" (15). His grandfather fears that Laurie wants to pursue a materially unproductive and therefore unmasculine career: "His music isn't bad, but I hope he will do as well in more important things" (55). What is important for his grandfather is that Laurie do well in business, as he had done.

It seems likely that Laurie's desire to be a musician and not a merchant would have met with a stern response not only from his grandfather but from many parents. Antebellum conduct books and Gilded Age success manuals never acknowledged art as a viable career for middle-class young men. Rather, these manuals endorsed typical preindustrial occupations, such as farmer, craftsman, and shopkeeper (Hilkey 110). Even the boys' fiction of the period rarely portrayed artistic occupations as possible careers for middle-class boys. Vocations such as musician—and the arts in general—were thought of as "less manly" because, as entertainment, they were outside the rigors of the marketplace. "Aesthetic contributions" to culture, Dubbert notes, were devalued compared to the contributions of businessmen and "men of action" (30–31). William Dean Howells, a contemporary of Alcott, learned to his dismay that a career in the arts was seen as a "female" vocation: "To pursue his interests," Rotundo observes, "he had to divide himself into male and female halves that could only flourish in different social realms" (170). In an 1878 manual, *Success in Life, and How to Secure It: or Elements of Manhood and Their Culture,* William Owen expresses a typical position on the value of the arts, one that echoes Laurie's grandfather's desire that Laurie do "well in more important things": "Let poets and preachers, [and] artists . . . bestow more time on material matters . . . and let our schools and colleges remember to make men—stalwart, invincible *men*" (cited in Hilkey 109).[6]

Norms of masculinity, as Kimmel and others have argued, are often created and enforced through the pressures placed on boys and men to enact certain behaviors, behaviors which usually either explicitly or implicitly involve capital.[7] Throughout the nineteenth century, boys like Laurie were often expected to enter their father's business:

> I ought to be satisfied to please grandfather, and I do try, but it's working against the grain, you see, and comes hard. He wants me to be an India merchant, as he was, and I'd rather be shot; I hate tea, and silk, and spices. . . . Going to college ought to satisfy him, for if I give him four years he ought to let me off from the business; but he's set, and I've got to do just as he did, unless I break away and please myself, as my father did. (144)

But this dream of breaking away, Alcott says, is difficult for both sexes to realize; pleasing oneself, to use one of her favorite phrases, is an "air castle" that must be abandoned by little men and women alike. Here, as elsewhere, Alcott dramatizes a central claim of many critics who study masculinity: culture has its designs on male fulfillment (Dubbert 1–11; Kimmel 1–10). So, like many young men, Laurie is not free to pursue the career he wants, for it would be "working against the grain" of cultural expectations.

Dubbert's and Hilkey's discussions of advice literature for young men shows that manliness was synonymous with success in the market. A boy knew that he would never be viewed as a man unless he was fiscally productive (Dubbert 27–28; Hilkey 142–46); as success manuals repeatedly announced, "character was capital" (Hilkey 126). That a career as an artist would be counterproductive has already been forecast in the story of Laurie's father, a musician who "please[d] him]self" and ran away, only to end up dead (144). The narrator never tells us how and why he dies, but the implication is that his death results from his career choice; had he become an India merchant—as Laurie's grandfather surely would have wanted—a different outcome is easy to imagine. Though still only a young man, Laurie has been initiated into the male world of negotiation. He trades four years of his life in order to escape becoming an India merchant—a bargain that does not pay off.

Although many men likely fantasized about "breaking away," the pressure placed on them to succeed in business meant that most could not and did not. In reaction to pressure and violence directed at him by his grandfather, Laurie tells Jo he wants to run away to Washing-

ton. "What fun you'd have!" Jo replies. "I wish I could run off, too. . . .
If I was a boy, we'd run away together, and have a capital time; but as
I'm a miserable girl, I must be proper, and stay at home. Don't tempt
me, Teddy, it's a crazy plan" (212–13). In spite of the romance of escape, she believes that Laurie's interests are best served by remaining,
so she orchestrates a truce to keep him at home. Critics tend to take
Jo's comment as reiterating a cultural truth: boys can run away, but
girls must submit. Ann Murphy, for instance, claims that "as a boy, Jo
would be . . . able to . . . 'run away [with Laurie] and have a capital
time,' " even though the text tells us in no uncertain terms that Laurie
cannot (577). Running away is not an option for him, as it often was not
for middle- and upper-class young men. They typically were not the
ones who went out west in search of gold or to sea in search of whales
(Kimmel 63). Rather, they grew up to raise families and hold respectable middle-class positions; as Rotundo observes, parents discouraged
a "bold and daring code" for boys and young men and instead endorsed "the cautious, abstemious ethic of the clerk" (43).[8] Alcott herself often wished to run away, but she learned through her father, as
Laurie learns through Jo (and later Amy), to embrace the doctrine of
duty, labor, and submission; in a journal entry of August 1850, Alcott
said of teaching, "School is hard work, and I feel as though I should
like to run away from it. But . . . [I] do my best" (63). Although contemporary readers must have identified with Jo and Laurie's desire to
escape, they most likely agreed with Jo and Alcott that a boy must "do
[his] duty" (145).

John Crowley has argued that Laurie wants to run away in order to
escape domesticity, a claim that echoes much critical work characterizing male escape fantasies as longings to be free from women.[9] Novels
such as *Moby-Dick* and Cooper's Leatherstocking tales were canonized
by critics who felt that these texts advocated an ideal American manhood by celebrating the protagonist's flight from "feminizing" civilization, his refusal to submit to domesticity. Feminists rightly criticized
these critics' endorsement of the flight trope as misogynist, yet they
repeated the earlier critical mistake of assuming that domesticity was,
invariably, the crucial problem for men, the sole aspect of their daily
lives from which they wanted to escape. Although it is true that escape fantasies could be driven by an urge to reject what some men felt
as the confines of domesticity, recent scholarship on masculinity has
drawn our attention to the ways in which men have constantly fantasized about escaping the pressures of the market, the space Thoreau

called "a site of humiliation." It is more accurate and helpful to see
Laurie's desire for flight as representing the anxiety many boys and
men felt trying to live up to ideal male behaviors. And Jo tells Laurie's
grandfather that his resistance is not to domesticity but to business:
"He won't [run away] unless he is very much worried, and only threatens it sometimes, when he gets tired of studying" for college and preparing for his career (215).

Crowley goes on to suggest that Laurie has an "impulse to escape
the civilizing force of" domesticity because he is "completely surrounded by the woman's sphere" (393, 394). Yet it is male vocation and
violence he wants to flee.[10] In the early part of the novel, and by implication for many years before the action of the text begins, Laurie
has been completely surrounded by men: Mr. Laurence "keeps his
grandson shut up when he isn't riding or walking with his tutor, and
makes him study dreadful hard" (21). The narrator describes Laurie's
"sphere" in quite bleak terms: "it seemed a lonely, lifeless sort of
house; for no children frolicked on the lawn, no motherly face ever
smiled at the windows, and few people went in and out, except the old
gentleman and his grandson" (47). Quite the opposite of wanting to
escape domesticity, he yearns for it, saying to Jo:

> "I beg your pardon for being so rude, but sometimes you forget
> to put down the curtain at the window where the flowers are; and,
> when the lamps are lighted, it's like looking at a picture to see the
> fire, and you all around the table with your mother; her face is
> right opposite, and it looks so sweet behind the flowers, I can't
> help watching it. I haven't got any mother, you know"; and Laurie
> poked the fire to hide a little twitching of the lips that he could
> not control. (50)

The picture Laurie draws here evokes the conventional domestic tab-
leaux of so many Victorian novels and prints, an image that encodes
the values of domesticity: children gathered around their mother in
a scene lit by the glow of a fire. Later, Laurie again imagines his place
in the domestic realm using another visual genre, the landscape:
" 'Here's a landscape!' thought Laurie. . . . It *was* rather a pretty little
picture; for the sisters sat together in the shady nook, with sun and
shadow flickering over them. . . . A shadow passed over the boy's face
as he watched them, feeling that he ought to go, because uninvited. . . .
'May I come in, please?' " (139). Far from escaping domesticity, Laurie
knows that his life will be intimately involved with it. Though some

men and boys could and did flee what these images represented (Kimmel 44), escape into solitude (best represented by the misanthropic nomadism of Daniel Boone) or into male community *(Moby-Dick)* was a notion of male possibility more fantastic than real.[11] Alcott shows such masculine worlds as unsatisfying ideals and instead advocates a notion of male behavior that was more generally endorsed. Writing shortly before *Little Women* was published, the popular lecturer and conduct book author Josiah Holland summed up what middle-class culture expected of its boys: "One of the first things a young man should do is to see that he is acting his part in society . . . you can have no influence unless you are social. . . . The revenge which society takes upon the man who isolates himself, is as terrible as it is inevitable" (63–69). To be "social," then, meant to play a part in societal structures such as marriage, domesticity, and the market. To embrace these structures was the conventional expectation for young men.[12]

In a crucial and often-cited scene in *Little Women,* Mr. Bhaer convinces Jo to give up her dream of being a "sensational" writer. The scene begins with Jo's defense of sensation stories, but after listening to Bhaer's attack on such "trash," she feels "horribly ashamed" (356). The shame Jo feels from seeing herself through, as she calls it, his "moral spectacles" (356) causes her to throw all her "lurid" stories into the stove. Though these stories are profitable and give her the opportunity to experience imaginatively a life she is denied, Jo must stop writing them because such a profession is incompatible with the way in which the novel conceives of "womanhood" (356). Thus Mr. Bhaer acts as a kind of enforcer for the text's values, shaming Jo into sacrificing her desires. But rarely referred to are the scenes in which Amy, acting like Mr. Bhaer, shames Laurie into giving up his dreams of life as an artist, and the moment in which Laurie, echoing Jo's destruction, destroys his own manuscripts. The striking resemblance between these scenes suggests that Alcott wants to draw our attention to the similar sacrifices that boys and girls must make in order to fit into narrowly defined adult roles.[13]

In order to make Laurie into a man, Amy constantly reminds him of his distance from cultural ideals of masculinity.[14] Elaine Showalter observes that Jo's German husband, Mr. Bhaer, is "unconfined by American codes of masculinity" (xxvii), but she misses the way in which Alcott shows us how Laurie, as an American boy, is all too confined by such codes. Amy sees it as her job to awaken the sleeping "young

knight" from his boyish illusions and bring him into conformity with
these norms.[15] She even concludes her sermon by promising, "I won't
lecture any more, for I know you'll wake up, and be a man" (411). As
Jo's "lurid" literary aspirations are in conflict with the way the text
imagines her as a woman, so too are Laurie's boyish artistic dreams
incompatible with the way it imagines him as a man.

An essential part of Amy's shaming of Laurie involves renaming
him; as his friends had called him "Dora" to emphasize his failure
to measure up to their standards of masculinity, Amy calls him "Lazy
Laurence" to feminize him by emphasizing how unindustrious, and
therefore unmanly, he seems to her. Laurie's new name comes from
Maria Edgeworth's didactic story "Lazy Lawrence," published in a
popular collection called the *Parent's Assistant*.[16] The tale features two
boys, Jem, a model of masculine ambition, and Lawrence, a model of
idleness. Like Laurie, Lawrence dreams, dismisses ambition, and en-
joys "amusements," but eventually he converts to the ways of industry.
As Anthony Rotundo observes, one of the key "deficiencies of character that [was] thought to cause failure . . . was laziness. Again and
again we have heard men exhort one another to 'industry,' 'persistence,' 'hard work.' . . . Each of these popular phrases stood not only as
an exhortation to positive behavior, but as a warning against negative
behavior" (179). Amy's appeal to Laurie to be industrious, then, represents a typical exhortation to be successful, but also a warning to him
that if he continues on his present course he will be perceived as a failure. Like a success manual come to life, Amy attempts, as H. A. Lewis
attempted with his *Hidden Treasures,* to "awaken dormant energies in
ONE PERSON who otherwise might have failed" (cited in Hilkey 75).[17]

Though the name "Lazy Laurence" implicitly feminizes him, Amy
tries to make her assault on Laurie's masculinity explicit: "instead of
being the man you might and ought to be, you are only—" (408). But
before she can finish, Laurie interrupts her. He likely believes that
she would conclude with "a girl" or "a woman," and in fact she soon
says, "Aren't you ashamed of a hand like that? It's as soft and white
as a woman's, and looks as if it never did anything but wear Jouvin's
best gloves" (408). A physical sign of manliness is roughness, typically visible in a hand that has been shaped by labor; Daniel Boone's
nineteenth-century biographer, Timothy Flint, for example, railed
against men who lacked the "manly hardihood" of the pioneers, calling them "effeminate spirits, the men of soft hands" (cited in Kimmel
61). Laurie's job as an India merchant, even if it would not literally

rough up his hands, would be a job that made something happen, that would make a man out of him. Laurie is beginning to realize that he cannot become the kind of man that his culture and Amy demand if he continues to pursue his "effeminate" art.

Amy uses her art to further convince Laurie that he has yet to act "manfully." She shows Laurie "a rough sketch of [him] taming a horse; hat and coat were off, and every line of the active figure, resolute face, and commanding attitude, was full of energy and meaning. . . . [In] the rider's breezy hair and erect attitude, there was a suggestion of suddenly arrested motion, of strength, courage" (411). The image contains numerous codes of the "real man" as Amy and the novel conceive of him: active, resolute, in command, and sexually powerful.[18] Amy's sexualized image is like those offered in success manuals, in which writers often connect success and sexual potency: William Owen, for example, argues that "Unless man can erect himself, . . . how poor a thing is man" (cited in Hilkey 149). Amy's "suggestion of suddenly arrested motion," too, is typical; according to Hilkey, the manual writers believed that "only the virile could succeed, and then only by holding their inner powers in reserve for use at just the right moment" (149).[19] Even the kind of sketch Amy draws encodes manliness; it is "rough," in contrast to Laurie's "soft" feminine hands. She tells him that this picture represents him "as you were" and then compares it to a picture that could have been an illustration of Edgeworth's "Lazy Lawrence." But it is clear that Laurie never was such a man. Amy makes this claim in order to shame him by calling his virility into question. As she had used Edgeworth's story as a model for Laurie's life, here she uses her drawing to teach him "a little lesson."

When Amy says to Laurie, "instead of being the man you might and ought to be, you are only—," he concludes for her with "Saint Laurence on a gridiron" (408). The narrator tells us that this insertion "blandly finish[es] the sentence," but Laurie's invocation of one of the most famous Christian martyrs should not be so easily dismissed. That Laurie should see himself as Saint Laurence, a martyr who was burned to death, implies that he recognizes the renunciation of his "boyish passions" as a metaphorical death. The process of converting lazy Laurie into a man, the process that Amy begins, he concludes with a literal act of destruction—he destroys his manuscripts: "He grew more and more discontent with his desultory life, began to long for some real and earnest work . . . then suddenly he tore up his music-sheets one by one" (422).

Laurie's destruction of his manuscripts and the fiery death of his patron saint both implicitly refer to Jo's similar act of martyrdom: the extinguishing of her writerly self by burning her sensational tales. And it is crucial to realize that Amy's shaming of Laurie immediately precedes the destruction of his music. Playing on the fears that, as Kimmel notes, have "haunted" American men, fears "that they are not powerful . . . or successful enough" (8), she repeatedly calls Laurie's masculinity into question and invokes Edgeworth's "Lazy Lawrence" to rewrite his life to coincide with that script, a script whose ending he provides by following its narrative of idleness to industry: "I won't be a humbug any longer" (422).

But Laurie knows that simply destroying the manuscripts is not enough. The best way to prove to Amy and his grandfather that he is not a "humbug" is to do what men do: get a job. As critics have shown, male identity in the nineteenth century was intimately connected to work, and Laurie knows that if he fails to work he will be seen as unmasculine, as weak and feminine. He sends Amy a note addressed to "Mentor" from "Telemachus" in order to acknowledge the success of her "little lesson": " 'Lazy Laurence' has gone to his grandpa, like the best of boys" (412). Although Laurie literally goes to see his grandfather, the metaphorical "going" is most important. He has finally left his boyhood "air castles" and submitted to his grandfather. Like "the best of boys" he embraces the values of the patriarchy and abandons idle dreams in favor of "earnest work." The boy who earlier said he never wanted to be "bothered about money or business" now exclaims, "I'm going into business with a devotion that shall delight grandpa, and prove to him that I'm not spoilt. I need something of the sort to keep me steady. I . . . mean to work like a man" (457). This is perhaps the novel's most compact formulation of the cultural connection between masculinity and material productivity: to be a man is to work. Acting as Mentor, Amy is (to adapt the title of Edgeworth's collection) the "culture's assistant"; that is, she enforces its codes of masculinity. As Mentor educates Telemachus, she teaches Laurie that he can prove himself a man by putting his boyhood dreams behind him. And given Amy's use of Edgeworth's text in enforcing these codes— a use Laurie acknowledges when he says " 'Lazy Laurence' has gone to his grandpa"—it is difficult to understand Beverly Clark's claims that Laurie can rebel "against prescribed texts" (81). In fact, "Lazy Lawrence" acts as the master narrative for Laurie's story, his conversion from idleness to industry. Rather than rebel against this "prescribed text," Laurie accepts its dictates and decides to "work like a man."[20]

Amy thinks she is preparing Laurie to be a man so that he will be a suitable partner for Jo, but the novel has already told us that this pairing is not a possibility (411). Instead, she prepares him to fill the narrowly prescribed categories of middle-class husband, father, and businessman, the roles he ends up playing in her life.[21] As a young woman named Mollie Clark said to her suitor in the year *Little Women* was published, "I often think it is so different for men from what it is with us women. Love is our life[,] our reality, business yours" (cited in Rotundo 168). This perception, Rotundo argues, "was constantly reinforced by the people who made up a man's social world," just as Amy, Jo, and his grandfather reinforce it for Laurie (168). When Laurie marries Amy, he submits to convention, becoming a husband and accepting the reality of a life of business. Many critics have suggested that Jo's marriage to Mr. Bhaer is a kind of punishment. Rather than marry the erotic young Laurie, she ends up with the asexual older man.[22] Yet Laurie's marriage to Amy—the most traditional of all the March girls—instead of Jo could similarly be seen as a punishment. But, of course, Amy's conventionality is the point. His marriage to her signifies that he has proved his manhood to the novel's characters. He accepts convention by embracing domesticity and business.[23]

In an essay that imagines the relevance of *Little Women* in the twenty-first century, Christy Minadeo sees Alcott's novel as valuable only for what it can tell us about girls' experiences, in particular their struggles with cultural limitations. "The trajectory of girls' lives," she argues, "remains carefully defined, and that is why *Little Women* remains relevant to contemporary readers" (200). But Laurie is conspicuously absent from her gaze. When she mentions him, it is only in passing; he is not the subject of a single paragraph. To talk about *Little Women* and gender without including Laurie denies him, Alcott, and us his story. Alcott certainly could have written a very different narrative, one in which Laurie's life was more like Huck Finn's than Jo's. He could have "always had a capital time," perhaps even running away to the capital as he wanted. But like many boys and young men, Laurie was not Huck Finn.[24] He couldn't "light out" for the territory because there was another kind of "capital time" awaiting him: life as a merchant. The parallel between Laurie's and Jo's submission makes it clear that he is as crucial to *Little Women*'s exploration of gender as the March girls. As a novel about Laurie's and the March girls' submission, then, *Little Women* remains relevant to us as a story of how both boys and girls confront cultural limitations.

Notes

The author would like to thank Stephen Railton, Marion Rust, and the readers at *Children's Literature* for their valuable suggestions on earlier versions of this essay.

1. See also Joanne Dobson's reference to "the cultural ethos of feminine 'obedience' and 'subordination' " (Introduction xiv).

2. Ann Murphy's "The Borders of Ethical, Erotic, and Artistic Possibilities in *Little Women*" represents a more recent and influential example of scholarship on gender and the novel that fails to take Laurie into account. Her claims about "female subjectivity" and "sisters' pilgrimage" are based on assumptions that male subjectivity and male pilgrimage always have a fundamentally different structure. This assumption, however, misrepresents Laurie's life as the novel portrays it. Her argument that the text is about the "cultural limitations imposed on female development" (565), though certainly true in one sense, seems incomplete because it erases the way in which Laurie's development is impeded by similar limitations; the text repeatedly shows us how his tutor, grandfather, Amy, and Jo seek to control his development. Like Murphy, many critics who have examined the figure of the artist in the novel either ignore or dismiss Laurie, who, as a musician, deals with many of the same problems that Jo faces. (See, e.g., Fetterley's "Alcott's Civil War" and B. Clark, 95.) The inclusion of Laurie's story would compromise the force of such arguments by making the novel appear less exclusively concerned with feminist issues. Murphy and others have missed the point that the novel is about the ways in which cultural forces shape girls' and boys' lives; the structures and beliefs that condition subjectivity are even more pervasive than many critics have realized.

3. See also Keyser's *Little Women: A Family Romance,* 42–44, for a discussion of Jo, Laurie, and gender roles.

4. Anne Dalke's " 'The House-Band' " is one of two articles devoted to male characters in the book. Dalke examines the reciprocal process of education between males and females in order to counter Nina Auerbach's claim that the novel is about the "autonomous development of women" (571). In her extensive bibliography of *Little Women* scholarship, Ann Murphy does not include Dalke's article, probably because it does not address traditional feminist concerns (562–63). Jan Susina's "Men in *Little Women,*" the only article in the recent collection *Little Women and the Feminist Imagination* (1999) that focuses on male characters, takes a dismissive view of Laurie. Calling him an "awful character," an "unrealistic figure," an "eternal boy," a "token male," and not "a real boy," Susina sees Laurie as a mistake: "I certainly don't want to be Laurie" (169). Following earlier critics, he thinks of Laurie as an undifferentiated "fifth sister," but this erases the complexity of Laurie's life and negates Alcott's interest in how his life dramatizes problems that many boys faced. Other critics have also expressed a negative view of Laurie; Fetterley, for example, says, "If anything, Laurie is Jo's inferior" ("Alcott's Civil War" 381). But Alcott saw herself as a staunch defender of boys from a culture that she felt often neglected and mistreated them; see, e.g., her introduction to "My Boys," published in the first volume of *Aunt Jo's Scrap-bag.*

5. Because of its failure to look at male characters in the text, Greta Gaard's " 'Self-denial was all the fashion' " distorts many of the novel's claims. Gaard correctly notes that "child-rearing manuals [in the nineteenth century] . . . emphasized its [anger's] channeling in boys, but its complete absence in girls" (3), yet the connection of this absence to "the feminine quality of self-denial" that she argues is "the novel's . . . message"

is misleading (5). Although Laurie expresses his anger toward his grandfather, he also must eventually repress it and deny himself; the "dwarfing" and "diminution" of female subjectivity that she talks about equally applies to him (7). In *Little Men,* Jo makes sure her boys know that the "quality of self-denial" is essential to their lives; she tells them, "we will plant self-denial . . . and make it grow" (46).

6. See also Colleen Reardon's valuable discussion of Laurie and music, 80–82.

7. *We Boys,* an anonymous novel brought out by Alcott's publishers, Roberts Brothers, dramatizes this expectation. The narrator discusses the occupations of his and his best friend's fathers: "My father is [a] cashier . . . and I do think a cashier's is the stupidest business!" (7). But in the epilogue we learn that both boys—now men—have the same jobs as their fathers. "Training of Boys," an article in the *Mother's Journal and Family Visitant,* says that when a young boy imitates his father's employment, "labor becomes insensibly incorporated among his thoughts" (182). See Rotundo, 37, for a discussion about boys "imitating" their fathers' profession. See Zimet, 38, for a brief examination of this idea in textbooks of the period.

8. In an article that appeared in *Putnam's Magazine* shortly after *Little Women* was published, Rebecca Harding Davis describes how "the majority of young men . . . hop[e] . . . to become a good citizen, husband, and father . . . [and go] into business" (343).

9. See, e.g., the discussions of Melville and Twain in Fiedler's *Love and Death in the American Novel* and Judith Fetterley's reading of "Rip Van Winkle" (*Resisting* 1–11). Fetterley correctly notes that Rip's escape is motivated by a rejection of his wife, but she misses how it involves a desire to reject the pressures of work; as the narrator says, Rip wants "to escape from the labour of the farm and clamour of his wife" (32).

10. Violence often serves as a mechanism to enforce male submission. In order to create an environment in which the failure to submit has definite consequences, Laurie's grandfather uses violence. Though Jo does not think much of the grandfather's threat, Laurie, who has experienced violence in a way that Jo has not (he "thrashed" boys who had called him Dora), feels differently: "he privately thought she would have good reason to be a trifle afraid of the old gentleman, if she met him in some of his moods" (51). His grandfather "lectured and pummeled" Laurie when he refused to answer a question: "I've been shaken, and I won't bear it! . . . if it had been anyone else I'd have— . . . I'll allow no man to shake *me*" (211). Laurie's response to this violence is typical; he desires to inflict violence himself: "I'll thrash him with my own hands" (214). But, of course, Laurie can't do this, so he just "bears it."

11. Stories about Boone were immensely popular in the nineteenth century. He was celebrated in part because of his strident dismissal of materialism. Although this rejection seems to place him in opposition to the more conventional pro-market attitude (an opposition that Laurie shares in the first part of the novel), it is likely that his popularity derived from the fact that he offered men an imaginative rejection of the forces that so dominated their lives.

12. Holland's comments here represent the stance toward male submission advocated by fellow conduct manual writers Rufus Clark, Daniel Eddy, W. W. Everts, Harvey Newcomb, and others.

13. A similarity between Jo and Laurie that many critics have noted is their androgyny. Yet to see Laurie primarily as androgynous is to ignore the way he is also figured as one of the period's most conventional boy types: the bad boy. Alcott's narrator articulates what could stand as the quintessential definition of the bad boy: "Being only a 'glorious human boy,' of course he frolicked and flirted, grew dandified, aquatic, sentimental or gymnastic . . . talked slang, and more than once came perilously near suspension and expulsion. But as high spirits and the love of fun were the causes of these pranks, he always managed to save himself by frank confession, honorable atonement, or the irresistible power of persuasion which he possessed in perfection. In fact, he rather prided himself on his narrow escapes, and liked to thrill the girls with graphic

accounts of his triumphs" (238–9). Such a description could easily be of Tom Sawyer or Tom Bailey, the hero of Thomas Bailey Aldrich's *Story of a Bad Boy* (1870), whose narrator describes his young self as "an amiable, impulsive lad, blessed with fine digestive powers and no hypocrite. . . . In short, I was a real human boy" (7–8). Like the "mischievous Laurie," the bad boy commits pranks yet is always forgiven. Tom Sawyer, for example, continually misbehaves, yet his Aunt Polly "ain't got the heart to lash him, somehow" (10). The March girls call Laurie a "bad boy" (207, 213), but like Aunt Polly, feel "that it was impossible to frown upon him" (210). Laurie's theatricality, too, identifies him as a literary predecessor to Tom Sawyer. Laurie uses the kind of mock romantic posturing that characterizes bad boys like Sawyer, who goes to Becky Thatcher's house, lies underneath what he thinks to be her window, and revels in the fantasies of a wounded lover — all of which echo Laurie underneath Meg's window: "Laurie . . . seemed suddenly possessed with a melodramatic fit, for he fell down upon one knee in the snow, beat his breast, tore his hair, and clasped his hand imploringly . . . and when Meg told him to behave himself . . . he wrung imaginary tears out of his handkerchief, and staggered round the corner as if in utter despair" (225). Ignoring these similarities, Susina claims that Laurie is more like the "good boy" Sid Sawyer than his brother Tom (164). In his "*Little Women* and the Boy-Book," Crowley likewise overlooks such parallels.

14. Educational writers often endorsed shame as an effective method of discipline for boys. In "Discipline; School Government," published in *The American Journal of Education*, the author says, "An appeal to a boy's sense of shame, or to his manliness, may often be made with success" (Hamill 128). He refers to an incident in which he was able to get a boy to take an exam simply by saying, "Albert, I want you to be a man, and . . . pass your examination" (129).

15. In this chapter Amy and the narrator share a discourse that connects boyhood to dreaming and manhood to waking from these dreams. This shared language suggests how Amy acts as a voice for the novel's values. In a letter to Alfred Whitman, a childhood friend on whom Laurie was partially based, Alcott said that "there was always something very brave & beautiful to me in the sight of a boy when he first 'wakes up' & . . . resolves to carry [life] nobly to the end through all disappointments" (*Letters* 51).

16. Amy's use of Edgeworth as a moral authority puts her in good company; the most influential nineteenth-century American educator, Horace Mann, said that "Edgeworth was 'universally acknowledged' to be the foremost writer on education since Locke" (cited in Kett 113). Alcott's father, the transcendentalist and educator Bronson Alcott, also had his students read Edgeworth.

17. As Hilkey points out, success and failure were gendered: "the equation that linked manhood with success was built upon a corollary equation that linked the feminine with failure" (155). Thus Amy's attack on Laurie participates in a conventional gendered discourse, one that, as conduct and success manuals show, was often directed against young men.

18. Amy's emphasis on physical strength and its connection with character is echoed in advice and success manuals published during and after the Civil War. The historian Joseph Kett says of Daniel Eddy (author of *The Young Man's Friend*, 1865) that he "was so convinced of the challenge facing young men in the late 1860s that . . . [he called] for physical culture [and] he lapsed into rhetorical declarations of the value of force and energy" much like those in the narrator's description of Amy's drawing (163).

19. For a detailed discussion of this sexualized discourse in success manuals, see Hilkey, 146–51.

20. Clark also argues that "other males" can rebel "against prescribed texts" (81). Yet the other men in the novel — Brooke, the tutor and conventional husband, Laurie's grandfather, the typical business man, and Mr. Bhaer, the wise and gentle father — are fully in line with conventional expectations for middle-class men (81). Laurie even romanticizes his own act of not rebelling by figuring it in terms of one of the period's

most valorized "prescribed texts," heroic self-sacrifice: "the boy said to himself, with re-solve to make the sacrifice cheerfully, 'I'll let my castle go, and stay with the dear old gentleman while he needs me, for I am all he has' " (146). He mitigates his loss by figur-ing himself as the suffering hero in his grandfather's narrative, the story that replaces his "castle," his dream to be a musician.

21. It is curious that although Laurie is wealthy, he and Amy believe strongly that he must work. But as Francis Gund wrote in 1837, "Business is the very soul of an American: he pursues it, not as a means of procuring for himself and his family the necessary com-forts of life, but as the fountain of all human felicity" (cited in Kimmel 24). Like Amy, success manual authors worried about the boy who already had wealth: they felt that he was likely to lead a life of "emasculated idleness and laziness" (cited in Hilkey 91).

22. See, e.g., Spacks, *Female Imagination*, 101.

23. When Laurie appears in the later two novels of the March family trilogy, *Little Men* and *Jo's Boys*, he becomes like many fathers in nineteenth-century novels: an often absent provider. In *Little Men*, he makes a brief but telling comment about his vocation, a topic on which the text otherwise remains almost silent: "I get desperately tired of business" (191).

24. Murphy invokes Huck Finn as a point of contrast to the lives of the March girls, saying that Huck "may very well be a metaphor for white, middle-class male America" (567). But if Huck is a metaphor, it is only for the dreams of middle-class American men who wanted to escape the pressure and responsibility of their work, but, like Laurie, were expected to accept their role. Though *Little Women* presents a much more repre-sentative look at the cultural truths about boys and escape fantasies than do other texts (especially *Adventures of Huckleberry Finn*), for the last twenty-five years *Huck Finn* and *Moby-Dick* have been used by critics as representative of male experiences, concerns, and possibilities in the mid- and late nineteenth century. Critics have compared these texts to women's fictions in order to illuminate the restrictions placed on women in light of the autonomy given to Huck and Ishmael. Yet the experiences that both these texts chronicle have limited relevance to the lives of many middle-class mid-nineteenth-century boys and men. For some of the many comparisons with *Moby-Dick*, for example, see Tompkins, Afterword, 586, 593, and *Designs*, 147; Dobson, *Hidden Hand*, 239; Harris, *19th-Century American Women's Novels*, 20; Baym, *Woman's Fiction*, 14; Ammons, "Stowe's Dream," 157; Auerbach, *Communities*, 8.

Works Cited

Alcott, Louisa May. *The Journals of Louisa May Alcott*. Ed. Joel Myerson and Daniel Shealy. Boston: Little, Brown, 1989.
——. *Little Men*. Boston: Roberts Brothers, 1872.
——. *Little Women*. New York: Penguin, 1989.
——. "My Boys." In *Aunt Jo's Scrap-bag*. Vol. 1. Boston: Roberts Brothers, 1872.
——. *The Selected Letters of Louisa May Alcott*. Ed. Joel Myerson and Daniel Shealy. Bos-ton: Little, Brown, 1987.
Aldrich, Thomas Bailey. *The Story of a Bad Boy*. Boston, 1870.
Ammons, Elizabeth. "Stowe's Dream of the Mother-Savior: *Uncle Tom's Cabin* and Ameri-can Women Writers Before the 1920s." In *New Essays on Uncle Tom's Cabin*. Ed. Eric J. Sundquist. New York: Cambridge University Press, 1986. Pp. 155–95.
Auerbach, Nina. *Communities of Women: An Idea in Fiction*. Cambridge: Harvard Univer-sity Press, 1978.
Baym, Nina. *Woman's Fiction: A Guide to Novels by and About Women in America, 1820–1870*. Ithaca: Cornell University Press, 1978.

Clark, Beverly Lyon. "A Portrait of the Artist as a Little Woman." *Children's Literature* 17 (1989): 81–97.

Clark, Rufus W. *Lectures on the Formation of Character: Temptations and Mission of Young Men.* Boston, 1853.

Crowley, John W. "*Little Women* and the Boy-Book." *New England Quarterly* 58 (1985): 384–99.

Dalke, Anne. "'The House-Band': The Education of Men in *Little Women*." *College English* 47 (1985): 571–78.

Davis, Rebecca Harding. "Men's Rights." In *A Rebecca Harding Davis Reader.* Ed. Jean Pfaelzer. Pittsburgh: University of Pittsburgh Press, 1995. Pp. 343–61.

Dobson, Joanne. "The Hidden Hand: Subversion of Cultural Ideology in Three Mid-Nineteenth Century American Women's Novels." *American Quarterly* 38 (1986): 223–42.

———. Introduction to *The Hidden Hand,* by E.D.E.N. Southworth. New Brunswick: Rutgers University Press, 1988. Pp. xi–xli.

Dubbert, Joe L. *A Man's Place: Masculinity in Transition.* Englewood Cliffs: Prentice-Hall, 1979.

Eddy, Daniel C. *The Young Man's Friend.* Boston, 1855.

———. *The Young Man's Friend.* Rev. ed. New York, 1865.

Everts, W.W. *Manhood: Its Duties and Responsibilities.* New York, 1854.

Felski, Rita. *Beyond Feminist Aesthetics: Feminist Literature and Social Change.* Cambridge: Harvard University Press, 1989.

Fetterley, Judith. "*Little Women*: Alcott's Civil War." *Feminist Studies* 5 (1979): 369–83.

———. *The Resisting Reader: A Feminist Approach to American Fiction.* Bloomington: Indiana University Press, 1978.

Fiedler, Leslie. *Love and Death in the American Novel.* New York: Criterion Books, 1960.

Gaard, Greta. "'Self-denial was all the fashion': Repressing Anger in *Little Women*." *Papers on Language and Literature* 27 (1991): 3–19.

Hamill, Samuel E. "Discipline; School Government." *American Journal of Education.* 1 (1856): 123–33.

Harris, Susan K. *19th-Century American Women's Novels: Interpretive Strategies.* New York: Cambridge University Press, 1990.

Hilkey, Judy. *Character Is Capital: Success Manuals and Manhood in Gilded Age America.* Chapel Hill: University of North Carolina Press, 1997.

Irving, Washington. *The Sketchbook of Geoffrey Crayon, Gent.* New York: Penguin, 1988.

Kett, Joseph. *Rites of Passage: Adolescence in America, 1790 to the Present.* New York: Basic Books, 1977.

Keyser, Elizabeth. *Little Women: A Family Romance.* New York: Twayne, 1999.

———. *Whispers in the Dark: The Fiction of Louisa May Alcott.* Knoxville: University of Tennessee Press, 1993.

Kimmel, Michael S. *Manhood in America: A Cultural History.* New York: Free Press, 1996.

Minadeo, Christy. "Little Women in the 21st Century." In *Images of the Child.* Ed. Harry Eiss. Bowling Green: Bowling Green State University Popular Press, 1994.

Murphy, Ann. "The Borders of Ethical, Erotic, and Artistic Possibilities in *Little Women*." *Signs* 15 (1990): 562–85.

Newcomb, Harvey. *How to Be a Man: A Book for Boys.* Boston, 1850.

Reardon, Colleen. "Music as Leitmotif in Louisa May Alcott's *Little Women*." *Children's Literature* 24 (1996): 74–85.

Rotundo, E. Anthony. *American Manhood: Transformations in Masculinity from the Revolution to the Modern Era.* New York: Basic Books, 1993.

Showalter, Elaine. Introduction to *Little Women,* by Louisa May Alcott. New York: Penguin, 1989. Pp. vii–xxviii.

Spacks, Patricia. *The Female Imagination.* New York: Knopf, 1975.

Susina, Jan. "Men and *Little Women:* Notes of a Resisting (Male) Reader." In *Little Women and the Feminist Imagination: Criticism, Controversy, Personal Essays.* ed. Janice M. Alberghene and Beverly Lyon Clark. New York: Garland, 1999. Pp. 161–72.

Titcomb, Timothy. [Josiah Holland] *Letters to Young People.* New York, 1863.

Tompkins, Jane. Afterword to *The Wide, Wide World,* by Susan Warner. New York: Feminist Press, 1987. Pp. 584–608.

———. *Sensational Designs: The Cultural Work of American Fiction 1790–1860.* New York: Oxford University Press, 1985.

"Training of Boys." *The Mother's Journal and Family Visitant.* 10 (1845): 181–84.

Twain, Mark. *The Adventures of Tom Sawyer.* New York: Oxford University Press, 1993.

We Boys. Boston: Roberts Brothers, 1876.

Zimet, Sara Goodman. "Little Boy Lost." *Teachers College Record* 72 (1970): 31–40.

Drying the Orphan's Tear: Changing Representations of the Dependent Child in America, 1870–1930

Claudia Nelson

> *Little Orphant Annie's come to our house to stay,*
> *An' wash the cups an' saucers up, an' brush the crumbs away,*
> *An' shoo the chickens off the porch, an' dust the hearth, an' sweep,*
> *An' make the fire, an' bake the bread, an' earn her board-an'-keep.*
> — James Whitcomb Riley, "Little Orphan Annie"

The 1885 poem "Little Orphant Annie," by Hoosier versifier James Whitcomb Riley, profiles an orphan "bound out" to earn her own way in the world. In return for room and board, young Annie (based on a child who worked for the Rileys) serves as maid-of-all-work for a large family; at night, she tells ghost stories to her employer's offspring. After recounting what befalls bad children who demonstrate their inadequate respect for authority by mocking adults or refusing to say their prayers, she concludes with a message at once attractive to the powers that be and calculated to serve her own interests:

> You better mind yer parents, an' yer teachers fond an' dear,
> An' churish them 'at loves you, an' dry the orphan's tear,
> An' he'p the pore an' needy ones 'at clusters all about,
> Er the Gobble-uns'll git you
> 　　　Ef you
> 　　　　　Don't
> 　　　　　　　Watch
> 　　　　　　　　　Out! (ll. 41–48)

At once subservient and feisty, Riley's Annie uses oratory and imagination to convince her luckier peers of the existence of unseen powers who will avenge any unkindness offered her. Readers may notice, however, that these powers evidently see no reason to ameliorate her lot as a slavey. Ultimately, Annie is probably on her own.

Originally published (as "The Elf Child") in the Indianapolis *Journal* and later in considerable demand at verse recitations public and

Children's Literature 29, ed. Elizabeth Lennox Keyser and Julie Pfeiffer (Yale University Press, © 2001 Hollins University).

private, Riley's poem may have lent its name to another popular text, Harold Gray's comic strip *Little Orphan Annie,* which began its run in 1924. But the cartoon Annie is no bound-out girl. Despite a rocky start in a Dickensian orphanage and endless subsequent tribulations, she is always reunited with Daddy Warbucks, and her role in his household is not to care for chickens but to be cared for herself by the retinue consisting of Sandy, Punjab, the Asp, and especially Warbucks. Although the nouveau riche Mrs. Warbucks originally brings Annie into the mansion as a prop so that she herself can "impress her society friends with her charity" (Smith 11), the adoptive father's love for his new daughter is immediate and powerful. Bruce Smith proposes, indeed, that Warbucks—a self-made man whose fortune, as his name implies, comes from defense contracts awarded to him during World War I—is "a man with deeply hurt feelings who believed nobody liked him because he'd made money from the war"; thus "the orphan nobody wanted" becomes crucial to "the munitions maker nobody liked" because she is his connection to the world of feeling (13). And though his love attracts kidnappers and the jealousy of Mrs. Warbucks, it puts her at the family's center, not its margins.

The contrast between the situations of the two orphan Annies suggests the dramatic changes that took place over several decades in North American understandings of the function of the dependent (that is, adopted, foster, or institutionalized) child. Today's readers might find that dependent children of the 1870s and 1880s work to expose the limitations of domesticity in a day in which, as Ann Douglas has argued in *The Feminization of American Culture,* domesticity was next to godliness. For example, orphan novels such as *The Adventures of Tom Sawyer* (1876) or *Sara Crewe* (1887, expanded as *A Little Princess* in 1905) consciously critique respectability, showing its narrowness, its drabness, and its lack of sympathy. Mark Twain's Tom and Huck, Frances Hodgson Burnett's Sara and Anne (Sara's foil Becky was added in 1905) serve on one level to illustrate the callousness with which a culture that sentimentalized children could treat the young, in that they show that social class rather than need is the key factor in a child's adoptability. Middle-class Tom may rely on his aunt to fill the void left by his parents' deaths, and Sara's aristocratic demeanor attracts the attention of the wealthy guardian who has long sought his missing ward, but Huck is a pariah to the adults of St. Petersburg until he comes into money, and Anne exchanges life as a street waif for a congenial job rather than for adoption.[1]

Novels that expose the reluctance with which society makes room for its displaced children also remind readers that the benefits of belonging to a family are often bestowed arbitrarily and ungenerously— and that the sturdy child may well feel that he or she can do without them. But such independence is less a subversive literary device than a reflection of what nineteenth-century society expected of penniless young people. In a nation largely without child labor laws or welfare benefits, orphans without class standing had to be prepared to light out for the territories or earn their bread as servants. Even the waifs who are lucky enough to be adopted, such as Patches in Rosa Graham's 1876 *St. Nicholas* story by the same name, should expect to repay the benevolence shown them in a practical way: in later life, "industrious" Patches does "her best to lighten the labors of the good woman to whom she owed so much" (quoted in Gannon 162).

On the other hand, consider various early twentieth-century orphans, among them L. M. Montgomery's Anne Shirley (1908), Jimmy Bean in Eleanor H. Porter's *Pollyanna* (1913), and the title character in Josephine Lawrence's Linda Lane series of the 1920s.[2] All, like Riley's Annie, go to new homes "cal'latin' ter work, of course," as Jimmy puts it (81), but find, like Gray's, that their real work is emotional: they are to serve, in the sentimental words of Jimmy's once hard-bitten new father, as the "child's presence" without which no real home can exist (131). Indeed, their task is nothing less than to heal the adult world. Although these novels, too, critique domesticity and respectability, they suggest that households that can accept the dependent child can transcend their original limitations. Excavating the humanity in their dour benefactors, such children embody a national myth of orphan as transformative force that did not come into being until late in the century. Indeed, we may discern three overlapping eras in representations of orphans from the 1870s through the 1920s: an early period ending about 1890, in which children whose class or gender or age might make them difficult to integrate into the middle-class home are presented primarily in terms of their relation to work; a middle period lasting until about 1914, in which orphans regenerate adults emotionally but both adults and orphans continue to think in terms of practical work; and a late period in which the child's needs are considered paramount.

To some critics, to be sure, any differences are minor when considered alongside orphans' similarities: from Horatio Alger hero to Superman, orphans early and late exude competence, decency, and a near-magical ability to fulfill society's needs. Thus, for instance, noting the omnipresence of orphans in classic children's books in this country, Jerry Griswold identifies an "ur-story" (4) of orphan trial and triumph that animates novels as disparate as *The Wizard of Oz* (1900), *The Secret Garden* (1911), and *Tarzan of the Apes* (1914). To Griswold, the most compelling explanation for what he deems the striking uniformity of orphan narratives is psychological; he sees in their programmatic humbling of parent figures a peculiarly American oedipal fantasy (10–13). In the present article, though, I propose that we consider the historical context of the attitudinal shift that occurs in orphan literature on either side of the turn of the century, an era when "nonrelative adoptions [were] expand[ing] steadily" (Silverman and Feigelman 187). Children's fiction of the late nineteenth and early twentieth centuries often uses the dependent child, whose presumed defenselessness and lack of authority may make him or her seem particularly "childlike,"[3] to illustrate and endorse important new approaches toward children as a group, especially the redefining of the child's value as emotional rather than practical and the increased interest in the desires and feelings of the young.

Orphan fiction recapitulates the late-nineteenth-century debate about what to do with the dependent child, a debate in which the impulse to nurture the parentless slowly vanquished the impulse to hire them. Orphanages, once lauded for efficiency, were increasingly chastised for being insufficiently homelike (the 1909 complaint of the president of the National Conference of Jewish Charities, Emil G. Hirsch, that "the inmates are of necessity trimmed and turned into automatons" [*Proceedings* 87] is typical); orphans themselves, formerly warehoused alongside delinquents and vagrants by the judiciary system, were becoming respectable.[4] Nor, in an era of high adult mortality, were orphans just convenient psychological emblems. After all, they were much more common in real life than is the case today—as Eileen Simpson points out, there were more than ten times as many full orphans in 1920 as there were in 1953 (231). In times of economic struggle, such as the depression of the 1890s, children might also lose their parents temporarily or permanently to poverty rather than death. Arguing that orphan asylums served as "the poor man's boarding school," Judith Dulberger notes that in New York State alone the asylum population grew from 18,000 in 1870 to more than 65,000 in 1895 (8–9).[5] When Theodore Roosevelt told Congress in 1909 that, as of 1904, nearly 100,000 children were living in orphanages (*Proceed-*

ings 5), his figure may have been overly conservative, as may that of Edward P. Savage of the Children's Home Society of Minnesota, who estimated in 1895 that perhaps 200,000 children had been abandoned nationwide (Ashby 51). Whatever the accuracy of these statistics, they suggest that there was intense concern in the late nineteenth and early twentieth centuries about the perennially beleaguered American family and about the development and training of the equally beleaguered American child. Anxiety about immigration rates, the perceived dilution and degeneration of the "American" gene pool, and the effects of institutionalization on citizens-in-training colors discussions of dependent children in fiction and nonfiction alike.

Simultaneously, orphan fiction reflects a crucial change in the orphan's status as worker, in that earlier orphans—Alger heroes, for example—are less likely than their later counterparts to find families and more likely to find jobs. By the turn of the century, argue historians Susan Downs and Michael Sherraden, America was feeling the effects of an "oversupply of child labor" (274). As their role in the workforce shrank following the passage of anti–child labor legislation in an assortment of states around the 1890s and 1900s, orphans, even more than most children, needed a new social function. Orphan fiction of the middle and late periods identifies that function as emotional. That these stories frequently describe the waif as belonging to a higher order than his or her adoptive parents—marked by unusual talent (such as that characterizing Anne Shirley and Alice B. Emerson's series heroine Ruth Fielding), strength of character (as with Linda Lane and the comic-strip Little Orphan Annie), or membership in a higher socioeconomic class (which turns out in *Pollyanna Grows Up* [1915] to be the case with Jimmy Bean)—helps to establish symbolically that by rights it is the adoptive parent who ought to work for the child, not the child for the adult. Natural aristocrats, orphans "should" belong to the leisured class.

Matters were not always thus. Under the poor-law tradition that America inherited from Britain (a country that did not enact an adoption law comparable to those of the United States until 1926), the chief motive for taking on an extra child was presumed to be the need for its labor (Carp 5–6). Nor was this desire censured until well along in the nineteenth century; Marilyn Holt observes that in the 1850s "sturdy workers were part of the advertised benefits to the receiving families" but that fifty years later, advertisements' emphasis was, rather, on the needs of the child (138–39). Indeed, by the 1880s, as the number of hours that all Americans worked shrank, child-placement officials were already decrying prospective parents whose aim was to gain an unpaid hand rather than to fill an empty nest. "The great majority of those who apply for children over nine years old are looking for cheap help," sniffed one Michigan orphanage superintendent in 1885; an Iowa colleague of his complained, "The average family with us wants a child for what they can get out of it in the way of work" (*Care* 203, 204).

Despite such expressions of disapproval, which both fueled and grew out of the Progressive Era campaign against child labor, and despite the "oversupply of child labor" noted above, change in the orphan's lot was slow; the practice of sending dependent children to earn their keep in foster homes or factories continued for decades. The glass-bottle factories of New Jersey and other states were notorious and brutal employers of orphan boys aged twelve and up, as the journal *Charities* detailed in articles of 1903 and 1904 (see Dale; Kelley). The New York Catholic Protectory put boys as young as seven to work in its shoe shop, printing office, chair and stocking factories, and tailor shops; New York Charity Organization Society founder Josephine Shaw Lowell reported of the latter in 1886 that 125 seven- to ten-year-olds were producing 5,200 pairs of pantaloons and sixty-five ten- to sixteen-year-olds were turning out 3,000 suits and 4,200 shirts annually, as well as repairing 300 garments a day for the Protectory's inmates (*Care* 196).

Or consider Charles Loring Brace's orphan train movement, which transplanted roughly 100,000 young people from urban poverty to the farms or hamlets of the Midwest and the South between 1854 and 1924. Throughout, Brace seems to have cared more about easing the assimilation of immigrants and paupers into "American" respectability than about serving anyone's emotional needs.[6] As he wrote in 1872, the major reason for placing waifs on farms, besides the farmer's perennial quest for laborers, was that farm workers, as live-in help, must "share in [farmers'] social tone" (225). Although by the turn of the century Brace's Children's Aid Society warned would-be adopters that " 'under no circumstances will a child be placed with people who wish chore boys or kitchen drudges,' " Holt finds that "using them for farm labor was still a common reason for taking in these children" (139). Indeed, as late as 1900 Henrietta Wright approvingly noted that in weighing child-placement options, the Society always considered whether a given situation would be likely to instill in an urban orphan "the same reliance which makes the country boy, on the whole, the best *wage earner* that the city ever sees" (120, emphasis added).

Thus it is not surprising that the boys and girls featured in orphan fiction at the turn of the century expect to work, even if their creators ultimately soften their lot. Jean Webster's Judy Abbott (*Daddy-Long-Legs,* 1912) receives a college education from a mysterious benefactor (the "Daddy" whom she eventually marries) on the understanding that she will use her training to earn her living as a writer. Gene Stratton-Porter's Freckles (1904) is initially a nameless graduate of a foundlings' home who gains an adoptive father by demonstrating his willingness, despite his missing hand, to take on what would be "a trying job for a work-hardened man" (9). Eleanor Porter's Jimmy, who has run away from an orphanage in search of "folks" (*Pollyanna* 78), explains that he's not asking for a handout; anyone who adopts him will get the benefit of his labor, and, he points out, he's "real strong" (79). (Indeed, even though his eventual father is a millionaire who can well afford to hire help, Jimmy has his "Saturday morning task" around the mansion, presumably assigned to him as character-building rather than necessary labor [199].) In contrast, a later Porter orphan, the violin-prodigy hero of *Just David* (1916), is taken aback to find that he must perform "useful labor" by weeding the garden, filling the woodbox, and poisoning the potato bugs to earn his keep from the forbidding elderly couple who have taken him in (64). This later narrative suggests that the boy's astonishment is as much a product of the remoteness and backwardness of the New England town in which he finds himself (his talent goes unrecognized for a considerable time) as it is evidence of his own social isolation: his dead father, a musician and hermit, deliberately reared David to know nothing of the "ugliness" of everyday life, presumably including the common treatment of waifs.

Other, earlier children are more socially savvy than David. The ten-year-old hero of Kate Douglas Wiggin's *Timothy's Quest* (1890) seeks an adoptive home for baby Gabrielle merely on the grounds that she is "dear" and "pretty,"[7] but adds that "you needn't have me too, you know, unless you should need me to help take care of her" (52). And indeed, his interlocutors promptly send him off to apply for a job with the local squire (64), although the squire refuses to hire so young a hand. Montgomery's Marilla and Matthew Cuthbert plan to adopt an orphan *boy* "old enough to be of some use in doing chores right off" (6). When their order is garbled and they receive a girl instead, Anne turns out to have led a "life of drudgery and poverty and neglect" (41), and at Green Gables, too, she expects and receives only "odd half hours" by way of playtime (63). And even in L. Frank Baum's *The Marvelous Land of Oz* (1904), the erstwhile Princess Ozma has undergone a magical sex change and grows up as a boy named Tip, reared by a sorceress for whom "he" carries wood, hoes the cornfield, and tends the livestock, for all his tendency to rebel by loafing. When the sorceress announces her plan to turn him into a garden ornament, Tip appeals to practicalities, not sentiment, responding, "What use'll I be then? . . . There won't be any one to work for you" (26). All these narratives disapprove the uses to which the children are put—much as the Boston child-placement official Gertrude Freeman describes in 1903 her rejection of would-be foster parents Mr. and Mrs. B., who "believe in teaching children to work," in favor of Mr. and Mrs. R., who have a "real longing for a child in the home" to replace their own dead son ("Placing-Out" 507)—but all nonetheless assume that most foster parents expect children to earn their keep.

In contrast, later novels typically distance orphans from work from the outset, hinting at the shift in assumptions during this time. Had Porter's David not accidentally come to a town "buried in this forgotten valley up among these hills," he would not have met with chores but with "friends, relatives, an adoring public, and a mint of money" (321), all of which he deserves not only because of his talent but also because of his innocence, sweetness, and power to transform others' unhappy lives. Similarly, Emerson's series opener *Ruth Fielding of the Red Mill* (1913) brings Ruth to the home of a miserly great-uncle who informs her, "I expect all cats to catch mice around the Red Mill. Them that don't goes into the sluice. There's enough to do here. You won't be idle for want of work" (55). Unlike earlier authors, however, Emerson paints this attitude as retrograde, eccentric, and downright mean-spirited, even while Ruth is notable for her industry and application, which eventually transform her into a Hollywood screenwriter, director, producer, and star. Ruth's professional success is certainly the focus of the series overall, but one of Emerson's points is that her heroine's dedication and determination are gifts to be used for Ruth's own advancement, not properties to be owned by another in exchange for a home. Significantly, Ruth's labors ultimately take place in the entertainment industry, a field that doesn't look like "work" at all to retrograde souls such as her great-uncle. As Anne Morey observes, Ruth's form of production, which requires her to attend exclu-

sive schools and visit country clubs so that she can acquire the necessary social tone, looks very like consumption (77). Nevertheless, the
narratives repeatedly stress how arduous Ruth's life is, a neat way for
Emerson to allow her protagonist to function simultaneously as eter-
nally laboring orphan and as Cinderella after the ball.

Similarly critical of the "put 'em to work" spirit is Webster's *Dear
Enemy* (1915), an epistolary romance relating how a newly minted B.A.
takes over and reforms an orphanage. The methods of the protagonist,
Sallie, recall those of Clara Spence (founder of what has since become
the Spence-Chapin Agency), which Virginia Gildersleeve described in
1923 as follows:

> You must take the children and keep them in hygienic surround-
> ings and clothe them properly and feed them with suitable diet,
> and you must investigate prospective parents and find that they
> are respectable and reliable. . . . The Spence-Baker method, I
> gathered, did all this with proper technique; but what a vast deal
> more! They put heart and spirit and imagination into it; they
> made the children not only healthy and clean but adorable. They
> dressed them in pretty clothes and tied their hair with pink rib-
> bons . . . so that they warmed the hearts of the prospective par-
> ents with enthusiasm and affection, and they managed to give to
> each home, not only a child, but also a love of childhood and ap-
> preciation of what a privilege it was to receive a child into one's
> household. (quoted in Abbott 215)

Given her up-to-date emphasis on emotion, Sallie waxes sardonic
about having heard "from a couple of farmers, each of whom would
like to have a strong, husky boy of fourteen who is not afraid of work,
their object being to give him a good home. These good homes appear with great frequency just as the spring planting is coming on"
(60). Whereas the boys in Alger's 1874 orphan-train novel *Julius, or
The Street Boy Out West* cheerfully go to "farmers and mechanics who
needed a boy on the farm or in the shop" (52), Sallie's charges are not
"to be placed out unless the proposed family can offer better advantages than we can give. . . . I am very *choosey* in regard to homes, and
I reject three-fourths of those that offer" (61, emphasis in original).
Were Sallie to figure in *Anne of Green Gables,* Marilla's utilitarian attitude toward orphans would disqualify her from fostering Anne.

In keeping with their emphasis on work, the stories of the middle
period dwell on the reluctance with which caregivers accept orphans

into their lives, as the dour adults who populate these tales typically doubt the children's use value and take them out of duty, not love. Agreeing to take baby Gabrielle, Wiggin's Miss Avilda Cummins complains that she has been badgered into this decision by her fellow villagers, who "wanted to . . . be so dretful charitable all of a sudden, and dictate to me and try to show me my duty" (160). Marilla acquiesces in raising Anne because the alternative is to hand her over to a "terrible worker and driver" who will "expect [her] to earn [her] keep, and no mistake about that" (Montgomery 44, 45); in the circumstances, Marilla sees it as "a sort of duty" to keep the child herself, though as she tells Anne, the shrewish Mrs. Blewett "certainly needs you much more than I do" (47). Pollyanna's Aunt Polly disapproves of her niece's very existence because Pollyanna's mother married against Polly's wishes, and though as the child's only living kin she has to take her, she has no answer to the little girl's question, "Isn't there *any* way you can be glad about all that—duty business?" (44). Indeed, pre-war aunts and uncles seem especially apt to distance themselves from the children wished on them by fate, as we also see in *Rebecca of Sunnybrook Farm* (1903), *The Secret Garden,* and *The Wizard of Oz*—recall that Aunt Em, who initially "would scream and press her hand upon her heart whenever Dorothy's merry voice reached her ears" (13), leaps into the storm cellar without waiting to find out whether her ward is following her. All these adults resist loving their charges until an emergency forces emotion, as when Pollyanna is hit by a car, Matthew dies and leaves Marilla bankrupt, Timothy runs away from home, and Dorothy miraculously returns after having been snatched up by a cyclone.

Brace wrote an 1873 article for *Harper's* on his orphan trains, categorizing the applicants for children: "Farmers come in . . . looking for the 'model boy' who shall do the light work of the farm and aid the wife in her endless household labor; childless mothers seek for children that shall replace those that are lost; housekeepers look for girls to train up; mechanics seek for boys for their trades; and kindhearted men, with comfortable homes and plenty of children, think it is their duty to do something for the orphans who have no fair chance in the great city" ("Little Laborers" 330). Of these five types, only the bereaved mothers are motivated by sentiment rather than by duty or self-interest. They too have their counterparts in early and middle-period orphan novels, in which foster parents unrelated to their charges often adopt them as substitutes for "a lost loved one," as the catchphrase went. But even here, the adults seem curiously reluctant. Jimmy's adoptive father *really* wants Pollyanna, whose mother he loved, and takes Jimmy only to please the little girl. Magazine fiction tends to follow the pattern of Lucy G. Morse's "Cathern," published in *St. Nicholas* in 1877, a story detailing how the rich Mrs. Percy fosters a waif to replace a daughter who has died but initially finds Cathern an inadequate stand-in. In real life, foster children awaiting adoption might be returned to stock if they did not measure up to the standard set by the dead rival (see, for example, Dulberger 125–26); similarly, early orphan tales suggest that being an adult's second choice is chancy because adults find it hard to love someone else's child. By the 1890s, of course, the spiritual payoffs for the adult far outweigh any practical assistance that the child may provide; as Wiggin puts it in *Timothy's Quest,* "in that sweet embrace of trust and confidence and joy, the stone was rolled away, once and forever, from the sepulchre of Miss Vilda's heart, and Easter morning broke there" (188). Instead of Old Testament duty and narrow rectitude, we have a New Testament revelation, a gospel of love—but this conversion is not easily achieved.

Still, even when it comes painfully, love almost always burgeons between foster child and caregiver in the classic orphan novel, however stern the adult and however troublesome the orphan in question. The transformative nature of family life for both parties is signaled by the apparently universal moment in such narratives when the orphan receives a new wardrobe from the caregiver, a moment that symbolizes both the change (financial or emotional) in the child's situation and the new eyes with which the adult will eventually learn to view his or her charge. Porter's David takes over the wardrobe formerly belonging to his benefactors' son, now grown up and estranged from his parents, a sign of the second and more successful chance at parenting that has been vouchsafed to the Hollies. Similarly, Mary Lennox's mourning, Tip/Ozma's boy's garb, Anne Shirley's skimpy wincey, Judy Abbott's second-hand wardrobe, Freckles's "roughest of farm clothing" (7), and Pollyanna's gleanings from the missionary barrel are all discarded at the beginning of the children's sojourns in their new environments. In Anne's case the clothes undergo a further upgrade when Matthew replaces the stiff, ugly, "serviceable" garments into which Marilla inserts the girl with an attractive and fashionable brown gloria with puffed sleeves. Matthew's Christmas gift is a telling one, suggesting as it does that Marilla's rigid insistence on attempting to force Anne to conform to an unrealistic and uncomfortable model is giving way to a new mode of child-rearing in which Anne's own wishes will be gratified, even when they strike Marilla as frivolous and worldly.

Clothing scenes in other narratives are equally significant. Burnett's Little Lord Fauntleroy (1886), for instance, a fatherless child living apart from his surviving parent, appears throughout the novel in his infamous black velvet suit with lace collar—an outfit that offended the masculine sensibilities even of boys of his own generation. The suit is originally made out of an old skirt of his mother's and segues, after his move to his grandfather's castle, into a more expensive one boasting "a large Vandyke collar of rich lace" (172); that the replacement is so strikingly similar in style to its predecessor emblematizes the crucial point that even in the lap of luxury, Fauntleroy will continue to embody his mother's social vision and her plans for him. Another child of ambiguous appearance, the title character of Alger's *Tattered Tom* (1871), is a twelve-year-old female street waif whose gender is initially uncertain: "The head was surmounted by a boy's cap, the hair was cut short, it wore a boy's jacket, but underneath was a girl's dress" (10). "Tom"'s benefactor, Captain Barnes, hands her over to his sister for a makeover and training in feminine ways, but his plans to outfit Tom (henceforth "Jenny") in new garments arouse the jealousy of his niece Mary, who steals a gold pencil to augment her own wardrobe and puts the blame on Tom. Back in the streets again, Tom encounters an old nemesis, her soi-disant "Granny," who is herself clad in new garments. Because "she [is] now, in outward appearance, a very respectable old woman; and appearances go a considerable way," Granny manages to abduct the child despite the presence of a policeman (227). But when the denouement reveals Tom to be the missing heiress Jane Lindsay, the outwardly decent and inwardly corrupt Mary and Granny get their comeuppance, since Jane has achieved the best appearance and most loving home of all. The story's erstwhile distrust of clothing as an indicator of value has itself been transformed.

Finally, consider Ruth Fielding, whose great-uncle causes her much distress by *losing* her only trunkful of clothes and refusing (for many chapters) to replace them. Here again, the episode mirrors an important fact of the narrative, namely, that in moving to the Red Mill, Ruth, unlike most orphan protagonists, is exchanging a good emotional situation for a bad one: she is having to leave a beloved relative who can no longer afford to shelter her. Ruth's clothes, however, are replaced multiple times and by different people, including herself, in the course of the story, each occasion suggesting a new stage in the evolution of her emotional relationships within and around the Mill. In all these cases, clothing (as has long been the case in fairy tale and real life; see, for example, Scott) stands for a much wider and richer array of cultural codes relating to human ties, social position, and perception of character; significantly, orphans' wardrobes almost always improve,[8] and the change in sumptuary status frequently reflects the authors' point that these heroes and heroines are natural aristocrats, deserving of the best.

Early and middle-period novels, I have argued, typically contain adults who have considerable difficulty perceiving the innate worth of their charges; the new clothes may sometimes be long in coming and hard-earned. In contrast, later novels depict the orphan's primary task, the emotional satisfaction of an adoptive parent, as simple. Take 'Lias Brewster of Dorothy Canfield Fisher's *Understood Betsy* (1917), who is mistreated by a drunken stepfather. The sympathetic community spruces him up to make him, as they think, more adoptable by the wealthy and childless Mr. Pond, but this prospective patron takes no interest in him until the boy is found in rags, weeping because his stepfather has stolen the new clothes. His heart touched, Mr. Pond sweeps 'Lias up, buys him everything in sight, and removes him from the narrative to a life of luxury; the episode informs us that the adoptive parent's happiness comes from benefiting the child and that parental love may instantly be triggered, not by a child's personality or efforts, but simply by its need. Nor are those who nurture orphans permitted to revel in their own charity, since benevolence is supposed to be its own reward: Betsy and her schoolmates, sewing away on 'Lias's new wardrobe and picturing themselves as young Ladies Bountiful destined to win the approbation of all, are chastised for this self-aggrandizing vision by Betsy's Cousin Ann. As the unremunerated fosterers of Betsy herself, Ann and her parents ask neither for gratitude from the child nor for praise from the neighbors. Merely having a child around and doing their duty by her is all they want. And although on her arrival in Vermont Betsy is neurotic, helpless, and painfully timid, hardly the ideal inmate of a hard-working farming family, her very failings seem to make her desirable to her Putney cousins, in that she becomes yet another crop to be cultivated into thriving sturdiness. Betsy learns to work and to show initiative, but plainly the Putneys consider that she is acquiring these skills for her own present and future benefit, not for theirs.

Or consider Linda Lane, who at thirteen finds a home with a dress-maker. In such a household, there can be no question about whether the new clothes—and the emotions for which they stand—will show up in a timely fashion. The two take to each other at once, Linda be-cause Miss Gilly respects her feelings, Miss Gilly because a child can remedy her loneliness and give her an interest in life. Deidre John-son points out that the Linda Lane books differ from their predeces-sors in that "from the very beginning when Miss Gilly resolves to 'take a little girl and try to make her happy' (unlike Marilla or Aunt Polly who acquire their female charges by fate, not choice), she already pos-sesses the capability of loving a child" (63). Although Linda instantly starts helping out by washing the dishes and feeding the chickens like Riley's Orphan Annie, these chores are her own idea (Lawrence, *Linda* 37). The two quickly form what Johnson sees as a feminist commu-nity. Their menage is so idyllic that by the end of the series, when Linda finds herself mentoring an older girl named Mary, it is clear that Linda's life as an adopted orphan is far more fulfilling than Mary's as the oldest of many children of one living parent. It is Mary, not Linda, who is a household drudge, starved of affection and drearily anticipat-ing a lifetime of unrewarding labor.

And though Linda follows an earlier orphan, the protagonist of Carolyn Wells's 1899 *St. Nicholas* serial *The Story of Betty*,[9] in construct-ing a larger adoptive family that includes in each case a destitute old woman for grandmother, a brother, and a two-year-old girl, Betty is an heiress who acts on her own to "buy" a family; Linda acts in part-nership with Miss Gilly (who finances the effort) to create the family that she has always wanted. Betty is reunited with her long-lost mother at story's end, a moment that reveals the inadequacy of the artificial family she has purchased: "she was happy now, truly happy; and she realized that all her life she had been starving for true human affec-tion. This, she now understood, was the longing that had kept her hun-gry heart unsatisfied. . . . At last mother-love had made for Betty a home" (1024). Mothers, here, cannot be bought or adopted; only the genuine article will do. Twenty-five years later, however, Linda finds Miss Gilly and the other members of the family wholly satisfactory and proclaims that it feels "nice!" to be adopted (*Experiments* 16). Like the children whom Sallie McBride places in homes in *Dear Enemy*, Linda shows that the point of adoption is love, not work, and that this love is at least as strong as the love that grows from a biological relationship.

To be sure, Linda—unlike the siblings she acquires, whom the neighbors consider foolish luxuries because they are too young to be useful—*is* a worker, and the series presents this quality as a major part of her charm. If Anne Shirley, Rebecca Randall, and Pollyanna Whittier are characterized by their imagination or optimism, through which each "produc[es] a change of heart or outlook in those who began as her antagonists," to quote Shirley Foster and Judy Simons (153), Linda is remarkable for her energy and sense. She can calm quarrelsome children, run a millionaire's house when the servants quit, cook good food, and occupy leadership roles at school. Nevertheless, the series presents her as admired rather than exploited, loved rather than used. And unlike Miss Gilly, whose meekness allows others to impose on her, Linda enters the series asserting that she is no "doormat" (11)—and her work always finds recompense.

Foster and Simons, Griswold, Johnson, and Perry Nodelman have all noted the family likeness of classic North American orphan tales, in which, as Nodelman writes, the child "shocks, and then delights, repressed or unhappy grown-ups . . . makes them more natural, and brings an end to the artificial repression of their overcivilized values" (32). Orphans, he adds, are "symbols of childhood and its virtues," manifestations of a Wordsworthian insistence on youth's transformative innocence (34). Even so, the orphan's undeniable symbolic qualities change over time. Orphans of the pre–Civil War period, such as Ellen Montgomery in Susan Warner's 1850 bestseller *The Wide, Wide World,* do not typically change the adults around them, but rather adapt themselves to adult society. Their immediate successors, similarly, are less likely to transform their environments than they are to better their own lots in a material sense. In the final third of the nineteenth century, years in which America experienced intense anxiety about the need to absorb vast numbers of working-class immigrants into its fabric, literary orphans, like the ideal immigrant, are often represented as infinitely flexible, upwardly mobile, and potentially useful, even when authors simultaneously establish that the child's rightful social class "should" always have exempted him or her from labor, as in the case of Burnett's Sara, Baum's Tip/Ozma, Wells's Betty, Alger's Tom/Jenny, and many others. Such works reassure readers not only about orphans' worth and salvageability but also about their ability to survive in an era in which children had little legal protection.

Conversely, the stories of Anne Shirley and her turn-of-the-century kindred could not be told before the Victorian sentimentalization of childhood and the lessening need for children in the workforce turned children themselves, as opposed to the physical services they might perform, into a commodity. It is not until the 1890s that the utility of even the working-class dependent child is commonly represented as emotional rather than practical, but the tales of the 1920s, in which adults are eager to satisfy the child's needs instead of demanding the reverse, suggest the extent to which conceptions of orphans— and children in general—had changed. Even in the brief span of years between *Anne of Green Gables* and *Linda Lane,* the depictions of the ease with which love between adult and orphan burgeons, and the corresponding understanding of the child's function and labors, are strikingly different.

And, of course, changes in the fashioning of the dependent child continue to occur. As Claudia Mills has observed, "The effervescent, exuberant orphans of the century's early years give way to the passive, polite orphans of the 1940s and early 1950s, culminating in the angry, bitter 'orphans' (often actually foster children) of more recent fiction" (228). To trace the evolution of the literary orphan over the last 150 years is to discern an uneven oscillation between sweetness and feistiness, inhibited and demonstrative behavior, physical and moral energy. It is also to gain insight into American attitudes toward childhood as a stage at once powerful and vulnerable—qualities also perceived within the larger nation. In portraying the orphan, children's writers were commenting on America as well.

Notes

I thank Southwest Texas State University and the National Endowment for the Humanities for grants supporting this project and the larger work of which it is a part; I am also grateful to Marilynn Olson for her suggestions.

1. I speak here of one level of the stories, not of all. It goes without saying that Huck, and to a lesser extent Tom as well, are at least as dubious about "sivilization" as it is about them, a point developed more extensively in *The Adventures of Huckleberry Finn* (1884). Huck's freedom from the trammels of family and domesticity excites Tom's envy in the first novel and helps Huck himself to move in the sequel from identity to identity until he "becomes" Tom Sawyer himself—a fluidity that is again presented as admirable. But the boys' point of view is not that of the dominant society, which holds that identity should be stable; that family, home, and schooling are privileges rather than shackles; and that it owes the waif nothing.

2. Anne, of course, differs from the other orphans discussed here in that she hails from Canada, not the United States. Although in real life the Canadian orphan experience was more strongly inflected by British custom than was the case south of the border, I venture to include Anne among my examples because Montgomery's work is clearly indebted to such American predecessors as *Rebecca of Sunnybrook Farm* and because it, in turn, found its largest readership in the United States. Canadian critics may legitimately be offended by this categorization; I plead in my defense that this article

does not seek to provide close readings of the texts it examines (and a close reading of *Anne of Green Gables* would necessarily grapple with the work's Canadianness) but rather to provide contexts and trace family likenesses. As one of the most familiar orphan novels surviving in today's literary marketplace, Montgomery's text provides a useful piece of context for readers unacquainted with some of the out-of-print titles cited in this essay.

3. Perry Nodelman, similarly, argues that orphan girls such as Heidi, Anne Shirley, Pollyanna, Rebecca of Sunnybrook Farm (technically a half-orphan but separated from her one living parent), and Mary Lennox are presented as "purely and essentially child-like . . . pure manifestations of qualities that would be muddied in less detached children" (34).

4. For a useful summary of the history of adoption, see E. Wayne Carp's recent study (3–35). He sees 1851, when Massachusetts passed "the first modern adoption law," as a watershed: for the first time, the statute emphasized "the welfare of the child—it made the adopted person the prime beneficiary of the proceeding—and the evaluation of the adopters' parental qualifications" (11). It is nevertheless important to remember that even as the Massachusetts statute wrote into law shifts that had already occurred in Americans' understanding of childhood (with its new emphasis on "the needs of children" [11]), it took another quarter-century for another twenty-five states to pass similar legislation (12), and longer still for foster-care providers to give even lip service to the idea that the child's needs might trump their own.

5. Writing in the *North American Review* in 1900, Henrietta Wright complained of the evils of the New York State "Children's Law" of 1875, "which contained a clause providing that all children committed to institutions should be placed in those controlled by persons of the same religious faith as the parents of the children." The assurance that one's child would be appropriately churched, Wright implies, is the sole factor influencing the enormous post-1875 rise in institutionalized children, "most of the commitments being made by parents anxious to be relieved of the care of their children, until the wage earning period was reached" (116–17).

6. Brace estimated, as Carp points out, that perhaps 47 percent of his exports had at least one living parent, "poor and degraded people, who were leaving them to grow up neglected in the streets" (quoted in Carp 10). Or, as Brace put it in an 1882 article in *St. Nicholas,* New York City was threatened by children "who have been taught only in the schools of poverty, vice, and crime; whose ways are not our ways . . . and who, if they grow up thus, will be more dangerous to this city than wolf or tiger to the villages of India. But, fortunately for us . . . though wolves in human shape have brought them up to crime and sin, they can be saved and made into reasonable human beings" by being sent to "kind-hearted farmers in the West" as (initially) unpaid apprentices to learn Christianity and virtue ("Children" 544, 552).

7. As various commentators around the turn of the century noted, attractive toddler girls were in high demand: "Curiously," wrote Mabel Potter Daggett in 1907, "all the world is waiting for just one child. It is a two-year-old, blue-eyed, golden haired little girl with curls" (510). Adoptees of this ornamental type were not expected to work. Older boys, however, were considerably less prized as objects for sentiment; prospective parents of this period typically focused on such children's health, strength, and capacity for labor. Daggett's article heralded a lengthy campaign on the part of the magazine in which it appeared, the *Delineator* (a Butterick publication then edited by Theodore Dreiser), to find loving homes—not employment—for a series of adoptable boys and girls of all ages.

8. One measure of Huckleberry Finn's radicalness is that although he acquires a number of handsome outfits from various kindly adults in the course of his travels, he consistently loses or rejects them, just as he passes up chance after chance to be adopted into homes that would appeal to more conventional orphans. The clothes that have his

loyalty are the rags associated with his upbringing by Pap, whose chief virtue in Huck's eyes is his wish that Huck *not* accomplish any kind of social rise.

9. I owe my acquaintance with this serial to a paper presented at the 1997 meeting of the Children's Literature Association by Phyllis Wong.

Works Cited

Abbott, Lawrence F. "A Unique Memorial." *Outlook* 136 (6 February 1924): 214–15.

Alger, Horatio. *Julius, or The Street Boy Out West.* 1874. Rpt. in *Strive and Succeed: Two Novels by Horatio Alger.* New York: Holt, Rinehart and Winston, 1967.

———. *Tattered Tom; or, The Story of a Street Arab.* 1871. Philadelphia: Henry T. Coates, n.d.

Ashby, LeRoy. *Saving the Waifs: Reformers and Dependent Children, 1890–1917.* Philadelphia: Temple University Press, 1984.

Baum, L. Frank. *The Marvelous Land of Oz.* 1904. New York: Dover, 1961.

———. *The Wonderful Wizard of Oz.* 1900. New York: Dover, 1960.

Brace, Charles Loring. *The Dangerous Classes of New York and Twenty Years' Work Among Them.* 1872. Washington, D.C.: National Association of Social Workers, 1973.

———. "The Little Laborers of New York City." *Harper's New Monthly Magazine* 47 (August 1873): 321–32.

———. "Wolf-Reared Children." *St. Nicholas* 9 (May 1882): 542–54.

Burnett, Frances Hodgson. *Little Lord Fauntleroy.* 1886. New York: Puffin, 1981.

Care of Dependent Children in the Late Nineteenth and Early Twentieth Centuries. Intro. Robert H. Bremner. New York: Arno, 1974.

Carp, E. Wayne. *Family Matters: Secrecy and Disclosure in the History of Adoption.* Cambridge: Harvard University Press, 1998.

Daggett, Mabel Potter. "The Child Without a Home: A Cry from the Little Human Derelicts Cast up on the Tide of Our Great Cities." *Delineator* 70, no. 4 (October 1907): 505–10.

Dale, Florence D. "Foster-Children and the Shop: A Study of the Inter-Action of Placing-Out Standards and Child-Labor Laws in Different States." *Charities* 12, no. 13 (2 April 1904): 343–46.

Douglas, Ann. *The Feminization of American Culture.* 1977. New York: Doubleday, 1988.

Downs, Susan Whitelaw, and Michael W. Sherraden. "The Orphan Asylum in the Nineteenth Century." *Social Service Review* 57 (June 1988): 272–90.

Dulberger, Judith A. *"Mother Donit fore the Best": Correspondence of a Nineteenth-Century Orphan Asylum.* Syracuse: Syracuse University Press, 1996.

Emerson, Alice B. *Ruth Fielding of the Red Mill; Or, Jasper Parloe's Secret.* New York: Cupples and Leon, 1913.

Fisher, Dorothy Canfield. *Understood Betsy.* 1917. New York: Grosset and Dunlap, 1946.

Foster, Shirley, and Judy Simons. *What Katy Read: Feminist Re-Readings of "Classic" Stories for Girls.* Iowa City: University of Iowa Press, 1995.

Gannon, Susan R. "'The Best Magazine for Children of All Ages': Cross-Editing *St. Nicholas Magazine* (1873–1905)." *Children's Literature* 25 (1997): 153–80.

Griswold, Jerry. *Audacious Kids: Coming of Age in America's Classic Children's Books.* New York: Oxford University Press, 1992.

Holt, Marilyn Irvin. *The Orphan Trains: Placing out in America.* Lincoln: University of Nebraska Press, 1992.

Johnson, Deidre A. "Community and Character: A Comparison of Josephine Lawrence's Linda Lane Series and Classic Orphan Fiction." In *Nancy Drew and Company: Culture, Gender, and Girls' Series.* Ed. Sherrie A. Inness. Bowling Green: Bowling Green State University Popular Press, 1997. Pp. 59–73.

Kelley, Florence. "A Boy Destroying Trade: The Glass Bottle Industry of New Jersey, Pennsylvania, Ohio, Indiana, and Illinois." *Charities* 11, no. 1 (4 July 1903): 15–19.

Lawrence, Josephine. *Linda Lane.* New York: Barse and Hopkins, 1925.

———. *Linda Lane Experiments.* New York: Barse and Co., 1927.

Mills, Claudia. "Children in Search of a Family: Orphan Novels Through the Century." *Children's Literature in Education* 18 (winter 1987): 227–39.

Montgomery, L. M. *Anne of Green Gables.* 1908. New York: Bantam, 1979.

Morey, Anne. "Fashioning Hollywood, Fashioning the Self: Industry Outsiders and Film, 1916–1934." Ph.D. diss., University of Texas, 1998.

Nodelman, Perry. "Progressive Utopia: Or, How to Grow Up Without Growing Up." Rpt. *Such a Simple Little Tale: Critical Responses to L. M. Montgomery's "Anne of Green Gables".* Ed. Mavis Reimer. Metuchen, N.J.: Scarecrow, 1992. Pp. 29–38.

"Placing-Out Work." *Charities* 11, no. 22 (28 November 1903): 505–8.

Porter, Eleanor H. *Just David.* New York: Grosset and Dunlap, 1916.

———. *Pollyanna.* 1913. New York: Puffin, 1987.

Proceedings of the Conference on the Care of Dependent Children Held at Washington, D.C. January 25, 26, 1909. 1909. New York: Arno, 1971.

Scott, Carole. "Magical Dress: Clothing and Transformation in Folk Tales." *Children's Literature Association Quarterly* 21, no. 4 (winter 1996–97): 151–57.

Silverman, Arnold R., and William Feigelman. "Adjustment in Interracial Adoptees: An Overview." In *The Psychology of Adoption.* Ed. David M. Brodzinsky and Marshall D. Schechter. New York: Oxford University Press, 1990. Pp. 187–200.

Simpson, Eileen. *Orphans: Real and Imaginary.* New York: Weidenfeld and Nicolson, 1987.

Smith, Bruce. *The History of Little Orphan Annie.* New York: Ballantine, 1982.

Stratton-Porter, Gene. *Freckles.* 1904. Bloomington: Indiana University Press, 1986.

Webster, Jean. [Alice Jane Chandler] *Dear Enemy.* 1915. New York: Dell, 1991.

———. *Daddy-Long-Legs.* 1912.

Wells, Carolyn. *The Story of Betty.* Serialized in *St. Nicholas* 26 (January–October 1899).

Wiggin, Kate Douglas. *Timothy's Quest: A Story for Anybody, Young Or Old, Who Cares to Read It.* 1890. Boston: Houghton Mifflin, 1893.

Wright, Henrietta Christian. "State Care of Dependent Children." *North American Review* 171 (1900): 112–23.

The "Disappointed" House: Trance, Loss, and the Uncanny in L. M. Montgomery's Emily Trilogy

Kate Lawson

The three novels that make up the *Emily* trilogy—*Emily of New Moon,* *Emily Climbs,* and *Emily's Quest*—were written by L. M. Montgomery from 1923 to 1927. The *Emily* series is a marked departure for Montgomery from what had become the "stale" *Anne* books. Although similar in tracing the growth and development of an orphan girl from childhood through adolescence to adulthood, the *Emily* trilogy as a whole hints at darker forces of personality and identity than are evident in *Anne of Green Gables* and its immediate successors.[1] This essay examines the repeated psychic or supernatural experiences in Emily's life and argues that they point to or figure a traumatic lack and absence. Seen through the lens of Freud's paradoxical notion of the *unheimlich,* Emily's uncanny experiences reveal that the familiar world in which she lives is also inhabited by figurations of loss and estrangement. Freud claims that the uncanny is a disturbing combination of dread and horror in which the "homelike" and the "unhomely," the familiar and the unfamiliar, the known and the unknown, the human and the inhuman merge.[2] Arguably, Emily's supernatural vision in each of the three novels relates to a house or homelike space that resonates strongly with her imaginative sense of the familiar: in *Emily of New Moon,* Beatrice Burnley is returning happily home to her husband and baby when Emily "sees" her meet her tragic death; in *Emily Climbs,* Emily claims to "own" the empty house that a boy, Allan Bradshaw, has inquisitively explored and then found himself unable to escape; in *Emily's Quest,* Teddy Kent is returning home to Canada from Europe when Emily, thousands of miles away, prevents him from boarding a fatal ship. The clearest connection between the uncanny stories is the idea of leaving and returning home and of that home being unhomely, "inhabited" by emptiness and loss. Each of Emily's visions involves a light-hearted, innocent, even joyous journey that meets, or almost meets, with disaster rather than with a safe return to the familiar and reassuring. Each trip thus involves a perilous detour, indicat-

Children's Literature 29, ed. Elizabeth Lennox Keyser and Julie Pfeiffer (Yale University Press, © 2001 Hollins University).

ing that the return to the homelike, and therefore the home itself, is fraught with complication and danger.

In one sense, Emily seems to be a third party to these dangerous returns home, since her visions could be read as magical and self-less "good deeds" that assist others in clearing away painful misapprehensions or preventing tragic loss. In *Emily of New Moon* she heals the Burnley family by recovering the truth about their dead wife and mother, Beatrice; in *Emily Climbs* she assists a family by finding their lost and dying son; in *Emily's Quest* she prevents her friend Teddy from boarding a doomed ship. Save perhaps the last event, which involves her fraught relationship with Teddy Kent, these experiences seem largely unconnected to Emily's own psychic life. Further, Emily herself, unlike other characters, seems to avoid dangerous journeys to the unhomely by remaining attached to New Moon; although she lives in or visits other houses—the house in the hollow that she shared with her father, her Aunt Ruth's house in Shrewsbury, where she attends college, her great-aunt Nancy's house, Wyther Grange—Emily is and remains "Emily of New Moon"; she is not, like Anne of Green Gables, later linked to other or larger homes—Avonlea, Island, or "House of Dreams." Whereas Emily's friends Ilse, Teddy, and Perry leave the Blair Water area, whether for Charlottetown, Montreal, or Europe, Emily refuses the offer to pursue her career in New York and remains "of" New Moon, bound to one place and one home. The other houses that play an important role in Emily's psychic life are all, significantly, empty houses: the Old John house, where she and her friends seek shelter from a snow storm, the shore house that she feels she "owns," and the "Disappointed" house that she and Dean lovingly furnish during their engagement. Thus although Emily is strongly connected to the homelike and familiar, the many empty houses with which she is linked offer an ambiguous sense of the homelike in her own life. Although each empty house allows Emily to imagine the potential home-like space it might become, it also acts as an uncanny mirror reflecting back to Emily the potential void or lack, the unhomely, that resides within the familiar.

Critics have tended to examine the uncanny and supernatural elements of the *Emily* trilogy as evidence of both a political and a personal struggle against the forces of male domination and as a link to her role as creative artist. For instance, Lorna Drew analyses Gothic conventions in the *Emily* novels as tropes that signify "a critique, if not a collapse, of family and its much touted values" (20); Emily's psychic experiences, like her writing, situate her "closer to that maternal space of difference" (21) which Drew describes as "a source of plenitude and pleasure" (20). Elizabeth Epperly also reads Emily's psychic experiences as liberating: "it is only Emily's gift of second sight that saves her from the control and silence that characterise the lives of many women, even (perhaps especially?) women of great talent" (186). Ian Menzies, too, sees Emily's second sight as redeeming: "In a female messianic way, [Emily's vision in *Emily of New Moon*] brings peace and love not only between Ilse and her father, but between Emily and the patriarchal Aunt Elizabeth" (59–60). In addition to figuring liberation or redemption, Emily's supernatural experiences are also read as figuring poetic rapture: "her psychic experiences . . . belong to Emily the artist," since "[t]he psychic experiences are to her intuition what the flash is to her visions of beauty: Emily touches the artistic realm within and beyond the world of appearance" (Epperly 166–67). Emily is shaped by what Elizabeth Waterston calls "the world of words" (211) in the novels; like a true romantic, she inhabits a world where words—signifiers—point to experiences beyond the conventional realm. Her Wordsworthian "flash"—where the "curtain" or "veil" that separates the ordinary world from "the enchanting realm beyond" is lifted (*Emily of New Moon* 7)—suggests the power of words to signify transcendently. As a writer, Emily has privileged access to a rich world of imagination and beauty not available to people like her rigid and disapproving Aunt Elizabeth or her loving but unimaginative Aunt Laura.

But Mr. Carpenter, her nurturing teacher and harshest critic, sounds a warning note; admitting Emily's promising literary talent at the end of *Emily of New Moon,* he cautions, " 'the gods don't allow us to be in their debt'—she will pay for it—she will pay" (350). What might be called the dark side of the *Emily* trilogy records the repayment of this debt and demonstrates the costs associated with being a romantic visionary, for the image of the lifting of the veil and the drawing of the curtain are not only used as metaphors for the creative imagination or for personal freedom, but to suggest that in her uncanny experiences Emily comes into contact with a dark world beyond ordinary reality where she is "possessed" by influences and events she cannot control. These uncanny experiences can be traumatic rather than liberating; Emily finds that drawing "aside the veil of sense and time and [seeing] beyond" (*Emily's Quest* 94) is not, or not only, an experience of joy or beauty but also one of disturbance and anxiety. During these visionary but distressing experiences, Emily feels like the "instrument" (*Emily Climbs* 199) of special and frightening powers of knowledge and vision; it is, she says, "as if I were marked out in some uncanny way—I don't feel human" (*Climbs* 199–200). Thus this paper, rather than examining the psychic as a means of Emily's liberation, considers the uncanny as an inhuman and estranging experience both of possession and of emptiness in the midst of the familiar.

The Uncanny

Montgomery's interest in the uncanny arguably began in childhood experience. In a journal entry from January 7, 1910, when she was thirty-six years old, Montgomery looks back over certain memorable childhood events and records a curious experience during a bout with typhoid fever when she was five or six years of age. She became ill while on a visit to her Grandfather Montgomery's house during one of her father's rare visits. Her maternal grandmother, Lucy Macneill, the woman who raised her after the death of her mother and the departure to western Canada of her father, visited the sick child, but the young Lucy Maud was unable to recognize her. Having been told by her father that her grandmother had left her side, she believed that "this tall thin woman by the bed" (370) could not be her grandmother but must be the unwelcome housekeeper: "she was Mrs Murphy and I would not have her near me" (370). This lack of recognition persisted for several days until one day, "it simply dawned on me that it really was grandmother. . . . I remember stroking her face continually and saying in amazement and delight, 'Why, you are *not* Mrs Murphy after all—you are grandma'" (1:370). In her autobiographical work *The Alpine Path* (1917), Montgomery retells the story and comments: "Nothing could convince me that it was Grandmother. This was put down to delirium, but I do not think it was. I was quite conscious at the time" (21). Relying on her father's assertion—"Father, thinking to calm me, told me that she had gone home"—Lucy Maud "believed it implicitly—too implicitly" (21), refusing to believe the evidence of her own senses. Montgomery does not comment further on this story, yet it remained strongly in her mind, presumably because of its uncanny power. A familiar and accepted part of everyday life— her grandmother—suddenly became an unrecognized and unwanted presence at her sick bed.

Freud's discussion of the uncanny sheds light on the nature of this childhood experience. In his 1919 essay "*Das Unheimliche,*" Freud investigates both literary and clinical experiences of the uncanny and the linguistic usage of the word and concludes that although *unheimlich* (literally, "unhomely") may seem to be the opposite of *heimlich* (homelike), in fact, "*heimlich* is a word the meaning of which develops in the direction of ambivalence, until it finally coincides with its opposite, *unheimlich. Unheimlich* is in some way or other a sub-species of *heimlich*" (347). This curious state of affairs means that uncanny experiences that arouse "dread and horror" (339) because of their extraordinary and alien nature are in fact, Freud argues, precisely the experiences that are habitual and known: "the uncanny is that class of the frightening which leads back to what is known of old and long familiar" (340). In experiences of the uncanny, the subject fends off "the manifest prohibitions of reality" (363) through repression: "something which is familiar and old-established in the mind . . . has become alienated from it through the process of repression" (363–64).

The young Lucy Maud's estranging experience of her grandmother operates in much the same way as does the *unheimlich* in Freud's discussion; an intimate family member suddenly becomes unrecognizable, revealing the strange and anomalous nature of the homelike itself. In Montgomery's case, the logic that explains this repression is not difficult to trace. Her beloved father is on one of his rare visits to Prince Edward Island from his home in Prince Albert, Saskatchewan; her grandmother Macneill, the woman with whom she has lived since age two, is habitually cold and disapproving.[3] What better way to ensure the presence of the loving father by her side during illness than to disavow any knowledge of the grandmother, to deny the reality principle by repressing her familiar and certain knowledge. Upon her recovery, the reality principle once again reasserts itself and "recognition" occurs.

Unlike many experiences of Montgomery's childhood, this uncanny experience of nonrecognition is not directly assimilated into the *Emily* trilogy.[4] The novel is in fact plotted in such a way that the reality principle must assert itself; Douglas Starr *is* dead, and thus Montgomery cannot "stage" his return and an ensuing nonrecognition of Aunt Elizabeth by Emily (the most exact parallel the novel could offer). Even Emily's connection to a fantasy version of her father is broken late in the first novel when Aunt Elizabeth reads Emily's "letters" to him and thus destroys her sense of closeness to him.

Nevertheless, it is clear that the phenomena of the uncanny continue to have a strong grip on Montgomery's creative imagination; this continued ambivalent fascination in her adult life can perhaps be attributed to her perception of an uncanny element in her husband's mental illness. Having just completed the typescript of *Emily Climbs,* Montgomery recorded in her journal a fresh outburst of Ewan Macdonald's religious melancholia. Although she had once promised herself to be silent on the subject—"I did not mean to write anymore concerning my feelings during these attacks" (3:170)—she found herself compelled to do so on March 16, 1924:

> Nothing is more curious than the way he forgets, in these attacks, the fact that he has recovered from many similar attacks during these five years—nothing, except the way he forgets, when he is well, that he ever had such attacks at all. . . .
>
> The suddenness of these attacks is so uncanny. Two weeks ago, Ewan was well, jolly, and care free—a fine looking man with a pleasant, open face and friendly, twinkling eyes. Yesterday he sat or lay all day—unshorn, collarless, hair on end, eyes wild and hunted, with a hideous imbecile expression on his face. . . . There *is* an alien personality in Ewan during these attacks. He is an utterly different creature from the man I married. The touch of his hand on me seems like a profanation. (3:169–70)

Montgomery finds it "curious" that her husband cannot remember himself well when ill, or ill when well. It is thus not surprising that she imagines that there is "an alien personality" which inhabits Ewan Macdonald, and that the sudden shift from the familiar personality to the alien one is, for her, "so uncanny" that a touch of her husband's hand becomes a "profanation" of her flesh. Montgomery's experience of her husband's illness may at least partially explain Emily's seeming distance from the troubled events in her visions: the death of Ilse's mother, the lost boy, Teddy boarding a train. As with Emily's visions, Montgomery is in one sense a looker-on at the misery of another; she herself is not in direct jeopardy. And yet Montgomery, like Emily, finds herself drawn into the experience of the other, and is in fact the only one to experience fully the uncanny effects of her husband's madness since it is *she* who witnesses and remembers the eruptions of the alien within the familiar. Thus although Montgomery is not herself inhabited by an "alien personality," as Emily is, her ability to remember her husband's normal personality in the midst of his slide into melancholia produces the uncanny effect.

It may thus be argued that the uncanny discovery of the estranging within the familiar that Montgomery experienced in both her childhood and her marriage and found clearly connected to her own psychic life, *is* mirrored in Emily's experiences and Emily's psyche, albeit indirectly. The uncanny in the novels becomes the route for discovering the hidden and estranging truth that lies within Emily's familiar world, as it does in Montgomery's. Freud, quoting Schelling, notes that the uncanny comes from "something which ought to have remained hidden but has come to light" (364). When the young Lucy Maud Montgomery sees her grandmother as an unwelcome stranger, she has a true apprehension of her own lack of affection for the cold, unresponsive woman who is at the center of the only home she has known. When the mature Montgomery finds the touch of her mad husband's hand to be profane, she has a deep and disturbingly intimate experience of the familiar touch becoming alien. When Emily declares of a previously unseen house, "That house belongs to me" (174) in *Emily's Quest,* and then the missing child Allan Bradshaw is discovered in that house, she experiences a distressing connection between her own familiar and "owned" psychic space and the space of an imprisoned child. Further, when her would-be lover Teddy reminds her that witches were formerly burned for revealing this kind of hidden knowledge (*Quest* 100) and her best friend Ilse says, "It makes me a little afraid of you, Emily" (*Climbs* 199), Emily must understand that her uncanny experiences are perceived by those close to her not as "alien" but as an anomalous and unnerving part of who she is, of the inner "house" that she "owns" and inhabits. In linking the homelike with the unhomely, the uncanny is a helpful paradigm for understanding how experiences that seem foreign to Montgomery and to Emily are in fact intimately related to their own essential selves.

It is worth noting, however, that Freud's essay on the uncanny does not end with his discussion of the linguistic merging of the meanings of the words *heimlich* and *unheimlich,* of the discovery of the estranging that resides in the midst of the homelike. Rather the essay, controversially, goes on to ground the uncanny in the castration complex, primarily through a reading of E. T. A. Hoffman's uncanny story "The Sand-Man" as an allegory of repressed castration anxiety. Although feminist critics have disagreed both with Freud's reading of the Hoffman story and, more profoundly, with his stress on the castration complex as the basis of human sexual difference,[5] Jacques Lacan's reformulation of the idea of castration has provided fruitful grounds for feminist interpretation. Lacan points out that Freud stresses "the sub-jective import of the perception of the female genital organ" and thus its "essential link with the function of representation as such" (Lacan 113). The experience of the uncanny is a frightening apprehension of lack, an apprehension shared by the boy and the girl, for although the presence or absence of a penis comes to figure sexual difference, this lack or absence refers not to the real but to the symbolic order: "there is nothing missing in the real" (Lacan 113). Elizabeth Bron-fen argues that this fundamental experience of lack can be under-stood not only as the entry into the symbolic order but also "in ref-erence to real loss such as the actual death of a beloved person, or the fact that from birth onwards, existence is coterminous with the actual threat of dying" (44). The uncanny experience is thus inter-preted as an inevitable confrontation, at once familiar and estranging, with lack, loss, or absence. Consequently, though Montgomery's par-ticular childhood and marital experiences of the uncanny may par-tially explain the force of the uncanny in her work, Lacan's and Bron-fen's arguments clearly place a perception of the uncanny at the center of all human subjectivity.

The "Disappointed" House

Emily of New Moon opens with an archetypal return home; Emily, the romantic visionary, is dancing over the fields at night with her friend the "Wind Woman," joyfully in touch with a magical realm beyond the "veil": "It had always seemed to Emily, ever since she could remem-ber, that she was very, very near a world of wonderful beauty. Between it and herself hung only a thin curtain; she could never draw the cur-tain aside—but sometimes, just for a moment, a wind fluttered it and then it was if she caught a glimpse of the enchanting realm beyond— only a glimpse—and heard a note of unearthly music" (*New Moon* 7). The enraptured Emily returns home only to be met at the threshold by the unloving housekeeper Ellen Greene, who grimly informs her, "your pa has only a week or two more to live" (*New Moon* 8). Her loving father dies in the next chapter, and Emily's safe and loving home is lost. Emily's experience in the opening chapters of the novel is thus one of ecstatic vision and of a safe return to the familiar being obliter-ated by traumatic loss, of a yawning void that opens suddenly within the homelike.[6]

Emily's encounter with the supernatural at the end of the novel repeats some of the associations from the first chapter. Emily has been both fascinated and horrified by the secret story of her friend Ilse's mother, Beatrice Burnley, a woman who seems to have eloped with her childhood lover one night, leaving her husband and infant child behind. Returning home to New Moon from a visit to great-aunt Nancy's with the secret and scandalous knowledge of the story of Beatrice Burnley, Emily falls ill and becomes delirious with a high fever.[7] In her delirium she "sees" the woman with "the ace of hearts on her forehead" (the identifying mark of Beatrice Burnley) dancing over the fields at night, and calls out: "she is coming so gladly—she is singing—she is thinking of her baby—oh, keep her back—keep her back—she doesn't see the well—it's so dark she doesn't see it—oh, she's gone into it—she's gone into it!" (333). Emily's narrative of Beatrice Burnley's death—of the mother's joyful return home to her baby tragically cut short by a fall into an uncovered well—recalls her own dancing and joyful return home in the first chapter, only to have that home, as she reaches its threshold, metaphorically cast into an abyss by the sudden fact of her father's imminent death. The deep, dark well in which Beatrice Burnley dies is thus in one sense a figuration of lack, of the antithesis of home, and of the sudden dizzying trauma associated with its loss.

Emily's uncanny exploration of Beatrice Burnley's death thus could be said to function as a repetition and resolution of Emily's own traumatic return home. Her "solution" to the puzzle of Beatrice Burnley's death allows Beatrice to be reintegrated into the network of community relations—"That which had been found in the old Lee well had been buried in the Mitchell plot at Shrewsbury and a white marble shaft, 'Sacred to the memory of Beatrice Burnley, beloved wife of Allan Burnley,' had been erected" (*New Moon* 337)—a restored relationship that could be said to mirror Emily's own growing sense of "belonging" at New Moon. Emily's delusion also reestablishes the untainted innocence of the laughing, singing Beatrice Burnley—"She was a bright, beautiful, merry creature—we thought her close friendship with her cousin natural and harmless. We know now that it was so," says Aunt Laura (*New Moon* 338)—and thus may reestablish the possibility of joyful innocence and the homelike that had been cast in doubt by her traumatic loss of the paternal home. Nevertheless, at the end of the novel Emily's growing maturity suggests that her uncanny access to knowledge of Beatrice Burnley's death has left a certain taint; Mr. Carpenter notes that she looks "less childlike, with great grey shadowy eyes that had looked into death and read the riddle of a buried thing, and henceforth would hold in them some haunting, elusive remembrance of the world beyond the veil" (*New Moon* 341). Having come face to face with an irremediable lack beyond the veil of the homelike and familiar, Emily cannot entirely re-veil the place of loss and trauma. That the two later novels continue this theme of the perilous journey home indicates a level of unresolved anxiety in Emily's experience of the homelike.

In the second novel, *Emily Climbs,* Emily once again has a supernatural encounter, but on this occasion her trance comes not with fever but in sleep. She and Ilse are walking through the countryside selling magazine subscriptions door-to-door to help pay their way through college. Through a series of misadventures they become lost and cannot find the house in which they were welcome to spend the night. This detour from the homelike means that they must spend the night in a hay-stack, an episode that is not terrifying or distressing but rather an occasion for Emily, again, to be struck by the beauty of the natural world and her sense of close communion, and communication, with it: "She was afraid to move or breathe lest she break the current of beauty that was flowing through her. Life seemed like a wonderful instrument on which to play supernal harmonies" (*Emily Climbs* 171). After this ecstatic experience she and Ilse make their way the next day on the mundane task of subscription sales until they hear at one house that a small boy, Allan Bradshaw, has been missing from his home for two days. Emily is struck by the fact that as she was lying "in the ecstasy of wild, free hours" (173–74), the boy's mother must have passed a night of anxious horror; of the boy himself and his fate, she can hardly bear to think. The pitiful story of the boy haunts her for the rest of the day. Again, then, the stage is set for the supernatural encounter by the haunting juxtaposition of fullness, innocence, joy, and beauty with loss, trauma, and suffering.

Emily's distress is alleviated for a moment, though, when she and Ilse pass a beautiful, striking, and isolated small house on the shore, a sight that brings her sudden declaration: "That house belongs to me" (174). Emily clarifies this for the puzzled Ilse: "Of course, I don't *own* it. But haven't you sometimes seen houses that you knew belonged to you no matter who owned them?" (175). The empty shore house is paradoxically the epitome of what is homelike. Emily rapturously says:

"That house is full of [personality]. There isn't a line or a corner that isn't eloquent, and those casement windows are lovable — especially that little one high up under the eaves over the front door. . . . You dear friendly thing, I love you — I understand you. As Old Kelly would say, 'may niver a tear be shed under your roof.' . . . If I lived in you, beloved, I'd always stand at that western window at evening to wave to some one coming home. That is just exactly what that window was built for — a frame for love and welcome." (175)

At the end of the day chance leads the girls to ask at the Bradshaw house if they, strangers, may stay the night. They are admitted into the troubled household and given beds. When they awake in the morning Emily finds a sketch in her "Jimmy-book" of the house she "owns" with a "black cross" and an inscription indicating "*Allan Bradshaw is here*" (194). Although she disclaims any ability to draw, the sketch can only have been made by Emily since the inscription is in her own hand. The house is searched and — again — Emily's premonition proves true; the lost child is found, and although he is weak and at the point of death, he recovers and eventually returns home to his elated and relieved mother.

If Emily's first psychic experience is related to the traumatic loss of her paternal home and the difficulty of establishing a new home for herself at New Moon, the second experience seems to indicate a new level of traumatic conflict for Emily regarding the nature of the homelike. At one level, the house in this story — the shore house that she calls her "beloved" — is a clear contrast with the house she shares with her Aunt Ruth in Shrewsbury. Her room at Aunt Ruth's is "such an ugly one. She hated it at sight. The door wouldn't shut tight; the slanting ceiling was rain stained, and come down so close to the bed she could touch it with her hand. . . . 'I can *never* feel at home here,' said Emily" (91–92). Not only does her unhomely room lack privacy — the door won't close — it also seems as cramped as a prison cell. Aunt Ruth's attempts to restrict Emily's visitors again emphasize its prison-like nature.

Emily may feel metaphorically imprisoned at Aunt Ruth's; however, the lost child, Allan Bradshaw, is literally imprisoned in a room that is the antithesis of Emily's own. Having found his way into the empty house through a cellar window, the child had, according to one of his rescuers, "pulled [a] closet door tight in some way and the spring lock

made him a prisoner. The window was too high for him to reach. . . .
The white plaster of the closet wall is all marked and scarred with his
vain attempts to get up to the window" (198). Whereas Emily's room
has a door that will not shut, the child is imprisoned by a door that
will not open; whereas Emily feels crowded by the ceiling she can almost touch lying in bed, the child cannot reach the window, let alone
the ceiling. The house with which Emily claims a psychic connection,
which "belongs" to her, seems to contain a homelike space where the
restrictions she feels most bitterly at Aunt Ruth's are lifted, and yet it
is ironically capable of imprisoning a terrified child. In particular, the
"lovable" high window that Emily feels is a "frame for love and welcome" is perhaps the window that the child cannot reach to attract
attention. Whereas Emily imagines the window "high up under the
eaves" as a place where she would "always stand . . . at evening to wave
to some one coming home," for the child this is in reality an empty
house to which no one ever returns. Her wish for the shore house—
"may niver a tear be shed under your roof"—is ironically and horribly
reversed as the child wails and scratches fruitlessly for help. The idea
of comfortable, familiar homelike space, a space that is Emily's own,
is thus undercut by an uncanny doubling of the home as a space of
prison and confinement. That the home with which Emily feels a psychic bond is not only believed to be empty but actually contains a prisoner desperate to escape suggests that Emily's own dreams of fulfillment and home may be in some sense contaminated at their source.

   This idea receives further development in *Emily's Quest,* in which
Emily's freedom and the difficult nature of both romantic vision and
her relationships with Dean Priest and Teddy Kent are at the center of
the narrative. Although Elizabeth Waterston claims that *Emily's Quest*
"marked the author's retreat from her experimental venture" in the
previous novels (213), it could be said, whatever its weaknesses, to engage at times compellingly with an adult woman's problematic experience of loneliness, fear, and lack of fulfillment, and to do so in the
context of the uncanny.[8] In this last novel, it is Emily's relation to the
"disappointed" house that symbolizes the same paradoxical sense of
entrapment and freedom in a homelike space as was presented in the
previous novel. The disappointed house was built many years before
by Fred Clifford—a distant relative of Emily's—for his bride according to a plan she chose (*New Moon* 77); when his would-be bride jilted
him, he boarded over the unfinished house and left it in the state that
Emily felt intuitively at first sight to be "Disappointed" (*New Moon* 67).

That the disappointed house is so intimately connected with a failed marriage makes it an appropriate setting to explore Emily's lack of fulfillment and sense of positive entrapment as she anticipates her marriage. That the house was being built according to the bride's plan and then left unfinished because of her actions, moreover, brings Emily's own equivocal desires into question.

Although *Emily's Quest* opens with Emily "thrilled" by her friend Teddy's use of the plural "we" in relation to their future lives (13), she finds herself inexplicably estranged from him. Unlike Valency Stirling, the oppressed and dejected heroine of Montgomery's novel *The Blue Castle*, who nevertheless finds the strength of will to leave her family and propose marriage to a man who is almost a stranger,[9] the strong-willed and outspoken writer Emily cannot find words to express her affection to Teddy, a companion she has known since childhood. Certain that "she always knew she wanted Teddy" (39), she nevertheless writes letters to him that are chilled with "frost" (40) at the first sign that he may be losing interest in her.

Her other male friend, Dean Priest, dashes her hopes of ever being a writer by telling her that her first novel is nothing but "a pretty little story" and her characters "only puppets" (57, 58). Discouraged, she burns the manuscript, and then in a fit of remorse runs from her room blinded with tears, steps on Aunt Laura's sewing scissors, and falls down the stairs at New Moon. Brought to the seeming nadir of her fortunes, she is gravely injured, is estranged from Teddy, and loses her essential connection to the poetic realm.

In her slow recovery only Dean Priest is there to comfort her; eventually she agrees to marry him. Yet given his demanding personality, she feels trapped and even afraid; she looks guiltily at the wedding ring on her finger, which with its "great, green emerald winking on her finger seemed like a fetter" (85). The freedom symbolized by her writing and by her flights of imagination is lost in her engagement. Dean's purchase of the disappointed house, clearly a symbol of the coming failure of their engagement, provides the most joy of their shared lives. When Dean promises that the house "isn't going to be Disappointed any longer" (77), Emily's delighted reaction links her more strongly to the house than to Dean: "I've always loved that house. . . . I've always longed to see that house fulfilled" (77). As in the previous novel, the vacant house symbolizes for Emily both the reality of lack and emptiness, and the possibility of fulfillment and compensation for loss. Emily guiltily admits to herself this profound connection to the house; she is "more interested than ever in her little grey house, which meant so much to her—'more to me than Dean does,' she said to herself once in . . . despairing honesty" (85–86).

Emily's joy lies in imagining a recovery of the place of disappointment and loss, of seeing the uncannily familiar but empty space of the house transformed into a homelike and loving place. It is thus in tune with the darker tone of this novel that this proposed recovery and transformation does not take place; rather, the house is the setting for the event that breaks their engagement. She is alone in the furnished but uninhabited house, looking into the "gazing-ball" bequeathed to her by her Aunt Nancy, and finds herself—not delirious, not asleep—but in a trancelike state "among throngs of people" looking at Teddy at a ticket window, with "amazed recognition in his eyes" (94). Knowing that he is "in some terrible danger—and that *she* must save him" she says only, "Teddy. *Come*." He "follows" her through the crowd until she finds herself "back in her chair staring fixedly into Aunt Nancy's gazing-ball" (95). News comes that the ship on which Teddy was to have sailed hit an iceberg and sank. Teddy himself then writes to Emily saying that as he was buying his ticket for the boat-train, he "saw" Emily in the crowd and followed her until he missed the train and the connecting passage on board the ship. Teddy thanks her for saving his life, but then adds, ambiguously: "I heard a queer story of you long ago—something about Ilse's mother. I've almost forgotten. Take care. They don't burn witches nowadays, of course—but still—" (100).

Emily's visionary encounter leads her to break her engagement with Dean since she now understands the depth of her connection with Teddy. As Elizabeth Epperly argues, "Emily's psychic experience with Teddy shows her the foundation of her spirit, and she is true after that to both of its dictates: the critical standards of the writer and those of the lover who knows only one choice" (190). In this optimistic reading of the novel, Emily and Teddy have now had a shared visionary experience; no longer does Emily alone see "ghosts." Further, in this experience she acts not as a channel for knowledge to be transmitted unconsciously, in delirium or in sleep, but as an agent with conscious knowledge and choice; she understands the danger and by speaking—"Teddy. *Come*."—is able to reach out to make contact with the man she desires. Finally, whereas Emily's other psychic encounters were apprehensions of the past (Beatrice Burnley's death) and of the present (the location of the lost child), this encounter is oriented toward the future, toward a shared vision that allows suffering to be averted.

But this last uncanny experience also reasserts the reality of the empty and unhomely spaces that endure within Emily's familiar existence, of the disappointed or imprisoning house that "belongs" to her. In breaking her engagement with Dean, Emily may be true to Teddy but she is also repeating history by "jilting" the expectant groom and again leaving the house disappointed: "So this is still to be the Disappointed House. Verily, there is a doom on it. Houses, like people, can't escape their doom, it seems," says Dean (104). Thus Dean' wedding gift of the "Disappointed" house to Emily and Teddy adds a note of disquiet to the novel's belated "happy" ending. Although the narrator asserts in the novel's final line that "the beloved grey house . . . is to be disappointed no longer" (235), that fulfillment is never dramatized, and many readers have been left unconvinced by the suggestion that Emily's problems of loneliness, loss, and artistic integrity will be resolved by her union with Teddy. Mary Rubio argues that Emily's life with Teddy in the disappointed house "will sink into grey domesticity within" (30). Elizabeth Epperly, noting the span of time which passes before Emily and Teddy become reconciled ("Year after year the seasons walked by her door" [*Quest* 228]), acutely comments that "[w]ith so many years of sorrow and loneliness behind her, Emily's eventual marriage to Teddy is a relief rather than a positive joy" (190). Marie Campbell argues darkly that the final novel "hints that Teddy actually *steals* or usurps Emily's creative talents" through their shared psychic connection (141). For all his artistic ability, Teddy is a pallid and prosaic hero,[10] seemingly a puppet of the women in his life—his mother, Ilse, and Emily. Any fulfillment for the disappointed spaces in Emily's life, any reparation for the pain of loss, is very belated.

The disappointed house with its sense of doom thus speaks strongly to Emily's psyche because it corresponds to a place of emptiness, loss, and disappointment at the center of Emily's own life, emptiness that begins with her initial bereavement at the death of her father and continues in more muted form through the other two novels. In this sense the disappointed and other empty houses in the novels are a kind of crystallization of Emily's three psychic experiences. What Emily calls "that horrible power or gift or curse" (*Quest*, 96) of her uncanny abilities reveals a pattern of loss or unfulfilled potential in the space that "belongs" to her. Her vision of Beatrice Burnley's death in the well re-

peats the moment of traumatic knowledge of her father's death. Her
sketch of the imprisoned child Allan Bradshaw echoes her adolescent
sense of lost freedom and frustrated potential. Her vision of the well-
traveled artist Teddy returning from an education in Paris ironically
mocks her own self-chosen enclosure in the small world of New Moon
and the loss of artistic potential symbolized by her burned book. Even
though Teddy's death would have been another catastrophic loss, his
return to Emily with its promise of fulfillment seems tenuous. Thus the
estranging and dismaying power of Emily's psychic experiences comes
from their very familiarity or intimacy in her life. By forcefully representing the space of the unfamiliar and unhomely, these uncanny experiences point to the gaps, losses, and disappointments that mark the
heroine's life.

Montgomery too had a disappointed house at the center of her psychic life. From her earliest home with cold and disapproving grandparents to her marital home with a man liable to sudden possession
by an "alien personality," Montgomery was clearly aware that the fantasy of a home that is a "dear friendly thing" may be precisely that—
a fantasy. Addressing the empty home on the shore, Emily says: "If
I lived in you, beloved, I'd always stand at that western window at
evening to wave to some one coming home. That is just exactly what
that window was built for—a frame for love and welcome." For Montgomery also, the home is presumably the place in which one belongs,
and from which one could hail the loved one returning home. And
yet who does return home to her? Her absent father rarely made the
trek to the family home in Prince Edward Island from Saskatchewan
after his second marriage; when the adolescent Montgomery went to
his home, she felt like an unwelcome alien, an intruder. Equally important, her marital home was fraught with anxiety and regret, not only
for her, but for her husband as well, since she interpreted her husband's melancholia as a response to living in the wrong house and in
the wrong community. Writing in her journal in Leaksdale on April 12,
1921, Montgomery analyzed the cause of her husband's attacks:

> Looking back over his attacks I find they have always come on
> suddenly when he was disappointed or homesick. Evidently his
> disappointment and loneliness were repressed in his subcon-
> scious mind and began playing tricks with his nerves, as psycho-
> analysis has recently discovered such things do. . . . I am con-

vinced that his suppressed disappointment [at not being "called"
to a new church] brought on his last and worst attack. If he were
now to get a call to a place he liked this old rankling disappointment might be rooted out and he would be perfectly well. (3:2)

Her analysis of her husband's illness makes it clear that in her view the
home is a locus of repression; his attacks come on when he is "disappointed or homesick." But in the instance that follows, his homesick-
ness is not for a place he has *lost* but for a place he has never been,
a place that he is disappointed not to have attained. Montgomery
believed that Ewan Macdonald too had a "Disappointed" house, an
imagined place of fulfillment, a place where "he would be perfectly
well." But as Montgomery's journal records, his life was a series of "old
rankling disappointment[s]," so the hoped-for perfect wellness never
occurred, even when he *was* "called"; the family left Leaksdale for
Norval in February 1926, and only a month later, Montgomery again
wrote, "Ewan is far from well" (3:293). This new home was presumably another disappointment. Montgomery recorded in March 1924
that her husband told her that one of the "voices inside his head" said:
"A house divided against itself cannot stand" (3:179; Matt. 12:25). For
Ewan Macdonald and for his distressed wife, their house was clearly divided between the imagined place where he, and they, could be "perfectly well" and the real home that inevitably contained disappointment.

Montgomery's domestic disappointments went beyond her fraught
relations with her father, her grandmother, or her husband. Her anxiety about her growing sons, for instance, is also clearly recorded in
her journals of these years.[11] Further, other miserable events crowded
the years leading up the publication of the *Emily* trilogy; the Great
War, the death of her close friend Frederica Campbell MacFarlane in
1919, and her protracted legal battles with L.C. Page Co. all contributed to the somber tone of the novels. The empty and disappointed
houses that inhabit the trilogy, combined with Emily's disturbing visions of failed, blocked, and traumatic returns home, clearly indicate
that for Montgomery, the home is at once a place of imagined fulfillment and a place that clearly registers the reality of loss and estrangement. As Freud says, "*heimlich* is a word the meaning of which develops
in the direction of ambivalence, until it finally coincides with its opposite, *unheimlich.*" *Emily's Quest* ends with Emily, the deed to the "Disap-

pointed" house in her hand, waiting for Teddy to join her, an apt image of happy expectation and coming fulfillment that already "owns" the moment of loss and disappointment.

Notes

1. In a journal entry from August 20, 1921, L. M. Montgomery writes: "This morning I wrote the first chapter of my new book—*Emily of New Moon*. . . . And it is such a relief to be done of the 'Anne gang.' I had gone so stale on them" (3:16).

The successors to the *Anne* books I have in mind are those published immediately after *Anne of Green Gables* (1908): *Anne of Avonlea* (1909) and *Anne of the Island* (1915). The later volumes, *Anne's House of Dreams* (1917), *Rainbow Valley* (1919), and *Rilla of Ingleside* (1921), are all, as Elizabeth Waterston says, "shadowed by war" (209) and thus bear evidence of the same disquiet that marks the *Emily* series. Several critics (Epperly 145–46; Gammel 40) have noted that Montgomery began the *Emily* series as she was recopying her childhood journals; these journals at once provided the forty-nine-year-old writer with the freshness of the adolescent voice and evidence of the inevitable struggles of the young Montgomery to understand her perplexing and exacting roles of daughter, step-daughter, granddaughter, and niece—all roles that Emily herself must play. One can also note, however, that as early as 1908, Montgomery wrote in her journal: "Thank God, I can keep the shadows of my life out of my work. I would not wish to darken any other life—I want instead to be a messenger of optimism and sunshine" (1:339). Perhaps all of Montgomery's work can be read as successful or unsuccessful attempts to keep the "shadows" of her life at bay.

2. No translation is perhaps fully satisfactory, but I am using "homelike" and "unhomely" as translations of the words *heimlich* and *unheimlich* in Freud's essay "The 'Uncanny.'" James Strachey, in his translation, notes that *unheimlich* is "literally 'unhomely,'" although "[t]he English term is not, of course, an exact equivalent of the German one" (Freud 339 n). Because "homely" means "simple, plain; uncomely" (*Oxford English Dictionary*), the word "home*like*" is closer to the meaning of *heimlich*. The negative "unhomely," however, seems to be a negation of obsolete and archaic meanings of "homely": "of or belonging to the home or household; become as one with the household; familiar, intimate." For instance, the *OED* offers the following citation from *The Athenaeum* (1871): "Everything in the picture is neglected and unhomely and coarse." For this reason I have chosen to retain Strachey's "unhomely."

Freud's essay is in part a linguistic analysis of the words themselves, in German and other languages, the paradoxical conclusions of which I report briefly in this paper.

3. Lucy and Alexander Macneill appear as stern grandparents in Montgomery's journal. On February 27, 1890, Montgomery writes: "Grandpa and Grandma always seem so averse to my going anywhere" (1:17); on July 1, 1890, "I have enjoyed it all [a concert], although, as usual, it was somewhat embittered for me by the fact that grandpa and grandma did not approve of it—why I cannot say. It just seems that they never do approve of anything which means the assembling of young folks together" (1:21–22).

4. See, e.g., the incident that immediately precedes this account in Montgomery's journal, when she grabbed a hot poker by mistake and burned her hand badly. This event is transposed directly into *Emily of New Moon* 11.

5. Jane Marie Todd, for example, returns to Hoffman's story to suggest ways in which Freud himself overlooked or repressed aspects of the narrative; she suggests that in not analyzing the role in the story of the female doll or automaton, Olympia, Freud failed to note that "Olympia's 'castration' signifies nothing other than [the] social oppression

of women" (525). Sarah Kofman, in her broader critique of Freud's theory of female sexuality and the girl's experience of the castration complex, argues that Freud's own argument bears a neurotic complexion: penis envy, the experience at the center of the girl's castration complex, becomes for Freud "a delirious speculation . . . an idée fixe, an idea that has become more and more 'fixated' to the point of replacing all other ideas" (171); for Kofman, penis envy is simply an "extravagant 'false solution' " (174).

6. Emily's traumatic loss of the paternal home is a good example of Montgomery's direct transposition of her own traumas into fictional form. Not only did Montgomery not live with her father throughout her childhood and adolescence, but her year-long stay with him and with her step-mother when she was fifteen proved to be bitterly disappointing. Emily's traumatic apprehension of the father's loss is thus reflective, not of the facts of Montgomery's life, but of the distance, both physically and psychically, at which he lived. Montgomery is clearly aware of the significant parallels; in her journal she writes: "*New Moon* is in some respects but not all my own old home and 'Emily's' inner life was my own, though outwardly most of the events and incidents were fictitious" (3:147).

7. Emily's first night at great-aunt Nancy's house, Wyther Grange, is spent in a "haunted" room so that the formerly interesting house "suddenly became a dreadful, uncanny place" (*New Moon* 254). In the morning Emily, like many Gothic heroines, discovers that the eerie sounds had an ordinary source, in this case, birds in the chimney behind her bed. It is back in the familiar New Moon that the "real" ghost—Beatrice Burnley—appears.

8. Montgomery had a great deal of difficulty in writing this last novel. In her journal she writes that she "resumed" work on *Emily's Quest* at the end of May 1924 (3:184) but then writes of the novel in April 1926: "I *must* get down to work. . . . The book will be poor stuff I fear" (3:292); in June 1926: "I wonder if I shall *ever* get that book done" (3:298); and finally in October 1926: "Yesterday morning I actually finished *Emily's Quest*. . . . Thank heaven it is the last of the Emily series" (3:310). Irene Gammel comments that Montgomery completed *Emily's Quest* "[a]mid journal entries recording her loneliness, unhappy marriage, and 'gnawing mental pain' that she is able to obliterate 'only by an opiate' (3:209)" (39). Contrast this to her enjoyment on commencing the series: " 'Emily' is a dear little soul and I have some good experiences waiting for her" (3:16).

9. Montgomery's difficulty in writing *Emily's Quest* led her to begin *The Blue Castle*. She published *Emily Climbs* in 1924, started *Emily's Quest* in the same year, but turned to *The Blue Castle*, which she completed in 1925, and finished *Emily's Quest* in 1926. Rubio argues that *The Blue Castle*, "an unadulterated and bitter assault on the patriarchal system," allows Montgomery to "[blow] off the steam that had been gathering as she faced the unhappy prospect of marrying off Emily" (31–32). Unlike Emily's attachment to real, empty houses, the heroine of *The Blue Castle* dreams of finding fulfillment in a beautiful but thoroughly imaginary "blue castle," one that is eventually realized in the unlikely form of a small cabin on a remote lake. Thus at the end of the respective novels, Valancy's extravagantly imagined homelike ideal finds a real psychical embodiment, whereas Emily remains trapped in the confines of her "Disappointed" house.

10. In her journals of 1924 Montgomery mentions that she has a horse named "Teddy" (3:165). It is unclear whether she had the same horse when she began writing *Emily of New Moon*, but it is hardly a confident declaration of a hero's abilities to give him a name evidently suitable for a horse.

11. She was anxious not only about her sons' schooling and future prospects but also about a possible hereditary aspect of her husband's illness. In her journal she notes that if she had known of her husband's melancholia, she would never have married him: "I could never have had the courage to marry a man under such a doom; nor, if I had

dared, would I have thought it right to do so because I hold that no man or woman ought to bring children into the world under the curse of such hereditary tendency" (3:115).

Works Cited

Bronfen, Elizabeth. "Castration Complex." In *Feminism and Psychoanalysis: A Critical Dictionary*. Ed. Elizabeth Wright. Oxford: Blackwell, 1992. Pp. 41–45.

Campbell, Marie. "Wedding Bells and Death Knells: The Writer as Bride in the *Emily* Trilogy." In *Harvesting Thistles: The Textual Garden of L. M. Montgomery*. Ed. Mary H. Rubio. Guelph, Ont.: Canadian Children's Press, 1994.

Drew, Lorna. "The Emily Connection: Ann Radcliffe, L. M. Montgomery, and 'The Female Gothic.'" *Canadian Children's Literature* 77 (1995): 19–32.

Epperly, Elizabeth Rollins. *The Fragrance of Sweet-Grass: L. M. Montgomery's Heroines and the Pursuit of Romance*. Toronto: University of Toronto Press, 1992.

Freud, Sigmund. "The 'Uncanny.'" In *Arts and Literature*. Harmondsworth: Penguin, 1953, 1985. Vol. 14 of *The Pelican Freud Library*.

Gammel, Irene. "'My Secret Garden': Dis/Pleasure in L. M. Montgomery and F. P. Grove." *English Studies in Canada* 25 (1999): 39–65.

Kofman, Sarah. *The Enigma of Woman: Woman in Freud's Writings*. Trans. Catherine Porter. Ithaca: Cornell University Press, 1985.

Lacan, Jacques. "The Phallic Phase and the Subjective Import of the Castration Complex." In *Feminine Sexuality: Jacques Lacan and the école freudienne*. Ed. Juliet Mitchell and Jacqueline Rose. Trans. Jacqueline Rose. New York: Norton, 1982.

Menzies, Ian. "The Moral of the Rose: L. M. Montgomery's Emily." *Canadian Children's Literature* 65 (1992): 48–61.

Montgomery, L. M. *The Alpine Path: The Story of My Career*. 1917. Markham, Ont.: Fitzhenry and Whiteside, 1997.

———. *Emily Climbs*. 1924. Toronto: McClelland and Stewart, 1977.

———. *Emily of New Moon*. Toronto: McClelland and Stewart, 1923.

———. *Emily's Quest*. 1927. Toronto: McClelland and Stewart, 1989.

———. *The Selected Journals of L. M. Montgomery*. Ed. Mary Rubio and Elizabeth Waterston. Toronto: Oxford University Press, 1985. 4 vols.

Rose, Jacqueline. "Introduction II." In *Feminine Sexuality: Jacques Lacan and the école freudienne*. Ed. Juliet Mitchell and Jacqueline Rose. Trans. Jacqueline Rose. New York: Norton, 1982.

Rubio, Mary. "Subverting the Trite: L. M. Montgomery's 'Room of Her Own.'" *Canadian Children's Literature* 65 (1992): 6–39.

Todd, Jane Marie. "The Veiled Woman in Freud's 'Das Unheimliche.'" *Signs* 11, no. 3 (1986): 519–28.

Waterston, Elizabeth. "L. M. Montgomery, 1874–1942." In *The Clear Spirit: Twenty Canadian Women and Their Times*. Ed. Mary Quayle Innis. Toronto: University of Toronto Press, 1966.

Once upon a Time in Aframerica: The "Peculiar" Significance of Fairies in the Brownies' Book

Fern Kory

> *Little Annabelle was lying on the lawn, a volume of Grimm before her.*
> *Annabelle was 9 years of age, the daughter of a colored lawyer, and the*
> *prettiest dark child in the village. She had long played in the fairyland of*
> *knowledge, and was far advanced for one of her years. A vivid imagination*
> *was her chief endowment . . .*
>   *"I wonder," she said to herself that afternoon, "if there is any such thing*
> *as a colored fairy? Surely there must be, but in this book they're all white."*
>   —Fenton Johnson, "The Black Fairy"

The *Brownies' Book* (January 1920–December 1921) was a groundbreaking but short-lived monthly children's magazine created in part to provide African American children like Annabelle with "colored" fairies. It was the brainchild of W. E. B. DuBois, the only African American founding member of the National Association for the Advancement of Colored People, and since 1910 the managing editor of the NAACP's official organ, *Crisis: A Record of the Darker Races*. The *Brownies' Book* grew out of the popular annual "Children's Number" of *Crisis,* published each October starting in 1912. In this special issue, dozens of photographs of African American children submitted by readers visually framed the usual coverage of political, cultural, and social issues. Each "Children's Number" also included a story explicitly directed to a child audience, either an African folk tale or an original fairy story like the one quoted in the epigraph.[1]

    The fact that the first stories offered to children by the editors of *Crisis* were folktales and fairy stories suggests that these genres were central to their conception of an African American children's literature. This idea is played out even more fully in the *Brownies' Book*—not just in stories featuring fairies and elves but also in poems (including "Fairies" by Langston Hughes in the January 1921 issue), illustrations, letters from readers, advertisements, and, of course, the magazine's title, which pointedly appropriates a European folk character,

Children's Literature 29, ed. Elizabeth Lennox Keyser and Julie Pfeiffer (Yale University Press, © 2001 Hollins University).

the brownie. But to understand the rhetoric of the choices made by
those responsible for first the title and then the content of the *Brownies'
Book,* it is necessary to understand the literary-historical context in
which these choices were made. Only then can we fully appreciate
the rhetorical ingenuity of the editors, authors, and illustrators who
tried to make a place for African American children in children's literature by revising the materials of mainstream children's literature
"'authentically,' with a Black difference" (Gates xxii). Specifically, I
want to argue that they did so in the *Brownies' Book* by self-consciously
"signifying" on the folk and fairy tale conventions that were an integral
part of the Eurocentric pattern of American children's literature.

My terminology here reflects that of Henry Louis Gates Jr. in *The
Signifying Monkey,* in which he discusses the use of "signifying" ("intertextual revision") by African American writers as a culturally specific
rhetorical strategy. In this book, Gates focuses his critical lens on revision of previous African American writers by African American writers within that same tradition. But he recognizes that "black writers
most certainly revise texts in the Western tradition" (xxii) and that
"[a]nyone who analyzes black literature must do so as a comparativ-
ist, by definition, because our canonical texts have complex double
formal antecedents, the Western and the black" (xxiv). In the context
of American culture's conflation of European fairy tale and children's
literature, the editors and writers of the *Brownies' Book* had compelling
reasons to respond to the Western canon of children's literature.

By the time W. E. B. DuBois launched his monthly magazine for
African American children, fairy tales had come to be seen as the literature of American childhood. This assumption—for it is not quite a
fact—is dramatized in literature published by the venerable *St. Nicholas
Magazine* (established 1873) between 1900 and 1920, in which allusions
to fairy-tale characters and conventions are common. Such allusions
are in fact quietly ubiquitous in poetry, realistic fiction, and even nonfiction published in *St. Nicholas* during this period. There is a poem
about "fairy folk" by a fourteen-year-old boy (November 1919: 90)
and a rhymed didactic fairy story by an adult writer ("The Discon-
tented Prince," December 1919: 160). Even more typical are nature
poems that allude to "the fairy mists of morn" (November 1919: 11) or
"fairy forests" (February 1920:329), characters in realistic fictions who
describe their benefactor as a "fairy godmother" (November 1919:
62) or describe a friend as like "the anxious sister in the fairy tale"
(December 1919: 207), and biographers who declare that a life story

like Jenny Lind's "reads like a fairy tale" (October 1920: 1077). With some regularity, characters in *St. Nicholas* say—one way or another—that it "sounds like a fairy-story to me" (April 1920: 516).

These allusions to a literature with its roots in European folklore reveal the mutually sustaining relation of mainstream (white) American children's literature and that tradition. As Jack Zipes points out,

> by the beginning of the twentieth century, the fairy tale had become fully institutionalized in England and America, and its functions had shifted and expanded. The institutionalization of a genre means that a specific process of production, distribution, and reception has become regularized within the public sphere of a society and plays a role in forming and maintaining the cultural heritage of that society. Without such institutionalization in advanced industrialized and technological countries, the genre would perish, and thus the genre itself becomes a kind of self-perpetuating institute involved in the socialization and acculturation of readers. Thus it is the interaction of writer/publisher/audience within a given society that makes for the definition of the genre in any given epoch. The aesthetics of each fairy tale will depend on how and why an individual writer wants to intervene in the discourse of the genre as an institution. (Introduction xxvi)

The scarcity of original fairy tales and the ubiquitousness of allusions to traditional fairy tales in a cultural institution such as *St. Nicholas* (which in its heyday in the nineteenth century had published the original American fairy tales of Frank Stockton and L. Frank Baum)[2] offers evidence that by 1920 these mainstream publishers and writers were not at all motivated to "intervene" in this discourse.

Instead, the unself-conscious Eurocentrism of fairy tale seems to reinforce the racist assumptions of the writers and editors of *St. Nicholas,* in which African American child characters are almost nonexistent and African American adults function as features of the settings in which white American children act.[3] This is abundantly clear in *St. Nicholas,* even when we limit examples to 1920 and 1921, the two years that the *Brownies' Book* was published. Examples of such static characterizations include the "dark cooks" (October 1920: 1081) who are described as one of the amenities of a private train car in an adventure story, as well as the character in a boarding school story who is described as "Old Tom Juniper . . . the colored man who worked on the place" (May 1920: 627). In an adventure story set in northern Mississippi, a young girl who had ridden into town to head off a bandit "threw the reins to a negro who was lounging there" (November 1920: 424), clearly dramatizing the functional subservience of adult African Americans to white children. Conversely, in "Peter to the Rescue" (May 1921), an adult white male revisits his "old plantation home" (636) and finds himself "touched by the . . . loyalty" of a "dusky lad" (637) who, though he is only eight years old, helps save his home and his life and seems to feel he was put on earth to do so. In the drawings and photographs and stories they contributed to the "St. Nicholas League," child readers of *St. Nicholas* marginalize African Americans in the same way. One reader submitted to a contest with a "Homecoming" theme a drawing with an African American porter in the background of a scene set at a train station (June 1920: 762). Another young reader submitted a photo of several unnamed bootblacks (April 1921: 570) to a contest with a "Sun and Shade" theme.

Not all of the racism in children's literature was even this subtle, of course. A 1914 editorial in *Crisis* analyzes the slippery logic used by the editors of the *Youth's Companion* to defend their practice of spelling "Negro" with a lower-case *n* (May 1914: 28–29). And the underlying racism of *St. Nicholas* became more, not less, pronounced as it entered the 1920s. This is clear in a slapstick comic strip by E. W. Kemble, "The Soft Step," in which an African American adult and child serve as the stereotypical "comic darkies." In this three-panel cartoon an African American mother sneaks up on her "rapscallion" of a son, who is fishing, sitting on a board set across a narrow stream. When she steps "softlike" on the end of it, her son is catapulted safely away from her while she is smacked in the face by the board. The third panel shows her in the stream yelling threats in the estranging dialect common in mainstream literature of this period: "Neber you min', honey! Your mammy gwine ter be home dis ebenin' some time" (August 1920: 898).

Throughout *St. Nicholas,* various distancing strategies—linguistic, geographic, temporal—insulate its readers from confrontations with contemporary African Americans, even fictional ones. In the index to *St. Nicholas* for the years up to 1920, many of the stories with African American characters are classified as historical fictions under the heading "Civil War Stories." Others are under the descriptor "Plantation Stories," a category that foregrounds an extreme regional specificity. By depicting African Americans almost exclusively in stories set in the South, the editors elide the "Great Migration" from the South to the North that took place after World War I. And they effectively avoid any discussion of "the problem of the color line" (DuBois, *Souls* 107). The categorization of other stories with African American characters as "Recitations—Negro dialect" segregates whites and blacks linguistically and also reflects the survival of the minstrel tradition into the 1920s, something that is particularly striking in a 1920 *St. Nicholas* pageant called "America the Beautiful," which anachronistically represents slaves singing "Swannee" and "longing for the old plantation" (June 1920: 741). As one literary historian notes, "[t]his subconscious acceptance of white superiority was reflected in many books published between 1900 and 1940" (Allen 55). But this consistent evasiveness is particularly noteworthy in the case of *St. Nicholas* since the editorial stance of the magazine was not apolitical, as evidenced by the fact that it addressed the tensions surrounding immigration editorially and through "Americanization" efforts like the pageant described above.

The fact that many middle-class African American children consumed this propaganda along with the white children who were its implied audience exacerbated the problem. The roster of African American child readers of *St. Nicholas* who later wrote for the *Brownies' Book* includes Yolande DuBois, daughter of W. E. B. DuBois (Lewis 458), and Julian Elihu Bagley (Bagley, *Welcome,* 6). Effie Lee Newsome, a poet who published in *Crisis* and the *Brownies' Book* (and after 1921 wrote a children's page for *Crisis*), as a child read "the Bible, poetry, fairy tales, and children's magazines" (Bryan 802). DuBois's famous statement in "Criteria of Negro Art" (1926) that "all Art is propaganda and ever must be" certainly applies to much of the children's literature of his day. The *Brownies' Book* is a response in keeping with DuBois's belief that the real problem is "propaganda . . . confined to one side while the other is stripped and silent" (66).

In the October 1919 *Crisis* "Children's Number," DuBois argues that "[t]o educate [our children] in human hatred is more disastrous to them than to the hated; [but] to seek to raise them in ignorance of their racial identity and *peculiar situation* is inadvisable—impossible" (emphasis mine). Here DuBois's phrasing recalls descriptions of slavery as the "peculiar institution," a powerful reminder that although the institution of slavery has been abolished, African Americans still occupy a "peculiar" place in American society. Significantly, DuBois also suggests that children need to be brought up to understand not just their "racial identity" but also their social—and rhetorical—situation. As a step toward this goal, he proposed the creation of "a little magazine for children—for all children, but especially for ours, 'the Children of the Sun.' " It will "seek to teach Universal Love and Brotherhood for all the little folk—black and brown and yellow and white" (286). In the same article, titled "The True Brownies," DuBois announced that the magazine "will be called, *naturally, The Brownies' Book*" (286, emphasis mine). The rhetoric of this choice of title, which DuBois emphasizes by referring to it as natural, responds to a very specific literary-historical context. The brownie is a figure from "Scottish and North of England folklore . . . , an elf-like creature, said to come out at night and finish the housework left undone in the day, in return for a reward of milk or cream and food" (Carpenter and Prichard 85–86). Given that African Americans figured in mainstream American children's literature of this period almost exclusively as servants, the image of the African American child as the "True Brownie" seems at first to reinforce limiting stereotypes. This seems less true, however, if we look at this decision rhetorically, as an act of African American signification in an oppressive literary-historical context.

As Gates explains, "[t]o Signify . . . is to engage in certain rhetorical games" (48). Paraphrasing Roger D. Abrahams, Gates states that in African American usage, "one does not signify something [as in Standard English]; rather, one signifies in *some way*" (Gates 54, emphasis in original). Another scholar defines signification as "the art of expressing ideas, opinions, feelings, and so forth, by indirection" and as "a culturally specific form of irony": "one signifies on a particular work, author, form, or tradition, by copying central elements of practices, even while revising them in some significant way. The repetition implicit in this form of signifying criticizes or extends the previous and frequently (though not exclusively) white literary or cultural source by setting it within the context of African American expressive culture" (Mason 665). Signification is thus a Bakhtinian double-voiced discourse in which "[t]he audience . . . is meant to hear both a version of the original utterance as the embodiment of its speaker's point of view . . . *and* the second speaker's evaluation of that utterance from a different point of view" (Morson, quoted in Gates 50, emphasis in original). Of course, it follows that decoding double-voiced discourse requires "shared knowledge" and awareness that "signifying is occurring" (Mitchell-Kernan, quoted in Gates 86). When DuBois addresses his remarks to the adult readers of *Crisis* in his announcement of the *Brownies' Book* in 1919, presumably the necessary understanding exists. And because it is one of DuBois's stated goals to prepare African American children to negotiate their "peculiar" rhetorical situation with similar sophistication, he gives their magazine a title that signifies on one of the most visible representatives of American children's culture: *St. Nicholas.*

DuBois's title signifies on the title (specifically) and through it on the ideology of *St. Nicholas,* a leading magazine of the dominant culture and therefore a logical parodic analog to the *Brownies' Book.* Like the *Brownies' Book,* which reflected the ideology of *Crisis, St. Nicholas* reflected the ideology of its adult precursor, *Scribners' Monthly.* It tried to present "life as it is"; however, as one critic points out, "life" seemed to be narrowly defined as "reality as perceived by a well-educated, well-established segment of upper-middle-class American society" (Erisman 380).[4]

The title signifies on *St. Nicholas* by repeating it with a difference, almost literally "a black difference" in this case, given the emphasis on color in DuBois's title. Saint Nicholas, or Santa Claus, was a "well-known figure" by the early nineteenth century in America and "the only 'fairy' that immigrants were to bring over from the Old World" (Avery 2). A jolly, white-haired, pale-faced northern European elf, he brings presents to good children. This makes him a fitting icon for a magazine whose privileged readership is assumed to share northern European descent and to be able to afford to underwrite the activities of this mythical figure.

The brownie, on the "other" hand is, appropriately, a creature with a "dual nature" (Briggs 38) — a phrase that evokes DuBois's idea that African Americans in American society necessarily possess a "double-consciousness" that reflects both their own identity and the perception of them by others (*Souls* 102). Its duality is seen in characterizations of the brownie in literature as an "industrious and helpful household spirit" that is "laborious, grotesque, touchy . . . , capable of affection and even devotion," but also "tricksy, touchy, and easily driven away," capable of "active mischief" and potentially "dangerous" (Briggs 28, 90, 39). This makes the brownie a fitting ancestor of the signifying monkey of Gates's title, who is himself a trickster figure and a symbol of indeterminacy. DuBois's implicit contrast between this earthy and colorful imp and the fat and happy St. Nicholas may well be intended as a double-voiced in-joke between him and the adult readers of *Crisis* to whom he addressed the remark that his magazine "will be called, naturally, the *Brownies' Book.*" Although the editors of both magazines believed that children like "to now and then . . .

step over to fairy-land" (Dodge 353), DuBois recognized that African American child readers would need a bridge to get from the mainland to a fairy land that would nurture their imaginations.

DuBois's title also probably reflects his awareness of an English children's book by Juliana Horatia Ewing, *The Brownies and Other Tales* (1865). The first story embedded in this novel's realistic frame story is an anti–fairy tale about brothers who learn that the brownies of folklore are figurative: in reality, "all children are Brownies . . . [w]hen they are useful and considerate" (Ewing 27–28). More than fifty years after its publication, Ewing's story inspired the "adoption of the name 'Brownies' for junior Girl Guides, and the first handbook for Brownies (1920) opened with an abridged version of the tale" (Carpenter and Prichard 86).

The use of the phrase "True Brownies" to refer to his readers suggests that DuBois is familiar with Ewing's book, at least by reputation. The child in that book who goes looking for a "domesticated Brownie" (Ewing 21) to do his chores learns along the way that he and his brother are the only "real" brownies (43). In a relatively straightforward way, the association of helpfulness and personal responsibility with brownies is very much in keeping with DuBois's sense of mission and may well have led to a sympathetic appropriation of this figure for his readers. One of his stated goals in publishing the *Brownies' Book* is "to inspire [readers] to prepare for definite occupations and duties with a broad spirit of sacrifice" ("True Brownies" 286). And in practice, this idea comes through in the editorial comment attached to a picture from the May 1920 issue showing a group of African American children dressed as fairies for a dancing school performance. The caption describes these children as "truly little fairies," "not the make-believe fairies of the story book, but real fairies who get lots of happiness out of doing good for others" (May 1920: 153). A story by the poet Georgia Douglas Johnson, "The Story of the Little Tin Horn" (December 1920), has a similar thrust in that the boy hero becomes the "child of all the fairies" because he chooses to share his toys "freely and joyfully" (Johnson-Feelings 1996, 177). But however sympathetic the appropriation, the claim that African American children are the "true Brownies"—and that the British children in Ewing's tale and frame story or their North American cousins are *not*—adds a significant edge to this sleight of hand appropriation.

The ubiquitous brownies of author-illustrator Palmer Cox are another context for DuBois's appropriation of this character. The illustrated adventures of Cox's elflike creatures appeared in *St. Nicholas* from 1883 to 1914 and in numerous books. Attention to this manifestation of fairies in popular culture supports the idea that though the fairy tale retains a basic Eurocentrism in early twentieth-century American children's literature, it has in other ways entered a kind of public domain in which it has been stripped of much of its cultural specificity.[5] In the case of Palmer Cox's Americanized brownies, it has been commodified as much as it has been adapted.

Cox's books about brownies were a commercial phenomenon. Palmer Cox brownies appeared in magazines and books at first; later they appeared on stage, in a variety of advertisements, and in the form of "toys, games, and educational items" as well as "household articles" (Cummins 101–2). By 1920, the remarkably long heyday of the brownies was largely past. But as one literary historian observes, "eleven [Cox titles] were in print at his death [in 1924], and still drawing a handsome royalty"(Cummins 49). It is difficult to imagine that DuBois was unaware of the creatures Cox described in the foreword to each of his books: "BROWNIES, like fairies and goblins, are imaginary little sprites, who are supposed to delight in harmless pranks and helpful deeds. They work and sport while weary households sleep, and never allow themselves to be seen by mortal eyes" (quoted in Cummins 62). As Cummins points out, Cox "retained characteristics found in the brownies of folklore, but he made notable changes"; his brownies are "gregarious" and do not "confine themselves to domestic work" though they are willing and able to do "deeds of kindness" (62–63). Cox's brownies are not characterized as homebodies, but as travelers, as suggested by the titles of books such as *The Brownies Around the World* (1894), *The Brownies Abroad* (1899), and *The Brownies in the Philippines* (1904). These attributes might all appeal to DuBois's broader, pan-African vision.

Cox's vision, however, did not encompass African American children as implied audience or as subject matter, which is surprising given his emphasis in illustration and text on broadly distinguished "types" of people. Recurring brownie characters included ethnic or national types (an Irishman, an Italian, and an "Indian") as well as characters defined by their profession or lack of same (a policeman, a cowboy, and a "dude" or dandy). All were male. The only dark-skinned character is the Native American. In eliding the African American in his depictions of "the American scene" (quoted in Cummins 51), Cox is following the trend of his era.[6] Like others of his time, Cox is com-

fortable mirroring the immigrant heritage of America and mytholo-
gizing of the Native American but is either unwilling or unable to portray African Americans.

Through his choice of title, DuBois was signifying on the exclu-
sionary ideology of these "other" brownies and promising the adult
readers of *Crisis* that his magazine for children will rework the most
visible materials of popular culture into a mirror that can begin to
reflect its child readers back to themselves. Like Cox, DuBois appropriates only the positive aspects of brownies. And he assures the parents of African American children that their children are the "*true*
Brownies," though they were neither included nor imagined as audience or subject by these other authors, who themselves appropriated
these traditional characters for their own purposes.

In the twenty-four issues of the *Brownies' Book* there are numerous
works that follow through on the promise of DuBois's title, winking
significantly at readers as they intervene in the discourse of American
children's literature. From the start, however, DuBois shared editorial
responsibilities with Jessie Fauset, the literary editor of the *Brownies'
Book* (and the literary editor of *Crisis* from 1919 to 1926). In its second year, Fauset officially took over from DuBois as managing editor
of the *Brownies' Book,* though she had probably been responsible for
the day-to-day editorial work since the beginning.[7] DuBois's most obvious contributions to the *Brownies' Book* during these years included a
regular unsigned current events column, "As the Crow Flies," a story
("Honey," a nature fantasy, August 1920), and an essay ("Taboo," May
1921). Fauset put her name to many poems and a story (a translation from the French in April 1920); she also contributed a regular
unsigned feature titled "The Judge," in which persona she discusses
moral and ethical issues with a set of fictional representative children
of various ages.

Given Fauset's role as literary editor, it is almost certainly her voice
that is heard most consistently in the magazine, and the stories published in the *Brownies' Book* reflect her complex literary relationship
with fairy tale. On one hand, in the very first "Children's Number"
of the *Crisis* Fauset recommended canonical European fairy tales to
African American children as "the first aids to the intellect" and "to
the exercise of the imagination" (*Crisis,* October 1912: 295). And as
"The Judge," she focused two columns in the *Brownies' Book* on the
question of what children should read—"the question in comparison
with which all other kiddie matters fade into insignificance"—and "of

course" recommended "fairy tales—Andersen's and Grimm's and the collections of Andrew Lang," as well as "dear 'Uncle Remus'" and a "nice little book published by one of us,—A. O. Stafford's 'Animal Fables of the Dark Continent'" (*Brownies' Book,* June 1920: 176). In a later column, she recommended Czechoslovakian fairy tales to young readers as well as some other books "by colored writers, mostly about colored people" (July 1920, 214). In each case the European works are recommended more enthusiastically than those by African American writers on African American subjects.

But on the other hand, in a story serialized in *Crisis* from August to October 1920, Fauset overtly signifies on fairy tales such as "Cinderella" and "Sleeping Beauty," suggesting that the implicit messages of these tales are particularly dangerous for African American women. The heroine of "The Sleeper Wakes" is a young woman of unknown parentage whose adoptive parents are "colored." She runs away from home as a teenager, under the influence of "fairy tales read to her in those long remote days when she had lived with the tall proud woman" (who gave her up for adoption) and popular movies based on them in which girls who are "pretty" and "poor" marry men who are "tremendously rich" (Fauset 3). She eventually marries her prince, a rich older man with "very white skin" whose "suggestion of power" intrigues her (8). This sleeper only begins to shake off her passivity when her husband threatens a young black servant with violence, at which point she confesses her ambiguous heritage. Months after their subsequent divorce, she discovers that although her ex-husband's love and respect for her has died, his passion for her survives. At that point, she wakes up. Her "youth" and "illusions" (20) die and she comes to see her fairy-tale marriage as a form of prostitution or slavery. She then works to buy herself back from her ex-husband symbolically by reimbursing him for all alimony he paid her. Finally, she decides to move back "home" to her adoptive family and vows to throw in her lot with colored people.

This fable makes a strong statement about the ways canonical and popular narratives are "not always true to life" (4) and points out that African American women who attempt to participate in these cultural narratives are particularly vulnerable to being misread. The narrator explains that when the protagonist's husband thought she was poor and white, it was "just the kind of romantic story to appeal to a rich powerful man" (9). But when her husband believes she is poor and black, the story turns out to be about sex. This story offers evidence that Fauset—perhaps as a result of her months as literary editor of the *Brownies' Book*—is rethinking how fairy tales affect African American readers.[8] But the fact that she published it in *Crisis* and not in the *Brownies' Book* suggests that Fauset thought that the story was not appropriate for the *Brownies' Book* audience of "Kiddies from Six to Sixteen."

It is difficult to gauge with certainty the effect Fauset's ambivalence about fairy tales had on individual stories published in the *Brownies' Book*. It is indisputable, however, that under her literary editorship the magazine regularly published what one reader referred to as "splendid stories about fairies" (August 1920: 256). These innovative stories offered readers a change from the overt didacticism of the nonfiction written specifically for African American children at this time,[9] though the *Brownies' Book* also built on that tradition, regularly including biographical sketches of contemporary and historical African American adults and children. But the editors also expanded the canon of African American children's literature in many directions by including stories, plays, and poems written specifically for children and, in a number of cases, by children.[10] Before the *Brownies' Book*, fiction for African American children was rare and fantasy—outside of folklore—equally unusual, even including the experiments in this form in three of the annual "Children's Numbers" of *Crisis* that preceded the *Brownies' Book*.

As we've seen, in 1920–21 *St. Nicholas*, though full of allusions to European fairy tales, rarely published fairy stories. The fairy stories published in the *Brownies' Book*, on the other hand, were original stories in which authors and illustrators tried to use the characters and conventions of fairy tale " 'authentically,' with a Black difference" (Gates xxii). But their success at evading the rhetorical traps behind the transparent assumptions of the dominant culture is mixed, at least partly because the expectations of the readers—and writers—of the *Brownies' Book* had been formed by their reading of literature written for white children.[11] As Gates notes, when faced with "a deafening silence in black literary antecedents" (133) authors sometimes have to fit their vision into generic shapes taken from white literary traditions. Looking at the use of fairy-tale characters and conventions in some of the original stories published in the *Brownies' Book* offers a fascinating glimpse into the opportunities and pitfalls of this peculiar rhetorical situation.

For example, the first story in the first issue of the *Brownies' Book*

—"Pumpkin Land" (January 1920) by Peggy Poe—and its sequel—
"The Watermelon Dance" (September 1920)—are a problematic hybrid of the most didactic sort of fairy story and a conventional plantation story.[12] The central character, Happy, is "a little colored boy"
who lives with his Mammy in the "Land of Sure-Enough, away down
South, in a most wonderful land named Georgia" (3). In the secondary fantasy world embedded in this domestic frame, we meet conventional nature characters—"Mister Bumble Bee" and "Mister Rabbit"—
as well as the allegorical "Mister Temp-ta-tion" and an "elf," "Pumpkin
Man" (4). The stories convey the presumably harmless overt moral of
the blandest sort of children's story (one should always "T-R-Y"). But
they eventually betray their plantation roots through each tale's external focalization—the way the narration looks *at* the child Happy and
not *from* his perspective—and its naïve narratee, for whom the South
is a foreign country. Both of these features could, however problem-
atically, merely reveal the urban northern bias of this pre–Harlem Renaissance magazine. But the distance between the child reader and the
child subject of these stories turns perverse when Happy is described
as seeing someone the text refers to as "Captain Jones' colored boy"
(6). If Happy were white (as we find out in the second story his two
little friends are), the story's narrational perspective would make more
sense.

There are other stories that betray a lack of editorial self-consciousness about the baggage carried by the characters and conventions
of fairy tale, as we can literally see in the sentimental one-act play
"Tommy and the Flower Fairies" by Eulalie Spence. The protagonist
is described in the culturally generic text as "Eight year old Tommy
. . . the much spoiled and petted only child of wealthy parents" (April
1921, 122). The full-page illustration by Hilda Rue Wilkinson, a regular
contributor, shows an African American child in a sailor suit waking
(within his dream) to find himself surrounded by stereotypically pale
fairies with long straight blonde hair. The frontispiece to a later issue
of the *Brownies' Book*—a photograph of a group of African American
school children from Birmingham, Alabama, who performed this play
—highlights the inappropriateness of this image to a script for African
American children (December 1921). To compound matters, this illustration appears only a few pages before an advertisement for "Madame
C. J. Walker's Superfine Preparations for the Hair and for the Skin,"
which are touted as "The Gift of the Good Fairy" to "unfortunate ones
whom nature had not given long, wavy hair" (back cover).

But there are many other tales that exhibit more self-consciousness about their role in a magazine dedicated to enhancing the self-esteem of African American children. For example, the illustrations for "The Fairies' Flower Garden" (May 1920: 131), an otherwise culturally generic story, include both children and fairies of color. The issue of color is addressed both visually and textually in the story "Dolly's Dream" (November 1920) by Nora Waring, in which the main character's fairy godmother grants her wish to have "long, golden curls" instead of her " 'cwinkley' . . . black ringlets." Dolly learns to regret this wish because no one recognizes her after the change, which also changes her "little, dimpled face of rosy tan" to "pinky white skin" and leaves her with the "blue, blue eyes" of her favorite doll (Johnson-Feelings 1996, 42). By the end, Dolly exclaims with dismay "I'm not me" and finds she desperately wants to change back so her friends and relatives "will always know [her]" (43), a resolution that hints at the interconnectedness of personal, familial, and racial identity.

In the last issue of the *Brownies' Book,* in a story called "The Land Behind the Sun" by Yolande DuBois, the female protagonist exclaims in surprise "Why! . . . , everybody's brown" when she sees the dark-skinned inhabitants of this fairyland in her dreams. Her fairy escort, a lady-in-waiting named Topaz, tells Madalen that "we are the Brownies —we are all brown, even our Queen" (December 1921: 332). This young woman's surprise dramatizes the need of African American children to hear the implicit message of these stories—that the symbolic power and beauty and nobility of fairies need not be tied exclusively to whiteness.

In spite of their differences, these stories illustrate one of the most common narrative strategies used by African American writers of fairy stories for the *Brownies' Book:* they make the fantasy itself part of a dream and embed it in a domestic frame in which realistic African American children are the leading characters.[13] The most significant advantage of this framing was that it inscribed contemporary African American children in children's literature—something mainstream children's literature had not even tried to do—thus making good on the promise implicit in DuBois's title. The frame also offered readers contemporary African American child characters they could relate to more directly than to fairies, even brown ones. And though the frame offered the reassuring return to reality typical of domestic fantasies, it often functioned additionally as an opportunity for the author to offer a call to action in the real world. In these stories, the readers of the

Brownies' Book are encouraged to become the "true Brownies," ener-
gized by the "Joy! Love! Hope!" (April 1921, 124) that will allow them
to contribute to the advancement of the race, as Tommy is ready to do
after his dream of the flower fairies.

The framed story that offers the *Brownies' Book*'s most sophisticated
rhetorical model for fledgling "New Negroes" is "The Story-Telling
Contest" by Julian Elihu Bagley, in which Bagley signifies on European fairy tale and offers readers a vision of a living African American folk tradition to take its place.[14] Bagley wrote five stories for the
Brownies' Book, all with the same basic frame tale: little Cless comes to
his Granny with a problem, in response to which she tells him a story,
which he learns from her and later retells. There are several interesting
features to this frame. The first is that Cless and his grandmother live
in a Harlem apartment on 135th Street (November 1920: 323). (Cless's
father is in Florida working at a Palm Beach hotel; no information
about his mother is provided.) But the tales that grandmother tells
are set in the South—a swamp in Virginia, for example (as in "How
Br'er Possum Learned to Play Dead," January 1921)—or in Africa (as
in "How Mr. Crocodile Got His Rough Back," November 1920) or in
the less clearly defined "land of sunshine" (as in "Once 'Twas a Little
Pig," June 1921). Thus, the setting of the frame tale and the settings
of the embedded tales work together to tie the contemporary urban-
dwelling African American child represented by Cless to his or her
roots in the American South and Africa, even as they evoke fantasy
and distance.

In "The Story-Telling Contest" (November 1921, 303), a Thanksgiving story that appeared in the penultimate issue of the *Brownies'
Book,* Granny tells Cless "a story that will just fit in for the contest," a
story the reader does not "hear" until later in the story when Cless tells
it to his classmates during the contest. In the context of Bagley's story,
the European fairy tales told by the children who precede Cless—
which include "The Three Bears" and "Little Red Riding Hood"—are
boring stories that are "old as the hills." Cless wins the contest because
he tells "a really *new* story" (emphasis in original). This "new" story,
modeled on African American folktale, centers—as the storytelling
contest does—on the question of who will get the prized turkey drumstick. Cless's story begins "Once a long, long time ago, the day before
Thanksgiving, Br'er Bear, Br'er Fox, Br'er Rabbit and Br'er Wolf met
together to lay plans for their Thanksgiving dinner." Cless's story, in
which Br'er Rabbit the trickster successfully appropriates the drum-

stick, has the room "literally roaring with applause," in contrast to the "groans" that greeted the anemic, twice-told European tales. Cless, as a result, wins the turkey drumstick, which he wraps up to take home to Granny.

In this story and in the others Bagley published in the *Brownies' Book*, Granny's tales are presented as part of a living oral tradition; they are, paradoxically, "new," though they are presented to Cless as if they were preexisting tales. It is clear, however, that Granny is making up these stories rather than remembering them because each is tailored to Cless's particular situation. Granny's insistence on telling Cless "the best [story] for Thanksgiving Day" and not, as Cless requests, "the best for any day" shows that Granny is self-conscious about her own rhetoric, as Gates suggests that African Americans have had to be (xi) and as the "peculiar" rhetorical situation of the writers for the *Brownies' Book* demanded they be. And in each story, Bagley shows Granny using her rhetorical flexibility to empower her grandson as a teller of African American folktales. In the same way, Bagley's tale empowers Cless's peers, the readers of the *Brownies' Book*, by giving them tellers of African American folktales as role models. This valorization of the African American folk tradition would become a major thrust of the Harlem Renaissance just a few years later and would be associated especially with writers such as Zora Neale Hurston, who in "Characteristics of Negro Expression" (1934) said, "Negro folklore is not a thing of the past. It is still in the making. Its great variety shows the adaptability of the black man: nothing is too old or too new, domestic or foreign, high or low, for his use" (84). She also observed that "it is obvious that to get back to original sources is much too difficult for any group to claim very much certainty. What we really mean by originality is the modification of ideas" (86). This observation is in line with Gates's sense of how African American writers signify, by "repeating received tropes and narrative strategies with a difference" (217).

Bagley's story does not just signify on European fairy tale; it also repeats the narrative strategies of Joel Chandler Harris's *Tales of Uncle Remus* (1880) with a significant difference. The African American folktales collected and published by this white journalist as "Uncle Remus" stories were embedded in a plantation frame in which the tales are told to amuse and instruct a young white boy. Bagley signifies on Harris's Uncle Remus by replacing him with Granny, an African American woman who adapts her tales to the needs of a contemporary African American boy instead. Bagley's adaptation of features old, new, domestic, foreign, high and low allows him to signify successfully on European fairy tale—itself "an appropriation [of] oral storytelling tradition" (Zipes, Introduction xii)—while simultaneously intervening in Joel Chandler Harris's similar appropriation of African American folklore. In the process, Bagley clearly directs African American children back to their cultural roots and their elders, presciently pointing to the vernacular tradition as the most flexible tool available to the "New Negro."

Dianne Johnson-Feelings has rightly called the *Brownies' Book* an "experiment in pedagogy and propaganda aimed at African-American youth" (1996, 336). It was undertaken in the middle of an exciting time for mainstream children's literature: 1919 saw the first National Children's Book Week and the establishment of the first children's book department at a major publisher. The Newbery Medal was established in 1922. It was an exciting time for Aframerica too, a crisis time, following as it did the race riots and lynchings of the "Red Summer" of 1919. The *Brownies' Book* was created at the intersection of these moments. When we look closely at one set of experiments contained within the *Brownies' Book*—those involving re-visions of folk and fairy tale motifs—the complexity of the rhetorical situation in which African American writers wrote becomes clearer and we can appreciate the way they meet the challenge offered by an institutionalized European fairy tale and avail themselves of "the new possibilities of subversion" (Zipes, Introduction xvi) it offers.

"Children's literature" always entails a complex rhetorical relation between the child reader and the adults who write, edit, and publish literature for children, a relation that is further complicated by the layer of adults—parents, teachers, librarians, and so on—who provide children with much of their access to literature. This rhetorical imbalance has led theorists such as Jacqueline Rose to posit the fundamental impossibility of children's literature. But for writers of African American children's literature, the need to subvert the subtle and not-so-subtle messages of a body of racist children's literature inspired them to try innovative strategies to bridge these rhetorical gaps. Writers and illustrators for the *Brownies' Book* revised the materials of mainstream American children's literature in order to create something "new" that would allow African American children—the newest Negroes—to win the storytelling contest in spite of the fact that everyone else was telling the same old story. The twenty-four issues of the *Brownies' Book* are the site of the rhetorical struggle over fairyland that

W. E. B. DuBois began with his choice of title. Close attention to the rhetoric of these tales reveals the complexity of the peculiar situation in which early twentieth-century African Americans found themselves decades after the "peculiar institution" of slavery was abolished.

Notes

The author gratefully acknowledges the assistance of Ruth Hoberman, who read multiple drafts of this essay, and the Council on Faculty Research at Eastern Illinois University.

1. In this essay I use the term *folk tale* to refer to the tales in the *Crisis* "Children's Numbers" and the *Brownies' Book* that are presented to the reader as oral tales told within a specified culture. This terminology is in line with Zipes's description of *folktale* as a term that "clearly signifies that the people were the *carriers* of the tale" (*Breaking* 23, emphasis in original). My choice also reflects the practice of the editors of the *Brownies' Book,* who offered this comment in the introduction to a Ugandan folktale published in the second issue: "the story is very old and has come down from father to son for many generations and has probably met with almost no changes. Such a story is called a *folk tale*" (February 1920: 46). I also follow both Zipes and the editors of the *Brownies' Book* in using the term *fairy tale* to refer to "literary" versions of specific European tales "*adapted* by bourgeois or aristocratic writers in the seventeenth and eighteenth centuries . . . for educated audiences" (Zipes, *Breaking* 23, emphasis in original).Jessie Fauset, literary editor of the *Brownies' Book,* specifically recommends "fairy tales" of this description in a June 1920 column (176) quoted below. My use of the term *fairy story* is more idiosyncratic but, I hope, useful for distinguishing from these traditional tales the original stories published in the *Brownies' Book* that borrow some of the generic characters of folk and fairy tale—specifically brownies, elves, fairies, and fairy godmothers—without reference to their roots in any specific culture or their previous appearance in specific tales.

2. L. Frank Baum in his 1908 preface to *American Fairy Tales* (1901) promised "to offer our wide-awake youngsters modern tales about modern fairies" (ix) and set the first tale "on Prairie avenue in Chicago" (15). Baum's *American Fairy Tales* are not consistently American in setting, however, and his only story featuring "black people" is set in Africa, "[o]n one of the upper branches of the Congo river" (Baum 94, 93). This displacement of African Americans by Africans is another example of the pattern of evasion and elision of African Americans in mainstream American children's literature of the early twentieth century.

3. Critics including Violet Harris have already demonstrated that the *Brownies' Book* "challenged a selective tradition in children's literature" that "provided children with pejorative portraits of Black culture and Black people" (4) and "reflected the values and power of the gentry class" (10), excluding African Americans. Harris has given the most sustained attention to the *Brownies' Book* in her dissertation, The Brownies' Book: *Challenge to the Selective Tradition in Children's Literature.* Some of her core ideas are also presented in "Race Consciousness, Refinement, and Radicalism." But the first scholar to contribute to the literature was Elinor Sinnette in *"The Brownies' Book:* A Pioneer Publication for Children." Sinnette was also the first to compare the *Brownies' Book* to *St. Nicholas* magazine. Courtney Vaughn-Roberson and Brenda Hill offer another comparative approach in *The Brownies' Book* and *Ebony Jr!* Dianne Johnson-Feelings has not only given scholarly attention to the *Brownies' Book* in *Telling Tales,* with noteworthy attention to the importance of its illustrations, but has also recently made it available to a new

generation of readers in *The Best of* The Brownies' Book (1996). This anthology contains an impressive number of selections from the twenty-four issues of the magazine and a complete facsimile of the April 1921 issue from front cover to advertisements.

4. In its own way, the *Brownies' Book* too represented the views of its well-educated editors (both DuBois and Fauset had advanced degrees) and the largely middle-class readership of *Crisis,* a group DuBois referred to collectively as the "talented tenth" of contemporary African American society. It has also been pointed out that much of the fiction in the *Brownies' Book,* perhaps self-consciously, presented atypically affluent African American families (Harris, *Brownies' Book,* 112–14, 221–25).

5. There is evidence that by 1920 titles in the canon of traditional European fairy tales were no longer clearly associated in the popular mind with the specific cultures or authors that produced them. For example, in one early twentieth-century American series book by Inez Haynes Irwin, the children who buy inexpensive books of "fairy tales" from *Maida's Little Shop* (1909) get an undifferentiated mix of English, French, and German tales including "The Three Little Bears," "Puss-in-Boots," "Jack-and-the-Beanstalk," "Jack the Giant Killer," "Cinderella," "Bluebeard," "Little Goody-Two-Shoes," "Tom Thumb," "The Sleeping Beauty," and "The Babes in the Wood."

6. The same is true of the Maida books (cited above), in which there are many Irish American characters but the only adult African American characters are servants and the closest thing to an African American child is a "statue of a negro boy with his arms lifted above his head [who] seemed to beg the honor of holding the reins" (Irwin 19). This example is particularly poignant because Effie Lee Newsome, writing in *Crisis* about a recent reprint of *Maida's Little Shop,* thought she detected African American characters in it (October 1927:260), mistakenly over-reading a description of two brown-eyed Irish immigrant children who were compared to "brownies" (Irwin 71).

7. Carolyn Wedin, author of the only book-length biography of Jessie Fauset, claims that "Fauset wrote hundreds of signed and unsigned stories, poems, dialogues, biographies, and articles, as well as handling all of the correspondence with contributors and all of the editing" (337). As literary editor of these two publications Jessie Fauset nurtured many of the young talents who would contribute to the Harlem Renaissance, including Langston Hughes, who published in both *Crisis* and the *Brownies' Book* during these years, and Nella Larsen. Hughes would later call Fauset one of the "midwives" of the "New Negro Renaissance" (218). In many ways, the *Brownies' Book* is a defining project of the Renaissance. In addition to soon-to-be-famous writers such as Hughes, Larsen, and Fauset herself (who published one of the first novels of the Harlem Renaissance in 1924), contributors included Laura Wheeler Waring (one of many African American artists), folklore scholars Arthur Huff Fauset (Jessie's half-brother), Elsie Clews Parsons, and A. O. Stafford, and a host of less well-known writers, including child reader-writers such as Bertie Lee Hall and John Bolden.

8. This story can be seen as a study for Fauset's novel *Plum Bun* (1929), the plot of which is structured ironically around a nursery rhyme ("To market, To market . . .") and signifies on fairy tale and romance conventions (for more on this see Deborah McDowell's 1990 introduction to the Beacon Press "Black Women Writers" edition of *Plum Bun*). See also her earlier *Crisis* story (serialized in April and May) "There Was One Time," the story of a "typical American girl done over in brown" (April 1917:273) who takes a day off from teaching to live out a story from a French "fairy-tale" (272).

9. An advertisement for some of the books available to African American children appears on the inside back cover of many issues of the *Brownies' Book* (including the April 1921 issue, available in facsimile in Johnson-Feelings 1996). There is some poetry by Paul Laurence Dunbar on this list and one realistic novel: *Hazel* by Mary Ovington White, a white woman who was one of the founders of the NAACP. Nonfiction offerings include *History of the Negro* by Benjamin Brawley, *The Negro* by DuBois, *The Negro*

in Literature and Art by Brawley, and *A Child's Story of Dunbar* by Julia Henderson. For more extensive information on the history of African American children's literature, see Johnson-Feelings's "Children's and Young Adult Literature."

10. The editors comment that "there wasn't a market for *our* stories and biographies and poems, but now we have THE BROWNIE'S BOOK and 'Little People of the Month'" as a forum "for each little Brownie who succeeds" (November 1920: 349). This choice is connected to the magazine's mission of providing its readers material they can read "with pride" and, in DuBois's terms, "emulation" (*Crisis,* October 1919: 286). In order to press home this point, the story "A Visit to Fairyland" by Bertie Lee Hall is accompanied by a picture of its young female author (February 1920: 37). This is one of twenty-five photographs of African American children in the first issue of the magazine alone. There is also a photograph of John Bolden, who "adapted" "The Three Golden Hairs of the Sun-King" (September 1920: 276). This treatment contrasts with that of child writers in *St. Nicholas,* in which children's contributions were relegated to the back of the magazine and published in smaller print. Contributions to the *Brownies' Book* were integrated into the magazine and illustrated by the same artists who embellished the works of adult writers. This empowering of child readers is another feature of the *Brownies' Book* that was prefigured in the earlier "Children's Numbers" of *Crisis:* the October 1914 story "The Fairy Good Willa" was written by a ten-year-old child.

11. Children whose letters were published in "The Jury" commented on their enjoyment of its fairy stories (November 1920: 350). On the evidence of the letters they sent to the *Brownies' Book,* readers participated in the general understanding of the conventional features of fairy tales. One reader says she can imagine "all the princesses in the fairy-tales standing tall and white in the corners" and refers to specific characters such as "Tom Thumb," "Puss in Boots," and "sister Anne—she was Bluebeard's wife's sister, you know" (September 1920: 282). A child in a story by an adult writer imagines that a friend is "a beautiful lady in distress" and that a cow is "a ferocious dragon ready to spring on her"; he is "an armoured knight" (November 1920: 329). Fauset herself structured one of her columns around young Billy's wish "that a fairy would come along and give [him] three wishes" so that children wouldn't have to go to school any more (April 1921; Johnson-Feelings 1996, 108).

12. Violet Harris has also commented on Poe's stories as "analogous to the plantation image" (*Brownies' Book* 226). Saul identifies Poe as one of the authors and illustrators who had already contributed to the *Crisis* before writing for the *Brownies' Book* (60).

13. This explains why Violet Harris found only five "self-identified" folk or fairy tales to discuss in her study of the *Brownies' Book* (243–246): "others that contained the elements of fairy tales were categorized as stories" (244).

14. Bagley (who died in 1981 at age eighty-eight) published a children's book in 1971 that contained illustrated versions of some of these stories and others without a frame story. One of many forgotten Harlem Renaissance writers, he also published in *The Southern Workman* and *Outlook* before the *Brownies' Book,* and for *Crisis* and *Opportunity* during the 1920s.

Works Cited

Allen, Marjorie N. *One Hundred Years of Children's Books in America.* New York: Facts on File, 1996.

Avery, Gillian. *Behold the Child: American Children and Their Books, 1621–1922.* Baltimore: Johns Hopkins University Press, 1994.

Bagley, Julian Elihu. *Candle-Lighting Time in Bodidalee.* New York: American Heritage Press, 1971.

————. *Welcome to the San Francisco Opera House.* Interview by Suzanne Riess. Berkeley: Bancroft Library Regional Oral History Office, 1973.

Baum, L. Frank. *American Fairy Tales.* 1901. New York: Dover, 1978.

Briggs, K. M. *Fairies in Tradition and Literature.* London: Routledge and Kegan Paul, 1967.

Bryan, T. J. "Effie Lee Newsome." In *Notable Black American Women.* Ed. Jessie Carney Smith. Detroit: Gale Research, 1992. Pp. 802–4.

Carpenter, Humphrey, and Mari Prichard. "Brownie." In *Oxford Companion to Children's Literature.* New York: Oxford University Press, 1984.

Cummins, Roger W. *Humorous But Wholesome: A History of Palmer Cox and the Brownies.* Watkins Glen, N.Y.: Century House Americana, 1973.

Dodge, Mary Mapes. "Children's Magazines." *Scribner's Monthly,* July 1873: 352–354.

DuBois, W. E. B. "Criteria of Negro Art." In *Within the Circle: An Anthology of African American Literary Criticism from the Harlem Renaissance to the Present.* Ed. Angelyn Mitchell. Durham, N.C.: Duke University Press, 1994. Pp. 60–68.

————. *The Souls of Black Folks.* 1903. In *Oxford W. E. B. DuBois Reader.* Ed. Eric J. Sundquist. New York: Oxford University Press, 1996.

————. "The True Brownies." *Crisis,* October 1919: 285–86.

Erisman, Fred. "*St. Nicholas Magazine.*" In *Children's Periodicals of the United States.* Ed. R. Gordon Kelly. Westport, Conn.: Greenwood Press, 1984: 377–88.

Ewing, Juliana Horatia. *The Brownies and Other Tales.* 1865. London: G. B. & Son, 1927.

Fauset, Jessie. "The Sleeper Wakes." *Crisis,* August–October 1920. Also available in *The Sleeper Wakes: Harlem Renaissance Stories by Women.* Ed. Marcy Knopf. New Brunswick: Rutgers University Press, 1993: 1–25.

Gates, Henry Louis. *The Signifying Monkey: A Theory of African-American Literary Criticism.* New York: Oxford University Press, 1988.

Harris, Violet. "*The Brownies' Book:* Challenge to the Selective Tradition in Children's Literature." Ph.D. Diss., University of Georgia, 1986.

————. "Race Consciousness, Refinement, and Radicalism: Socialization in *The Brownies' Book.*" *Children's Literature Association Quarterly* 14, no. 3 (winter 1989): 192–96.

Hughes, Langston. *The Big Sea.* 1940. New York: Hill and Wang, 1963.

Hurston, Zora Neale. "Characteristics of Negro Expression." In *Within the Circle: An Anthology of African American Literary Criticism from the Harlem Renaissance to the Present.* Ed. Angelyn Mitchell. Durham, N.C.: Duke University Press, 1994. Pp. 79–94.

Irwin (Gilmore), Inez Haynes. *Maida's Little Shop.* New York: Grosset and Dunlap, 1909.

Johnson, Fenton. "The Black Fairy." *Crisis,* October 1913: 292–94.

Johnson-Feelings, Dianne. "Children's and Young Adult Literature." In the *Oxford Companion to African American Literature.* Ed. William L. Andrews, Frances Smith Foster, and Trudier Harris. New York: Oxford University Press, 1997. Pp. 133–40.

————. *Telling Tales: The Pedagogy and Promise of African American Children's Literature.* Westport, Conn.: Greenwood Press, 1990.

————, ed. *The Best of The Brownies' Book.* New York: Oxford University Press, 1996.

Lewis, David Levering. *W. E. B. DuBois: Biography of a Race.* New York: Henry Holt, 1993.

Marcus, Leonard S. "Mother Goose to Multiculturalism: Through More Than a Century of Change and Growth, Children's Book Publishing Remains a Cyclical Business." *Publisher's Weekly* 244, no. 31 (July 1997): 62+.

Mason, Theodore O., Jr. "Signifying." In *Oxford Companion to African American Literature.* Ed. William L. Andrews, Frances Smith Foster, and Trudier Harris. New York: Oxford University Press, 1997. Pp. 665–66.

Newsome, Effie Lee. "Child Literature and Negro Childhood." *Crisis,* October 1927: 260+.

Rose, Jacqueline. *The Case of Peter Pan, or The Impossibility of Children's Literature.* 1984. Philadelphia: University of Pennsylvania Press, 1993.

Saul, E. Wendy. "*The Brownies' Book*." In *Children's Periodicals of the United States*. Ed. R. Gordon Kelly. Westport, Conn.: Greenwood Press, 1984. Pp. 62–68.

Sinnette, Elinor. "*The Brownies' Book:* A Pioneer Publication for Children." *Freedomways* 5 (winter 1965): 133–42.

Vaughn-Roberson, Courtney, and Brenda Hill. "*The Brownies' Book* and *Ebony Jr.!* Literature as a Mirror of the Afro-American Experience." *Journal of Negro Education* 58, no. 4 (fall 1989): 494–510.

Wedin, Carolyn. "Jessie Redmon Fauset (1882–1961)." In *Notable Black American Women*. Ed. Jessie Carney Smith. Detroit: Gale Research, 1992. Pp. 336–40.

Zipes, Jack. Introduction to *Spells of Enchantment*. Ed. Jack Zipes. New York: Viking, 1991. Pp. xi–xxxii.

———. *Breaking the Magic Spell*. Austin: University of Texas Press, 1979.

How They Do Things with Words: Language, Power, Gender, and the Priestly Wizards of Ursula K. Le Guin's Earthsea Books

Laura B. Comoletti
Michael D. C. Drout

> *She had fled the Powers of the desert tombs, and then she had left the Powers of learning and skill offered her by her guardian, Ogion. She had turned her back on all that, gone to the other side, the other room, where the women lived, to be one of them.*
>
> —Ursula K. Le Guin, *Tehanu*

"Now that I know that even in Fairyland there is no escape from politics, I look back and see that I was writing by the rules," writes Ursula K. Le Guin in her Oxford lecture "Earthsea Revisioned." Inherited "rules" shaped the imaginary world of the first three of Le Guin's Earthsea books: *A Wizard of Earthsea, The Tombs of Atuan,* and *The Farthest Shore.* In *Tehanu: The Last Book of Earthsea,* published nearly twenty-five years after the original trilogy, Le Guin negotiates not only the genre traditions she inherited from Western culture but also the internal logical and metaphysical structure she inherited from her own first three Earthsea books.[1] In this essay we identify the most important of Le Guin's cultural inheritances and investigate the ways in which she (after coming to regard them as ideologically and politically unacceptable) adapts them in the final book. We conclude that, contrary to Perry Nodelman's assertion that Le Guin is attempting to "blot out" the past novels and "reinvent history" in *Tehanu* (179–81), the author is undertaking a feminist intervention into her secondary world that works well within the tradition of extrapolation-within-constraints that characterizes science fiction. Le Guin's Tenar may say that she has "turned her back on all that"—the masculinist powers of the wizards of Earthsea—but in *Tehanu* Le Guin has in fact found ways to assert the power and importance of women without overturning the logical structure of the secondary world she has created. And, follow-

Children's Literature 29, ed. Elizabeth Lennox Keyser and Julie Pfeiffer (Yale University Press, © 2001 Hollins University).

ing both that existing logical structure and her own predilection for belief in a feminist "Mother Tongue," Le Guin, like her priestly wizards in Earthsea, has accomplished her transformation by examining and changing the ways people do things with words.

Wizards: Medieval Christian Priests

The most significant cultural inheritance Le Guin imports into Earthsea is the one that seems perhaps the most unlikely for a self-proclaimed Taoist who also has called herself a "congenital non-Christian" (*Language* 55) and who sees her hero as being "outside the whole European heroic tradition" (*Revisioned* 8).[2] Le Guin notes that she "followed the intense conservatism of traditional fantasy in giving Earthsea a rigid social hierarchy of kings, lords, merchants, peasants" (*Revisioned* 8). It is in this pseudomedieval matrix that the mages of Earthsea assume the social and cultural roles and powers of medieval Christian priests, celibate males, trained in a textualized lore managed in a central location, holders of specific ranks in a centrally managed hierarchy, and (often) wanderers who depend on the charity of local people. Most significant, wizards and priests alike are able to perform speech-acts by which they can change not only social reality but the physical world as well.[3] Using words, a wizard can transform a pebble into a diamond or a person into a bird; using words, a priest can transform bread and wine into the body and blood of Christ.[4] Wizards and priests have powers beyond those of ordinary people that allow them, in the words of J. L. Austin, "to do things with words."

In Earthsea, as Le Guin notes, "the fundamental power, magic, belongs to men; only to men; only to men who have no sexual contact with women" (*Revisioned* 9).[5] As Aunt Moss explains in *Tehanu*, accepting and binding oneself to celibacy is absolutely necessary if a wizard is to exercise power (*Tehanu* 107–8).[6] In the Middle Ages, priests were required to be celibate, not only by canon law but also as an "implied" part of their consecration and hence as a basic prerequisite of the power of celebrating the sacraments (*New Catholic Encyclopedia* [*NCE*] 3:366–67).

The education of wizards in Earthsea is managed by a centralized hierarchy (*Wizard* 24) composed of a sort of college of nine "Masters" on the Island of Roke at the School of Wizardry—"true wizards are made only on Roke" (*Shore* 13–14).[7] The school at Roke, which John

Algeo cleverly describes as "a kind of Advanced Institute for Magic and Naming" (63), is led by one "Archmage" who is elected by the Masters but is their absolute superior, answerable to none and serving for life after his election (*Wizard* 64; *Shore* 24). The Masters and the Archmage hold social rank in the wider world, just as cardinals are called "princes of the church" and the pope claimed rank above that of even the highest secular rulers (*Dictionary of the Middle Ages [DMA]* 10:31–32).

After their training at Roke, wizards in Earthsea "went commonly to cities or castles, to serve high lords who held them in high honor" (*Wizard* 76). Each small town would have at the very least a magic worker, a "plain sorcerer" perhaps, who had studied for years at Roke but had not earned his staff and become a full-fledged "Mage" (*Wizard* 76). In small towns such as Low Torning, where the young wizard Ged, the protagonist of *A Wizard of Earthsea,* is first posted, the villagers support the wizard through gifts or tithes of food, lodging, clothing, and other necessities (*Wizard* 76–79). Every medieval town had at least one churchman who could officially establish contact between the "superhuman world and the human community" (*NCE* 11:766). In the same way in which Chaucer's Parson serves his parish, mages serve as intermediaries between the powers of magic (although these "powers" are not "gods" in the strictest sense of the term) and the lives of ordinary men and women.

When Ged leaves his appointment in Low Torning and wanders through Earthsea, his life becomes similar to the lives of clerics in the medieval mendicant (begging) orders. This group of peripatetic clerics, which included Franciscans and Dominicans, traveled from town to town without possessions, living by the good will of the people they encountered (*DMA* 8:273–74).[8] Like these friars, Ged relies on the good will of strangers. In *The Tombs of Atuan,* after Tenar and Ged have journeyed through the western mountains, Tenar asks the mage if wizards often beg. Ged answers: "Well, yes. I've begged all my life, if you look at it that way. Wizards don't own much, you know. In fact nothing but their staff and clothing, if they wander. They are received and given food and shelter, by most people, gladly. They do make some return" (130). That "return" is the gift of supernatural power harnessed for the good of the believing individuals of the community, the same "return" medieval parishioners believed that they received from their priests.

Languages of Power

The most important and most telling connection between wizards and priests can be found in the languages that they speak and the way these languages can be used to change the nature of the physical world. For medieval priests and for Earthsea's mages, bilingualism is an essential and necessary component of their vocations, and in both cases the second language learned (Latin for priests, the Old Speech for wizards) is both older and more powerful than the vernacular.[9] Both second languages enable private communication within a select group of bilingual initiates, and mastery of the secondary language also provides wizards and priests with the knowledge encoded in texts. Most important, both second languages allow their users in certain specific situations to change the physical nature of reality—although in Earthsea this power is ascribed to magic, whereas for priests it is interpreted as a sign of God's power.

Unlike Latin, the Old Speech of Earthsea is a creation language.[10] Like the universe in Genesis, Earthsea is created by the use of language. A creator named Segoy "made the islands of the world, and the language of . . . lays and songs, spells, enchantments, and invocations" (*Wizard* 47). Just as the Old Testament God named the light "day" and the dark "night" and in so naming, created them, Segoy's speech in the "language of the Making" brings Earthsea into being (*Tombs* 107). The creation of Earthsea by means of the language of a creator is obviously parallel with the familiar Judeo-Christian creation myth: by *saying* "let there be light," God brings the light into being. Likewise Segoy *speaks* the first word and the islands of Earthsea rise from beneath the waters.[11]

"At the beginning of time, all things bore their own true names" (*Tombs* 107). These names are words in the "Old Speech" or "True Speech" of Earthsea, the native tongue of dragons and once the cradle tongue of people. But over time speech changed, and now in Earthsea the people of the inner isles speak Hardic as a cradle tongue, the people of the Kargish Empire speak Kargish, and the people of Osskil speak Osskilian.[12] Just as Latin slowly changed to form the Latinate vernaculars, so too the Old Speech has mutated into Hardic (the antecedents of Kargish and Osskilian are not explained).[13]

The key parallel between Latin and the Old Speech is the ability of each nonnative language, in the mouth of an authorized speaker, to change the physical world. In Earthsea the Master Hand explains the power of the Old Speech after Ged has asked him how to change a pebble permanently into a diamond rather than merely presenting an illusion:

> The Master Hand looked at the jewel that glittered on Ged's palm, bright as the prize of a dragon's hoard. The old Master murmured one word, *"Tolk,"* and there lay the pebble, no jewel but a rough grey bit of rock. . . .
>
> "This is a rock; *tolk* in the True Speech. . . . It is itself. It is part of the world. By the Illusion-Change you can make it look like a diamond—or a flower or a fly or an eye or a flame—. . . But that is mere seeming. Illusion fools the beholder's senses; it makes him see and hear and feel that the thing is changed. But it does not change the thing. To change this rock into a jewel, you must change its true name. . . . It can be done. Indeed it can be done. It is the art of the Master Changer, and you will learn it, when you are ready to learn it." (*Wizard* 43–44)

The "true arts of Summoning and Change" (*Wizard* 44) allow wizards to change one thing into another thing by renaming it in the Old Speech, or to summon the great powers of light, heat, magnetism and the physical characteristics of things, "real powers, drawn from the immense fathomless energies of the universe" (*Wizard* 53–54).

Christian priests in the Middle Ages used Latin invocations to draw on the power of the Christian God to transform bread and wine into the body and blood of Christ. That the priest's actions in the Eucharistic ritual were understood throughout the medieval Christian populace (not merely in the schools of theology) to in fact alter the physical world is clear from numerous sources, most obviously the descriptions of female mystics such as Mary of Oignies, Ida of Louvain, Agnes Blannbekin, Christina Ebner, and Angela of Foligno, who all claimed to see or feel physical changes take place in the bread and wine or even tasted actual flesh and blood when they partook of the Eucharist (Bynum 119–126, 142).

But though words are the effective means by which the priest alters the physical world, words are not enough. For not anyone could say "Hoc est corpus meum" ("This is my body") and transform bread into Christ's body. And not only was this power reserved to priests, but it was reserved to them in the very strict context of the Mass. The invocation of God's power in the Christian Mass, then, is a specific kind of "speech act" (after the terminology developed by J. L. Austin, John R.

Searle, and others) only available to specific speakers in a specific set-ting.[14]

Speech acts or, to use Austin's original term, "illocutionary acts," are human utterances that affect the social world. Theorists have developed complex categorizations of speech acts, but for the purpose of this article we need focus on only one type, the "performative."[15] A "performative" is a speech act in which the very issuing of an utterance is the performing of an action in which, to paraphrase Austin, saying makes it so: a social change comes about due to the performance of words (4–8). As Austin notes, "there must exist an accepted conventional procedure having a certain conventional effect, the procedure to include the uttering of certain words by certain persons in certain circumstances" (26–27).

Those certain people in certain circumstances are what Austin calls "felicity conditions" (26–32). When the felicity conditions are met and a speech act is performed, an utterance has the ability to change social reality. To use Searle's terminology, the world is changed to fit the word. Felicity conditions are social and to a degree political: the person performing the speech act has to have been socially sanctioned to have his or her utterances validated as effectively performed speech acts (Searle 150, 111–34).

The felicity conditions necessary for the Eucharistic rite include the following: the person performing the rite must be an ordained priest (officially sanctioned by the hierarchy of the church); he must therefore be male. The celebrant must also be blessing the proper (unleavened) bread and wine (with a bit of water added), and he must do so in an appropriate manner (*NCE* 5:600–7). When these conditions are met, the effect of the Eucharistic rite (obviously within the belief system in which it operates) is fundamentally different from that of any other speech act: the physical nature of the bread and wine is actually changed by the speech act. The physical (not merely the social) world changes to fit the word.

Le Guin adopts for Earthsea the conceit of physical change being brought about by purely verbal means. And whereas the ability of priests to change the *physical* world though speech acts is limited to the Eucharistic rite, Earthsea's mages can use speech acts to change the physical world of Earthsea in any number of contexts. Wizards have to meet felicity conditions of their own in order for their magical speech acts to be successful. First, they must have power, intrinsic, inborn power (*Wizard* 3–5).[16] Second, they must have knowledge of how to utilize that power, for in Earthsea, Le Guin notes, "need alone is not enough to set power free: there must be knowledge" (*Wizard* 8). Although that knowledge includes specific spells and gestures, its key component is a specific, often secret, name in the Old Speech: "there are spells to learn, of course, ways to use the words," Ged tells Tenar, but the key element is knowledge of the name of the thing to be changed or summoned by the spell (*Tombs* 107–8). Wizards also must have some proximity, it seems, to the things they wish to control: the further away from Roke a wizard travels, the less sure he is in his spells, and animals and forces of nature far away from the archipelago do not "know" their true names and do not respond to wizardly power (*Wizard* 160, 175, 181).

The speech acts of wizards, then, are enabled by the Old Speech, presumably because it is a creation language. Unlike real human language, which is arbitrary in nature, the Old Speech of Earthsea is perfect because its vocabulary is able to describe thoughts, actions, things —the world in all its complexity—precisely. The Master Namer says (though this may be in jest) that every drop of water in the ocean has its name in the Old Speech; certainly not jesting, he says "there is no end to that language" (*Wizard* 46–47).

Signifier/Signified Relationships

Just as speech act theory clarifies the ways wizards do things with words, so does Ferdinand de Saussure's analysis of the distinction between the signifier and the signified help to explain the workings of the Old Speech. Saussure's linguistic "sign" is made up of two parts: the signifier, the sound or image that is tied to a particular concept, and the signified, the concept that we wish to communicate (70–71). The "bond between the signifier and the signified is arbitrary"; thus the choice of the signifier is that of an established linguistic community: "every means of expression used in society is based . . . on collective behavior or—what amounts to the same thing—on convention" (72).

The Old Speech is profoundly anti-Saussurian. In the Old Speech the creator Segoy named all the objects in the world, creating them as he named them. Thus the relation between the signifier and the signified is *not* arbitrary; Saussure's rules do not apply.[17] In fact, not only is the relation between signifier and signified not arbitrary in Earthsea, but under certain conditions the signifier and signified actually collapse into *the same thing*.[18] When a wizard says "tolk" and a rock appears in his palm, the difference between the name and the thing named has effectively disappeared. The Old Speech thus has the ability both to describe the world perfectly and to change it.

The Earthsea tetralogy presents a series of meditations on the nature of the signifier/signified relation and the power of authorized speech acts; these meditations widen in scope as the series unfolds. The first book, *A Wizard of Earthsea,* is primarily concerned with delineating the principles of magic in Earthsea by portraying the maturation and struggle of Ged, who, through careless magic, has accidentally loosed a terrible shadow on the world. In the course of the novel Ged must learn the art of naming in order to set the world right again. Indeed, much of *Wizard* focuses on the idea of naming and the use of speech acts in the Old Speech as a means of both knowing the world and controlling it.

When Ged attempts to summon an old heroine of Earthsea back from the dead by calling her true name, he only succeeds momentarily before accidentally loosing a "shadow," or "gebbeth," that hunts him all over Earthsea, seeking to possess him. In order to defeat the shadow, Ged must find out its true name. The Archmage Gensher tells Ged that, owing to its evil nature, the shadow has no name: it is "the shadow of your arrogance, the shadow of your ignorance, the shadow you cast" (66). But Ged's teacher, Ogion, believes otherwise: "'*All* things have a name,' said Ogion, so certainly that Ged dared not repeat what the Archmage Gensher had told him, that such evil forces as he had loosed were nameless" (127).

Ged eventually discovers that both Ogion and Gensher are correct: his creation, the shadow, has a name, but not a unique one: it has the same name that Ged does. Just as the word *"tolk"* can be the essence of the rock itself, Ged discovers that the shadow is actually another manifestation of his own essence, and in his final struggle with it, he recognizes that he and the shadow are in fact one. "Aloud and clearly, breaking that old silence, Ged spoke the shadow's name and in the same moment the shadow spoke without lips or tongue, saying the same word: 'Ged.' And the two voices were one voice . . . Ged reached out his hands, dropping his staff, and took hold of his shadow, of the black self that reached out to him. Light and darkness met, and joined, and were one" (*Wizard* 179).

By having her hero not destroy the shadow but rather embrace and become one with it through the performance of a magical speech act,

Le Guin illustrates the nonarbitrary relation between the signifier and the signified. Because no two different things can have the same name and, conversely, the same name can not name two different things,[19] Ged brings about union between himself and his shadow by applying one name to two entities, thus fusing the two into one.

The Tombs of Atuan shifts the focus of language from the individual to the community, in this case, a community of priestesses living in the non-Hardic-speaking Kargad Lands who worship some of the Old Powers of the Earth. The Kargish people have an organized state religion and do not believe in magic at all. The protagonist is a high priestess who has had her name taken from her in a ceremony in which socially authorized (but, as we shall see, not magically authorized) speech acts proclaimed her Arha, the Eaten One. She is accepted as a reincarnation of the high priestess who came before her and all previous high priestesses of the tombs. Through Arha, Le Guin explores the nature of the signifier and the signified in a culture that does not have the myth of creation language or nonarbitrary language (the Old Speech).

The Kargish priestesses who live and work at the Tombs of Atuan worship mysterious gods that they call the Nameless Ones. The name of the gods alone provides a stark contrast to the common belief on the archipelago. Much of the priestesses' worship centers on empty ritual in front of an empty throne, chanting words that *have no meaning:*

> Then it was dark of the moon, and the ceremonies of the darkness must be performed before the Empty Throne. Arha . . . danced for the unseen spirits of the dead and the unborn and as she danced the spirits crowded the air around her . . . she sang the songs whose words no man understood, which she had learned syllable by syllable, long ago, from Thar. A choir of priestesses hidden in the dusk behind the great double row of columns echoed the strange words after her . . . (*Tombs* 42)

Words seem to have no true meaning or purpose even for the priestesses, who chant tunes made up of babble: the speech acts themselves are authorized and perhaps magical, but they cannot work to change the physical world because the signifiers used by the priestesses are not magically linked to any specific signifieds. The religion of the Kargs, then, is one of meaningless words and ritual; no one in the Kargad Lands keeps his or her given name a secret because names appear to have no power there. As W.A. Senior points out, linguistic exchanges with the Nameless Ones are unidirectional: the speaker receives nothing in return (106). Speech acts are performed, but no one, it seems, is listening.

Le Guin here presents a language, and even a culture, that has no intimate connection between the signifier and the signified. Instead, it seems that the priestesses, worshipping nameless gods, have signifiers (the empty throne, the meaningless words) without any one thing being signified: the gods are unnumbered, undifferentiated, unnamed. One signifier can stand for any number (or no number) of signifieds. The relation is not only arbitrary but impossible to delineate.

Although the Kargs clearly live in a world that has magic—as seen when Ged comes and makes "werelight" in the Undertomb of the Nameless Ones—their state religion does not permit them to believe in any kind of magic, and they define reading, even in Kargish, as "one of the black arts" (*Tombs* 112). Shippey points out that the Kargs are the "first skeptics to appear in Earthsea" (155). Yet just as Ogion tells Ged that all things have a name, Ged tells Arha that the Nameless Ones have names, too, a fact with which Le Guin completely undermines the Kargish religion and belief system.[20]

Le Guin seems to suggest that language with this lack of magical linkage between the signifier and the signified eliminates the supernatural potential of speech acts and creates a society that, because it cannot differentiate between good and evil, is as a consequence completely enslaved to power. Arha begins to have doubts about the morality of the gods she serves when Ged comes secretly to the tombs in an attempt to steal the ring of Erreth-Akbe and she finds light and love instead of the evil she expects from him. She is further confused when Ged returns her birth name to her (96). Arha later despairs when she finds that her rival, the priestess Kossil, is unharmed by the Nameless Ones after desecrating their Undertomb with light. In the treasury of the Tombs, after Ged gives her birth name back to her, Arha's doubt solidifies into full-blown disbelief: " 'I am not Tenar. I am not Arha. The gods are dead, the gods are dead' " (104).

With the return of her birth name, Tenar/Arha is caught in an onomastic situation the converse of that of Ged and his shadow in *Wizard*. Whereas the signifier "Ged" applies to two separate signifieds— Ged and his shadow—that are eventually joined, the signifiers Tenar and Arha refer to the same signified. Since a single thing cannot have two names, Tenar/Arha is forced to choose: as Ged says, "You must be Arha, or you must be Tenar. You cannot be both" (113). Tenar finds her true self only when Ged gives her back her name—her signifier—which allows her to know her essential, uneaten self.[21]

Critics have identified in Arha/Tenar the "empty signifier" that is a common trope of feminist criticism. Barrow and Barrow say that Arha is an "identity created only by the death of the true self, Tenar" (34), but Tenar's true self never dies. Even as the One Priestess she has the capability of differentiating between good and evil: she knows that what she has done to the prisoners is wrong; she recognizes in Kossil a bottomless desire for power over others that she equates (correctly) with evil; and when weighing Penthe's kindness against the unhappy young girl's blasphemy, she sides with her friend. It seems, therefore, that Arha/Tenar does not fit the trope: she is not an empty signifier into which others can project their desires, but rather she is a signified without a proper individual signifier so that she exists in her own being but cannot be named by others or even name herself. She cannot properly receive the social speech acts of others, speech acts that may proclaim solidarity, or friendship, or love, because there is no signifier onto which others can attach their signifieds. And even though Tenar's recovery of her true name is a triumph over evil, it is also a painful and sad moment. Tenar weeps for the "waste of her years in bondage to a useless evil" (141) and in fact starts her life anew, regressing almost to the point where her birth name was first taken from her: when she and Ged reach Havnor she walks into the city "holding his hand, like a *child* coming home" (146, emphasis added).

In *The Farthest Shore,* the effects of language disequilibrium are applied to the global rather than the local community. Owing to the actions of Cob, a death-fearing sorcerer, the magic is running out of Earthsea, and people are forgetting the words of the Old Speech. As a result of Cob's spell of immortality, the Old Speech is shifting from a nonarbitrary relation between things and their names to one that—like normal human language—is arbitrary. As they sail the Dragon's Run, Arren and Ged cannot agree on the meaning of a sound coming from a cave: "Sparrowhawk listened; he glanced at Arren and back at the cave. 'How do you hear it?' 'As saying the sound *ahm.*' 'In the Old Speech that signifies the beginning, or long ago. But I hear it as *ohb,* which is a way of saying the end' " (151). The arbitrariness of names and words prevents communication and agreement.

Cob's spell offers the promise of eternal life to people if they will only give up their true names. But this promise is false; the people who give up their names do not gain eternal life but rather become mere signifiers without signifieds, signifiers that, circularly, refer only to other signifiers. As Ged says to Cob:

> My name is no use to you. You have no power over me. I am a living man; my body lies on the beach of Selidor, under the sun, on the turning earth. And when that body dies, I will be here: but only in name, in name alone, in shadow. Do you not understand? Did you never understand, you who called up so many shadows from the dead, who summoned all the hosts of the perished, even my lord Erreth-Akbe, wisest of us all? Did you not understand that he, even he, is but a shadow and a name? (*Shore* 180)

The names of the dead, and their images, are merely markers of something that is not there, an absent signified no longer linked to the signifier or name or ghost image. In essence the falling, decaying world of *The Farthest Shore* is a world of dramatized Derridean relationships where the signifiers refer only to other signifiers in an endless empty cycle without any connection to reality. In Le Guin's world this self-referential structure is exposed as fundamentally hollow. The difference between Earthsea and the mundane world has been that the relation between signifier and signified is not arbitrary but grounded in a firm physical reality. Anything that upsets this dualistic relation unbalances the very physics and metaphysics of the world: societal confusion ensues and Earthsea becomes depressingly like our current world. Fortunately, Ged is able to defeat Cob and return the signifiers to their proper signifieds, thus restoring balance and order to Earthsea.[22]

A Feminist Speech Act Intervention Through Creation Language

Tehanu works as a feminist reaction to the Earthsea trilogy. Here Le Guin makes explicit the relations of gendered power and domination through culture and language that were implicit in the metaphysics of Earthsea. As Le Guin herself notes, "instead of using the pseudo-genderless male viewpoint of the heroic tradition, the world [in *Tehanu*] is seen through a woman's eyes. This time the gendering of the point of view is neither hidden nor denied" (*Revisioned* 12).

In *Tehanu*, Le Guin extends the underlying idea of a creation language in such a way as to work women and their powers and speech into the cosmological and metaphysical workings of Earthsea. The focus of the speech acts of magic becomes not the *how* of the acts (as it is in the first three books) but the *who* of the speakers. The novel picks up Tenar's story years after her arrival in the Hardic-speaking archipelago after fleeing the Tombs of Atuan with Ged. The use of the Old Speech as a language with nonarbitrary relations between the word and the thing, between signifier and signified, becomes complicated by an essentialist conception of gender in which women use their speech for communication and nurturing while most men use their speech acts to dominate, control, and perpetuate violence. By examining the felicity conditions of magical speech acts, Le Guin continues to explore the equilibrium that the Old Speech maintains.

As is *The Tombs of Atuan, Tehanu* is written from the point of view of Tenar, who, after her husband's death, lives with various other women in a rural farming community on Ged's native island of Gont. Now a middle-aged woman, Tenar's "eyes have been opened, and she finds herself repeatedly questioning and condemning the laws, traditions, and policies that have caused women to be second-class citizens in Earthsea" (Littlefield 251).[23]

The men who interact with Tenar, including men who speak in the Old Speech, use a genderlect that shows their dominance and superiority. After Ogion has died, leaving his true name with Tenar, the other wizards come to pay their respects to Ogion's body. They remark that it is a shame that he died without telling anyone his true name:

> "His name was Aihal," Tenar said. "His wish was to lie here, where he lies now." Both men looked at her. The young man, seeing a middle-aged village woman, simply turned away. . . .
> "And," said the older man, "—and he told you—?" . . .
> To her consternation she saw from their expressions that in fact they had not heard the name, Ogion's true name; they had not paid attention to her. (28–29)

The same men also refuse to believe that Tenar could know any of the Old Speech or have been Ogion's apprentice when she was younger.[24] Here Le Guin suggests that the wizards use the Old Speech not only to exert power over their surroundings but also to control others, especially women, who are not permitted to share their knowledge of the Old Speech.

This suggestion becomes a full-blown illustration of the capacity of the Old Speech to enable men's violence-driven power over women when the evil wizard Aspen puts a spell on Tenar that, among other things, causes her to think of burning herself. The focus of the curse is language, and the trigger appears to have been Tenar's use of the Old Speech to teach Therru the word "tolk":

> [S]he knew there was a spell on her. It had been laid waiting for her. She had said the word, the true name of the stone, and it had been flung at her, in her face—in the face of evil, the hideous face—She had dared not speak—She could not speak—
>
> She thought, in her own language, *I cannot think in Hardic. I must not.*
>
> She could think, in Kargish. (135, emphasis in original)

Tellingly, Tenar is able to avoid the worst aspects of the spell by thinking in Kargish, thus changing the mental signifiers that must go along with the communication of Aspen's evil speech act. But Aspen's terroristic threats do accomplish their goal of driving her almost into the grasp of Handy, the man who had raped and burned Therru.

Whereas men's speech works to generate violence against women, women's speech is presented as being the language of simple communication, of understanding. Le Guin illustrates this communicative process not only through the interactions of Tenar, Moss, and Therru, but most powerfully through Tenar's interaction with the feminized Ged, who has lost his magical ability after the fateful battle with Cob to restore the words to the people of Earthsea, to rebalance the linguistic equilibrium. Ged returns to Gont to live with Tenar, and their speech is surprisingly simple, direct, and nurturing. As Littlefield notes, "[Ged] must confront his own powerlessness. To a certain extent he has been symbolically feminized. Significantly, it is Tenar who . . . restores to him a different kind of potency . . . emotionally, she teaches him to learn to find happiness and fulfillment outside of wizardry and in connections with other people instead" (253).

As do *The Tombs of Atuan* and *The Farthest Shore*, *Tehanu* presents a world that is out of balance. But the difference is that the equilibrium is thrown off by socially constructed gender inequality rather than by an extrasocial metaphysical force. As Littlefield suggests, the imbalance is in the wizards (252). In their position of social authority, some of them abuse their knowledge of the Old Speech to unjustly dominate women (and weaker men). And even those who are fundamentally good, like Ged (until the dramatic intervention of Kalessin at the end of the novel), are incapable of understanding the possibility of gender equity. For example, the kind sorcerer Beech, who suggests that Therru be trained as a witch, refuses to understand the clear implications of Ogion's last words about the child and instead interprets them to mean that Ogion meant for Therru not to be trained in the "High Arts"—even though Ogion had said "teach her all" (175–76). And though the Master Patterner has foretold that the next Archmage will be "a woman on Gont," the Masters of Roke are obtusely incapable of taking—or, as Littlefield says, they "rigidly refuse to accept" (252)—his words at face value and instead pursue tortured linguistic circumlocutions in order to avoid the obvious conclusion that the next Archmage will be a woman (*Tehanu* 155–59).[25] Ged himself tries to argue away the possibility: "No woman can be Archmage. She'd unmake what she became in becoming it. The Mages of Roke are men—their power is the power of men, their knowledge is the knowledge of men. Both manhood and magery are built on one rock: power belongs to men. If women had power, what would men be but women who can't bear children? And what would women be but men who can? (219–20).[26]

By emphasizing the perceived link between wizardry and masculine power, Le Guin emphasizes one of the external felicity conditions of wizardly speech acts—the condition that in order to perform "true" magic the speaker of a spell must be male—rather than on the internal constitution of the naming-summoning process. She thus reifies the masculine, priestly power that she has inherited from the genre traditions that end up making her mages socially and culturally isomorphic to medieval Christian priests. In the first three books of the Earthsea series an extrahuman authority, the very nature of the universe (analogous to the laws of physics or, in the Christian *weltanschauung*, God's laws for the universe), determines whether the felicity conditions for a spell have been met. But in *Tehanu* Le Guin begins to reconsider her ideas about the morality of the magical "technology" of Earthsea and hints that in fact felicity conditions that seem to be part of the nature of the universe (no women are wizards) are in fact socially constructed through the improper uses of power.

Just as some contemporary Catholics may question the all-male constitution of the priesthood, so too does Le Guin call into question her all-male hierarchy of wizards. In her emphasis on the necessity of the "male-speaker" felicity condition, or rather, in the strong emphasis put on the condition by male wizards, Le Guin challenges the perceived metaphysics of Earthsea that she has inherited both from her culture's traditions and from her earlier books. For if women are not excluded from power by the basic laws of creation but merely because men restrict their access to the school of Roke (likewise if women are not excluded from the priesthood by God's laws but by the human tradition of interpreting sacred texts), then the entire gender order of Earthsea is not only illegitimate, but also, and perhaps more important, subject to revision.

And in fact Tenar begins to bring about a revision or revolution in the gender order, through one act of caring and nurturing. By saving Therru, whom Tenar adopts and mothers, Tenar has saved an enormously powerful being who, it seems, will eventually become Archmage. Therru, it turns out, is both dragon and human, and therefore the Old Speech is her native tongue. Like a true wizard, she has the power to recognize a person's true name without being told: "the one called Aspen, whose name was Erisen" (244). Ogion, the witch Ivy, and other individuals skilled in sorcery have recognized in her immense power (23, 179–81). Her true name is Tehanu, the Kargish name of a certain star (197). But rather than having the name given to her by someone else (Ged interprets Kalessin's speaking the word "Tehanu" to her as giving a name), it seems more likely that, as Tenar says, "she had been Tehanu since the beginning. Always she has been Tehanu" (248–50).[27] She is, it seems, the "child" of Kalessin, who apparently is also Segoy, the creator of the world (249).[28] In other words, Tehanu's name is not bestowed upon her by another human but is instead an intrinsic part of her being. The true names of Ged, Tenar, Ogion, and every other human being in the archipelago are mediated socially: they are given by a human wizard. Tehanu, on the other hand, either has had her name, as Tenar says, "since the beginning" or, as Ged suggests, has received her name "from the giver of names" (250). At the deepest core of her being, her true name, she is independent of human beings and the gender-asymmetric social world constructed by them.

So Tehanu is both dragon and human dragonlord (a person to whom the dragons will speak). She is a woman but is possessed of enormous power for a magery that has been defined as masculine. She is maimed and crippled yet, it seems, able to speak familiarly to the most powerful being in Earthsea, its creator. Her speech acts will be felicitous because she speaks in what is for her a cradle tongue but what is for Earthsea a creation language wherein signifier and signified can become one.

Le Guin seems to suggest that by means of Tehanu Earthsea will be rebalanced, that the disequilibrium that had allowed Cob to perform his spell of madness will be righted.[29] The Old Speech will be returned to its proper use, not to estrange communication between the sexes, between those with the true speech and those without, between men and women, but as a creative force used to keep all things in balance. In the person of Tehanu the human and dragon halves of the children of Segoy, separated since almost the beginning of time, are joined. This joining may reunite the speakers of the Old Speech — the dragons, wild — and the learners of the Old Speech — the humans, wise — into creatures whose whole beings are both human and dragon (*Tehanu* 10–14).

Lebannen, as a good king, has begun to heal the political and social life of the archipelago (175, 178, 225–26). Interestingly enough, he seems to give more credence to the possibility of a female Archmage than any of the Masters of Roke: when Tenar is alone with Lebannen and stumbles through a few sentences that hint that there might be a female Archmage-to-be on Gont, Lebannen tells her that "it may be" (160–61). If Lebannen has renewed the mundane life of Earthsea, and he is open to the possibility of female power, then Tehanu, perhaps, will renew the magical life, demonstrating female power and bringing about a new and better gender order for Earthsea.

Making Tehanu the future Archmage rather than, say, the first female lower-level mage, also makes a powerful feminist political statement. Not content with merely incremental change in gender roles, or the promise of some far-off day when equality will be achieved, Le Guin modifies her social order right at the top. And this modification — since it relies not on the goodwill or accommodation of the masculine wizards but simply on the superior power of Tehanu — serves to make a powerful counterclaim against the inherited sociocultural structure that shaped Le Guin's first three Earthsea books. Le Guin is not content to make Tehanu the first female "priest": the dragon woman will be the first female "pope."

Conclusion: A Successful Intervention

The problem of inherited materials is one of the most complex a cultural critic can face. Even the most original speculative fiction can contain and communicate cultural constructs and ideological patterns its author would never espouse.[30] Nor would most authors want to so escape, since so much of the resonance of a work of literature relies on stirring deeply embedded cultural patterns, whether these be Jungian archetypes (as so many critics seem to believe is the case for the Earth-sea books) or simply long-standing historical and sociocultural patterns of social behavior.[31] As Le Guin herself puts it: "The tradition I was writing in was a great one, a strong one. The beauty of your own tradition is that it carries you. It flies, and you ride it. Indeed, it's hard not to let it carry you, for it's older and bigger and wiser than you are. It frames your thinking and puts winged words in your mouth" (*Revisioned* 10).

Le Guin has called herself "un-Christian" (*Language* 55) and has been recognized as developing a feminist consciousness (Hatfield 60 and passim; Nodelman 199). Yet she has in her masculine wizards imported into the pseudomedieval milieu of Earthsea the figure of medieval Christian priests, and in fact the stories are dependent on their speech acts and language.

Lois Kuznets states Le Guin's problem nicely: "Women do not automatically write feminist books, especially when they are using mainly the traditional materials of a patriarchal culture" (32).[32] Faced with the realization that nearly thirty years ago she had created a patriarchal secondary world that reified gender roles that her more recent work has struggled to call into question,[33] Le Guin in *Tehanu* has made a particularly courageous feminist intervention.[34] She could have, as Nodelman incorrectly suggests she has done, reinvented a past in which for "almost 20 years . . . there was *no* explicit subversion of patriarchy" (180, emphasis in original), creating as Hatfield suggests a new metaphysics that would valorize a "mother tongue" (43).[35] But instead, working in the best tradition of the logical rigor of science fiction, Le Guin has not simply thrown to the wind the previously developed metaphysics of Earthsea. Rather, she had struggled with the cultural constructs that she had inherited from her culture and from her previous work, finding in the interstices and implications of that previous structure a place from which to challenge her own earlier (unconscious, perhaps) assumptions about gender.

Since Le Guin had worked out in such detail the operations of magic in terms of the signifier/signified relationships and the speech acts of her priestly wizards, she really did not have the freedom to modify these aspects of Earthsea's metaphysics without doing violence to the logic of the structure she had created. But though the internal linguistic structure of the speech acts that are spells were, by their detailed descriptions, relatively fixed, and though Le Guin had inherited the traditional masculine gender of her priest-wizard

speakers, the fact that she had not in detail described the felicity conditions that enabled the speakers to do magic or the possible identity of the speakers as related to those conditions allowed her a freer
play of ideas. Combining this freedom with unexplored implications
of the power of the Old Speech as a creation language and the fact that
dragons speak these words of power as their native tongue, enabled
Le Guin to work women into the equations without, as it were, erasing
the blackboard.[36]

And Le Guin's intervention also suggests a revision of her views
on knowledge, power, and mastery. As Nodelman has pointed out,
the Earthsea trilogy works to undermine the very didactic message of
being rather than doing that Le Guin's wise wizards so explicitly state:
"the endings of both *Wizard* and *Tombs* seem to contradict what they
most obviously try to persuade us of" (188). Manlove's contention that
in the trilogy the accent is on magic's "not changing the nature of the
world, except in cases of real need" (293) is undercut by the very fact
that the situations Le Guin chooses to illustrate are precisely those in
which magic is used to change the nature of the world. And though
critics such as Robert Galbreath accept Le Guin's contention (*Wizard*
180–81) that Ged "does not 'defeat' or 'subdue' the Shadow by naming it" (264), Ged does in fact conquer the shadow (the two signifieds
may be merged, but we see only the persona of Ged directing his actions; the shadow is gone). And Ged defeats Cob and saves the world
through an exercise of power and knowledge: "with all the skill of his
life's training and all the strength of his fierce heart, Ged strove to shut
that door" (*Shore* 183).[37] Mason Harris's suggestion that "Ged's attempt
at omnipotence [when he releases the Shadow in *Wizard*] is the passionate impulse of an adolescent" (54) could be extended throughout
the trilogy to all of Ged's actions. In every case Ged succeeds through
his integrity and his passion, both particularly adolescent virtues, and
both more accessible to adolescents, who are otherwise not provided
by our culture with very many means by which they can access social
power.

The original Earthsea trilogy is perhaps so well loved by children
because it communicates the idea that the relatively powerless will
be rewarded with power if they seek knowledge. Priests and wizards
receive their authority and knowledge from their participation in a
hierarchy. In the first three Earthsea books, children are invited to
enter into a hierarchy of knowledge, power, and obedience, replicat-
ing the journey of Ged from fierce, rebellious independence to fully

assimilated, legitimated (even, perhaps, domesticated; certainly co-opted) leadership of the hierarchy. They can achieve social integration (or perhaps co-option) by seeking knowledge through books, like Le Guin's.

"To tap into [the power of Earthsea's magic], one must patiently master the true name and nature of everything, including oneself. Nothing could more directly contradict the quick material fix" writes Jeanne Walker, approvingly ("High Fantasy" 114–15). A "quick material fix" it may not be, but learning—and learning oneself—can be accomplished by children with little social power but with access to books and their own thoughts, thus allowing many children, in many different material conditions, to imagine themselves to be like Ged. This message of the equivalence of knowledge and power, and the desirability of both, is summed up by Cordelia Sherman as "You too . . . can be as wise as Ged . . . if only you are willing to know and master yourself" (195).

Such links between knowledge and power certainly help explain the love that intelligent children (the sort who read complex high fantasy at an early age) have for the Earthsea trilogy. Knowledge is easily acquired by an intelligent, reading child. The abilities of children to master abstruse knowledge—the Latin names of dinosaurs or fish or plants, the batting averages of baseball players, the current market value of Beanie Babies—is a continual source of amazement to parents. If the trilogy communicates to children that the pursuit of knowledge will lead to one thing that children have always lacked, social power, it is easy to see the appeal of Earthsea to young readers.

But the power that the metaphysics of Earthsea offers has a price. And parents and children's librarians can find in Le Guin's focus on mastery, obedience to older and wiser "masters," and the restraint of passionate impulses a subtext of constraint and control. Hatfield asserts that Le Guin presents two views of authority, which he calls "masterly" and "masterful" and then aligns with the adult versus the child view of authority. Ogion's silence and seeming passivity is the model for the "adult," or masterly, view of authority, whereas Ged's challenge of Jasper is the "arrogant," adolescent masterful form. Though Hatfield follows the postmodern trope of asserting that the opposition cannot be reduced to an "either-or division," it would seem that both he and in fact Le Guin (and likely the parents and librarians reading the Earthsea trilogy) would assert the moral superiority of the "adult" mode (47). Sherman argues that the Earthsea books teach a child how to be a "good" adult. Because, in general, adults possess more knowledge than do children, links between knowledge and power reinforce an ideology of obedience certain to be popular in a culture that fears children's exercises of freedom.[38] That his obedience is to the internalized ideology of "equilibrium" promulgated by his superiors, rather than to individual superiors themselves, does not make Ged any more free.

The equation of knowledge with power and the consequent logical conclusion that knowledge legitimates the exercise of power, though perhaps socially unquestioned at the height of the technocratic mainstream culture of the late sixties and seventies, is, at least since Foucault, a politically difficult position to take. The powerful wizard who understands the equilibrium and only does what he must has to be at least balanced with the cultural facts of the existence of powerful but ignorant bureaucrats, amoral scientists, "experts" for sale to the highest bidders in business and government, and the exclusion (whether an aim in itself or a by-product of other relations) of women from power. In *Tehanu* Le Guin illustrates the price paid for power in the sufferings of others, and she challenges the heroic masculinity of the first three books while at the same time holding out the hope for an equitable but still magical future for Earthsea. By calling attention to the socially constructed gender roles that limit the exercise of power by women, Le Guin manages to call the social structure of Earthsea into question without simultaneously undercutting the idea that knowledge itself, particularly self-knowledge, is a way to pass *through* power and into wisdom.

Walker argues that *A Wizard of Earthsea* acts in itself as a potential rite of passage for children ("Rites"181–83 and passim). We agree. And we believe that although the original Earthsea trilogy will retain its importance as a work of children's literature, *Tehanu* is unlikely to become as beloved a work. In our thoroughly subjective estimate, *Tehanu* as a work of art is inferior to the original trilogy (although we would assert that this weakness has nothing to do with the feminist content of the book).[39] But as an intellectual exercise, as speculative fiction, as a work that attempts to apply the rigorous standards of the logical extrapolation of fundamental assumptions (generally associated with the best science fiction) to fantasy literature, *Tehanu* is a triumph. Le Guin illustrates that after the rite of passage is completed the child must settle into the difficult, frustrating chore of being an adult, fighting the endless tiny existential social battles—be they struggles against gender oppression, inequities of power, illegitimate domination, and the enforcement of ideology on unwilling minds, or the crises of conscience, losses of motivation, and fears of failure—that make up adult life. As Dunn notes, the Earthsea books, even those written before *Tehanu,* dramatize that "the process of maturation is not something that ends at a given age or stage of life, and that it is not something which, once successfully completed, is completed forevermore. The challenge to grow continues as long as we live" (1983, 58).

In rewriting Earthsea through *Tehanu,* then, Le Guin has continued that growth, and she has not betrayed the promise of the first three books. Furthermore, she has not, contra both Hatfield and perhaps Le Guin's own published statements,[40] merely rewritten a patriarchal story as a feminist-essentialist "Mother Tongue" that somehow rejects the previous "Father Language" (Hatfield 60–61). Nor has she, as Nodelman argues, merely reversed "supposedly universal archetypes" (199).[41] Rather, Le Guin's feminist intervention illustrates a courageous and creative willingness to refuse to deny, toss away, or curse one's cultural inheritance (no matter how problematic it may be) but to intervene and improve on it in the hope that the future can be bettered without ignoring or eliminating the past. Le Guin has shown that a future in which women exercise power for the purpose of justice and balance can be imagined and delineated through logical extrapolation: a feminist future, even in children's fantasy, need not be a mere flight of fancy.

Notes

The authors would like to thank Candace Castro, Gabriel Cunningham, Jennifer Johnson, Jeniffer Hargroves, Teresa MacNamara, Emery Samuels, and Aaron Smith, all participants in the Wheaton College Spring 1999 Senior Seminar, "The Sources and Use of Fantasy Literature," for helping us develop and refine the arguments we present here. Beverly Lyon Clark, Mary F. Dockray-Miller, and Sylwia Ejmont provided invaluable criticism of early drafts of this article.

    1. These works are hereafter abbreviated as *Wizard, Tombs, Shore,* and *Tehanu.*

    2. Perhaps Le Guin's avowedly Taoist metaphysics has clouded the link between Earthsea and Christianity. Or perhaps Le Guin's failure to make explicit important metaphysical concepts until the publication of *Tehanu* obscured the issue for previous critics. In any event, we do not intend to dispute the contention, put best perhaps by Wytenbroek, that Le Guin illustrates important Taoist principles in the Earthsea books (179). Rather, we would like to suggest that in Le Guin's presentation these principles are fully compatible with the Christian influences we detect in the series.

    3. Other critics have noted in passing connections between Le Guin's Earthsea and

Christianity, but none has developed the idea in detail. See, e.g., Sherman (195), Filmer (12), and Shippey (150).

Patricia Dooley notes a link between the power of words in Earthsea and Adam's naming of the beasts in Genesis (106). Nodelman states that "traditionally, the ability to speak, to name, and to have the name you give accepted is a pure form of mastery, the strongest evidence of authority—like God's originary speech that simultaneously gives a name to light and produces it, or like Adam's naming of the beasts" (189). Nodelman, who does not cite Dooley's previous invocation of Adam's naming actions, also links Earthsea to Christianity, stating that "'Agni Lebannen' contains something so much like agnus, the Latin word for lamb. Like Christ, Arren is lamblike in his lack of sinful thoughts and his innocence. He is the child Ged sends before him into the dark . . . as Christ is the child that God sends into the dark world to announce his salvation. If Ged as wielder of light and speaker of words parallels God the father, then Arren, who becomes king of the world through resisting aggressive action and following God's word, is Christ" (197–98).

Though suggestive, the passage cannot withstand close scrutiny. "Agnus"—part of the Christian liturgical phrase "agnus dei" ("the lamb of God")—is commonly used to refer to the self-sacrificial aspects of Christ's ministry on earth (*NCE* 1:209). But it is Ged, not Arren, who sacrifices himself. The reading of Christianity in this case is superficial and replicates the fourth-century Arian heresy. (Arians believed that the persons of God the Father and Christ the Son were separate individuals.)

Francis J. Molson had previously argued that "'agni' appears to be a variant of Agnen, the rune of Ending" indicating that "the prince's becoming king is the end the quest has always pointed to" (145–46). But no other person or thing appears to have either a metaphoric true name or a noun-epithet formula for a name. A simpler explanation supported by a closer reading of the passages in which Arren is called "Agni Lebannen" strongly suggests that "agni" simply means "king" in the Old Speech.

4. Obviously, this transformation cannot be substantiated scientifically. But within the *weltanschauung* within which medieval priests operated (the same *weltanschauung* that informs that literature of the period and hence the tradition of English literature) the physical substances of bread and wine were changed in their true beings (*NCE* 14:259).

5. Apparently, celibacy is only required for full mages, not mere sorcerers. In *Wizard*, the sorcerer on the island of Vemish has a daughter (152), and Arren's father is a "wizardly man" who has studied at Roke and has the ability to say the spells of increase over the lambs (*Shore* 3–4).

6. Edward Carpenter suggests that the "androgyny" of priests or wizards may derive from the "matriarchal" character of early religions (51), though Barry Weller calls this anthropology "questionable" (238). Barbara J. Bucknall asserted in 1989 that wizardly celibacy was more a matter of time management than necessity: "It is absurd to think of [Ged] as having a love affair. Too much demands his attention" (63). Sandra J. Lindow calls wizardly celibacy a "genre tradition" but does not discuss whence the tradition has arisen (11).

7. The education of medieval priests was not quite as centralized as that of Earthsea wizards: priests did not have to travel to Rome to be educated, but they did nonetheless perform the same rites and study the same texts, rites and texts promulgated, edited, and overseen from the central Apostolic See (*NCE* 1:699–700, 4:539–40).

8. Chaucer's Friar is a member of a mendicant order, though he does not obey all the precepts of poverty, chastity, and obedience (*General Prologue* 208–69).

9. It is surprising that the link between the Old Speech and Latin has not been previously noted, since the model of the Latin-vernacular high-low speech has been present in fantasy literature at least since Tolkien (whose essays "On Fairy Stories" and "*Beowulf:* The Monsters and the Critics" are enormously influential in the criticism of fantasy lit-

erature). Tolkien, in a 1954 letter to Naomi Mitchison published in 1981 in his collected letters, explicitly refers to Quenya, the language of the "High Elves," as "a kind of 'Elven Latin' " (*Letters* 175–76).

10. Medieval literary theory and theology recognized Hebrew as the creation language (Dante 157).

11. The other obvious parallel is "et tenebrae super faciem abyssi" ("and darkness was on the face of the waters") (Genesis 1:2, Vulgate).

12. Le Guin does not explain why things no longer bear their true names or how Hardic evolved out of the Old Speech. In Christian theology the reason for the fragmentation of human languages is the episode of the Tower of Babel. Dante understood all other languages as a corruption, a "forgetfulness of the former language" of the "true" Hebrew (160).

13. Though, logically, these languages must also have derived from the Old Speech.

14. Mary Louise Pratt provides a good short overview of speech act theory in *Toward a Speech Act Theory of Literary Discourse* (80–86).

15. Doris Myers briefly links performative speech acts and Earthsea wizardry in her 1982 article " 'True Speech' in the Fantasies of Tolkien and Le Guin" but does not further develop the idea (95).

16. As C.N. Manlove notes, the power must be developed through education. But nevertheless the raw power must be already present in the putative wizard (294).

17. Shippey recognized that the Old Speech violates the Saussurian principle of the arbitrary nature of the signifier/signified relationship, calling the connection of word to thing the "Rumpelstiltzkin" theory of language and noting that its presence in primitive cultures was brought to prominence by early modern anthropology (151).

18. Edith L. Crowe says that "In Earthsea's magic the name *is* the thing," but she does not further develop the idea (66).

19. There is, however, an unresolved contradiction in Le Guin's metaphysics here, for both Yarrow/Kest and Arren/Lebannen bear names that are also the names of things in the real world: "kest" is a minnow (*Wizard* 169) and "lebannen" a rowan tree (*Shore* 28). It is not clear how the powers of magery are able to distinguish between "Kest" the person and "kest" the minnow, though perhaps the powers of the earth possess some way (beyond capitalization) of distinguishing proper names from common nouns. This potential contradiction might be resolved if, as discussed above, a wizard needs to be within some arbitrary proximity to the thing he is trying to control through its name. In that case, one major function of a spell in the Old Speech is to encode an appropriate set of deictic markers.

20. We can find no evidence to support Barrow and Barrow's contention that after the joining of the Ring of Erreth-Akbe, "the religion of Tenar's fair-skinned people will then complement the magic of the dark-skinned dwellers of the Inner Lands" (32). Certainly the Master Patterner is a Karg, but we see no evidence that he continues to practice the Kargish religion on Roke or that people of the Inner Lands adopt the Kargish worship of the Nameless Ones, Twin Gods, or Godking.

21. This recovery of self is neither easy nor immediate. Tenar almost falls back into the worship of the Nameless Ones when, in the cave at the edge of the sea, she considers stabbing Ged as he sleeps in a "last act of darkness" (*Tombs* 139–40). Contra Talbot, Tenar never "attempts to stab" Ged (143). She holds the knife at her waist, but she never moves it toward the wizard (*Tombs* 139–40).

22. Shippey contends that "Cob (like Arha) has forgotten his true-name, but . . . Ged, who says he can remember it, never restores it to him" (161). But it seems reasonable to infer that when Ged whispers to Cob after shutting the door between death and life he is either restoring to Cob his true name or renaming him the way he renames Akaren of Lorbanery by whispering into her ear. To be fair, it is also possible to read the passage as suggesting that what Ged whispers to Cob is "the word that was spoken

at the making of things," though we would argue that since Ged has summoned Cob "by the word that will not be spoken until time's end"—a word he obviously does not say directly—he does not have to actually pronounce "the word that was spoken at the making of things" in order to allow Cob to go and join the dead. Ged says "Go free!" before he whispers in Cob's ear, suggesting that the spell finished by "the word that was spoken at the making of things" is already complete when he whispers to Cob (*Tombs* 85, 184–85).

23. Barrow and Barrow assert that "magic in *Tehanu* is a secondary interest largely because it is seen as a corrupt aspect of male hegemony and sexuality" (41 n. 1).

24. The idea that women cannot be mages may be implicit throughout the first three Earthsea books, but it is called into question by the power of Serret, the sorceress in Osskil, to change her form into that of a gull. The power of change of form is one of the "true arts of Summoning and Change" (*Wizard* 44), and the possession of the knowledge to accomplish this feat is beyond the skill of the "prentice" mages on Roke and learned only by the more advanced students, who have been promoted to "sorcerer" (*Wizard* 57). Interestingly, and nowhere explained in the tetralogy, Serret appears to be able to accomplish magic using Osskilian words (*Wizard* 120). A conversation between Ged and Tenar suggests that she too could have practiced "art magic" at the level of a mage (*Tehanu* 94–95).

25. This scene contains the only unresolvable inconsistency between *Tehanu* and the original Earthsea trilogy that we have been able to locate. In *The Farthest Shore* we learn that Thorion, the Master Summoner whom Ged and Arren meet wandering in the land of the dead, has come back to life in time for Ged's and Arren's journey to Roke on Kalessin's back: "the Summoner, gaunt and frail, only one day risen from his bed, had come" (195). But in *Tehanu* King Lebannen tells Tenar that the Master Summoner "did not come back" to the land of the living, and we learn from the Master Windkey that the Changer still hoped for the Summoner's return (155–56). We can find no way to resolve the inconsistency and so simply note it here.

Another potential inconsistency arises if we attempt to determine the gender of Segoy/Kalessin. In *The Farthest Shore*, Ged says of Kalessin's gender "I say 'he' but I do not even know that" (151), yet previously, as Alice Mills notes (5), the narrator of *Shore* refers to Segoy with a masculine pronoun (*Shore* 128). If Kalessin and Segoy are the same being, then Kalessin must be masculine. This determination of gender, however, is not actually inconsistent. Ged says that he does not know the dragon's (and hence, the creator's) gender. Of course, it may be that referring to the creator with a masculine pronoun is simply a tradition of Earthsea songs. Le Guin herself says that "I don't know if Kalessin, the Eldest, is male or female or both or something else. I choose not to know" (*Revisioned* 24).

26. In Matthew 16:18 Christ says to Peter, "tu es Petrus et super hanc petram aedificabo ecclesiam meam" ("you are Peter, and upon this rock I will build my church"). Le Guin is perhaps (consciously or unconsciously) linking Christian priests and Earthsea mages through masculine power.

27. Tehanu, it seems, will be beyond the power of the Mages of Roke as well. Every person on Roke has a true name given to him or her by a wizard (*Wizard* 14–15). In addition, every person who enters the walls of the School of Wizards must give the Master Doorkeeper his or her name (*Wizard* 34; *Shore* 20). The Master Doorkeeper, then, and by extension the rest of the Masters of Roke, know the true name of every trained wizard on Earthsea, thus giving the Masters power to protect themselves from the actions of their former students (it is perhaps for this reason of security, as well as his presumed ability to detect power in likely wizards, that the Doorkeeper is one of the Masters of Roke). Since every single person's name has been given by some wizard or another, and since every wizard is, due to the Doorkeeper's knowledge of his true name, magically subject to Roke, it would stand to reason that, at least theoretically, every named per-

son in Earthsea is subject to Roke. But Tehanu has not been given her name by a wizard and has never encountered the Master Doorkeeper. Thus she is a being of great power outside the control of the hierarchy of wizards and the power of the Masters of Roke.

28. We believe that Talbot may be misreading the passage in question when he suggests that Tehanu calls Ged by the name Segoy (146). Ged says to the dragon "Now I know who called thee, Eldest." Tehanu replies: "I did . . . I did not know what else to do, Segoy." At this point it seems reasonable that Tehanu could be addressing Ged, but the next line, "she *still* looked at the dragon and she spoke in the language of the dragons, the words of the Making" shows that Tehanu has been and still is addressing Kalessin/Segoy (*Tehanu* 249, emphasis added).

29. In *Tehanu* Tenar wonders aloud whether the problems in the world were not so much a result of Cob's spells as a symptom of problems afoot in the world because of Cob's influence (159–60).

30. For example, the sources used by Susan Cooper in *The Dark Is Rising* series work to communicate imperialistic ideologies that appear to be directly contradictory to the author's explicitly stated political ideals (Drout 234–38 and passim).

31. As Nodelman puts it: "in the first three Earthsea books [Le Guin] was merely taking for granted what her culture believed, and expressing it in metaphors her culture commonly used" (198).

32. Kuznets criticizes *The Tombs of Atuan* for depicting the "suppression" of a female cult (32). Though it is indeed true that many historical female cults are misrepresented in misogynistic reportage, in the case of the worship of the Nameless Ones the female cult is, in the context of the information Le Guin has provided, in fact evil. Kuznets is correct in noting that "Earth spirits" are generally recognized as female, but in *Tombs* they are given no gender and are not misrepresented as evil but are actually devouring, dark, and vicious (they desire the deaths of the innocent). The female world of the Place of the Tombs, one of "jealousies and miseries and wasted passions" (*Tombs* 83) that is based on hierarchy and on physical and partially sexualized punishment and domination, seems hardly the sort of community that feminists would support. We should also note that the women in the all-female community in Atuan are there not by choice but to serve the purposes of *men*, particularly the Godking in Awabath, whom they worship.

33. Alexei Kondratiev notes that *Tehanu* develops Le Guin's "feminist voice" in a way that had been evident in her more recent work but was lacking in the Earthsea trilogy (54).

34. Though Sandra J. Lindow's labeling Le Guin's apparent political change of heart as "moral *development*" is perhaps a bit judgmental (1, emphasis added).

35. See also Le Guin, *Dancing* 147–60.

36. John R. Pfeiffer had, in 1979, noted the implications of the Old Speech as both native tongue of dragons and creation language: "dragons are not only the users of the Old Speech, but also its makers . . . and the Old Speech creates the world. It must be that the dragons, then, create the world" (126).

37. Filmer argues that "there is no concept of 'winning' and 'losing' in Earthsea" (46), but, as demonstrated above, Ged defeats the shadow (although there could be some argument about this point). It is difficult to read, however, the scene at the dry spring as indicating "self-acceptance and harmony with the rhythms of the universe" (46). At the dry spring Ged defeats Cob against Cob's will—harmony and balance are restored to the universe by Ged's action of willful domination because Ged *forces* Cob to accept the harmony and balance of death and life.

38. See, e.g., Drout 243–45. A particularly virulent form of this fear of freedom and a mostly unquestioned and uncriticized impulse to extend authoritarian regimes of surveillance to nearly every aspect of a child's or adolescent's life has been visible in the mainstream media culture in the wake of the 1999 Columbine High School killings in Littleton, Colorado.

39. This view of Tehanu's aesthetic inferiority is shared by all members of the seminar in which the ideas of this paper were developed.

40. It is important to note that the quotations Hatfield analyzes are not direct comments on *Tehanu* (61 n. 1). Even if they were, an author is not always the best critic of his or her work.

41. If *Tehanu* is merely such a "reverse discourse," then it is a particularly ineffective one, since Le Guin could just as easily have completely rewritten the rules of magic to make them explicitly feminist and closer to a putative "Mother Tongue."

Works Cited

Algeo, John. "Magic Names: Onomastics in the Fantasies of Ursula Le Guin." *Names* 30.2 (1982): 59–67.

Alighieri, Dante. De Vulgari Eloquentia. *A Translation of the Latin Works of Dante Alighieri.* Trans. A. G. F. Howell. New York, Greenwood Press, 1969.

Atteberry, Brian. "On a Far Shore: The Myth of Earthsea." *Extrapolation* 21.3 (1980): 269–77.

Austin, J. L. *How to Do Things with Words.* Cambridge: Harvard University Press, 1962.

Barrow, Craig, and Diana Barrow. "Le Guin's Earthsea: Voyages in Consciousness." *Extrapolation* 32.1 (1991): 20–44.

Benson, Larry D., et al., eds. *The Riverside Chaucer.* 3d ed. Boston: Houghton Mifflin, 1987.

Bucknall, B. "Rilke and Le Guin." *Mythlore* 16.2 (1989): 62–65.

Bynum, Caroline Walker. *Fragmentation and Redemption: Essays on Gender and the Human Body in Medieval Religion.* New York: Zone Books, 1992.

Carpenter, Edward. *Intermediate Types Among Primitive Folk.* 1931. New York: Arno Press, 1975.

Crow, John H., and Richard D. Erlich. "Words of Binding: Patterns of Integration in the Earthsea Trilogy." In *Ursula K. Le Guin.* Ed. Joseph D. Olander and Martin Harry Greenberg. New York: Taplinger, 1979. Pp. 200–24.

Crowe, E. L. "Integration in Earthsea and Middle Earth." *San Jose Studies* 14.1 (1998): 63–80.

De Bolt, Joe, ed. *Ursula K. Le Guin: Voyager to Inner Lands and to Outer Space.* Port Washington, N.Y.: Kennikat Press, 1979.

Dooley, Patricia. "Magic and Art in Ursula Le Guin's Earthsea Trilogy." *Children's Literature* 8 (1980): 103–10.

Drout, Michael D. C. "Reading the Signs of Light: Anglo-Saxonism, Education, and Obedience in Susan Cooper's *The Dark Is Rising.*" *The Lion and the Unicorn* 21 (1997): 230–50.

Dunn, Margaret M. "The Dragon Is Not Dead: Le Guin's *Earthsea Trilogy.*" In *Forms of the Fantastic: Selected Essays from the Third International Conference on the Fantastic in Literature and Film.* Ed. Jan Hokenson and Howard Pearce. New York: Greenwood Press, 1986. Pp. 175–80. Vol. 20 of *Contributions to the Study of Science Fiction and Fantasy.*

———. "In Defense of Dragons: Imagination as Experience in the *Earthsea Trilogy.*" In *Proceedings of the Ninth Annual Conference of the Children's Literature Association.* Ed. Priscilla A. Ord. Boston: Children's Literature Association, 1983. Pp. 54–59.

Filmer, Kath. *Skepticism and Hope in Twentieth Century Fantasy Literature.* Bowling Green, Ohio: Bowling Green University Popular Press, 1992.

Galbreath, R. "Taoist Magic in the Earthsea Trilogy." *Extrapolation* 21.3 (1980): 262–68.

Harris, M. "The Psychology of Power in Tolkien's *The Lord of the Rings,* Orwell's *1984* and Le Guin's *A Wizard of Earthsea.*" *Mythlore* 15.1 (1988): 46–56.

Hatfield, Len. "From Master to Brother: Shifting the Balance of Authority in Ursula K. Le Guin's *Farthest Shore* and *Tehanu*." *Children's Literature* 21 (1993): 43–65.

Kondratiev, A. "Tales Newly Told: A Column on Current Fantasy." *Mythlore* 16.4 (1990): 54–55.

Kuznets, Lois R. " 'High Fantasy' in America: A Study of Lloyd Alexander, Ursula Le Guin, and Susan Cooper." *The Lion and the Unicorn* 9 (1985): 19–35.

Le Guin, Ursula K. *Dancing at the Edge of the World: Thoughts on Words, Women, and Places.* New York: Grove Press, 1997.

———. *Earthsea Revisioned.* Cambridge: Children's Literature New England, 1993.

———. *The Farthest Shore.* New York: Bantam Books, 1972.

———. *The Language of the Night.* Ed. Susan Wood. New York: HarperCollins, 1989.

———. *Tehanu: The Last Book of Earthsea.* New York: Bantam Books, 1990.

———. *The Tombs of Atuan.* New York: Bantam, 1970.

———. *A Wizard of Earthsea.* New York: Bantam Books, 1968.

Lindow, S. J. "Ursula K. Le Guin's Earthsea: Rescuing the Damaged Child." *New York Review of Science Fiction* 9.5 (1997): 1–10.

Littlefield, Holly. "Unlearning Patriarchy: Ursula Le Guin's Feminist Consciousness in *The Tombs of Atuan* and *Tehanu.* Extrapolation 36.3 (1995): 244–58.

Manlove, C. N. "Conservatism in the Fantasy of Le Guin." *Extrapolation* 21.3 (1980): 287–98.

Mills, A. "Burning Women in Ursula K. Le Guin's *Tehanu, the Last Book of Earthsea.*" *New York Review of Science Fiction* 7.1 (1995): 3–7.

Molson, Francis J. "The Earthsea Trilogy: Ethical Fantasy for Children." In *Ursula K. Le Guin: Voyager to Inner Lands and to Outer Space.* Ed. Joe de Bolt. Port Washington, N.Y.: Kennikat Press, 1979. Pp. 128–49.

Myers, Doris T. " 'True Speech' in the Fantasies of Tolkien and Le Guin." *Forum Linguisticum.* 7.1 (1982) 95–106.

Nodelman, Perry. "Reinventing the Past: Gender in Ursula K. Le Guin's *Tehanu* and the Earthsea 'Trilogy.' " *Children's Literature* 23 (1995): 179–201.

Pfeiffer, John R. " 'But Dragons Have Keen Ears': On Hearing 'Earthsea' with Recollections of 'Beowulf.' " In *Ursula K. Le Guin: Voyager to Inner Lands and to Outer Space.* Ed. Joe De Bolt. Port Washington, N.Y.: Kennikat Press, 1979. Pp. 115–27.

Pratt, Mary Louise. *Toward a Speech Act Theory of Literary Discourse.* Bloomington: Indiana University Press, 1977.

Saussure, Ferdinand de. "A Course in General Linguistics." In *The Structuralists from Marx to Levi-Strauss.* Ed. Richard DeGeorge and Fernande DeGeorge. New York: Doubleday, 1972. Pp. 59–79.

Searle, John R. *Mind, Language, and Society: Philosophy in the Real World.* New York: Basic Books, 1998.

Senior, W. A. "Cultural Anthropology and Rituals of Exchange in Ursula K. Le Guin's 'Earthsea.' " *Mosaic* 29.4 (1996).

Sherman, Cordelia. "The Princess and the Wizard: The Fantasy Worlds of Ursula K. Le Guin and George MacDonald." In *For the Childlike.* Ed. Roderick McGillis. Metuchen, N.J.: Children's Literature Association and Scarecrow Press, 1992. Pp. 195–205.

Shippey, Thomas A. "Magic Art and the Evolution of Words: Ursula Le Guin's Earthsea Trilogy." *Mosaic* 10.2 (winter 1977) 147–63.

Talbot, Norman. " 'Escape!': That Dirty Word in Modern Fantasy: Le Guin's Earthsea." In *Twentieth-Century Fantasists.* Ed. K. Filmer. New York: St. Martin's Press, 1992. Pp. 135–47.

Tolkien, J. R. R. "*Beowulf:* The Monsters and the Critics." In *Interpretations of* Beowulf. Ed. R. D. Fulk. Bloomington: University of Indiana Press, 1991. Pp. 14–44.

———. *The Letters of J. R. R. Tolkien.* Ed. Humphrey Carpenter and Christopher Tolkien. Boston: Houghton Mifflin, 1981.

————. "On Fairy-Stories." In *The Tolkien Reader*. New York: Ballantine Books, 1966. Pp. 25–84.

Walker, Jeanne Murray. "High Fantasy, Rites of Passage, and Cultural Values." In *Teaching Children's Literature: Issues, Pedagogy, Resources*. Ed. Glen Edward Sadler. New York: Modern Language Association, 1992. Pp. 109–20.

————. "Rites of Passage Today: The Cultural Significance of *A Wizard of Earthsea*." *Mosaic* 13.3–4 (1980): 179–91.

Weller, Barry. "Wizards, Warriors, and the Beast Glatisant in Love." In *Novel Gazing: Queer Readings in Fiction*. Ed. Eve Kosofsky Sedgwick. Durham, N.C.: Duke University Press, 1997. Pp. 227–48.

Wytenbroek, J. R. "Taoism in the Fantasies of Ursula K. Le Guin." In *The Shape of the Fantastic: Selected Essays from the Seventh International Conference on the Fantastic in the Arts*. Ed. Olena H. Saciuk. New York: Greenwood Press, 1990. Pp. 173–80. Vol. 39 of *Contributions to the Study of Science Fiction and Fantasy*. Ed. Marshall Tymn.

"Never overlook the art of the seemingly simple": Crockett Johnson and the Politics of the Purple Crayon

Philip Nel

When *Barnaby,* the first collection of Johnson's comic strip, was published in 1943, Dorothy Parker wrote, "I cannot write a review of Crockett Johnson's book of Barnaby. I have tried and tried, but it never comes out a book review. It is always a valentine for Mr. Johnson." That Parker, known for her caustic wit, could summon only praise explains in part why few have written about Johnson—indeed there is only one moderately extensive piece on him, running a mere eight pages in length.[1] His work tends to be optimistic, a fact that may frustrate critics, whose job is, after all, to be critical. They may also be daunted by the diversity of his creative output. To readers of children's literature, Crockett Johnson—the pen name of David Johnson Leisk—is best known for his seven books about Harold and the Purple Crayon. But Johnson, who was born in 1906 and died of lung cancer in 1975, wrote or illustrated twenty-four others and did much more besides. In the '30s, he wrote editorial cartoons for the *New Masses.* In the '40s, he contributed a comic strip to *Collier's Weekly* and wrote the syndicated "Barnaby" comic, which gained national attention in magazines such as *Time, Life,* and *Newsweek* as well as praise from as diverse a group as Parker, Duke Ellington, Louis Untermeyer, and W. C. Fields.[2] During his last decade, Johnson took up abstract painting, some of which was exhibited in museums.[3]

If any concept unifies his vast and diverse body of work, it is this: outwardly upbeat narratives and visually simple drawings investigate the ideological implications of the imagination. Johnson described his style of illustration as "simplified, almost diagrammatic, . . . avoiding all arbitrary decoration" (Kingman, Foster, and Lontoft 126) and, truly, simplicity defines his style to such a degree that, often, one character looks like the next: the boy from Ruth Krauss's *The Carrot Seed* (which Johnson illustrated) looks a lot like Harold, and both could be cousins of Barnaby (figure 1).[4] If this "simplified" style also explains the critical neglect of Johnson, then we should heed something

Children's Literature 29, ed. Elizabeth Lennox Keyser and Julie Pfeiffer (Yale University Press, © 2001 Hollins University).

Figure 1. The boy from *The Carrot Seed,* Barnaby, and Harold. *The Carrot Seed* (Harper, 1945): text copyright © 1945 by Ruth Krauss, illustrations copyright © 1945 by Crockett Johnson, copyright © renewed 1973 by Crockett Johnson. *Harold's Trip to the Sky* (Harper, 1957): copyright © 1957 by Crockett Johnson, copyright © renewed 1985 by Ruth Krauss. Both used by permission of HarperCollins Publishers. "Barnaby" is from Crockett Johnson's *Barnaby* (Holt, 1943), p. 47.

else Johnson said: "Never overlook the art of the seemingly simple" (quoted in *Animating Harold*).[5]

Following his advice, this essay examines the ideas that lie behind Johnson's "seemingly simple" artwork. To recover the politics of his books for children, I trace his social concerns—and his methods for addressing them—across his career, from the *New Masses* cartoons, through "Barnaby," up to the children's books about Harold, Ellen, and others. In the 1930s and 1940s, Johnson blurred the boundaries between imagined and material worlds to deliver particular arguments on specific political topics, but, in the 1950s and 1960s, he used this same device to advance a more general critique of societal structures of power. Using perceptual shifts to ask, *how do you know what's real?* Johnson invited his readers to raise larger questions about U.S. policy and society. For example, his emphasis on a socially constructed world challenged cultural stereotypes of gender. Suggesting that the "real world" is susceptible to the imagination, his works encourage the

"Aw, be a sport. Tell the newsreel audience you still have faith in the Lawd and good old Franklin D."   CROCKETT JOHNSON

Figure 2. Johnson, "Aw, be a sport. Tell the newsreel audience. . . ." From Robert Forsythe, *Redder than the Rose* (Covici, Friede, 1935), p. 232. First printed in *The New Masses* of 28 Aug. 1934, p. 7.

child's (and the adult's) impulses to explore alternatives to that world. And yet, though the imagination has power in Johnson's work, this power is not always cause for celebration: it can critique or reinforce the "real world"; it can both empower and threaten.

Johnson began exploring the line between real and imaginary during the 1930s, when he—then in his twenties—was writing editorial cartoons for the leftist newspaper *The New Masses:* one from August 1934 charges newsreels with distorting public reaction to Roosevelt's New Deal programs (figure 2). The director tells a starving family about to be filmed, "Aw, be a sport. Tell the newsreel audience you still have faith in the Lawd and good old Franklin D." When reprinted the following year in *Redder Than the Rose* (1935), a collection of *New Masses* columnist Robert Forsythe's essays, the cartoon accompanies "All Hectic Along the Potomac," an article that argues, "The capacity for illusion is endless and there are experts abounding on Pennsylvania Avenue to declare that all would be well if only Herbert Hoover were back, but neither Hoover, Roosevelt, nor the Great God Jehovah will cure the maladies of capitalism" (227). Johnson's cartoon suggests that newsreels promoted this "capacity for illusion," concealing public discontent by fostering the belief that even the most destitute still "have faith in the Lawd and good old Franklin D." Recalling photographs of sharecroppers by Walker Evans, Margaret Bourke-White, and Dorothea Lange, Johnson's drawing sympathetically depicts a starving family; unlike these photos, Johnson steps back, including the photographer—or filmmaker—in the frame. As Lange and Bourke-White do in other photographs,[6] Johnson displays an awareness of media's ability to manipulate the real world. This *New Masses* cartoon differs from *Harold* and *Ellen* in its specific message and its desire to enforce a clear boundary between imagined and material worlds, but resembles these books in its argument that imagined worlds can have real, and potentially harmful, effects.

Like the *New Masses* cartoons, the comic strip "Barnaby" often aims at a clearly defined target. "Barnaby," however, more closely resembles Johnson's children's books in its willingness to deliver its critique by effacing the line between "fictional" and "real" worlds. A precursor to Bill Watterson's "Calvin and Hobbes" strip,[7] "Barnaby" addresses "adult" topics through the adventures of a little boy, Barnaby, and an "imaginary" friend, Mr. O'Malley, Barnaby's cigar-champing fairy godfather. Like Hobbes, O'Malley is never (or rarely) seen interacting with adults; unlike Hobbes, O'Malley isn't imaginary—as Barnaby, his child friends, and the reader all know. In one memorable storyline, O'Malley becomes a Wall Street tycoon not through shrewd investing but because of the speculative nature of market economics. When a character that adults regard as imaginary uses purely imaginary assets to become a wealthy financier, Johnson blurs the boundary between "real" and imagined to make the troubling assertion that free-market capitalism is inherently precarious.

The episode, which ran from February through May 1945, begins when O'Malley phones stockbrokers to ask about purchasing 51% of Hunos-Wattall, Ltd., but unknowingly talks only to an office boy. The office boy thinks O'Malley is a "bigshot" and word gets out that the "international financier" O'Malley is starting a new company ("Barnaby," 21 Feb. 1945). Since no one wants to admit to never having heard of him, a financial newsletter reports that "J.J. O'Malley plans a big postwar industrial expansion program," and, without even meeting Barnaby's fairy godfather, financiers back his company, real people

Figure 3. Johnson, "Barnaby" from *PM* of 23 Feb. 1945.

begin running it, and the stock of O'Malley Enterprises soars (23 Feb. 1945). (See figure 3.) But speculation becomes the company's undoing, too.

When O'Malley offers to pay tailors Cuttaway and Sons *in cash* for his trousers, they're insulted that he's not charging it to his account (24 April 1945). Word spreads that his credit is no longer good, and the stock of O'Malley Enterprises plummets, bringing down the company with it (25 April 1945). Given that the strip ran only a few years after the Great Depression "officially" ended, when many worried that the end of World War II might also end wartime prosperity, this "Barnaby" episode made a very serious point: it highlighted structural flaws in the market system when people very much needed to believe in that system. As O'Malley says about two weeks prior to O'Malley Enterprises' collapse, "I'll admit, Barnaby, at times I nourish misgivings about the entire venture" (9 April 1945). (See figure 4.) His (accurate) misgivings offer troubling predictions for the postwar economy: O'Malley Enterprises, which is supposed to be converting wartime industries to peacetime ones, turns out to be all hype and no substance —an imaginary business, based on imaginary capital, run by a Pixie only children see.

With the exception of the illustrations for Constance Foster's *This Rich World: The Story of Money* (1943),[8] Johnson's children's books never directly satirize capitalism, but they do—like the *New Masses* cartoon and this "Barnaby" episode—often depict a reality in flux, a place always subject to change without notice. Put another way, the world of "Barnaby" and the *New Masses* enters the world of Harold and Ellen not through economics but through a similar conception of power. Like O'Malley Enterprises, Harold's purple-crayon universe hangs together by dint of chance and imagination; for Harold, as for O'Malley, there is both possibility and peril in this "fact."

Figure 4. Johnson, "Barnaby" from *PM* of 9 April 1945.

In *Harold and the Purple Crayon* (1955), when Harold draws a "frightening dragon" that "even frightened Harold," his "hand holding the purple crayon shook," creating the wavy surface of the sea. Harold backs into it, and soon he is "over his head in an ocean." This scene represents a genuine threat; but, saved by his ability to adapt, Harold "came up thinking fast," and draws himself a "trim little boat," into which he promptly climbs. In the same book, when Harold draws a mountain to help him see his bedroom window, he climbs to the top and slips: "And there wasn't any other side of the mountain. He was falling, in thin air." Here, too, Harold finds himself at the mercy of forces he cannot control. Again, his skill at responding to an ever-changing situation saves him: "But, luckily, he kept his wits and his purple crayon. He made a balloon and grabbed on to it. And he made a basket under the balloon big enough to stand in" (figure 5). And off he goes once again. There are many such scenes in the *Purple Crayon* books: Harold on an out-of-control flying carpet, Harold falling from a tightrope, Harold in a lion's cage, Harold encountering a "thing" in a "flying saucer." In each, Harold experiences a power dynamic that shifts arbitrarily and, in each, Harold adapts.

In scenes such as these, Johnson presents situations—with the possible exception of the flying saucer (which will be discussed in the following section)—that may not have clear political referents but that do have political implications. Each depicts circumstances over which a child has little control and, for children, subjection to the power of others is a condition of being. Johnson's work registers this fact and provides a way for the child to respond: Harold's adventures suggest that embracing eclecticism and improvisation is one way to survive in a precarious—and even pernicious—power dynamic. Significantly, psychologists who study resiliency in children have shown that these very factors—the ability to improvise, to respond creatively—can help

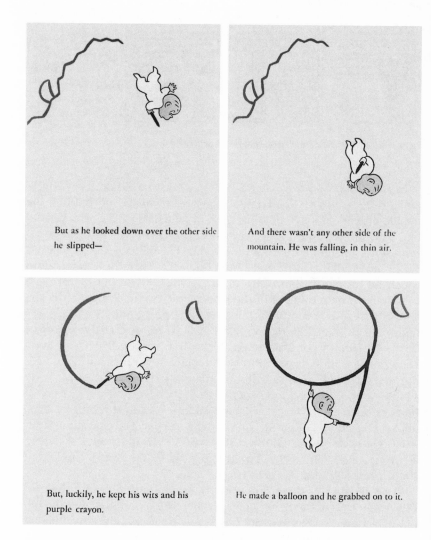

Figure 5. Johnson, from *Harold and the Purple Crayon* (Harper, 1955), pp. 40–43. Copyright © 1955 by Crockett Johnson, copyright © renewed 1983 by Ruth Krauss. Used by permission of HarperCollins Publishers.

Figure 6. Johnson, "Mr. Hearst says he'll buy your farm articles if. . . ." from *The New Masses* of 28 May 1935, p. 26.

a child to overcome adverse circumstances. As Luthar and Zigler's review of resiliency research (1991) indicates, children with a sense of humor, "effective problem-solving skills," and "high faith in their control over their environment" tend to be more resilient, better able to bounce back (15).[9] Johnson's work appears to agree, and offers an enabling strategy for children in an uncertain world.

To encourage both child and adult readers to be more critically aware of that world, Johnson deploys shifts in perspective that rearrange what a reader or character had thought to be true. Though he uses this device both with and without political referents, this section focuses more on the former—in particular, his critique of anti-Communist paranoia. Let us begin with two early examples of this technique, one that takes on anti-Communists and one that does not. A criticism of the Hearst International News Service appears in a cartoon from the *New Masses* of May 28, 1935 (figure 6). In the illustration, a secretary from Hearst's International News Service hands an article

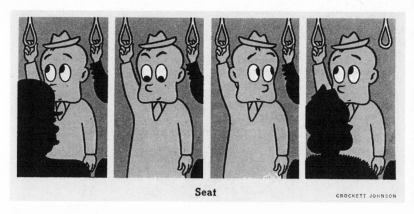

Figure 7. Johnson, "Seat." From *Collier's* of 18 July 1942, p. 56.

back to its writer. She says, "Mr. Hearst says he'll buy your farm articles if you'll just change 'Arkansas,' 'Louisiana,' 'California' and so on, to Soviet Russia." In addition to reminding the reader that the values of a publisher shape which "news" gets reported, the cartoon shows how a minor textual difference reveals a major ideological one.

Though it rarely refers to specific political events, Johnson's "The Little Man with the Eyes" cartoon (which ran in *Collier's* from 1940 to 1943) also relies on subtle shifts in perspective to deliver its joke: in four or five panels, the frame of each panel remains static, using movement within that frame to tell the story (figure 7). In "Seat," the reader must notice that the male silhouette in the first panel has been replaced by a female silhouette in the final one, and that the arm next to the little man's head is absent from the final one: only then can we understand that the little man's glance, first toward the seat and then to the face beyond the arm, indicates his wish for the lady to have the seat. Since, in all of these strips, the little man "speaks" only with his eyes and never in words, subtle visual changes convey all of the meaning. Though the *New Masses* cartoon emphasizes media power, and the "Little Man" cartoon emphasizes narrative power, the power itself rests in the ability of minor changes in text or illustration to effect major changes in meaning.

Falling midway between the blunt criticism of his *New Masses* work and the apolitical charm of "The Little Man with the Eyes" are the "O'Malley Committee" episode (1943) from "Barnaby" and children's

books such as *Harold's Trip to the Sky* (1957) and *Who's Upside Down?*
(1952). These works deploy perceptual power as a critical tool, but
they use it with greater nuance than the *New Masses* cartoons and with
greater purpose than "The Little Man." Prior to his Wall Street adventures but after his election in November 1943, Representative O'Malley forms the O'Malley Committee, Johnson's deft mockery of the Dies
Committee. Five years earlier, Martin Dies, Democratic Congressman
from Texas (1931–1945 and 1953–1959), had established and become
chair of the House Un-American Activities Committee, investigating
both real and imagined threats to America's national security. Like
the Un-American Activities Committee of the 1950s, the "Dies Committee" (as it was known during his tenure) made charges sometimes
founded on solid evidence but often based on hearsay, circumstance,
or anti-Communist zeal. For example, on June 23, 1942, Dies accused
the Union for Democratic Action of being a front for Communist
organizations seeking to "discredit" and "obliterate" Congress (Lapica
197). On the following day, a member of the Dies Committee dis-
sented, charging the committee with "name-calling" and noting that
people have the right to disagree with the committee "without being
branded as subversive and un-American" (203). A political cartoon by
Dr. Seuss—which, like Crockett Johnson's "Barnaby," ran in the newspaper *PM*—depicted Dies's prosecutorial zeal as misguided, excessive,
and ridiculous.[10] Seuss's drawing of June 28 shows Dies as a wild cowboy in pursuit of a tiny bird, calling for Uncle Sam's help: "After, him,
Sam! It's a Robin RED-Breast!"

In the summer of 1943, Dies's zeal caused John Bovingdon, a
Harvard-educated economist, to be fired from the Office of Economic
Warfare, a story that made the front page of the *New York Times* on August 5.[11] One might think that his ability to speak French, German,
Japanese, Russian, and Spanish would be an asset, but these skills,
coupled with Bovingdon's hobby of "rhythmic gymnastics," led Dies
to see the economist as a security risk: though Bovingdon was not
a ballet dancer, Dies pronounced, "this is no time for the appointment of ballet dancers to fill positions which require the best of brains
and ability from our people" ("Bovingdon" 36; "Gymnast" 21). If a
Harvard-educated economist can be investigated and fired, then why
not Santa Claus? In November 1943, the O'Malley Committee—consisting of Barnaby, Jane, O'Malley, and Gus the Ghost—decides to investigate St. Nick, whom O'Malley denounces as "a hoax perpetrated
on kiddies!" ("Barnaby," 25 Nov. 1943). Echoing Martin Dies's hyper-

Figure 8. Johnson, "Barnaby" from *PM* of 25 Nov. 1943.

bole, O'Malley proclaims, "The O'Malley Committee seeks merely to learn the truth about Santa Claus. . . . Is he a myth masquerading as a man? . . . Or vice versa? . . . [M]y unbiased committee will find out whether this Claus is a rogue taking fraudulent credit for the Christmas benevolence you children enjoy, or whether he IS to blame for this practice which spoils and softens up our youth." When Barnaby begins to speculate on how the investigation might hurt Santa Claus, O'Malley interrupts, "Barnaby! We mustn't prejudge things. This investigation is to be conducted in a fair and impartial manner" (30 Nov. 1943). Since both of O'Malley's options fault Santa Claus for something—falsely taking credit for "Christmas benevolence" or softening up youth—this final claim of impartiality underscores Johnson's satire.

As the strip from November 25 illustrates, the O'Malley Committee also toys with our perceptions by setting up several imaginary levels, one on top of the next (figure 8). On one level, an imaginary pixie investigates a myth: that is, though we know O'Malley is real, Barnaby's parents (and all adults) almost never actually see his fairy godfather and so consider O'Malley a myth. On another level, the strip inverts our expectations of who believes in Santa Claus. In "Barnaby," adults want their children to believe in Santa Claus, but the children know better, feigning belief only to humor their parents.[12] After O'Malley says he'll find some "clever pretext for you and your mothers to visit the toy section of the department store," Barnaby explains that there's no need: "We'd have gone to see Santa Claus anyway. . . . We wouldn't spoil all our mothers' fun" (5 Dec. 1943). So, when an "imaginary" pixie's committee accuses an "imaginary" man of fraud, Johnson implies not only that the Dies Committee cannot distinguish imagined enemies from real ones but that others are susceptible to believing in fictions, too.

In the O'Malley Committee episode and the *New Masses* cartoons, there's a clear political import to Johnson's art, but what about in his children's books? Though no book of Johnson's is as blunt in its social criticism as Dr. Seuss's *The Butter Battle Book* (1984) or *The Sneetches* (1961), his work does speak to the sociopolitical circumstances of its production. Consider, for example, *Harold's Trip to the Sky* (1957) and its version of rocket science. In *Trip to the Sky*'s opening pages, Harold "remembered how the government has fun on the desert. It shoots off rockets. Harold decided to go to the moon. On a good fast rocket, he figured he could get there and back in time for breakfast." Unfortunately, Harold overshoots the moon, lands on Mars, and meets an alien "thing." As Barbara Bader points out, *Harold's Trip to the Sky* dramatizes "night fears" as "fears of the Fifties": "To Jung and others," she says, "the widespread sighting of UFO's at the time stemmed from fear of nuclear destruction, and the whole of *Harold's Trip to the Sky* can be seen as an expression of [these] anxieties, absorbed and transformed" (437). But the book does more than transform such anxieties, because Harold takes an active role in responding to them—and his responses empower both him and the narrative. If we accept the reading of the "thing" in the space ship as representative of a nuclear anxiety, then we should note that Harold both calls it into being and disables it from acting on himself or others. He draws it and returns to destroy it, putting "a completely damaging crack in the flying saucer." Suggesting, accurately, that fears of the '50s were both real and imagined (justified fear of the Soviets' H-bomb and unjustified anti-Communist hysteria, for example), Johnson gives the child a way of productively encountering these fears and, through the imagination, counteracting them.

In addition to providing the child with a sense of agency, the book's shifting perspectives suggest that the "facts" of the world are neither absolute nor fixed, but subject to revision. If, to paraphrase Roland Barthes, ideology is opinion or belief naturalized as truth, then the *Harold* books show that what appears to be natural may in fact be a social construct. The books do not suggest that all problems are imaginary, but rather point to the role that perception plays in shaping them. For example, later in the book, Harold thinks he sees a flying saucer when, in fact, "He was mistaken. It wasn't a saucer. It was an oatmeal bowl" (figure 9). Like the alien in the space ship or Harold falling off of a mountain (in the first *Harold* story), this scene presents a serious problem. But these books suggest that few problems are insurmountable. Harold ultimately finds inspiration in the vagaries of

But, for a startled moment, he thought he saw a flying saucer. It was on the horizon, looking as if it had just come into land.

He was mistaken. It wasn't a saucer. It was an oatmeal bowl.

Figure 9. Johnson, from *Harold's Trip to the Sky* (Harper, 1957), pp. 58–59. Copyright © 1957 by Crockett Johnson, copyright © renewed 1985 by Ruth Krauss. Used by permission of HarperCollins Publishers.

his world; he uses the flexibility of his imagination to conquer what he must, and to succeed.

Like the *Harold* books, *Who's Upside Down?* (1952) presents strong examples of ideologically—and illogically—influenced perception and offers ways to overcome its effects. Unlike *Harold's Trip to the Sky*, however, *Who's Upside Down?* lacks an overt reference to events of the early '50s. But, as Jerome McGann has pointed out in another context, the effect of a work of literature "is profoundly related . . . to the reader or viewer's sense of history" (459).[13] So, if we consider Johnson's book in light of anti-Communist witch-hunts, loyalty oaths, and the anti-Soviet paranoia coursing through America in the early '50s, then *Who's Upside Down?* is more than a parable of perception. A kangaroo picks up a geography book and sees herself in Australia, on the bottom of the globe.[14] She had been "feeling on top of the world until she saw herself in the picture." Now, she exclaims, "I'm down underneath! And upside down!" Johnson's narrative continues,

> She couldn't really believe it at first. She looked again. Then she slowly said:
> "It certainly seems to be so!"

When a thing *seems* to be so, kangaroos usually hop to the conclusion that it *is* so. She believed she was upside down.
And once she really believed it, she began to feel upside down.

She spends most of the book believing herself to be upside down
and growing increasingly distressed about this "fact." Although the
book contains no specific reference to McCarthyism, if we read *Who's
Upside Down?* in this context, then the kangaroo's thought processes
resemble those of a paranoid person: "When a thing *seems* to be so,"
the kangaroo "hop[s] to the conclusion that it *is* so." The book, of
course, argues against hopping to such conclusions based on scant evidence; immediately after this moment and in a tone reminiscent of
A. A. Milne, Johnson explains that "animals who have their feet on the
ground any place in the world are not upside down, no matter how
they seem to be in this picture. And it is ridiculous for them to feel
upside down. Quite ridiculous." Allowing us to see how right-side-up
can seem to be upside down, Johnson's kangaroo dramatizes the logic
of paranoia.

Fortunately, the kangaroo's child offers a different perspective. In
response to his mother's tearful complaint that "Everything around
here is upside down!" the little kangaroo replies, "Everything? . . .
Then the book is upside down too, isn't it?" He turns the book around
and the kangaroos' self-perceptions do a 180-degree turnaround—literally. As in *Harold's Trip to the Sky*, a child's agile mind solves the problem. Johnson may hope that the imaginative flexibility of children
will serve as a necessary corrective to their parents, but he does not
idealize the child.[15] Instead, he credits characters like Harold and the
little kangaroo with the resourcefulness and the mental dexterity to
face their problems. If a flexible worldview makes success more likely,
Johnson's child characters maintain this flexibility because they have
not yet learned all the rules of behavior. In Foucauldian terms, Johnson's books present children who, having not yet fully absorbed the
structures of society, sustain a cognitive agility often lost in adulthood.
As *Who's Upside Down?* and *Harold's Trip to the Sky* illustrate, what appears
to be a fixed reality may—to a child—appear as a perceptual difference.

These books' lessons in perception apply not only to Cold War para-
noia but also to gender, a subject that emerges most prominently in
"Barnaby," *Ellen's Lion* (1959), and the *Harold* books (1955–63). Neither
Jane nor Harold seems confined by socially prescribed roles of mascu-

linity and femininity, and Ellen is most flexible of all, moving with ease between stereotypically masculine and feminine roles. Though Johnson's work is never actively sexist, his interest in gender may have been influenced by his relationship with Ruth Krauss, whom he married in 1939. Starting in the 1940s, Johnson began to register Americans' growing awareness (especially among women) in the years between Simone de Beauvoir's *Second Sex* (1949; English translation, 1953) and Betty Friedan's *Feminine Mystique* (1963) that women's reputedly biological need to find fulfillment solely in motherhood and family stood in conflict with a sense that this model of femininity was not enough. As Friedan wrote, though American women "*learned* that truly feminine women do not want careers, higher education, political rights" (16, emphasis added), many found that they could not "accept this role gracefully" (24). Krauss, author of classics such as *The Carrot Seed* (1945) and *A Hole Is to Dig* (1952), understood that children's books play a role in teaching girls and boys to adopt gender-specific behaviors. During the composition of *A Hole Is to Dig*, she accused Maurice Sendak of reinforcing gender-based stereotypes in his illustrations: "boys doing boy things, and girls (even worse!) doing girl things. 'God forbid, a boy should jump rope!'" he recalls her shouting ("Ruth Krauss and Me" 288).[16]

Whether influenced by Krauss or not, Johnson's work often depicts gender as a socially enforced construct that is therefore subject to revision. In drawings for children and for adults Johnson offers nontraditional depictions of women working in the home and advocates equal rights for female industrial workers. His illustrations for Margaret Wise Brown's *Willie's Adventures* (1954), for instance, show Willie's Grandmama with a hammer in her hand, constructing a wooden box (9). In that same book, Johnson twice pictures Willie's mother using tools: she uses a claw hammer to open a wooden box, and, with nail in mouth and hammer in hand, she constructs a fence for Willie's animal (19, 23). (See figure 10.) Though both of these illustrations directly challenge the idea that only men use tools, Johnson generally relies on two ways of depicting gender as a learned behavior—by emphasizing imaginative role-playing or by using a shift in perception to undermine a reader's stereotypes. The most striking example of the latter technique occurs in *Sister, you need the Union! . . .* And the Union Needs You!—a pamphlet Johnson illustrated for the International Union of United Automobile, Aircraft, and Agricultural Implement Workers of America. Published during World War II, the text

Figure 10. Johnson, illustration from Margaret Wise Brown's *Willie's Adventures* (William R. Scott, 1954), p. 23.

suggests that, where women are "organized into strong unions," they will have the power to address unequal pay, create better working conditions, and make a better postwar world. To drive home this point, Johnson depicts "THE GOOD OLD DAYS" as an angry foreman intimidating a child-sized woman; in contrast, beneath the heading "IT'S UP TO YOU," a woman holding a "United Auto Workers" sign towers over a child-sized foreman, demanding her rights (figure 11).

The pamphlet deploys perceptual shifts to illustrate the power of unionized women, and "Barnaby" uses the same technique to reveal apparently natural gender roles as socially constructed. In a comic from January 1943, when Barnaby and Mr. O'Malley describe their elaborate plans to enter the dangerous haunted house, Jane nonchalantly reveals that she has already been there (figure 12). "That old house up the road?" she asks. "The front door's stuck but I can get in a back window. Come on. I'll show you" ("Barnaby," 21 Jan. 1943).

Figure 11. Johnson, 2 illustrations from *Sister, you need the Union!* . . . <u>And the Union Needs You!</u> (UAW-CIO pamphlet, c. 1944).

Jane's remark not only illustrates that little girls being more timid or less practical than little boys is merely an expectation, but also challenges the reader by preparing him or her to anticipate the opposite response, withholding Jane's point of view until the final panel. O'Malley describes his "mission" to enter the "haunted house" as "fraught with danger," Barnaby reinforces this sense of risk, and one expects Jane to be as fearful. When she instead responds by matter-of-factly offering advice on how to enter the house, Jane proves more brave and powerful than her male friends.[17]

As Jane illustrates how girls can be brave, Harold shows that boys can be thoughtful. If, as Michael Kimmel has argued, traditional masculinity requires risk-taking, emotional reserve, and "devaluation of the feminine," then Harold is pleasantly unfettered by such "rules of masculinity" (261). In contrast to Max of Sendak's *Where the Wild Things Are* (1963) or Peter T. Hooper of Dr. Seuss's *Scrambled Eggs Super!* (1953), Harold is frequently thoughtful and expresses concern for others. Max sails off to the land of the wild things, romping recklessly with them, and Peter never considers the consequences of his quest for exotic eggs—Ali gets "jabbed" and "stabbed" by the "big pals" of the Mt. Strookoo Cuckoos, and the men who pry off a mountain top to get a Dawf's egg seem in danger of falling to their deaths. Though Harold's adventures, too, often involve risk-taking, Harold is careful to make sure that his actions do not cause harm. In *A Picture for Harold's Room* (1960), for example, he needs "rocks to step on" to climb "out of the sea and onto the hill" (26–27). But, immediately realizing that "the ship was too near the rocks," Harold "put up a lighthouse to warn

Figure 12. Johnson, "Barnaby" from *PM* of 21 Jan. 1943.

the sailors" (28–29). Likewise, in *Harold and the Purple Crayon* (1955), Harold "left a very hungry moose and a deserving porcupine" to finish the leftover pie; in *Harold's Trip to the Sky* (1957), he worries that the alien "thing" he's created "was about to fly to earth and scare somebody, maybe some little child" and so returns to damage the thing's flying saucer; and when, in *Harold at the North Pole* (1958), he draws a snowman who "didn't look cheerful" in the snowstorm (as Harold expected), Harold draws him "a muffler to wear."

Harold is not the sole thoughtful little boy in children's books of this period: one suspects that Ezra Jack Keats's Peter of *The Snowy Day* (1962) and Willie of *A Whistle for Willie* (1964) would get along quite well with Harold. As the behaviors of Harold and Ellen show, however, Johnson's characters do stand in marked contrast to those in many contemporary works. Dare Wright's *The Lonely Doll* (1957), reviewed on the same page of the *New York Times Book Review* as *Harold's Trip to the Sky,* features, in the words of the reviewer, a "patriarchal Mr. Bear" who chastises the little doll Edith for her imaginative role-playing (Buell 51). Contrary to Edith's experience, both Harold and Ellen enjoy a childhood in which little boys and little girls can be both nurturing and brave, gender is flexible, and multiple roles are possible.

What Harold achieves with his purple crayon, Ellen does with words and props—she imagines for herself a role as changeable as the malleable universe she creates. In contrast to Marcia Brown's *Cinderella* (1954) and John Langstaff's *Frog Went A-Courtin'* (1955),[18] the "Fairy Tale" episode from *Ellen's Lion* (1959) challenges the stereotypes found in fairy tales, approaching them more through the performance of identity than through the perceptual shifts found in "Barnaby." In *Gender Trouble* (1990), Judith Butler writes that "drag . . . mocks the

Figure 13. Johnson, first illustration in "Fairy Tale" from *Ellen's Lion* (Harper, 1959; repr. by Godine, 1984), p. 49. Reprinted courtesy of the Estate of Ruth Krauss.

notion of a true gender identity" by "displac[ing] the entire act of gender significations from the discourse of truth and falsity" (192). Although Ellen is not literally in drag, her role-playing allows her to change identities as easily as if she were changing clothes (figure 13). When "Fairy Tale" begins, Ellen is the "fairy godmother"; a few paragraphs later, she has become "the invincible knight"; near the end of the story, she turns into "the lovely princess"; and, finally, she becomes Ellen once again. Ellen's ability to shift effortlessly between masculine and feminine roles suggests that gender does not organize, guide, or limit her perception of the world. Unlike Brown's Cinderella, who seems confined by gender stereotypes, for Ellen, identity is portable, and gender is a mask that can be manipulated.

Johnson emphasizes the flexibility of Ellen's role-playing by giving the *Ellen* books a narrator whose subject position seems deliberately ambiguous. For example, "Fairy Tale" begins like this: "Once, twice, and thrice the beautiful fairy waved her wand and, before she spoke, she took another bite of muffin covered with raspberry jam" (48). In a single sentence, the narrator both inhabits and moves away from the structures of a fairy tale. The narrative voice first aligns itself with the point of view of a fairy tale (as reimagined by Ellen), then moves to an ironic distance to remind us that we are watching Ellen eat a muffin. In that same story, Johnson describes "the knight . . . , eating jam and muffin as she surveyed the besieging army across the wide moat" (50). Here, Ellen's narrator steps back to remind us that this is but a fairy tale, and then returns to narrate from the perspective of the fairy tale. In so doing, Johnson's work suggests not only that gender exists in the *roles* that a person inhabits but also that these "traditional" stories themselves can be transformed. As later work such as Anne Sexton's *Transformations* (1971), Angela Carter's *The Bloody Chamber* (1979), the many tales collected in Jack Zipes's *Don't Bet on the Prince* (1986), Scieszka and Johnson's *The Frog Prince, Continued* (1991), and Chris Van Allsburg's *The Widow's Broom* (1992) all do, Johnson's "Fairy Tale" episode revises and challenges the gendered assumptions of the better-known versions.

But more than these tales, Johnson's *Ellen* books value a girl's imagination when many (though not all) of his contemporaries do not. In Russell Hoban's *Bedtime for Frances* (1960), Father uses the threat of "a spanking" to silence Frances's unruly imagination; in Dr. Seuss's "The Glunk that Got Thunk" (from *I Can Lick 30 Tigers Today! and Other Stories*, 1969), little sister's imagination creates a dangerous Glunk that her brother must help her banish; and, in Laura Bannon's *Big Brother* (1950), Dick receives praise for his creativity and resourcefulness, but his little sister Sally has no imagination whatsoever. By contrast, at the center of each *Ellen* tale is a young girl's inventive mind. With her lion, Ellen climbs a mountain, becomes a doctor, and paints a picture; she and her lion also have more "everyday" adventures such as getting a drink of water at night or deciding who should take the blame after their space capsule (actually Ellen's tricycle) crashes into a table and breaks an ashtray. Though her creativity does sometimes lead to trouble, the stories emphasize imaginative play and not the negative consequences of little girls' imaginations (as Seuss's and Hoban's stories do). The *Ellen* books are not the only ones to portray a curious, active female character in a positive light, of course—Ludwig Bemelmans's *Madeline* series (1939–61), James Thurber's *Many Moons* (1943), Kay Thompson's *Eloise* (1955), and Robert McCloskey's *Time of Wonder* (1957)[19] all do—but, in their representations of gender, *Ellen's Lion* and *The Lion's Own Story* (1963) do locate Johnson among the more progressive children's book writers and illustrators of his day.

Crediting children with understanding and resourcefulness, Johnson encourages his readers to seek power in a creative response to their environment—a philosophy embodied by characters such as Ellen and Harold. Aware that fears that may be imaginary to adults can be very real to children,[20] Johnson creates in Ellen a character resourceful enough to respond to them. Indeed, *Ellen's Lion* and its sequel *The Lion's Own Story,* reportedly Johnson's personal favorites (Hopkins 123), are also two of his most interesting works in terms of their willingness to take seriously the mind of a child. In the story "Two Pairs of Eyes" from *Ellen's Lion,* Ellen enlists her lion's assistance in getting a drink of water at night—with him watching her back, she'll have "two pairs of eyes," she reasons (21). When he points out that his eyes are only "buttons," so he therefore "can't see very well in the dark," she replies:

> "Nobody can. . . . But the things don't know that."
> "How do you know they don't know?" said the lion.
> "I know all about them," said Ellen. "After all, I made them up in my head, didn't I?"
> "Ah," said the lion. "I said there were no such things."
> "But of course there are," Ellen said. "I just told you I made them up myself." (21–22)

Like Sendak's *Where the Wild Things Are* or Dr. Seuss's short story "What Was I Scared Of?" (1961, included in *The Sneetches and Other Stories*) in its approach to the imagination in general, *Ellen's Lion* knows that her imagined fears are serious and unavoidable. And, as Sendak and Seuss do, Crockett Johnson provides a way out. But, unlike Seuss in "Glunk," Johnson authorizes a little girl's imagination as a way to respond to these fears.

Ellen's Lion not only takes the imagination seriously but compels readers to do so, too. By means of an ambiguous subject position, both it and *The Lion's Own Story* interpellate the reader into the role of an active reader. For example, the very role of the lion keeps the reader guessing. Although the lion's status as stuffed animal is never in question, his ability to think independently varies: the lion appears both to be animated only by Ellen's imagination and to act independently of Ellen. In the first story of *Ellen's Lion*, "Conversation and Song," the lion's voice clearly is Ellen's because, when they sing a song, only one can sing at a time (9). Yet in "Afternoon Nap," from *The Lion's Own Story*, the lion becomes a kind of parent figure, advising Ellen to take her nap when she would rather play. Indeed, he often argues with Ellen, suggesting an existence independent of her. But in "Somebody to Blame" from *The Lion's Own Story*, the lion does not play the role of the adult, instead offering himself as a willing accomplice, ready to take the blame for her tricycle accident in the living room. By leaving open the question of the lion's reality (or fantasy), the book compels the reader to consider the possibilities that reside in this lack of distinction.

Encouraging an active reader is ultimately Johnson's goal. If the *Ellen* books rely on ambiguity to inspire active engagement with the world, both *Merry Go Round* and the *Harold* books involve the reader by suggesting that the books' action can continue after the last page. Designed and marketed as "A Story that Doesn't End,"[21] the twelve-page book *Merry Go Round* encourages participation in its deliberately circular structure. Its spiral binding allows the reader to keep turning the pages, and the almost punctuation-free text promotes continued reading because, like Joyce's *Finnegans Wake*, *Merry Go Round*'s last page—"ON HE RODE, PAST THE YELLOW SIGN, AND ON"—leads directly to the first page (also the book's cover), which has the words "AND ROUND AND ROUND AND ROUND AND ROUND" where Johnson's name normally would be (figure 14). Visually, too, the book keeps the reader's attention focused on the motion of the boy turning, around and around. It is as if a camera were attached at center of the ride, its lens fixed on the boy: with each turn of the page, he remains at the center, but the background shifts, recording his motion. Beneath the pictures, in all capitals, with minimal punctuation, the text proceeds, each page offering a line of almost exactly the same length:

> PAST THE GLASS HOUSE WITH FLOWERS IN IT
> PAST THE STATUE OF A HORSE AND A GENERAL
> PAST HIS MOTHER AND FATHER, WHO WAITED
> "ISN'T IT EVER GOING TO STOP?" THEY SIGHED

Like the sentence, the ride never ends, and the boy (referred to only as "he") turns around for as long as the reader keeps turning the pages.

Figure 14. Johnson, last page and cover of *Merry Go Round* (Harper, 1958). Reprinted courtesy of the Estate of Ruth Krauss.

The *Harold* books involve the reader beyond the final pages, but they do so by offering a nearly blank white page on which to draw. Many reviewers have given voice to the notion that, just as Harold draws in the white spaces, so might a child be encouraged to follow his example. In the *New York Times Book Review* in 1955, Ellen Lewis Buell wrote that *Harold and the Purple Crayon* "will probably start young-sters off on odysseys of their own" (34). In *The Horn Book* that same year, Virginia Haviland noted that *Harold*'s illustrations will "stimulate the imagination" and "suggest similar drawing adventures" (362–63). More recently, Deborah Solomon, biographer of Jackson Pollock and Joseph Cornell, named *Harold and the Purple Crayon* as the art book she recommends most for children because it suggests that "one well-worn, stubby crayon could allow you to dream up a whole universe. Which of course it can. There's no better art lesson than that" (25).

The *Harold* books' notion that what we imagine can become real is a powerful idea—for both good and ill—because it shows how theory can become practice, ideology can become fact, and nothing can be-come something. Though they may at first seem far removed from his children's books, Johnson's mathematically based paintings of the 1960s and 1970s emphasize the benefits of this idea most clearly. For example, his painting *Squared Circle* (1969, figure 15) offers a visual

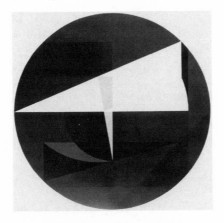

Figure 15. Johnson, *Squared Circle*. 48" × 48". 1969.

representation of his theorem "A geometrical look at $\sqrt{\pi}$," published in the *Mathematical Gazette* the following year.[22] Just as Harold uses a purple crayon to transform his ideas into realities, so Johnson's theorem embodies the notion of giving literal form to an abstract idea, such as a number or a mathematical constant. Indeed, Johnson devoted the last ten years of his life to these paintings because he enjoyed geometry's power to translate concepts from (what to him were) cloudy algebra onto a clear, visual plane. As Johnson writes in his essay "On the Mathematics of Geometry in My Abstract Paintings" (1972), "algebra . . . tends to make me lose a graphic grasp of a picture. Instead, as I did in approaching the problem of the squared circle, I played with what I knew in advance to be the elements of the problem, imagining them as a construction in motion, an animated film sequence with an infinite number of frames running back and forth between plus and minus limits across the point of solution" (99). For Johnson, then, geometry is a form of animation: as Gene Deitch's films of *A Picture for Harold's Room* and *Harold's Fairy Tale* turn Johnson's books into animated cartoons, these geometric paintings turn algebraic hypotheses into motion pictures. The painting of the square root of π, as Johnson explains, "is conceived as a construction 'moving' back and forth between close plus and minus limits across the point describing the solution" (98). In their power to make the abstract into something concrete, Johnson's artwork and his *Harold* stories echo William Carlos Williams's dictum from "A Sort of Song"

(1944): "(No ideas / but in things) Invent!" (145). In this oft-repeated line, the doctor-turned-poet affirms the illustrator-turned-mathematician's desire to literalize experience.[23]

As Williams's imagist poetry asks the reader to bring a lot to the reading process, so the clarity of Johnson's (and Harold's) line drawings presents a kind of tabula rasa onto which the reader may project his or her ideas. I noted earlier that Johnson's minimalist style gives us characters who are visually interchangeable. Harold, the boy from *The Carrot Seed,* the boy from *Merry Go Round,* Barnaby, Jane, Ellen, the children from *The Blue Ribbon Puppies*—all have oval-shaped eyes, one-piece outfits, heads as round as Charlie Brown's, and all are about the same height.[24] But this similarity is part of their appeal to both children and adults: in Maureen and Hugh Crago's *Prelude to Literacy* (1983), young Anna Crago's observation that Johnson's characters look alike occurs in the context of enjoying *The Carrot Seed;* and, during a laudatory review in *The Horn Book,* Virginia Haviland describes Ellen as "[l]ooking like a sister of Harold who owns the purple crayon" (379). Indeed, the very generic-ness of these characters increases the likelihood that readers may identify with them: just as each character could be any other, each character could be any reader. Their relatively neutral features function as a kind of empty space that readers can fill, a mirror in which readers may see themselves reflected, or a blank page on which they may draw. Perhaps, as Eliza T. Dresang notes in her *Radical Change: Books for Children in a Digital Age* (1999), this aspect of the *Harold* books makes them especially appropriate for contemporary readers. She writes, "The inclusion of white space to fill with thoughts and the empowerment of a small child, who is invited to draw his own life from his own imagination with his own crayon, speak directly to the digital age reader" (35). Although I am skeptical of Dresang's notion that cyberspace is a new or more critically promising way of thinking about the world, I agree that the radical instability of a universe such as Harold's can empower children with a sense of possibility. Like the Internet today, Harold's crayon-created world can be seen as an extension of the imaginative capabilities that we all possess—and, as such, invites us to imagine worlds of our own.[25]

Indeed, *Harold and the Purple Crayon* has inspired many, including the Purple Crayon of Yale, an improvisational comedy troupe whose founding members include actor Phil LaMarr (later of MAD TV and *Pulp Fiction*); Jane Marlin Shepard and others adapted it into a musical play, performed by Theaterworks USA in New York and across the country during the early 1990s (Ehrlich C36; Broadman 44; Obel); children's book editor Harold Underdown named his website the "Purple Crayon"; Maurice Sendak has praised the book's "supreme inventiveness" (289); and Chris Van Allsburg has not only named *Harold* as his favorite children's book but, in his 1982 Caldecott Medal acceptance speech, actually thanked "Harold, and his purple crayon."[26]

Van Allsburg has said that the best children's books include "any book or artistic experience that makes the young person question the nature of reality and the shape his or her own life has taken in it," and *Harold and the Purple Crayon* certainly meets this criterion (Van Allsburg, "A Western Canon, Jr."): it not only encourages children to "question the nature of reality" but empowers them to interact with that reality, to change it, to shape it—even falling through space, Harold "kept his wits and his purple crayon." Though imaginative power is certainly not all a person needs to succeed, it is an excellent start.[27] The *Harold* books in particular advise readers of all ages to remember: the world may not be as it appears, creative thinking can help change that world and, of course, always keep your wits and your purple crayon.

Notes

A much shorter version of this essay was presented at the Third Biennial Conference on Modern Critical Approaches to Children's Literature, Nashville, April 1999. For research assistance, thanks to Terri Goldich and Wendy Hennequin of the Northeast Children's Literature Collection, Thomas J. Dodd Research Center, University of Connecticut Libraries, Storrs, Connecticut; and, last but by no means least, very special thanks to Peggy Kidwell of the National Museum of American History, Washington, D.C.

1. To the best of my knowledge, Barbara Bader's "Crockett Johnson," a chapter in her *American Picturebooks,* (1976), is the only moderately extensive scholarly piece on Johnson, running eight pages in length. Ron Goulart's "A Little Bit of History . . . ," printed in Johnson's *Barnaby #1* (1985), offers a five-page history of "Barnaby"; Coulton Waugh's *The Comics* (1947) devotes four pages to "Barnaby"; Stephen Becker's *Comic Art in America* (1959) spends four to five pages on "Barnaby"; Maureen and Hugh Crago's *Prelude to Literacy* (1983) dedicates nearly as many pages to *Harold and the Purple Crayon.*

2. "O'Malley for Dewey," "Escape Artist," "The End of a Fairy Tale," *(Time);* "Cushlamochree!" *(Newsweek);* "Speaking of Pictures. . . ." *(Life).* For sources for Parker and Ellington, see the "Works Cited." Untermeyer is quoted on the dust jackets of *Barnaby* (the Holt edition) and *Barnaby and Mr. O'Malley* (1944); Fields's remarks appear on the dust jacket of the latter volume.

3. His "The Little Man with the Eyes" ran in *Collier's* from March 1940 through January 1943; "Barnaby" ran from April 1942 to February 1952, and again from September 1960 to April 1962. Johnson's art was exhibited at the Glezer Gallery (New York) in 1967, at the IBM Gallery (Yorktown Heights, N.Y.) in 1975, and as part of a show called "Theorems in Color" at the Museum of History and Technology (Washington, D.C.) in 1980

(Commire 144; Collier and Nakamura 1438). And his career was more varied than this brief résumé shows. As a young man, he played professional football; in 1955, he received a patent for a four-way adjustable mattress (Viguers et al. 135; Jones 22).

4. In *Prelude to Literacy* (1983), authors Maureen and Hugh Crago's daughter Anna thinks that the boy and Harold are the same (178), and at least one visitor to the Crockett Johnson Homepage has asked me this very question.

5. In "The Picture Book Animated" (1978), the animator Gene Deitch—the same person who supplies the quotation in *Animating Harold*—offers another variation on this phrase. He writes, "As I undertook *A Picture for Harold's Room* and *Harold's Fairy Tale*, Johnson warned me, 'Don't be fooled by the seemingly simple!' He was right. These films were devilishly difficult to make" (147). Johnson's "seemingly simple" line also appears in a blurb on the back of Sarah Perry's *If* . . . (1995), where Marilou Sorensen writes, "Crockett Johnson once said that the beauty of things was in "'*the seemingly simple.' If* . . . fits that description completely."

6. Other photographs by Bourke-White and Lange do exhibit an awareness of a frame, however. Lange's "Towards Los Angeles" (1937, also known as "NEXT TIME TRY THE TRAIN") and Bourke-White's "The Johnstown Flood" (1937, also known as "THE WORLD'S HIGHEST STANDARD OF LIVING") both use billboards to create the kind of juxtapositions that Johnson exhibits here. Both contrast images of prosperity (on the billboards) with a much bleaker material reality in order to expose the promise of American capitalism ("There's no way like the American way," Bourke-White's photographed billboard says) as an empty promise for many Americans (beneath the billboard, African Americans stand in line, waiting for relief).

7. In an interview for *Honk* magazine, Andrew Christie asks if Percy Crosby's *Skippy* influenced *Calvin and Hobbes,* but Watterson responds that he hasn't seen it. He continues, "I've had a couple of people write in comparing my work to *Barnaby* by Crockett Johnson, and that's another strip I've never seen. Or rather, with both of those I think I've seen one or two strips in anthologies, but I've never seen the work at any length." Watterson says that his main influences were Walt Kelly's *Pogo* and Charles Schulz's *Peanuts* (Christie).

8. One illustration, for example, notes that "Millionaire Cadwalader and thirty-dollar-a-week Tom Kent pay the same indirect taxes" (143).

9. At least one reader's experience concurs with this research. At Amazon.com's "Customer Comments" for *Harold and the Purple Crayon,* a reader from Dover, Delaware, reports, "I was a child of divorce. . . . My Grandparents, with whom we went to live, taught me to read. I began Kindergarten in 1957, and this book was on the shelf. I was stunned. I renewed it from our class library for the entire year. I lay in bed every night, holding that fat Crayola, waiting to climb out for an adventure. Forty years later, I think I've reached my goal."

10. Dr. Seuss' political cartoons ran in *PM* from April 1941 through January 1943.

11. See "Bovingdon."

12. In response to O'Malley's request for help, Barnaby and Jane ask their mothers to take them to see Santa Claus. After Mrs. Baxter (Barnaby's mother) agrees to take Barnaby, she remarks to Mrs. Shultz (Jane's mother), "I didn't think he believed in Santa Claus any more." Mrs. Shultz responds, "Jane never has. I've had to persuade her to take any interest at all in him." At that moment, Jane arrives to interrupt her mother with a request to see Santa Claus. In the final panel, Barnaby explains to his fairy godfather that he and Jane would not spoil their mothers' fun (4 Oct. 1943).

13. McGann's "Keats and the Historical Method" (1979) historicizes "To Autumn" (a poem often read ahistorically, in terms of an ideal romantic imagination) in order to make his point that "the governing context of all literary investigations must ultimately be an historical one. Literature is a human product, a humane art. It cannot be carried on (created), understood (studied), or appreciated (experienced) outside of its

definitive human context. The general science covering that human context is socio-historical" (459).

14. Why a kangaroo from Australia? In addition to mimicking the thought processes of a paranoid person, the kangaroo shares her country of origin with Harry Bridges, the Australian-born labor leader whom the U.S. government made six failed attempts to deport in the 1940s and 1950s (Klingaman 41). In 1951 (the year before Johnson's *Who's Upside Down?* was published), Bridges not only condemned the Korean War as "operation killer" but, as president of the independent International Longshoremen's and Warehousemen's Union, supported the three thousand longshoremen whose strike made front-page news in October ("Union Gains" 55). According to the *New York Times,* some of the ships affected "were being loaded with 'vital' cargo" destined for Korea ("Wildcat Strikers" 1). In December, Senator Joseph McCarthy himself claimed to have tape proving that Harry Bridges was part of a "leftist plot" intended to undermine the U.S. war effort (" 'Leftist Plot' Recited" 25). Although one cannot argue that Johnson intended to refer to Bridges by setting *Who's Upside Down?* in Australia, the prominence of the Australian—whom America repeatedly tried to send back to Australia—enhances the parallels between the misperceptions of both kangaroos and anti-Communists. That is, the fervor with which each clings to a belief results in an inability to distinguish a genuine threat from an imaginary one.

15. In his essay "Fantastic Companions" (1955) and in *Gordy and the Pirate* (1965) he displays an ability to satirize children effectively, too.

16. Krauss's work does not always live up to this ideal, however: *The Backward Day* (1950), illustrated by Marc Simont, stars an active little boy and a family (including a little sister) ready to cater to his whims; *A Very Special House* (1953), illustrated by Sendak, also features an active little boy—indeed, no girls appear in the book. But the Sendak-illustrated *A Hole Is to Dig* and *Open House for Butterflies* (1960) do exhibit an awareness of gender roles, with all children doing both "boy things" and "girl things."

17. This device recurs in the strip, starting with the moment when "Barnaby" introduces Jane: Mrs. Baxter tells Barnaby, "Remember she doesn't know us yet. She'll be timid." Directly after her words of advice, Jane calls out, "HEY, BARNABY!" and, without any trace of timidity, introduces herself (4 Dec. 1942). Her suggestions for games include the following: "We'll play house. You be the father and I'll be the mother and I'll be coming home late from working at the welding factory." When Barnaby refuses, she offers, "Then let's be Commandos . . . we'll sneak up on some Nazis" (6 Dec. 1942). Barnaby also rejects these ideas, but, significantly, both are not stereotypical. Her version of playing house includes herself in the paid workforce, and playing "Commandos"—a game one might expect little boys to prefer—strikes her as a suitable substitute for house. The following year, when she and Barnaby ride the train to Mrs. Krump's Kiddie Camp, Jane strolls up to the engineer's car to blow the whistle (27 and 28 July 1943); and, in general, Barnaby is more willing to believe his fairy godfather, but Jane remains consistently skeptical of Mr. O'Malley's plans. Throughout the "Barnaby" series, Jane's independent spirit leads her to challenge the "conventional wisdom" of others and to contradict gendered expectations.

18. Johnson is not the only writer or illustrator of his day revising fairy tales in ways that figure women and girls more positively, but books of this nature are a distinct minority. Much of James Thurber's *Many Moons* (1943), illustrated by Louis Slobodkin, focuses on the King's crisis of trying to get the moon for his daughter, but one could read the book as a lesson in the failure of experts (Lord High Chamberlain, Royal Wizard, Royal Mathematician) to listen to the Princess Lenore on her own terms. Indeed, a willingness to take seriously the little girl's imagination enables the Court Jester to get the moon; that his success depends on understanding the Princess Lenore suggests that her ideas are important. Many fairy tale books of the 1940s and 1950s do not retell their tales with the ironic awareness of Thurber or Johnson, however. Marcia Brown's

Caldecott-winning *Cinderella; or, The Little Glass Slipper* (1954) does reduce the violence of earlier versions but does not consider its messages about men's and women's roles. Its female characters seem to have three options: the self-sacrificing beauty (Cinderella) who can escape a life of drudgery only through marriage, the wish-fulfilling fairy godmother, and the mean, ugly stepmother and stepsisters. Like *Cinderella*, the following year's Caldecott winner also emphasizes the marriage plot and naturalizes oppressive gender roles. John Langstaff's *Frog Went A-Courtin'* (1955, illustrated by Feodor Rojankovsky) features a swaggering male frog who marries little "Mistress Mouse." Faithful to gender stereotypes, he is active, riding on his "high horse" with his "sword and pistol"; she is passive, "sit[ing] to spin" at her loom, and, when she does act, it is only to ask permission from her Uncle Rat, who approves the marriage immediately. Though its song and pictures are whimsical, the book's regressive ideologies of gender compare unfavorably with the more flexible gender roles found in Crockett Johnson's books.

19. Here I disagree with Alleen Pace Nilsen, who writes, "It is also interesting that in *Time of Wonder*, his two girls [McCloskey's characters are based on his daughters] are tremendously adventurous, even sailing across the bay by themselves, but when they get in a crowd of six boys who are diving from rocks, and swimming and surfing, the girls suddenly become very feminine as they play in the sand and sunbathe" (923). First, that the illustrations in question occur on four pages of a sixty-three-page book suggests that Nilsen exaggerates their importance. Second, the girls are *not* sunbathing: in the first two-page illustration, one girl climbs up the rock with the boys, while the other inflates a floating plastic fish (22–23); in the second, one girl carries a piece of wood, a second digs in the sand, and a third digs behind the second (24–25).

20. As Johnson reports in "Fantastic Companions" (1955), the "Barnaby" strip prompted parents to write him letters "telling of astonishing creatures that visited *their* homes." Though he invented Mr. O'Malley, "These writers were not inventing. They were reporting fact" (32). Despite Johnson's whimsical tone, "Barnaby" fan mail in the Smithsonian's archives indicates that parents did write letters about their children's "fantastic companions."

21. Since Johnson's name was not on the cover of the book, a paper banner was wrapped around it: on its front were the words "A Story That Doesn't End BY CROCKETT JOHNSON." This banner would have to be removed before the book could be read.

22. The paintings have been described as "large, vivid canvases, concentrating on geometric painting" (De Montreville and Hill 153) and as "large scale geometric designs in bold hues" (Collier and Nakamura 1438), and Johnson himself described the work as "non-objective, mathematic and geometric" (quoted in Marschall 449). A photograph of Johnson standing in front of *Squared Circle* appears on page 1436 of Collier and Nakamura's *Major Authors and Illustrators* (1993); a photo without Johnson appears on page 98 of Johnson's article "On the Mathematics of Geometry in My Abstract Paintings" (1972). Most of the paintings are held by the Smithsonian Institution's National Museum of American History, Division of Information Technology and Society.

23. The line "no ideas but in things" also recurs in Williams's *Paterson* (1946–58).

24. "Barnaby" may have been an influence on Charles M. Schulz's long-running "Peanuts" series, which made its debut in 1950—just two years before the last strip in "Barnaby's" original run ("Barnaby" was revived from 1960 to 1962). Like "Barnaby," Schulz's comic focuses on children not understood by adults (indeed, parents never appear in the strip) and features a "talking" dog (Snoopy's words appear in thought bubbles; Gorgon—Barnaby's dog—speaks out loud). Schulz himself said that "'Barnaby' was one of the great comic strips of all time" (back covers to *Barnaby #1, Barnaby #2, Barnaby #3, Barnaby #4, Barnaby #5,* and *Barnaby #6*).

25. Children appear to agree. In the Cragos' *Prelude to Literacy*, a study of their daughter Anna's responses to children's books, three-year-old Anna exclaims that Harold "is clever!" and, desiring to emulate Harold, soon wishes to exercise her own creativity

(205). During a walk with her father she asks, "How can I get up in the sky so I can draw on it with my purple crayon?" (206). While reading the book the following month, she remarks, "One day I will take a blue crayon out of mine [my pencil container] and draw on our path" (207). The Cragos note that though their daughter does not understand the "magic" of Harold's crayon, she has never "flatly denied the possibility of any of the book's happenings" (206) but instead has been inspired to undertake adventures of her own, to paraphrase Buell's *New York Times Book Review* appraisal of Harold. As a reader from Seattle wrote to Amazon.com, "With his crayon, [Harold] can meet any challenge, [and] climb any mountain. . . . It is a book that is both calming and empowering to kids, [because] it allows them to dream and imagine."

26. Van Allsburg's *Bad Day at Riverbend* (1995) seems most obviously influenced by *Harold and the Purple Crayon*. In it, cowboys drawn in coloring-book style come face to face with—and are defeated by—a little girl's crayons.

27. In this light, a comment Johnson once made about his "Barnaby" characters applies equally well to his readers. "As I go back over the former strips," he observed, "I am amazed and stand in awe as I see how the characters solved their problems, seemingly without any aid from me" ("Crockett Johnson, Cartoonist" 38).

Works Cited

Amazon.com: Customer Comments: *Harold and the Purple Crayon.* 20 March 1999. <http://www.amazon.com/exec/obidos/ts/book-customer-reviews/0060229357/>.
"Animating Harold." Five-minute documentary included on the videocassette *Harold and the Purple Crayon and Other Harold Stories.* Wood Knapp Video, 1993.
Bader, Barbara. "Crockett Johnson." In *American Picturebooks from Noah's Ark to The Beast Within.* New York: MacMillan, 1976. Pp. 434–42.
Bannon, Laura. *Big Brother.* New York and Chicago: Junior Literary Guild and Albert Whitman, 1950.
Becker, Stephen. *Comic Art in America.* New York: Simon & Schuster, 1959. Pp. 357–61.
Bemelmans, Ludwig. *Madeline.* 1939. New York: Penguin Putnam, 1967.
———. *Madeline's Rescue.* 1953. New York: Viking, 1981.
"Bovingdon, Ex-Dancer, Is Ousted By the OEW From Analyst Job." *New York Times,* 5 August 1943: 1, 36.
Broadman, Muriel. "Harold and the Purple Crayon." *Back Stage* 30 November 1990: 44.
Brown, Marcia, trans. and illus. *Cinderella; or, The Little Glass Slipper. A Free Translation from the French of Charles Perrault.* New York: Charles Scribner's Sons, 1954.
Brown, Margaret Wise. *Willie's Adventures.* Illus. Crockett Johnson. New York: William R. Scott, 1954.
Buell, Ellen Lewis. Review of *Harold and the Purple Crayon. New York Times Book Review* 16 October 1955: 34.
———. Review of *The Lonely Doll. New York Times Book Review* 13 October 1957: 51.
Butler, Judith. *Gender Trouble: Feminism and the Subversion of Identity.* New York and London: Routledge, 1990.
Carter, Angela. *The Bloody Chamber.* 1979. New York: Penguin, 1993.
Christie, Andrew. "Interview with Bill Watterson." *Honk.* c. 1987. <http://www.okidoki.nl/ calvin_and_hobbes/intrvw.htm>. 10 March 1999.
Collier, Laurie, and Joyce Nakamura, eds. *Major Authors and Illustrators for Children and Young Adults.* Detroit: Gale Research, 1993. Pp. 1436–38.
Commire, Anne, ed. *Something About the Author.* Vol. 30. Detroit: Gale Research, 1983. Pp. 141–44.
Crago, Maureen, and Hugh Crago. *Prelude to Literacy: A Preschool Child's Encounter with Picture and Story.* Carbondale and Edwardsville: Southern Illinois University Press, 1983.

"Crockett Johnson, Cartoonist, Creator of 'Barnaby,' Is Dead." *New York Times,* 13 July 1975: 38.

"Cushlamochree!" *Newsweek,* 4 October 1942: 102, 104.

Deitch, Gene. "The Picture Book Animated." *Horn Book,* April 1978: 144–49.

De Montreville, Doris, and Donna Hill, eds. *Third Book of Junior Authors.* New York: H. W. Wilson, 1972. Pp. 152–53.

Dresang, Eliza T. *Radical Change: Books for Youth in a Digital Age.* New York: H. W. Wilson, 1999.

Ehrlich, Phyllis. "For Children." *New York Times,* 16 November 1990: C36.

Ellington, Duke. "He Trusts Mr. O'Malley." *PM* 1 December 1942: 21. "The End of a Fairy Tale." *Time,* 28 January 1952: 77.

"Escape Artist." *Time,* 2 September 1946: 49–50.

Forsythe, Robert. *Redder Than the Rose.* New York: Covici, Friede, 1935.

Foster, Constance. *This Rich World: The Story of Money.* Illus. Crockett Johnson. New York: Robert M. McBride, 1943. Republished in a revised and expanded version by Metcalf Associates, 1952.

Friedan, Betty. *The Feminine Mystique.* 1963. With a new introduction by the author. New York: Laurel, 1984.

Goulart, Ron. "A Little Bit of History . . ." In Johnson, *Barnaby #1.* Pp. 209–13.

———, ed. *The Encyclopedia of American Comics: From 1897 to the Present.* New York: Facts on File, 1990.

"Gymnast for Health, Bovingdon Explains." *New York Times,* 3 August 1943: 21.

Harold and the Purple Crayon. Based on the book by Crockett Johnson. Adapted by Jane Shepard. Music by Jon Ehrlich. Lyrics by Robin Pogrebin and John Ehrlich. Theatreworks USA. 1992.

Haviland, Virginia. Review of *Ellen's Lion. Horn Book,* October 1959: 379.

———. Review of *Harold and the Purple Crayon. Horn Book,* October 1955: 362–63.

Hoban, Russell. *Bedtime for Frances.* Illus. Garth Williams. 1960. New York: Harper-Collins, 1996.

Hopkins, Lee Bennett. *Books Are by People: Interviews with 104 Authors and Illustrators of Books for Young Children.* New York: Citation Press, 1969. Pp. 121–24.

Johnson, Crockett. "Aw, be a sport. Tell the newsreel audience you still have faith in the Lawd and good old Franklin D." *The New Masses,* 28 August 1934: 7. Reprinted in Forsythe, *Redder Than the Rose,* 232.

———. *Barnaby.* New York: Holt, 1943; Garden City, N.Y.: Blue Ribbon Books, 1943.

———. *Barnaby and Mr. O'Malley.* New York: Henry Holt, 1944.

———. *Barnaby #1: Wanted: A Fairy Godfather.* New York: Ballantine, 1985.

———. *The Blue Ribbon Puppies.* New York: Harper, 1958.

———. *Ellen's Lion: Twelve Stories.* New York: Harper, 1959.

———. "Fantastic Companions." *Harper's,* June 1955: 32–34.

———. "A geometrical look at $\sqrt{\pi}$." *Mathematical Gazette* 54 (February 1970): 59–60.

———. *Gordy and the Pirate and the Circus Ringmaster and the Knight and the Major League Manager and the Western Marshal and the Astronaut; and a Remarkable Achievement.* New York: Putnam, 1965.

———. *Harold and the Purple Crayon.* New York: Harper, 1955.

———. *Harold at the North Pole: A Christmas Journey with the Purple Crayon.* 1958. New York: Reader's Digest Services, 1975.

———. *Harold's Circus: An Astounding, Colossal, Purple Crayon Event!* New York: Harper, 1959.

———. *Harold's Fairy Tale: Further Adventures with the Purple Crayon.* New York: Harper, 1956.

———. *Harold's Trip to the Sky: More Adventures with the Purple Crayon.* New York: Harper, 1957.

————. *The Lion's Own Story: Eight New Stories About Ellen's Lion.* New York: Harper, 1963.

————. *Merry Go Round.* New York: Harper, 1958.

————. "Mr. Hearst says he'll buy your farm articles if you'll just change 'Arkansas,' 'Louisiana,' 'California,' and so on, to Soviet Russia." *The New Masses,* 28 May 1935: 26.

————. "On the Mathematics of Geometry in My Abstract Paintings." *Leonardo* 5 (1972): 97–101, color plate facing p. 124. Reprinted in *Visual Art, Mathematics, and Computing.* Ed. Frank J. Malina. Oxford: Pergamon Press, 1979. Pp. 143–47, 306.

————. *A Picture for Harold's Room: A Purple Crayon Adventure.* New York: Harper, 1960.

————. "Seat." *Collier's,* 18 July 1942: 56.

————. *Sister, you need the Union! . . . And the Union Needs You!* UAW-CIO pamphlet. [1944].

————. *Who's Upside Down?* New York: William R. Scott, 1952.

Jones, Stacy V. "Inventor of Barnaby Gets Patent for 4-Way Adjustable Mattress." *New York Times,* 29 October 1955: 22.

Joyce, James. *Finnegans Wake.* 1939. New York: Penguin, 1976.

Keats, Ezra Jack. *The Snowy Day.* New York: Viking, 1962.

————. *A Whistle for Willie.* New York: Viking, 1964.

Kimmel, Michael. "Clarence, William, Iron Mike, Tailhook, Senator Packwood, Spur Posse, Magic, . . . and Us." *Rereading America.* 3d ed. Ed Gary Colombo et al. Boston: Bedford Books, 1995. Pp. 259–69.

Kingman, Lee, Joanna Foster, and Ruth Giles Lontoft, comps. *Illustrators of Children's Books, 1957–1966.* Boston: Horn Book, 1968. Pp. 126.

Klingaman, William K. *Encyclopedia of the McCarthy Era.* New York: Facts on File, 1996.

Krauss, Ruth. *The Backward Day.* Illus. Marc Simont. New York: Harper, 1950.

————. *The Carrot Seed.* Illus. Crockett Johnson. New York: Harper, 1945.

————. *A Hole Is to Dig.* Illus. Maurice Sendak. New York: Harper, 1952.

————. *Open House for Butterflies.* Illus. Maurice Sendak. New York: Harper, 1960.

————. *A Very Special House.* Illus. Maurice Sendak. New York: Harper, 1953.

Langstaff, John. *Frog Went A-Courtin'.* Illus. Feodor Rojankovsky. 1955. New York: Harcourt Brace, 1983.

Lapica, R. L., ed. *Facts on File Yearbook, 1942.* Vol. 2. New York: Facts on File, 1943.

" 'Leftist Plot' Recited." *New York Times,* 11 December 1951: 25.

Luthar, Suniya S., and Edward Zigler. "Vulnerability and Competence: A Review of Research on Resilience in Childhood." *American Journal of Orthopsychiatry* (January 1991): 6–22.

Marschall, Richard. "Barnaby" and "Leisk, David Johnson." *The World Encyclopedia of Comics.* Ed. Maurice Horn. New York: Chelsea House, 1976. Pp. 97–98, 448–49.

McCloskey, Robert. *Time of Wonder.* 1957. New York: Viking, 1985.

McGann, Jerome. "Keats and the Historical Method in Literary Criticism." In *Romantic Poetry: Recent Revisionary Criticism.* Ed. Karl Kroeber and Gene W. Ruoff. New Brunswick, N.J.: Rutgers University Press, 1993. Pp. 439–64. Reprinted from *Modern Language Notes* 94 (1979): 988–89, 1000–1032.

Nel, Philip. *The Crockett Johnson Homepage.* <http://www.cofc.edu/~nelp/purple>.

Nilsen, Alleen Pace. "Women in Children's Literature." *College English* 32 (May 1971): 918–26.

Obel, Susan B. Letter to the author. 27 October 1999.

"O'Malley for Dewey." *Time,* 18 September 1944: 50.

Parker, Dorothy. "A Mash Note to Crockett Johnson." *PM,* 3 October 1943: 16.

Perry, Sarah. *If. . . .* Malibu and Venice, Calif.: The J. Paul Getty Museum and Children's Library Press, 1995.

Sendak, Maurice. "Ruth Krauss and Me: A Very Special Partnership." *Horn Book* May–June 1994: 286–90.

————. *Where the Wild Things Are.* New York: Harper, 1963.

Seuss, Dr. "After, him, Sam! It's a Robin RED-Breast!" *PM*, 28 June 1942: 12.

———. *The Butter Battle Book*. New York: Random House, 1984.

———. *I Can Lick 30 Tigers Today! and Other Stories*. New York: Random House, 1969.

———. *Scrambled Eggs Super!* New York: Random House, 1953.

———. *The Sneetches and Other Stories*. New York: Random House, 1961.

Sexton, Anne. *Transformations*. 1971. Boston: Houghton Mifflin, 1979.

Sister, you need the Union! . . . And the Union Needs You! Pamphlet. Illus. Crockett Johnson. Detroit: International Union, United Automobile, Aircraft, and Agricultural Implement Workers of America, c. 1944.

Solomon, Deborah. "Beyond Finger Paint." *New York Times Book Review*, 17 May 1998: 24–25.

"Speaking of Pictures . . . 'Barnaby' Has High I.Q. for Cartoon-Strip Humor." *Life*, 4 October 1943: 10–11, 13.

Thompson, Kay. *Eloise*. Illus. Hilary Knight. 1955. New York: Simon & Schuster, 1983.

Thurber, James. *Many Moons*. Illus. Louis Slobodkin. 1943. New York: Voyager Books, 1991.

"Union Gains Cited by Harry Bridges." *New York Times*, 3 April 1951: 55.

Van Allsburg, Chris. *Bad Day at Riverbend*. Boston: Houghton Mifflin, 1995.

———. "Books I Remember." HomeArts. 1995. 20 March 1999. <http://homearts.com: 80/depts/ relat/allsbub1.htm>.

———. "A Western Canon, Jr. (Page 6)." HomeArts. 1995. 20 March 1999. <http:// homearts.com:80/depts/ relat/allsbub8.htm>.

———. *The Widow's Broom*. Boston: Houghton Mifflin, 1992.

Viguers, Ruth Hill, Marcia Dalphin, and Bertha Mahoney Miller, comps. *Illustrators of Children's Books, 1946–1956*. Boston: Horn Book, 1958. P. 135.

Waugh, Coulton. *The Comics*. New York: Macmillan, 1947. Reprint, Jackson: University Press of Mississippi, 1991. Pp. 306–10.

"Wildcat Strikers Make 15 Piers Idle." *New York Times*, 16 October 1951: 1, 26.

Williams, William Carlos. *Selected Poems*. Ed. Charles Tomlinson. New York: New Directions, 1985.

Wright, Dare. *The Lonely Doll*. New York: Doubleday, 1957.

Zipes, Jack. *Don't Bet on the Prince: Contemporary Feminist Fairy Tales in North America and England*. New York: Methuen, 1986.

Parodic Play with Paintings in Picture Books

Sandra Beckett

Many recent studies have pointed to the increasing influence on children's literature of the postmodern trends of adult literature, but few have explored in depth what some critics consider to be the most striking, that of parody. In her ground-breaking book *A Theory of Parody: The Teachings of Twentieth-Century Art Forms,* Linda Hutcheon has argued quite convincingly that parody is a characteristic shared by all the arts in the postmodern world (1). Hutcheon uses the term *parody* in the broad sense of a revisiting and recontextualizing of previous works of art, what is often referred to by the more neutral term *allusion,* but in this paper I would like to focus on parody in the more common sense of references with a comic or satiric intent.[1] Even in this stricter sense of the term, the functions of parody can range from respectful homage to biting ridicule, from serious criticism to playful mockery, but authors and illustrators who use artistic parody in children's literature tend to do so in a playful manner.

Hutcheon's theory of parody remains a more useful one for children's literature than more formalist approaches, such as Gérard Genette's, because she insists on the "pragmatic context": "the author's (or text's) intent, the effect upon the reader, the competence involved in the encoding and the decoding of parody, the contextual elements that mediate or determine the comprehension of parodic modes" (22), issues that are even more crucial in children's books than in adult literature. To appreciate parody, the reader must first recognize the intent to parody another work and then have the ability to identify the appropriated work and interpret its meaning in the new context. Many critics have pointed out the potential for elitism in parody, a danger that is even greater when children are the target audience. Like other forms of intertextuality, parody would seem to be inaccessible to most children in light of their limited cultural heritage. In spite of the heavy demands parody makes on the reader, however, it is not a new phenomenon in children's literature, as Lewis Carroll's *Alice* books clearly demonstrate.

Children's Literature 29, ed. Elizabeth Lennox Keyser and Julie Pfeiffer (Yale University Press, © 2001 Hollins University).

According to Hutcheon, the one thing on which all historians of parody agree is that it prospers "in periods of cultural sophistication that enable parodists to rely on the competence of the reader (viewer, listener) of the parody" (19).[2] In spite of widespread concerns about literacy rates, many critics have pointed to the increasing cultural so-phistication of children and children's literature at the turn of the millennium. In today's so-called Age of Information, children cer-tainly have access to, in fact they are inundated by, a vast cultural repertoire through their exposure to what the Canadian author Tim Wynne-Jones refers to as the "cybertower of Babel" (161).[3] Does this, in fact, make today's children more proficient readers and viewers of parody, as the increasing number of children's books using the tech-nique would seem to suggest? Based on my experience with my own three children, I am convinced that children today are able to decode more parodic allusions than the baby boom children. But I also think that the repertoire of allusions they recognize is at the same time nar-rower. In spite of their easy access to cultural information in the elec-tronic age, I am at once amazed and disconcerted to witness the extent to which their "cultural" education comes from programs such as *The Simpsons,* meaning not only that their repertoire of cultural icons tends to be limited largely to those they have seen on the popular show, but also that those icons have been assimilated in a parodic mode, making viewers more receptive to parody in other contexts. Authors and illus-trators such as Jon Scieszka and Lane Smith have plugged into the cul-tural phenomenon of the Simpsons generation.

Although today's children may be more proficient decoders of par-ody, it is obvious that authors and illustrators of the often quite sophis-ticated children's books currently on the market do not expect young readers and viewers to possess all of the codes necessary to understand all of the parodic allusions in their texts. As we shall see, parodies with multiple coding are often used to provide different levels of com-plexity for readers of all ages.

When parody's target text is another work of art, it is not necessarily in the same medium or genre, as Hutcheon's study clearly demon-strates. When picture-book illustrators parody paintings or sculptures, they engage in what she calls "cross-genre play." Although she cites only examples from texts for adults to support her claim that "litera-ture is famous for parodying non-literary discourse" (18), children's lit-erature also provides a wealth of examples. Picture books, which combine text and image, offer a particularly exciting medium for parody's "inter-art discourse" (2).

In the visual arts, parody can operate on either specific works or general iconic conventions. The simplest and most overt parodies are generally based on individual works of art or parts of them. As one would anticipate, it is this type that is most common in books for young readers. Allusions to the stylistic conventions of an entire genre, to the style of a period or movement, or to the characteristic manner of the entire oeuvre of an artist can also be found in picture books, although their decoding generally requires a much greater sophistication. Entire picture books may evoke a specific artistic movement, such as impressionism, expressionism, fauvism, surrealism, or primitivism. Perry Nodelman refers to this "scavenging of styles" for the narrative purposes of children's book illustrations in *Words About Pictures*. He cites a number of picture-book artists who "quote" styles to convey an atmosphere, an attitude, or a quality that is dependent on the new context (84). Some picture-book artists commonly "quote" the style of one particular artist, as in the case of Anthony Browne's frequent references to characteristics or elements of the work of Magritte. Although these types of general allusions to an artistic movement or an artist's style are common in children's books, they are less often parodic than are references to individual works, to which this paper is devoted.

It is hardly surprising that the most frequently parodied artworks, especially in children's books, tend to be those that are so well-known that they have become cultural icons in Western society. Among those in the visual arts, Hutcheon cites Leonardo da Vinci's *Mona Lisa* and paintings by Picasso (8). In picture books, these are also popular intertexts, as are the works of, among others, Monet, Van Gogh, Hals, Magritte, Chagall, and Dali. Less well-known artists, such as Henri Rousseau and Pollock, find their way into picture books because illustrators feel their style has particular appeal to children.

Parodic play with paintings (and to a lesser degree sculptures) seems to be a very widespread phenomenon in Western picture books. My first examples were deliberately chosen from the books of an author-illustrator who would be very familiar to most English-speaking readers, namely, Anthony Browne. In order to show that this is indeed an international trend, however, my other two examples are taken from works by award-winning picture-book artists from France and Nor-

way, Yvan Pommaux and Fam Ekman. It is noteworthy that all three
are both authors and illustrators of the books discussed, and this is
quite often the case in picture books that use this type of referen-
tiality. Other picture-book artists who come to mind are Jean Claverie,
Frédéric Clément, Maurice Sendak, and Chris Van Allsburg.[4] These
author-illustrators have challenged habitual thinking about the picture book and explored and developed the potential of the genre as
its own unique art form, one in which parodic metadiscourse on art
plays an important role. Their books appeal to adult readers, as well
as children, in part because of the high artistic quality, but largely because of the parody, with its particular brand of humor and irony. The
result is a new brand of sophisticated picture books that target all ages,
a trend that has been identified as one of the survival techniques of
children's books in the electronic age.[5]

Picture books have become big business. Have they also become
the newest form of high art? In an article on the Norwegian picture
book, Tone Birkeland states: "Nowadays, the most exciting events of
Norway's art world are just as likely to take place on the pages of an
illustrated children's book as on the walls of an art gallery" (11). In
some cases, as this study will show, the pages of picture books actually become the walls of an art gallery. What Eco calls the "inferential
walks" that the reader must make outside the text to gather intertextual support (32) take the readers of these particular books through
the world's great art galleries or into virtual museums.

The award-winning picture-book artist Anthony Browne often incorporates specific preexisting paintings into his illustrations. An interesting example of what René Payant refers to as "*citation*" (quotation) in painting (5) is the portrait hanging in the Piggots' living room
in *Piggybook,* an unmistakable rendition of Franz Hals's *The Laughing
Cavalier* (see figure 1). Although it is the Dutch master's most famous
painting, it is nonetheless unfamiliar to the majority of children and
even many adult readers. That doesn't prevent Browne from referring
to the same painting again, more than ten years later, in *Voices in the
Park.* In *Piggybook,* the portrait hangs above Mr. Piggot, who is sprawled
on the couch watching television with his two sons while Mrs. Piggot
attends to all the domestic tasks by herself. Not only is there a suggestive resemblance between the cavalier and Mr. Piggot (notably the
round shape of the head), but the father and one of the sons could
easily pass as Dutch. For readers who are at all familiar with Hals's
work, the portrait will evoke guild-hall paintings of Dutch merchants

engaged in endless communal banquets. Piggot, who seems to be eating or thinking about eating when he is not at his "very important job," is certainly a worthy modern descendant of that patriarchal society. The significance that Browne attaches to the portrait is made obvious by the fact that he has added other signs to assist the viewer in interpreting the parody. He humorously suggests the nationality of the Dutch master by choosing Holland's characteristic symbol, the tulip, to decorate the room. The portrait hangs on wallpaper printed with little pink tulips, and Mr. Piggot and his sons sit on a sofa with a flower pattern that also contains tulips. Browne's parodic intent is underscored by the fact that Hals's cavalier has an even more striking double in the form of the Piggot's cat, whose Cheshire-like smile and whiskers seem to reflect ironically the cavalier's smile and broad moustache. Piggot is framed between the laughing cavalier and the grinning cat, whose sprawl is not unlike his own, as if between two mirrors.

Many readers may still not have understood the parodic reference to Hals's masterpiece, but Browne uses a double-coded parody that provides a second level accessible even for very young children. The earlier living room scene *en rose* is repeated toward the end of the book *en bleu*.[6] In the latter, Mr. Piggot and his sons, who by now have been transparently identified as male chauvinist pigs, have been transformed into "real" pigs, and the metamorphosis is reflected in the painting, which replaces the laughing cavalier with a pig in the same dignified pose (see figure 2). *The Laughing Pig* is a parody "in the second degree," to borrow Gérard Genette's term,[7] because it parodies Browne's earlier version of *The Laughing Cavalier,* itself an ironic recontextualization of the original masterpiece. The earlier associations of the portrait with the room decor are confirmed because the pink tulips on the wallpaper have become little pink pigs' heads, as have the centers of many of the flowers in the pattern on the sofa. The august and noble bearing of the pig subject of the portrait contrasts strikingly with the undignified behavior of the Piggots as they "root" around on the floor looking for scraps.

Sometimes illustrators themselves may be unaware of potential interpretations of their multilevel parodies. Perry Nodelman's statement that illustrators who borrow styles "may even evoke ideas and attitudes of which they are not themselves consciously aware" (85) can also be applied to the appropriation of a single work of art. Although most readers, and perhaps even Browne himself, would be ignorant of the fact, certain knowledgeable readers may very well note that the

Figures 1 and 2. From *Piggybook*. Copyright © 1986 by Anthony Browne. Reprinted by permission of Knopf. All rights reserved.

iconic representation of the Piggot males' regression was chosen from the work of an artist whose penetrating insight into human nature is said to have "cut through the upper crust of culture" of "the recently civilized Gothic man" to reveal "a human soul on a simple, animal level" (Stites 633). The remarkable success of Browne's picture books is largely due to their ability to appeal to readers at opposite poles of sophistication.

Browne reworks a second painting in *Piggybook,* Thomas Gainsborough's *Robert Andrews and His Wife,* which will be even less familiar to many viewers than the Hals. While retaining all the formal aspects of Gainsborough's painting, Browne has substituted a pig's head for that of Robert Andrews and has eliminated his wife from the painting, leaving only the blank form of her contour sitting on the bench. This artistic allusion acts as a *mise en abyme,* mirroring events in the story. Once again, children and adults alike may not recognize the parodic allusion to Gainsborough's original, but Browne's playful treatment of it will nonetheless be meaningful. Even young children will realize that the absent feminine figure in the painting over the fireplace represents Mrs. Piggot, who has disappeared after leaving on the mantelpiece a note saying "You are pigs," which her husband picks up in his pig's hoof on the following page.

Browne's more recent *The Big Baby* offers examples of two different types of parodic allusions, although each functions as a playful *mise en abyme* of events and themes in the story. Two of the illustrations depict fairly faithful representations of recognizable works of art. Above the head of the bed, where John's sick father lies with a thermometer in his mouth and surrounded by medicine bottles and assorted remedies, hangs Edvard Munch's *The Sick Child.* There is certainly nothing the least bit humorous about Munch's painting of his sick sister, and its parodic function is entirely dependent on its recontextualization. The Munch painting positioned at the top of the page seems to provide a title for the scene below, as "the Sick Child" is a very appropriate, if somewhat less pejorative, description of Mr. Young, who, when he feels even slightly ill, becomes, in his wife's terms, "a Big Baby." Unlike many of Munch's better-known expressionist paintings, the one of his sick sister remains anchored in reality, as does the scene it mirrors of John's sick father. Later, Browne uses a painting by Dali to reflect the surreal situation that results when John's father drinks a whole bottle of "Elixa de Yoof" tonic, in his obsessive desire to stay young, and wakes up with a baby's body. No less than *The Sick Child,* Dali's painting is represented fairly accurately and the parody once again lies in the recontextualization. As John's mother carries the baby with the disproportionate, adult-sized head up to bed, she passes Dali's famous painting, *Sleep,* which depicts a large face sleeping propped up on crutches.

The third painting in *The Big Baby* is not nearly as well known but presumably has been chosen by the artist because it reflects a theme in the book. Unlike the two preceding paintings, this one is not reproduced faithfully but has been reworked in a playful, parodic manner similar to the Hals and the Gainsborough in *Piggybook*. Whereas many viewers might completely overlook the significance of the Munch or even the Dali, this less celebrated work is bound to draw their attention. When John's father, now "back to normal," calls Mrs. Young into his bedroom later to tell her about his "TERRIBLE dream," even young children will immediately notice that the painting hanging above the bed has changed, although they will not know that it is a parody of John Henry Fuseli's romantic work titled *The Nightmare*. For an elite of cultured readers, the title of the painting once again offers a highly appropriate heading for this scene of the book. Those incapable of naming the painting will nonetheless associate it with events in the book, because Browne has substituted John's baby-father for the little grinning demon that sits on the sleeping woman in the original. The luminescent horse's head that looks on in Fuseli's painting has also been replaced with a dragon's head, which children will consider more nightmarish.

In Yvan Pommaux's *John Chatterton détective,* as in Browne's *Piggybook,* an animal is substituted for the human subjects in the portraits and sculptures illustrated in the wolf's private art collection. In this parodic retelling of *Little Red Riding Hood,* which spoofs the mystery genre in a format that borrows from the comic book, the wolf is holding Little Red Riding Hood hostage to obtain from her mother the one painting he needs to complete his "collection of wolves." The portrait that hangs on the wall behind the wolf as he makes his ransom call on a cellular phone evokes vague reminiscences of the painting commonly known as *Whistler's Mother,* and more specifically the frequently reproduced detail that shows only the head and shoulders. Using the same austere whites, grays, and blacks that characterize the stark, ascetic canvas that Whistler titled *Arrangement in Gray and Black No. 1: Portrait of the Artist's Mother,* Pommaux has captured the same chilly austerity and Puritan look in his "*Wolf's Mother*." It is certainly not for-

Figure 3. From *John Chatterton détective*. Copyright © 1993, l'école des loisirs, Paris. Reprinted by permission of l'école des loisirs. All rights reserved.

tuitous that the ransom call to Little Red Riding Hood's mother is made in front of this particular picture, which evokes one of the art world's most celebrated mothers. The presence of the painting sets up an interesting parallel in the two frames juxtaposed on this page. In the first, the wolf's mother seems to watch from her portrait as the wolf makes his ransom demands to the little girl's mother, hinting perhaps at an unhealthy mother-son relationship.[8] Although only the wolf's arm is visible, his shadow on the wall seems to reflect the portrait of his mother, but the shadow is leaning forward in a more menacing pose with the mouth slightly open. The second frame focuses on Little Red Riding Hood and her mother, and the terrified "*Maman!*" that the little girl cries into the cell phone to her frantic mother clearly suggests a warm, loving relationship.

In the following double-page spread, the viewer's perspective is shifted to reveal a large portion of the wolf's very eclectic art collection, which ranges from Middle or New Kingdom Egypt to modern sculpture (see figure 3). The unifying theme of the collection, which includes French, Belgian, English, Flemish, Swiss, Spanish, Dutch, and American works of art from a wide variety of periods and movements, is, of course, the subject. The immediate effect is one of humor, but such a collection also suggests the wolf's narcissistic obsession with his own image. This is not just a case of a wolf collecting portraits of wolves as a human collects portraits of humans. The wolf stands in the middle of the room, surrounded by his collection of wolves, like so many mirror images of himself. This narcissism is humorously underscored in a manner that can be appreciated by young readers: the wolf himself is dressed in blue when he demands that Little Red Riding Hood's mother bring him a painting titled "Le loup bleu sur fond blanc" (Blue wolf on a white background) or he will devour her daughter.

The scene of the wolf's art collection appeals particularly to cultured adult viewers. All of the works in the wolf's collection seem to parody the paintings and sculptures of specific artists, and although Pommaux does not depict the originals as faithfully as Browne, an art amateur is nevertheless able to go around the room labeling many of them. There is a wolf posing, sword at his side, in a portrait reminiscent of Van Dyck, next to a wolf lounging in a Watteau- or Fragonard-like setting. The painting of the wolf's head pronouncing the word *loup* is clearly a parody of Magritte's word-images, many of which included the names of animals, in particular *cheval* (horse).[9] Franz Hals's *The Laughing Cavalier* seems to have made its way into this book as well, this time as a scowling wolf rather than a smiling pig. Giacometti's *Walking Man II* has become a "*Walking Wolf II*" that strides purposefully forward with rigid legs, square shoulders, and arms to the side, in a humorous imitation not only of the well-known sculpture but also of the stance of the wolf himself as he talks on his cell phone. The desire to reflect the broad-shouldered wolf would explain why Pommaux's parodic sculpture is not as elongated as Giacometti's figure, but it remains unmistakable, one of the most easily recognized pieces in the collection. The sculpture of the wolf howling, which contrasts with Giacometti's anthropomorphic wolf and the villain of the story, is reminiscent of Antoine-Louis Barye's realistic animal sculptures. In the corner stands an example of Dadaist sculpture and next to it a small cubist painting. A wrapped and tied wolf's head parodies the smaller wrapped objects of Christo, the Bulgarian-American master of *empaquetage* (wrapping). The wire sculpture of a wolf at the far right is clearly a parody of Alexander Calder's early wire sculptures, such as *Romulus and Remus under the she-wolf*. Pommaux's wolf seems to have a slight preference for Calder: the ominous-looking black sculpture in the foreground is not unlike the American's later large stabiles made out of heavy metal, one of which is aptly titled *The Black Beast*.

Like the first piece of the wolf's collection to be shown, the last is also isolated from the rest, with the result that our attention is drawn to the Egyptian mummiform effigy of a wolf on a pedestal. This is particularly amusing because the Egyptians did, of course, mummify animals, although a wolf mummy would be a rare artifact indeed! This piece takes on a thematic significance that the apparently gratuitous

Figure 4. From *Kattens Skrekk*. Copyright © 1992 by Fam Ekman. Reprinted by permission of J. W. Cappelen, Oslo. All rights reserved.

pieces on the previous double-page spread seem to lack. Protruding beyond the wall against which the mummy is displayed are the legs of the wolf, who lies unconscious (or quite possibly dead) on the floor. Children's fascination with ancient Egypt, confirmed recently by the box-office hit *The Mummy,* will allow many of them to appreciate the parodic intent in this scene.

In Fam Ekman's *Kattens Skrekk* (The cat's terror), the story of a cat who has an obsessive fear of dogs, canines are to be found everywhere, even "in the museum" (see figure 4). The curator is a dog, but so, too, are virtually all the subjects of the paintings and sculptures. The incorporation of the *Mona Lisa,* no doubt the best known and most parodied of all paintings, should allow most young readers to grasp the parodic intent and to enjoy a degree of empowerment they may not achieve from Pommaux's collection of less easily identified works. The only painting in the museum that has not been appropriated by dogs is Edvard Munch's *The Scream,* which is set apart from the others on a partition in the foreground of Ekman's illustration, where it seems to symbolize the cat's terror in the face of so many dogs.[10] *The Scream* is no doubt the most famous example of the very subjective painting of the expressionist movement, art "born out of anxiety," which "stressed the suffering of its protagonist, the artist (usually male, with a morbid fear of the female)" (Tansey 390). Ekman's appropriation of the painting to suggest the agony of her cat protagonist, who has a morbid fear, not of females, but of dogs, is obviously highly fitting. Whereas no external cause for the subject's anxiety is depicted in *The Scream,* in *Kattens Skrekk* the specific, concrete source of the cat's terror is not only manifest but obsessively portrayed. Munch's painting was familiar to many young people even before the image became an icon of popular culture thanks to *Scream,* the 1996 film that is itself an excellent example of the parody genre (*Scream 3* was released just before this article went to press). Children of all ages will now recognize the image, and its recent association with the horror genre makes it an obvious symbol of fear.

Fam Ekman's museum collection, like Pommaux's private collection, parodies specific works of art, and the choice of pieces in this case seems to be less fortuitous. The pose of the marble sculpture of a dog in a toga is unmistakably that of Gianlorenzo Bernini's marble sculpture of *David,* the fearless young conqueror of the giant Goliath to whom the protagonist will be compared in a later allusion. Immediately beside the fearful face of the cat peering in the doorway, two paintings seem out of place owing to the absence of a dog subject, unless the viewer recognizes them as allusions to Kasimir Malevich's *Black Square* and *Black Circle,* examples of what he called Suprematism, a style that sought to free art from the burden of the object and that the artist himself defines as "the supremacy of pure feeling in creative art" (Arnason 187). For the cat protagonist of Ekman's book, as for the suprematist, only feeling is significant. The paintings may also suggest, however, the supremacy that dogs seem to exercise over cats, even in the museum.

Just as the "pure feeling" of Malevich's early Suprematist works is expressed in black and white, "the cold, paralyzing intensity of the cat's feelings" in Fam Ekman's picture book is communicated visually in stark black and white wood engravings (Birkeland12). One illustra-

tion shows the cat watching his new dog neighbor unpack two paintings, one of which seems to be Fernand Léger's famous *The Polychrome
Divers,* playfully incorporated into a black and white illustration.[11] Although the vagueness of the painting itself prevents a positive identification, its context seems to confirm that it is an allusion to one
of Léger's paintings of divers falling through space. The cat's upside
down head is framed in the window like a picture, and in a sequel to
the scene, only the legs and tail of the cat can be seen in the window
as he falls from an upper story. In the second illustration, the painting
now hangs visibly on the wall immediately next to the window, where
it seems to mirror the diving cat framed by the window (the fact that
curtains have been hung somewhat reduces the frame effect).[12] In the
absence of color, it is the movement of the painting that is striking,
and even if viewers miss the subtle parodic play, they should be left
with the general impression of the whirling movement of a dog and
cat fight, as it is so often portrayed in comics or cartoons, where it becomes impossible, as with Léger's divers, to distinguish the owner of
individual body parts.

The black and white illustrations at the beginning and the end of
Ekman's book are in stark contrast with those that accompany the cat's
dream, embedded in the middle of the story. The dream is represented
in color, and the cat and its multicolored eastern costume are reminiscent of *Joseph and the Amazing Technicolor Dreamcoat,* although they
are, in fact, the colors of Henri Rousseau's visual world.[13] A forerun-
ner of the surrealists, Rousseau draws us compellingly into his dreams
and nightmares, as do the illustrations in the dream sequence of *Kattens Skrekk,* playful parodies of three of the French artist's best-known
works.

For the sequence in which the cat dreams that he is a shepherd
asleep in the desert after a hard day's work when a big dog comes along
and bites him, Ekman appropriates Rousseau's famous painting *The
Sleeping Gypsy,* with its fittingly dreamlike atmosphere (see figure 5).
The illustrator retains the formal elements of the original, but, by replacing the lion with a dog and the sleeping gypsy with the cat protagonist (she superimposes the cat's head on the gypsy's body), she
playfully inverts the position of the feline. Rousseau's sleeping gypsy
is now a fully awake shepherd, whose eyes are open wide and staring
directly into those of the dog. This modification suffices to transform
the extraordinary peace of the original scene into an atmosphere of
apprehension that is charged with the anticipation of the pending en-

Figure 5. From *Kattens Skrekk*. Copyright © 1992 by Fam Ekman. Reprinted by permission of J. W. Cappelen, Oslo. All rights reserved.

counter. A second illustration continues the parody of *The Sleeping Gypsy*, creating a kind of sequel, in a similar manner to Browne's second version of *The Laughing Cavalier*. Contrary to readers' expectations, the cat's reaction is not one of terror but of anger; no longer just awake, but upright, the cat uses the shepherd's staff, conveniently provided by Rousseau, to beat the crying dog for disturbing his peaceful sleep. The vertical lines of the two upright figures contrast strikingly with the horizontal lines of both Ekman's first illustration and Rousseau's original, but the rest of the scene remains unchanged. The substitution of a shepherd for the gypsy in Ekman's pictures reminds the reader of the dog/*David* sculpture in the museum and seems to cast the cat in the role of David in his dream. This scene seems to confirm that there may be some ambiguity in the Norwegian title *Kattens Skrekk,* which, like *katteskrekk,* could mean "being afraid of cats," as well as "what cats are afraid of."

A parody of Rousseau's *Portrait of a Woman* accompanies the next sequence of the dream, as the cat takes the dog home to tell his mother what happened. When Ekman introduces the cat, still wearing the sleeping gypsy's oriental costume, into her parodic rendition of *Portrait of a Woman,* she remains faithful, in a tongue-in-cheek kind of way, to the original, in which a tiny cat occupies the same position in the foreground. The dog is an entirely new element, as is the mother cat's yellow hat, borrowed from the painting that Ekman will parody in her next illustration. Such details are very witty and humorous, but, of course, they can only be decoded by a relatively small audience. When the cat's angry mother decides that as punishment the dog will be made to take them and all their relatives on a cart ride in a particularly hilly region, the trip takes place in *Old Junier's Cart,* another of Rousseau's more famous paintings (see figure 6). Once again, Ekman's parodic rendition retains the structure and general color scheme of the original, but the five human figures in the cart have been replaced by cats. This illustration offers an excellent example of the sophisticated dialogue in which an illustrator may engage with an artist, even though much of the playful parody may be lost on all but the most enlightened of viewers. The original painting by Rousseau was a cat's nightmare, as it contained three dogs, one in the cart, a tiny black dog in front of it, and a large black dog underneath it. In Ekman's parody, the dog that Rousseau insisted on painting under the cart in spite of suggestions that it was too large becomes even larger to replace the mare hitched to the cart, and the other two dogs are eliminated. Ekman seems to consider this illustration of key importance, since it was chosen for the cover of *Kattens Skrekk.*

In order for parody to be appreciated, the encoder and the decoder, in our case the illustrator and his or her viewer, must share the same cultural tradition. It has been suggested, however, that "the increased cultural homogeneity in the 'global village' has increased the range of parodic forms available for use" (Hutcheon 44). Contemporary Western illustrators certainly do not limit the artworks they parody to those that are indigenous. Anthony Browne includes a Gainsborough, but also a Hals, a Dali, and a Munch, and, as we know, he has a predilection for Magritte. Likewise, the Munch in the museum in *Kattens Skrekk* is the only Norwegian painting in a book that is structured around

Figure 6. From *Kattens Skrekk*. Copyright © 1992 by Fam Ekman. Reprinted by permission of J. W. Cappelen, Oslo. All rights reserved.

the works of Rousseau. If any artist is favored by Pommaux's wolf art collector, it seems to be the American, Calder. I have encountered more of this parodic play with paintings in picture books from Europe, which would certainly be understandable in light of its particularly rich and weighty cultural heritage.[14] Furthermore, the more cohesive culture of some European countries, such as France, where education is standardized, allows authors and illustrators to expect that allusions to a certain cultural repertoire will be recognized. But any edge European schoolchildren might once have had thanks to their proximity to many of the world's finest museums has been eliminated by World Wide Web Virtual Museums, the ultimate version of Malraux's "museum without walls," where "ONE CLICK takes you to the greatest art in the world!" There is certainly no doubt that artistic parody is becoming an increasingly common practice in picture books in North America as well.

Parodic codes must be shared by the encoder and the decoder for parody to be effective, yet we have seen that illustrators obviously do not expect young viewers, or most adults, to possess all of the codes necessary to grasp all of the parodies in their works. Parodies with multiple codings are commonly used in picture books in order to provide different levels of complexity for readers of all ages. Picture-book artists embrace strategies that facilitate the comprehension of parodic modes and ensure the complicity of their young readers. The substitution of animals for the human subjects of well-known works, used by all three of the illustrators examined here, is a common practice in picture books, as readers who are unable to decode the parody at more sophisticated levels, or to identify the target painting or sculpture, will at least recognize the intent to parody and can still appreciate the humorous and playful treatment of preexisting artworks. The repetition of allusions within an illustrator's own work is also a way of ensuring eventual decoding. A striking example is the numerous references throughout Browne's books to Magritte's *Ceci n'est pas une pipe,* in which he often substitutes a banana. The contextualization of parodic allusions is also very important. If the setting is a museum or an art gallery, children are likely to sense that the illustration incorporates artistic echoes of the past and that the reader is being called upon to make an "inferential walk" outside the text, even if they do not have the competence to recognize the art works and decode the parody. As we have seen, however, illustrations do not necessarily depict parodic paintings in frames on walls. In the case of the Rousseau parodies in *Kattens Skkrek,* or several of Browne's pictures in *Willy the Dreamer,* the illustration no longer merely includes the depiction of a more or less recognizable painting within a frame; the entire illustration becomes a parody of an individual painting or the aesthetic mode of a particular artist. These parodies are obviously more difficult to decode, since no frame surrounds them to act as a marker signaling a potential parody of a preexisting art work. The parody may then escape even very competent adult viewers.[15]

Carole Scott has argued convincingly that picture books "empower children and adults much more equally," since children are less hampered by accepted conventions, and their ability to deal with visual detail often outdistances that of adults (101). If we add to that the propensity for parody of the Simpsons generation, many children may decode parodic allusions as well as, if not better than, some adults. Browne's consistent use of this type of allusion shows that he obviously thinks that children are able to appreciate parody. In fact, it was through his "visual puns" that he hoped "to wrest [*Alice*] back from adults . . . and put it firmly back on children's bookshelves" (Marantz 50–51). These illustrators invite young readers to become, in Hutcheon's terms, "active co-creators of the parodic text" (93). As Rod McGillis pointedly states, this is a sign of respect for the young reader, who gains a sense of empowerment on recognizing the parody (124).

It is obvious, however, that picture-book artists also deliberately include parodic allusions for the amusement of adult co-readers. More subtle references may even target scholars, critics, and reviewers, not only in the hope of winning acclaim from the adult children's book establishment, but even of being legitimated by the adult literary system. And some illustrators may be engaged in a personal dialogue with an artist and care not a whit if the parody is decoded by any of their viewers. It is also possible that picture-book artists practice this type of parody as a form of playful revenge against the world of high art. When a pig or a cat or a wolf or a monkey is depicted in a well-known painting, the viewer obviously laughs at the new version, not at the original, but at the same time, high art loses its sacred aura and is made to look pretentious and ridiculous. Are these parodic allusions a way of getting back at "fine artists" who do "real art" and who get paid as much for one painting as an illustrator might get for an entire book that sells well? Speaking of the "small art" of children's books, Allan Ahlberg seems to state rather too insistently that his wife Janet "doesn't have any wish to frame pictures to hang on a gallery wall," although some of their illustrator friends might like to do so and consider that "a higher achievement" (Marantz 4, 6). Browne certainly seems to poke fun at high art in *Voices in the Park,* where the two paintings displayed for sale in a garbage-littered street beside a panhandling Santa with the sign "Wife and millions of kids to support" are the *Mona Lisa* and a very sad-looking *Laughing Cavalier*. A similar intent could explain the presence of Pommaux's wolf's large collection of parodied artworks in a picture book inspired by popular culture genres, such as the comic book and the crime thriller. On the last page of the book, the coveted painting "Le loup bleu sur fond blanc" adorns the wall of John Chatterton's rather run-down office, the detective's reward for solving the case of the missing Little Red Riding

Hood. The unframed painting has been hung hastily, with a common nail and a bit of string pulled out of a garbage box, cracking the paint on the wall, and one senses from the bemused expression on the detective's face that he perhaps prefers the blues his rat friend Charlie plays on his blue sax in the alley (dressed in blue overalls rather than the wolf/art collector's formal blue suit) to his newly acquired "Blue wolf" painting.

Perhaps these allusions to the world's great artworks are in fact an invitation to view picture-book illustrations as high art, or at least as equally important and worthy of acclaim as other art forms. Referring to his allusion to Millet's *Angelus* in *Anno's Journey*, Mitsumasa Anno says, "I await the day when today's children will be adults. They will go to see the paintings in the Louvre and will say: 'Millet did that after Mr. Anno!'" ("Anno" 56). Perhaps Browne hopes similarly that children who one day visit the Art Institute of Chicago will think that Magritte modeled *Time Transfixed* upon his illustration in *The Visitors Who Came to Stay!*

By incorporating parodic allusions to preexisting artworks into their picture books, illustrators introduce children to a rich cultural heritage, albeit in an often much-altered form. Even while subverting and inverting those works, parody guarantees their continued existence; it is, in Hutcheon's terms, "the custodian of the artistic legacy" (75). Whatever their reasons for parodying artworks, illustrators offer enlightened adult mediators a wonderful opportunity to introduce children to the original works to which they refer. Hutcheon rightly states that little attention has been paid to "the didactic value of parody in teaching or co-opting the art of the past by textual incorporation and ironic commentary" (27), a neglect that is even more surprising in the field of children's literature, which has so often been examined only from a didactic perspective. If these sophisticated picture books with their parodic play are indeed one of the book's survival techniques for the electronic age, the adults who share them with children would do well to view them as a valuable tool to be used in conjunction with the Internet's "WebMuseums" to interest the Simpsons generation in the world of high art.

Notes

I am indebted to my colleague Derek Knight, from the Department of Film Studies, Dramatic and Visual Arts at Brock University, for his invaluable assistance in identifying certain parodied works, and I am very grateful to Rolf Romören for his generous help with translation.

1. I am currently completing a much lengthier study on artistic allusions in children's literature.

2. There are no doubt some who would argue that parody is a sign of artistic impoverishment or decadence.

3. Eliza Dresang examines the types of books that are likely to appeal to this generation in *Radical Change: Books for Youth in a Digital Age*.

4. Joseph Stanton examines the surrealistic tendencies in Chris Van Allsburg's work in an article that appeared in volume 24 of *Children's Literature*.

5. In her speculations on the kinds of books that would make children want to continue reading in an electronic age, at the forum I organized for the Modern Language Association titled "The Status of Children's Books in this Millennium and the Next," Wendy Lamb, executive editor in the Books for Young Readers Department at Bantam Doubleday Dell, mentioned in particular sophisticated dual-audience picture books (172).

6. This change in color reflects the evolution of the work of the Dutch master, whose colors were bright in the earlier works and sober in the later ones.

7. I refer, of course, to the subtitle of Gérard Genette's *Palimpsests: Literature in the Second Degree*.

8. The painting seems to invite a psychoanalytical interpretation of the wolf's relationship with his own mother, especially for adult readers who know that Whistler's mother was a very domineering woman determined to control her son.

9. Anthony Browne also parodies one of Magritte's famous word-images on the title page of *Willy the Dreamer*.

10. One might wonder why Ekman did not turn Munch's screaming figure into a cat by adding ears and whiskers, but she may have wished to suggest that the cat's terror is no different from human fears, or perhaps she was merely afraid the painting would no longer be recognizable or that the cat would be mistaken for another dog.

11. Later versions by the artist do represent black and white divers on a colored background.

12. Léger insisted on the fact that his divers "are really *falling*" (de Francia 134).

13. The primitive, instinctive, childlike quality of the art of Henri Rousseau, also known as Le Douanier, an untrained painter unhampered by the influence of art school and academic doctrines, no doubt makes it an appealing choice for a picture book.

14. This finding has been confirmed by the children's librarians with whom I have spoken. Many museum shops in Europe, such as the one at the Musée d'Orsay, carry a good selection of such picture books from several countries.

15. In the case of *Willy the Dreamer*, all of the illustrations, including those which contain no reference to paintings, are framed in the same manner, so that the frame goes virtually unnoticed. The illustration that represents Willy dreaming that he's an explorer parodies a Rousseau painting by integrating Willy into the jungle scene in the same way Ekman embeds her cat protagonist into other works by the French artist. Willy also appears in one of Dali's strange landscapes. Once again, however, it is Magritte who predominates; when Willy dreams that he's a painter, the pictures in his studio are all parodies of Magritte's works. A salesperson in Chantelivre, a children's book store in Paris, told me shortly after the French edition of *Willy the Dreamer* was published that she and her colleagues had not yet been able to decode all of the illustrations.

Works Cited

Anno, Mitsumasa. "Anno 85–Anno 87." Remarks collected by Geneviève Patte and Annie Pissard and by Catherine Germain and Elisabeth Lortic. *La Revue des livres pour enfants* 118 (winter 1987): 53–57.

———. *Anno's Journey.* 1977. London, Sydney, Toronto: Bodley Head, 1978.

Arnason, H. H. *History of Modern Art.* 3d ed. New York: Harry N. Abrams, 1986.

Birkeland, Tone. "At the Crossroad—the Norwegian Picture Book." In *Norwegian Books for Children and Young People.* Lillehammer: Lillehammer Olympic Organizing Committee, 1994. Pp. 10–13.

Browne, Anthony. *The Big Baby: A Little Joke.* New York: Knopf, 1993.

———. *Piggybook.* New York: Knopf, 1986.

———. *Voices in the Park.* New York: DK Publishing, 1998.

———. *Willy the Dreamer.* Cambridge, Mass.: Candlewick Press, 1997.

Dresang, Eliza T. *Radical Change: Books for Youth in a Digital Age.* New York: H. W. Wilson, 1999.

Eco, Umberto. *The Role of the Reader.* Bloomington: Indiana University Press, 1979.

Ekman, Fam. *Kattens Skrekk* (The cat's terror). Oslo: Cappelen, 1992.

Francia, Peter de. *Fernand Léger.* New Haven and London: Yale University Press, 1983.

Genette, Gérard. *Palimpsests: Literature in the Second Degree.* Trans. Channa Newman and Claude Doubinsky. Lincoln: University of Nebraska Press, 1997 [1982].

Hutcheon, Linda. *A Theory of Parody: The Teachings of Twentieth-Century Art Forms.* New York and London: Methuen, 1985.

Lamb, Wendy. "Strange Business: The Publishing Point of View." *Signal* 87, special issue (September 1998): 167–73.

Marantz, Sylvia, and Kenneth Marantz. *Artists of the Page: Interviews with Children's Book Illustrators.* Jefferson, N.C.: McFarland, 1992.

McAfee, Annalena. *The Visitors Who Came to Stay.* Illus. Anthony Browne. London: Hamish Hamilton, 1984.

McGillis, Roderick. *The Nimble Reader: Literary Theory and Children's Literature.* New York: Twayne, 1996.

Nodelman, Perry. *Words About Pictures: The Narrative Art of Children's Books.* Athens: University of Georgia Press, 1988.

Payant, René. "Bricolage pictural: l'art à propos de l'art; I—La Question de la citation." *Parachute* 16 (1979): 5–8.

Pommaux, Yvan. *John Chatterton détective.* Paris: L'école des loisirs, 1993.

Scott, Carole. "Dual Audience in Picturebooks." In *Transcending Boundaries: Writing for a Dual Audience of Children and Adults.* Ed. Sandra L. Beckett. New York: Garland, 1999. Pp. 99–110.

Stanton, Joseph. "The Dreaming Picture Books of Chris Van Allsburg." *Children's Literature* 24 (1996): 161–79.

Stites, Raymond S. *The Arts and Man.* New York: McGraw-Hill, 1940.

Tansey, Richard G., and Fred S. Kleiner. *Gardner's Art Through the Ages.* 10th ed. New York: Harcourt Brace, 1996.

Wynne-Jones, Tim. "The Survival of the Book." *Signal* 87, special issue (September 1998): 160–66.

The End of Empire? Colonial and Postcolonial Journeys in Children's Books

Clare Bradford

To read children's books of the nineteenth and twentieth centuries is to read texts produced within a pattern of imperial culture. Works of the past, such as *Tom Brown's Schooldays, The Water-Babies,* and *The Secret Garden,* readily disclose the imperial ideologies that inform them. Thus, Hughes's depiction of schoolboy life at Rugby is framed by imperialism, not merely because Rugby's régime constitutes a training-ground for imperial adventures, as in the case of Tom's great friend East, who leaves the school to join his regiment in India, but also because the conceptual world in which the boys are located comprises two parts: home and abroad, center and margins, as Hughes's depiction of the tribe of Browns demonstrates: "For centuries, in their quiet, dogged, homespun way, [the Browns] have been subduing the earth in most English counties, and leaving their mark in American forests and Australian uplands" (13). In *The Water-Babies,* Kingsley's mobilization of imperial ideologies is distinguished by its convergence of categories of race and class. When Tom climbs down the wrong chimney to arrive in Ellie's room and catches sight of himself in a mirror, he sees "a little ugly, black, ragged figure, with bleared eyes and grinning white teeth" (19). Here, the grime of the chimney, a signifier of Tom's lowly position within the domestic economy, is mapped onto the blackness of peoples colonized by British imperialism.[1] Conversely, Tom's ascent to the middle class is coterminous with his transformation into a white imperial man: "[he] can plan railroads, and steam-engines, and electric telegraphs, and rifled guns, and so forth" (243–44). And in *The Secret Garden,* Frances Hodgson Burnett represents India as a space marked by disorder, danger, and sickness, so that Mary's return to Britain restores her to physical and psychic health (see Cadden; Phillips).

In these texts, the lands and indigenous peoples "out there" in the far reaches of the British Empire are "Othered" in order to produce and sustain an idea fundamental to colonial discourse: that Europe

Children's Literature 29, ed. Elizabeth Lennox Keyser and Julie Pfeiffer (Yale University Press, © 2001 Hollins University).

(and, in these three texts, Britain) is the norm by which other countries and peoples are judged. Not that the process of "Othering" is
an unproblematic one—indeed, colonial discourse is shot through
with anxieties concerning what Peter Hulme calls "the classic colonial triangle, . . . the relationship between European, native and land"
(1). Thus, for example, discourses of Christianity, some of which promote the equality of all people as children of God, frequently clash
with colonial discourse, which promotes the superiority of white over
colored peoples, and so validates the appropriation of land (see Bradford). Nevertheless, despite their moments of uncertainty and their
occasional resistance to dominant ideologies, colonial texts are by and
large organized through such binary oppositions as self and other,
civilized and savage, white and black.

Postcolonial texts are marked by a more complex and contradictory set of discursive practices, some of which this discussion seeks
to identify and analyze. Although the *post* of *postcolonial* is sometimes
read merely as a temporal marker separating a period of colonial rule
from the time after it, many theorists have pointed to the cultural and
historical differences that are concealed by such a monolithic term,
and to the fact that in countries with colonial histories (such as North
America, South Africa, India, Australia), the consequences of colonial
rule are played out in contemporary struggles over power and especially over land (McClintock 9–14; Dirlik 503–4; Ghandi 1–5). Accordingly, my use of the term *postcolonial* recognizes the shifting and uncertain significances that attend references to the imperial project.

A feature common in newly independent states after colonialism is
what Leela Ghandi terms "postcolonial amnesia" (4), in which painful
events of the colonial period are "forgotten." After Australia achieved
nationhood in 1901, for example, there followed what the anthropologist W. E. H. Stanner described in 1968 as "a cult of forgetfulness
practised on a national scale" (25), an eloquent silence regarding Aborigines and the violence and dispossession that they endured following white settlement. Most Australian children's texts produced in the
first few decades of the twentieth century omit Aborigines from accounts of Australian history or reconfigure historical events to produce stories of white heroism and black savagery, thus positioning
child readers to see themselves as citizens of a white Australia and the
inheritors of a tradition of pioneer endeavor. Such strategies seek to
elide aspects of the past in order to produce a new national identity.
But the past is not so easily forgotten, especially by peoples formerly

colonized. For as Edward Said notes, interpretations of the present frequently involve the rereading of the past in an attempt to discover "whether the past really is past, over and concluded, or whether it continues, albeit in different forms" (*Culture and Imperialism* 1). The colonial past is variously rehearsed, reinscribed, and contested in postcolonial children's texts, and it is increasingly a site of tension, producing different and conflicting significances. There are two reasons for this: first, the influence of subaltern writing, which seeks to recover the voices of colonized people and tell their stories; and, second, the fact that strategies of silence and forgetting merely repress colonial memories, the recovery of which is frequently painful and confrontational.

Tropes of journeying and travel are prominent in postcolonial texts, many of which rehearse, reexamine, and parody the historical journeys of colonialism. In this discussion I consider two British texts: Roald Dahl's *Charlie and the Chocolate Factory* (first published in 1964) and Penelope Lively's *The House in Norham Gardens* (1974), books as far apart from each other as can be imagined but that thematize aspects of the relations between empire and colonies. As instances of "the Empire writing back," I have selected two Australian texts, Pat Lowe and Jimmy Pike's *Jimmy and Pat Meet the Queen* (1997) and Tohby Riddle's *Royal Guest* (1993), and a New Zealand text, Paula Boock's *Sasscat* (1994). In all five texts, characters undertake journeys to or from Britain: the Oompa-Loompas, in *Charlie and the Chocolate Factory,* travel from Loompaland to the imperial center, located in Willy Wonka's chocolate factory; in *The House in Norham Gardens,* fourteen-year-old Clare becomes obsessed by the journey of her anthropologist great-grandfather to New Guinea in 1905. Both *Jimmy and Pat Meet the Queen* and *The Royal Guest* focus on visits by Queen Elizabeth to Australia, and in *Sasscat,* Win, a young New Zealander, travels to London, and her sister, Sass, dreams of becoming an astronaut. These journeys rework the themes of place and displacement that are so common in postcolonial literatures (see Ashcroft, Griffiths, and Tiffin 9), but the ideologies of the five texts are far from uniform. For although *postcolonialism* might seem to be invested with notions of progressivism and transition to a brave new world, in fact postcolonial texts display the heterogeneity of postcolonial cultures, with their traces of colonialism, their mix of complicitness with and resistance to colonial ideologies (Hodge and Mishra xi–xii), and their spasmodic irruptions of neocolonialism.

As Bob Dixon pointed out in his groundbreaking work *Catching Them Young* (1977), *Charlie and the Chocolate Factory* works as "a paradigm of imperialism" (110), with Willy Wonka exercising imperial power over the colonized Oompa-Loompas.[2] Dixon is quite correct to see *Charlie and the Chocolate Factory* as adhering to the ideologies of nineteenth-century novels of colonial adventure, but there are important distinctions to be made: Dahl wrote *Charlie* in the 1960s, well after the disintegration of the British Empire; and though the heroes of Haggard, Marryat, and Henty travel from Britain to the strange and barbaric lands "out there" in the empire and back again to the safety of Britain, the Oompa-Loompas are brought from their home in Loompaland to work in Willy Wonka's chocolate factory. Dahl's version of the journey thus involves the displacement of colonized people and their mass transportation to the imperial center, to be commodified as cheap labor. Indeed, the Oompa-Loompas signify two kinds of displacement: they displace the local workforce sacked by Willy Wonka, and they themselves are displaced from Loompaland. Dahl sidesteps the first kind of displacement by treating workers as mere cogs in Willy Wonka's machine, not as people and even less as individuals. And the Oompa-Loompas' displacement from their homeland is elided through Dahl's representation of Loompaland, in whose jungles lurk dangerous creatures such as hornswogglers, snozzwangers, and whangdoodles, and where the Oompa-Loompas can find nothing but green caterpillars to eat. In this way, Dahl constructs the home of the colonized as a place characterized by absence and poverty (specifically of cacao beans), so that the Oompa-Loompas' voyage to Willy Wonka's factory, smuggled in "large packing cases with holes in them" (68), is an insignificant price to pay for the privilege of working for Willy Wonka and of being supplied with cacao beans and alcoholic beverages such as butterscotch and buttergin.

Dahl's treatment of the Oompa-Loompas exactly conforms with Edward Said's description of the ways in which the West has rationalized colonial processes with claims that colonized people were "provided with order and a kind of stability that they haven't been able . . . to provide for themselves" (*Culture* 23). Within this fiction of Western benevolence and generosity, colonized peoples are represented as recipients of largesse; homogenized and robbed of individuality, they exist as a discursive figure, "them" as distinct from "us," whose duty it is to appreciate the magnanimity with which they have been treated. Such a "leap to essences and generalizations" (*Culture* 24) effectively elides the variety and specificity of colonial experience, suppressing, for example, the histories of colonized peoples sold to the slave trade or exploited as cheap labor in various parts of the British Empire. Willy Wonka's Oompa-Loompas are effectively enslaved, but through the mediating figure of Willy Wonka, Dahl positions children to read their enslavement as reward and privilege.

This strategy can be seen most clearly in the episode in which Willy Wonka relates the story of his discovery and "liberation" of the Oompa-Loompas. The children and adults who are taken on their tour of the factory first see the Oompa-Loompas from a distance, in a narrator-focalized sequence. The following exchange serves as a transition to Willy Wonka's first-person narrative:

> "Oompa-Loompas!" everyone said at once. "*Oompa-Loompas!*"
> "Imported direct from Loompaland," said Mr Wonka proudly.
> "There's no such place," said Mrs Salt.
> "Excuse me, dear lady, but . . ."
> "*Mr Wonka,*" cried Mrs Salt. "I'm a teacher of geography . . ."
> "Then you'll know all about it," said Mr Wonka. "And oh, what a terrible country it is. . . ." (66)

Whereas Mrs Salt is incontrovertibly an adult, Willy Wonka, an "extraordinary little man" (57), his face "alight with fun and laughter" (57), is attributed with qualities intended to persuade child readers that he is one of them, aligned with them against adults (and specifically teachers) such as Mrs Salt. The contrast between Mrs Salt and Willy Wonka is an epistemological one as well: whereas Mrs Salt knows theory (the "facts" of geography), Willy Wonka's knowledge is based on his practical experience of Loompaland. Through these strategies, Willy Wonka is established as a figure who speaks authoritatively to implied child readers about the Oompa-Loompas and their land.

Wonka's depiction of the Oompa-Loompas (66–68) proposes a series of oppositions between himself (as ideal and idealized imperialist) and his colonized workforce. Wonka is, first of all, *knowing*, whereas even the leader of the tribe of Oompa-Loompas is unable to understand anything beyond his physical symptoms of hunger. Contrasting values attach to place: Wonka's pride in the glories of his factory, compared with the Oompa-Loompas' readiness to leave their homeland. Wonka is an adult, the Oompa-Loompas perpetual children; Wonka an amused observer, the Oompa-Loompas objects of his colonizing gaze. Above all, the Oompa-Loompas are promoted to child readers as ideals of how colonized peoples should behave toward their imperial lords: they are satisfied, hardworking, and grateful; moreover, they never forget their colonial place, wearing the clothing that marks them as primitives: "They still wear the same kind of clothes they wore in the jungle. They insist upon that" (68). Racialized and objectified as Others, the Oompa-Loompas are thus distinguished from the book's implied readers, who are positioned as "normal" subjects, citizens whose clothing and way of life mark them as being *at home* in Britain in a way the Oompa-Loompas are not. Dahl's representation of colonized peoples suggests, by inference, that native peoples who turn against imperial rule, or who reject the subservience modeled by the Oompa-Loompas, contravene a model of social and imperial interactions naturalized as correct and appropriate. *Charlie and the Chocolate Factory,* produced in the decade following a dramatic increase in the migration of West Indian, African, and Asian people to Britain, and six years after the anti-black riots in Notting Hill and Nottingham, thus proposes a social and economic structure that treats colonial workers as unskilled and poorly paid factory fodder.

In its promotion of colonialism, its homogenization of the colonized, and its strategies of Othering, *Charlie and the Chocolate Factory* harks back to texts of the nineteenth century; in contrast, Penelope Lively's *House in Norham Gardens* displays many of the tensions and uncertainties of postcolonialism, within a complex and subtle narrative. Both texts play with what Mary Louise Pratt refers to as the "contact zone," the "space of colonial encounters" (6) where colonizers and those colonized meet and negotiate relations of power and influence. *Charlie and the Chocolate Factory* promotes the idea that colonial hierarchies are maintained "at home"—that is, in Willy Wonka's factory—just as they were "out there" in Loompaland. *The House at Norham Gardens,* in contrast, sets one contact zone against another through its shifts in time and place, between 1970s Britain and colonial New Guinea. Clare Mayfield, the protagonist of the novel, lives with her two great-aunts in an Oxford house that constitutes a time capsule of imperialism, for it is filled with the objects and records of Clare's great-grandfather, an anthropologist who "went to queer places and brought things back" (21). Clare discovers in the attic a tamburan, a carved shield from New Guinea, and becomes absorbed by the historical and cultural significances of this object, finally donating it to the Natural History Museum, where it is incorporated into the collection named after her great-grandfather. The tamburan is the central symbol within the novel's exploration of cultural and historical difference, a strand of meaning that intersects with two others: Clare's own sense of becoming an adult who is both like and unlike her fourteen-year-old self, and themes of aging, physical change, and death, centered on "the aunts."

Within its contrapuntal organization, *The House in Norham Gardens* circles around symbols and ideas connected with space and time. The house itself, a nineteen-room Victorian marooned among new buildings and old buildings converted into flats, is remote from modernity, since Clare's aunts live quietly in their library, reading and observing; the house is replete with the past in the form of old photographs, china, books and a lavatory "in brown mahogany with the bowl encircled in purple flowers and a cistern called 'The Great Niagara'" (18). While the narrative chronologically follows a few months (from winter to spring) in Clare's life, a series of flashbacks at the beginning of each chapter traces the process of colonization in the New Guinea village from which the tamburan originates: the coming of Europeans to the village in 1905, the destabilization of an ancient culture, the destruction of forests, the loss of cultural identity, the tribe's journey to modernity. Or, rather, this is how the narrative represents colonization, and the *how* of Lively's representation discloses the limitations of the epistemology on which it relies.

Whereas Dahl's treatment of the Oompa-Loompas trumpets the inferiority of the colonized, Lively's depiction of the New Guinea tribe is tinged with regret and nostalgia, as can be seen in the first of the novel's descriptions of the valley:

> There is an island. At the heart of the island there is a valley. In the valley, among blue mountains, a man kneels before a piece of wood. He paints on it—sometimes with a fibre brush, sometimes with his finger. The man himself is painted: bright dyes—red, yellow, black—on brown skin. . . . The year is 1900: in England Victoria is queen. The man is remote from England in distance by half the circumference of the world: in understanding, by five thousand years. (7)

The island, the valley, the mountains, the kneeling man, are objects of a Eurocentric gaze that describes and evaluates them in relation to their remoteness from England. The narrative itself, implying the existence of a knowing observer, inscribes the valley, and the painted man, as vulnerable to the encroachment of modernity. At the same time, the mobilization of a temporal contrast ("The man is remote from England . . . by five thousand years") enacts a vast and unbridgeable gap between the narrator and the painted man. In its authoritativeness, its knowingness, its emphasis on difference, this passage mobilizes the discursive strategies of Orientalism, which, in Said's terms, defines itself through "the whole complex series of knowledgeable manipulations" (*Orientalism* 40) through which it orders the study of the Orient. In Lively's descriptions of the village, the New Guinea tribesmen are represented, in their pre-colonized state, as living in a coherent and ordered society—they "celebrate the mystery of life with ritual" (37). But their culture is defined and fixed through its difference. They have "known no influences, learned no skills" (37)—that is, they have known no influences and learned no skills defined as such by the narrator, whose knowledge and ideological stance are naturalized as normative.

The system of knowledge invoked here is that of anthropology— more specifically, the model of social anthropology prominent in 1974, when *The House in Norham Gardens* was published. The following comments by the Australian anthropologist Gillian Cowlishaw describe how anthropology was mobilized in Australia to "manage" what was commonly called "the Aboriginal problem," but they refer more broadly to the uses to which it was put in former colonies: "From its establishment as a university based discipline there was an underlying, unstated moral task associated with studies of [indigenous] culture. This was that anthropology would supply expert knowledge about that culture that would be used to develop appropriate policy. . . ." (22). In exactly the same way, Lively's description of the New Guinea tribe constructs an "expert knowledge" of what is in the best interests of the tribe. Here is the final episode in the story of the tribe's colonization:

> Houses are built for the tribe, and roads. They learn how to drive cars, use telephones, tin-openers, matches and screwdrivers. They are given laws that they must obey: they are not to kill one another and they must pay their taxes. They listen to the radio and they make no more tamburans, but their nights are rich with dreams. The children of the tribe learn how to read and write: they sit at wooden desks with their heads bent low over sheets of paper, and make marks on the paper. One day, they will discover again the need for tamburans, and they will make a new

kind of tamburan for themselves, and for their children, and their children's children. (165)

The underlying assumptions of this passage are that Western laws will prevent bloodshed ("they are not to kill one another") and that the members of the tribe will embrace the icons of the Western lifestyle (houses, cars, telephones, tin-openers). If their entry into modernity precludes the making of tamburans, the gift of literacy will eventually enable the children of the tribe to "make a new kind of tamburan," but this will be possible only because of their deployment of Western systems of knowledge.

This story of colonization intersects with a series of dreams in which Clare observes the tribesmen seeking the return of their tamburan. As her dreams increase in urgency and intensity, they symbolize Clare's own groping after subjectivity; more important for this discussion, they expose the error of her great-grandfather in taking the tamburan from the tribesmen, who had at first believed that their European visitors were tribal ancestors. Significantly, Clare seeks a solution through an appeal to anthropological knowledge. Her Ugandan friend John Sempebwa is established within the text as an authority on native peoples: he is himself, he says, a "detribalized African" (75); moreover, he is a student of anthropology. When he tells Clare that the New Guinea tribes "stop making tamburans . . . as soon as they've jumped into the twentieth century. . . . They seem to forget how, or why they did it" (99), the principle of cultural discontinuity is promoted: that colonialism has effected a decisive split from the traditional culture of the painted man who created the tamburan. Clare's conclusion that "If it can't be where it belongs, then a museum is the best place" (169) implies that there is no longer any "where," so that the museum, and the disciplinary formations of anthropology, become custodians of the object and its cultural meanings.

Lively's representation of the New Guinea tribe is, of course, a far more progressive representation of colonial relations than that encoded in *Charlie and the Chocolate Factory*. But twenty-five years after its publication, its faultlines are clearly visible. The New Guinea tribesmen (and the figures of Clare's dreams are, true to the phallocentric traditions of anthropology, always male) are consigned to the past of primitivism; the sense of loss and regret that permeates Lively's depiction of the tribe enacts the meaning, implied throughout the novel, that the painted man represents the true and authentic culture of the tribe, a culture preserved only through anthropological knowledge, and specifically by museums. In Lively's descriptions of the colonization of the tribe, the New Guineans are attributed no agency, no capacity for reflexivity or adaptability, but wait passively for the return of the ancestors. Gillian Cowlishaw's summary of anthropological models of the 1960s and 1970s is strikingly close to the mood and tone that permeate Lively's depiction of the tribe: "The metaphor of destruction became intrenched, fixing the complex, ongoing events of colonisation into a one way process of collapse to which the appropriate response is passive sorrow" (25). The novel is thus caught between its contestation of the imperial past (exemplified by Clare's great-grandfather) and its privileging of modernity as a dynamic, protean, complex state that, paradoxically, *needs* primitivism as its opposite term, objectified as the embodiment of stillness, simplicity, and fixedness. *The House in Norham Gardens* concludes with Clare looking intently at her aged and beloved aunts and realizing that what she is doing is "learning them by heart," memorizing them against the time when they are dead. For the New Guinea tribesmen, on the other hand, there are dreams, but no memories; there is a dim consciousness of tradition and a nostalgia for it, but the culture is incapable of adapting and transforming itself.

In *Jimmy and Pat Meet the Queen,* written by Pat Lowe and illustrated by Jimmy Pike, colonization does not effect a rift of memory; instead, traditional knowledge, tested against the land of its production, constitutes a proof of tribal identity in contemporary Australia. Jimmy is "a Walmajarri man," from the Great Sandy Desert in Western Australia; Pat, his wife, "comes from England." The conjunction of histories and traditions exemplified in the partnership of Jimmy and Pat allows for broad comedy based on contrasted modes of speaking and thinking, but *Jimmy and Pat* is a hybrid text in other respects as well. It is at once a tract on land ownership in Australia and an illustrated book; its implied readers constitute a combination of older children, adolescents, and adults; its narrative combines the standard English of Pat with the Creole used by Jimmy in conversational exchanges; its illustrations draw on traditions of Aboriginal art but depict aspects of contemporary life. In these ways it exemplifies "transculturation," the term used by Pratt to describe how colonized and formerly colonized people engage in negotiations between their own culture and that of their colonizers (6).

As I've noted, an important line of resistance to earlier literary and cultural studies of colonialism is embodied in subaltern studies, described by Leela Ghandi as "an attempt to allow the 'people' finally to speak . . . and, in so doing, to speak for, or to sound the muted voices of, the truly oppressed" (2). *Jimmy and Pat Meet the Queen* alludes to the dispossession experienced by Aboriginal people, but its insouciance and subversive wit are anything but muted. On learning that the land of his people is regarded by kartiya (white) law as Vacant Crown Land, Jimmy invites the queen to prove her ownership by one concrete and decisive test: that she knows where to find water in "her" desert. The queen agrees to travel to Walmajarri country, and after a long search she concludes that she is indeed unable to locate any waterholes and that the land belongs to "the Walmajarri mob" (29).

In *The House in Norham Gardens,* tribal knowledge and traditions are represented as failing to survive colonization, so that they can be preserved only within systems of Western knowledge; in *Jimmy and Pat,* in contrast, Western epistemologies are pitted against the ancient and continuous traditions of the Walmajarri, whose knowledge is based on the land itself and on ritual journeys undertaken over many thousands of years. The nostalgia that informs Lively's depiction of the New Guinea tribe derives from an Orientalist emphasis on the primitive nature of their culture, which is quarantined in a past that is discontinuous with modernity. The Aboriginal culture promoted in *Jimmy and Pat* combines traditional beliefs and knowledge with elements of contemporary Western culture: Jimmy and Pat's letter asserting Walmajarri ownership of the land makes the sly suggestion that the queen "may be glad to get away from [her] family for a while" (9); the Walmajarri people follow their traditional journey in a Suzuki and a Toyota. This hybridity is a marker of a set of cultural forms at once fully Aboriginal and selectively modern.

Jimmy and Pat displaces colonial hierarchies through its juxtaposition of standard and Aboriginal English and its mobilization of intertextual references. Here, the queen meets Jimmy and Pat at their desert camp:

> Then a door in the [helicopter] opened, and out stepped the Queen of England.
>
> Jimmy and Pat walked forward to greet her. Jimmy held out his hand while Pat tried to do a curtesy in her King Gees.
>
> "Hello old woman," said Jimmy, and Pat gave him a hard nudge in the ribs.

The Queen took Jimmy's hand. "How do you do?" she said, with
her gracious smile.

"Do what?" Jimmy asked Pat.

"She means how are you going," Pat explained, on tenterhooks
in case either of them said the wrong thing.

Jimmy turned back to the Queen. "I'm right," he said. (12)

For Australian readers, this episode evokes the newsreels, photographs, news reports, and verbal commentaries that have always surrounded royal visits to this country. In particular, it recalls the iconic
moments when the queen emerges from car, plane or train, to be
greeted by her Australian subjects. Usually, such moments are pic-
tured within the broader context of a watching crowd or a line of
dignitaries awaiting their turn to be blessed by the royal presence;
here, the queen walks alone into the desert, so that the book's implied
readers are interpellated as the observers of a scene at once familiar
and strange. The queen enacts the rituals of royal visits through the
"gracious smile" that strategically ignores Jimmy's "Hello old woman"
and through the greeting "How do you do?," but in taking the final
"do" as a transitive verb, and responding "Do what?," Jimmy subverts
the queen's reliance on a formulaic phrase intended to maintain social
hierarchies and insists on locating speech within a context of interpersonal relations.

   Jimmy Pike's illustration of the camp where the trio sleep deploys an
aerial perspective (figure 1). For all its apparent artlessness, this picture subverts hierarchies of power and race through its positioning
of the queen, in her swag,[3] placed alongside the figures of Jimmy and
Pat in their shared swag, and against the white ground of the page. If
the queen is at the same level as Jimmy and Pat within a democracy
of desert life, she is allowed a signifier of royalty in the tiara that is
placed neatly by her, but this is not the only sign that distinguishes her
from her companions: her two corgis sleep near her, while Jimmy and
Pat's hunting dog sleeps at Jimmy's feet; and her high-heeled shoes,
so inappropriate to desert use, invite comparison with the serviceable
footwear of Jimmy and Pat. Pike's deployment of a limited number of
forms and participants is a feature common in traditional art, which
"[uses] a minimalist system of classification to establish a complex network of connections that in Western traditions is associated with metaphor" (Hodge and Mishra 96). In this picture, the key elements are
the human and animal participants, seen within a set of relations that

Figure 1. From Pat Lowe and Jimmy Pike, *Jimmy and Pat Meet the Queen,* pp. 16–17. By permission of Pat Lowe and Jimmy Pike.

displace Western notions of social status. The figure of the queen is smaller than those of Jimmy and Pat, suggesting that despite her tiara she is young in the ways of the desert and in need of the guidance of her companions.

When, finally, the moment of testing comes, and the queen must identify the waterholes that will prove whether she is the owner of the land, the broad humor of the following exchange relies on slippages and contrasts between registers:

> The Queen put her lorgnette up to her eyes and gazed out over the country, but for the life of her she couldn't see any water.
>
> "There *are* no waterholes!" she declared.
>
> "Bullshit!" said Jimmy, and Pat grimaced into the bushes. "There's a waterhole that way, and another waterhole that way, and another waterhole right there!" He flung out his arm in different directions as he spoke.
>
> "And cowpoo to you too!" said the Queen. "There's not a drop of water to be seen! This is a desert!"
>
> "Well, I'll show you!" said Jimmy. (27)

The queen's declarations "There *are* no waterholes!" and "This is a desert" insist on the primacy of Western (and queenly) knowledge, but her invention of "And cowpoo to you too," in response to Jimmy's "Bullshit!" traces a shift from "high English" to a demotic register, enacting a destabilization of hierarchies.[4] Following the group's collective action of digging in the region of a waterhole, her response to the discovery of water is a thoroughly colloquial one: " 'Well, I'll be buggered!' said the Queen" (29).[5]

The quest for water, with its associated competition between the queen and the Walmajarri people, can be understood within *schemata* of Western folk literature; but the outcome of the quest, and the narrative's validation of Walmajarri ownership of the land, are loaded with ironies that undercut notions of an ending in which all live "happily ever after." This is signaled on the inside front cover of the book, where conventional statements concerning the truth or otherwise of narratives are parodied in the following words: "All the people and places in this book are real. The story is true, although most of it hasn't happened yet." With considerable lightness of touch, Lowe here alludes to the historical and political contexts to which the narrative relates: the stories of dispossession and appropriation that it evokes and the long struggle by indigenous Australians for recognition as the original owners of the land and for continuing rights to it. Most of all, *Jimmy and Pat Meet the Queen* insists on the capacity of Aboriginal culture to transform its repertoire of textual and artistic forms. This is a far cry from Lively's representation of an indigenous culture reliant for its preservation on Western systems of knowledge.

Tohby Riddle's *The Royal Guest* also tells the story of a visit by Queen Elizabeth to Australia, but this text discloses another set of postcolonial significances that refer to Australia's history as a settler colony. Colonial distinctions between white settlers and Aborigines relied on hierarchies of value that placed Aboriginal people at the lower end of the Chain of Being and, following Darwin's *Origin of Species,* as a race locked into an early stage of human evolution. But distinctions of a different sort always attended comparisons between British people who settled in Australia and who gradually came to see themselves as "Australians," and inhabitants of the imperial center. Some of these distinctions manifest themselves in comparisons between the culture and refinement of Britain and a rough-and-ready Australian culture; others insist on the vitality and health of the New World, compared with an effete and exhausted Old World. Riddle's story, which comprises an

Figure 2. From Tohby Riddle, *The Royal Guest*, p. 3. By permission of Tohby Riddle.

account of "the last visit of the Queen," when "times were tough" and "people were wondering if the costs of such a visit could be managed," alludes to these comparisons and dismantles them.

The queen in *The Royal Guest* is parodically represented as a collection of features: she wears a sensible blue coat, serviceable brown shoes, white gloves, and a benign expression, and she carries a handbag (figure 2). Riddle's narrative, unfolded in a deadpan style, tells how "a Mrs. Jones of Padstow" offers to billet the queen during her visit to Sydney: "She had plenty of room and a comfortable inflatable mattress that the Queen was welcome to. She need only bring her sleeping bag." The *faux-naïve* quality of Riddle's text is replicated in the accompanying illustration (figure 3), which shows the figure of Mrs. Jones performing a deictic function by pointing to her house, which is defined by the details of its exterior as a working-class home of the 1950s: its neat, bungalow-type style, the featured cactus in a pot near the door, the decorative butterfly under the house number, the diamond-shaped panes of glass set in the front door, and the metal gate behind which Mrs. Jones stands.

Figure 3. From Tohby Riddle, *The Royal Guest,* p. 5. By permission of Tohby Riddle.

In the narrative that follows, the queen, carrying her rolled-up sleeping bag, arrives by plane and proceeds to the bus stop, where she catches the bus to Padstow, "go[ing] over her speeches to the nation in her head" during the trip. She spends the evening playing cards with Mrs. Jones and her friend; on the following day, after some moments of anxiety occasioned by the illness of Mrs. Jones's cat, the queen gives a public address before returning by train to Mrs. Jones's home. She is awoken the next morning by "the sound of cartoons on the television," but the Jones children are sent outside to play so as not to disturb her. To thank Mrs. Jones for her hospitality, the queen gives her one of her old crowns, and the narrative concludes with the queen continuing the royal tour to Melbourne, "where she would be staying with the Bradley family of Footscray," another working-class suburb. The comedy of *The Royal Guest* derives from the incongruities that it implies, particularly those between the queen's wealth, fame, and social class and her relocation within the habitus of working-class life. Catching a bus to Padstow, and seated behind a small boy licking an

Figure 4. From Tohby Riddle, *The Royal Guest,* p. 11. By permission of Tohby Riddle.

ice cream and in front of a sleeping elderly man (figure 4), the queen is represented as neither more nor less than an elderly woman, connected to the other participants in the illustration by their common use of bus travel, in which social status is subordinated to the physical organization of the public transport system. Similarly, the queen is incongruously incorporated into the Jones household, whose physical and social interactions are wildly different from those customarily associated with royal life. Thus, Mrs. Jones, her friend, and the queen sit cozily around the kitchen table playing cards; the queen is obliged to hold the family's sick cat on her knee as Mrs. Jones takes her to meet the prime minister; and the Jones children perch on the end of the queen's inflatable mattress as they watch their morning cartoons.

In different but related ways, *Jimmy and Pat Meet the Queen* and *The Royal Guest* construct ironic reversals of other journeys, colonial and postcolonial. In *Jimmy and Pat,* the queen is thrust into a landscape and culture that are alien to her and that expose the shallowness of her knowledge in comparison with the deep knowledge of the "Walmajarri mob"; shadowing the queen's displacement are the colonial stories in which Aboriginal people were removed from their lands and forced to live in alien country. *The Royal Guest* builds its understated comedy out of the queen's insertion into the frugal world of the Jones family, but through his deployment of 1950s settings, Riddle collapses two journeys: the triumphant progress of the young queen throughout Australia in 1954, following her coronation, and "the last visit of the Queen," when "times were tough." The scenes of adulation that surrounded the queen in 1954 thus shadow the surreal comedy of her visit to Padstow, plotting the social change that has seen a move toward republicanism and away from traditional associations with Britain. Nevertheless, the failure of Australians to approve the 1999 referendum on whether Australia would become a republic with an Australian head of state exemplifies the extent to which the colonial past signifies values such as "safety" and "reliability" at a time of rapid social change.

Most of all, both books insist on the radical instability of the sign "queen" in contemporary Australia. In *Jimmy and Pat,* the queen is associated with the legal category "Vacant Crown Land," a phrase that reflects Australia's dependence on the British legal system. In Jimmy's terms, the land is not vacant (being occupied by the Walmajarri people), and the idea that it belongs to the queen is patently silly in the face of her inability to locate waterholes, so that the sign "queen" signifies powerful tensions between colonial history and Aboriginal traditions. In both *Jimmy and Pat* and *The Royal Guest,* the queen is relocated in settings devoid of signifiers of royalty, power, and social class, except for the tiara that she discards for her desert journey and the "old crown" that she gives Mrs. Jones. Without such signifiers, she becomes merely a person—a somewhat inept tourist in *Jimmy and Pat* and, in *The Royal Guest,* a temporary member of the Jones family. And this separation of the sign "queen" from signifiers relating to Australia's historical links with Britain argues for a redefinition both of "queen" and of "Australia." Whereas Dahl's Oompa-Loompas are figures of fun within a schema that locates them at the margins of British culture, the Queen is displaced from the metropolitan center and reconstrued as a figure marginal to Australian and Aboriginal cultures.

Paula Boock's *Sasscat* thematizes a journey from New Zealand to Britain that involves another form of postcolonial displacement. Sass and Win Abbott have always preferred to believe that they are adopted; their parents Madge and Pete, whom they call "the Pets,"

seem to them to be so utterly ordinary, so devoid of sophistication and
good taste, that the girls have invented for themselves elaborate histories to account for their sense of having been "cruelly planted in a low
income, low IQ family in the backblocks of New Zealand" (8). In fact,
Win turns out to have been adopted as an infant, whereas Sass finds,
to her consternation, that she is the natural daughter of "the Pets."
Accordingly, Win journeys to London to search for her mother, while
Sass remains at home through her summer holidays, which are a time
of waiting: for Win to return, for the results of her School Certificate
examination, for her developing sense of a subjectivity that does not
depend on her relationship with Win. These months of apparent hia-
tus, like the similar period during which Clare dreams of New Guinea
tribesmen in *The House in Norham Gardens,* involve a sequence of significant moments when through empathy, self-assertion, and reflection
Sass becomes an active subject in her world.

The narrative see-saw between Sass and Win, signaled through the
letters and stories they exchange, enacts a set of comparisons and
contrasts between New Zealand and Britain, Arawa (where Sass lives)
and London, the Abbotts and the Lowells, Win's "other" family. Sass's
sense of imprisonment with "the Pets" is metonymic of her imprisonment within a New Zealand that seems parochial, backward, remote
from the metropolitan center. Conversely, Win's flight to discover her
mother is that most postcolonial of quests, a search for origins and beginnings that promises her a sense of her own reality. In the following excerpts, Win writes of her discovery of her mother, and Sass responds:

> They [the Lowells] live in Chelsea—it's very posh there. All I
> know is that Edward works in 'the City'—that's finance, and the
> twins go to public (that's private) school. Eleanor said of course
> you understand I was very young and it seemed the Right Thing
> to Do. . . . I love the name Lowell—don't you think it's much more
> literary than Abbott? Maybe it could be my pen name. . . . Any-
> way, I'll write more about the E-Lowells after tomorrow. You can
> pass this on to the Pets if you like—it saves me writing twice. (42)

> I am thrilled your mother is infinitely superior to all other
> mothers you've endured in the past. . . . Lowell is indeed a far
> more literary, aristocratic and intelligent, cultured, English,
> snooty bloody polo-playing surname than the lowly Abbott you've

suffered for the past eighteen years. It is of course the name of nobody remotely related to you, but then neither is Abbott . . . Sasha
Catriona Abbott (another pretentiously named peasant from the
colonies.) (46)

Win's description of the Lowells discloses a set of implied contrasts
with her New Zealand family: their "posh" Chelsea setting against the
Abbotts' humble home in Arawa; their wealth and privilege against
Madge and Pete's occupations (respectively, cleaner and bus driver);
the "literariness" that Win projects onto the name "Lowell," against
the "appalling Woolworths paintings" (13) with which Madge and Pete
decorate their home. And, of course, this cluster of contrasts constitutes part of the larger contrast between Britain as metropolitan
center and New Zealand as colonial outpost. Sass's response ironically accords with Win's view but dismantles it through her insistence
on the slipperiness of signifiers. Thus, the "poshness" that Win ad-
mires is re-visioned by Sass, who sees "Lowell" as a "snooty, bloody
polo-playing surname." And Sass's treatment of the signifier "mother,"
which carries the colonial associations of "mother England" as well
as of Win's discovery of her birth mother, insists on Madge's role as
adoptive mother (guiltily sidestepped by Win) and, most tellingly, on
Win's appropriation of a name (that of her birth mother's husband)
to which she has no connection. Sass's self-description as "another
pretentiously named peasant from the colonies" is a characteristically
postcolonial ploy, simultaneously acknowledging the marginality of
the colonial and mocking the center's pretensions. This exchange dismantles the colonial idea that self-realization can be achieved through
a return to the ancestral certainty of Britain; moreover, Sass's subversive reading of the name Lowell undermines the very notion of "center" and "margins."

At the end of the novel, Win returns to Arawa, though temporarily,
since she has obtained employment in London (ironically, through an
old friend of Pete's). To Sass's question concerning which name she
will use (Abbott or Lowell), Win responds as follows:

"Abbott," she said, "Abbott, Abbott, Abbott."
Sass gave a half-smile. "What's wrong with Lowell?"
"What's wrong with Lowell?" Win repeated. . . . "Lowell means
classist, sexist, racist. Lowell means stiff upper lip and hide the
illegitimate daughter. Lowell means what a shame about your ac-

cent dear, and here's a nice, fat cheque to keep you at a safe, un-embarrassing distance. . . . All in all, I think I had a lucky escape." (115)

Win's revised reading of the name Lowell accords with Sass's earlier interpretation and so privileges the latter's view from the margins. But whereas previously the comparisons between center and margins (focused on the opposition of Lowell to Abbott) was incorporated into larger oppositions between England and New Zealand, Win's decision to return to Britain discloses another possibility—that her return will not constitute a journey "home," to a lost mother, but to a site where Win will develop a subjectivity no longer limited to a choice between opposites. This type of subjectivity involves a mixture and fluidity of elements: that is, Win can be an Abbott, and a New Zealander, at the same time that she lives in London and embarks on a career.

Sass's realization of agency and self-determination involves a revisioning of herself and her world through her interactions with Win, her parents, her new neighbors, Hester and Jonathan, and a local "rich boy," Trent. The closure of the narrative enacts a mix of significances, centered around the moment when Sass receives her School Certificate results, which reassure her that she is intellectually capable of achieving her dream of becoming a scientist and of gaining a place in NASA's space course for young achievers: "There was a small smile appearing at the edges of Sass's mouth. Win grinned. 'I'll come visit you at NASA, promise.' And the whoops that followed had the entire neighbourhood, including Hester, looking skyward" (108). In one sense, the closure of *Sasscat* affords a quite conventional resolution in that a gifted but insecure adolescent learns to value herself, but Sass's projection of herself as an astronaut also constitutes a contemporary version of the postcolonial journey. While her dream of gaining a place at NASA seems to signal the substitution of one set of imperial relationships for another, the idea of space travel symbolizes a definitive escape from the smallness and remoteness of New Zealand, as well as from the fiction that Britain is the true psychological center for postcolonial subjects.

Colonialism is never over and done with, despite Dahl's attempt to persuade his readers that the Oompa-Loompas love the chains that bind them and Lively's nostalgic representation of a people who have lost their culture. There is thus no possibility of "the end of empire," so influential and pervasive are the effects of imperial rule on its former colonies; and children's books will inevitably continue to rehearse and revisit the events of colonization. Most significantly, the indigenous peoples of Britain's former colonies continue to experience the effects of their displacement and of the appropriation of their land, and it is highly likely that subaltern voices will continue to provide child readers with stories formerly suppressed or elided.

Notes

1. Such intersections of race and class were common during the second half of the nineteenth century: "T. H. Huxley compared the East London poor with Polynesian savages, William Booth chose the African pygmy, and William Barry thought that the slums resembled nothing so much as a slave ship" (McClintock 54). When visiting Ireland, Kingsley commented on the chimpanzee-like appearance of the Irish poor: "to see white chimpanzees is dreadful; if they were black, one would not feel it so much, but their skins, except where tanned by exposure, are as white as ours" (McClintock 216). Apes were commonly seen as figures straddling the margins of race and class; blackness "naturally" distinguished black people from white, but a special horror surrounds the figure of the hybrid who is both white and notwhite, enough like "us" to serve as a reminder about how "we" might descend to this level.

2. Dixon points out that the original American edition of 1964 and the first British edition of 1967 depict the Oompa-Loompas as black and as "imported direct from Africa" (112), whereas the revised 1973 edition removes these references.

3. The word *swag* is derived from a British dialectal term and refers to a bundle or roll containing the bedding and personal belongings of a traveler through the bush.

4. *High English* is glossed in *Jimmy and Pat* as "a form of English spoken by kartiya people, using long words and difficult expressions" (30).

5. "I'll be buggered" is a colloquial expression that means "I'll be damned."

Works Cited

Ashcroft, Bill, Gareth Griffiths, and Helen Tiffin. *The Empire Writes Back: Theory and Practice in Post-Colonial Literatures.* London: Routledge, 1989.

Boock, Paula. *Sasscat.* Melbourne: Hyland House, 1994.

Bradford, Clare. " 'Providence Designed It for a Settlement': Religious Discourses and Australian Colonial Texts." *Children's Literature Association Quarterly* 24, no. 1 (1999): 4–14.

Cadden, Mike. "Home Is a Matter of Blood, Time, and Genre: Essentialism in Burnett and McKinley." *Ariel* 28, no. 1 (1997): 53–67.

Cowlishaw, Gillian. "Studying Aborigines: Changing Canons in Anthropology and History." In *Power, Knowledge, and Aborigines.* Ed. Bain Attwood and John Arnold. Melbourne: La Trobe University Press, 1992. Pp.20–31.

Dahl, Roald. *Charlie and the Chocolate Factory.* 1964. Harmondsworth: Penguin, 1973.

Dirlik, Arif. "The Postcolonial Aura: Third World Criticism in the Age of Global Capitalism." In *Dangerous Liaisons: Gender, Nation, and Postcolonial Perspectives.* Ed. Anne McClintock, Aamir Mufti, and Ella Shohat. Minneapolis: University of Minnesota Press, 1997. Pp. 501–28.

Dixon, Bob. *Catching Them Young: Political Ideas in Children's Fiction.* London: Pluto Press, 1977.

Foucault, Michel, "The Order of Discourse." In *Untying the Text: A Post-Structuralist Reader*. Ed. Robert Young. Boston: Routledge & Kegan Paul, 1981. Pp. 52–64.

Ghandi, Leela. *Postcolonial Theory: A Critical Introduction*. Melbourne: Allen & Unwin, 1998.

Hodge, Bob, and Vijay Mishra. *Dark Side of the Dream: Australian Literature and the Postcolonial Mind*. Sydney: Allen & Unwin, 1991.

Hughes, Thomas. *Tom Brown's Schooldays*. 1856. Harmondsworth: Penguin, 1971.

Hulme, Peter. *Colonial Encounters: Europe and the Native Caribbean 1492–1797*. London: Routledge, 1986.

Kingsley, Charles. *The Water-Babies*. 1863. London: J. M. Dent, 1973.

Lively, Penelope. *The House in Norham Gardens*. 1974. Harmondsworth: Penguin, 1986.

Lowe, Pat, and Jimmy Pike. *Jimmy and Pat Meet the Queen*. Broome: Backyard Press, 1997.

McClintock, Anne. *Imperial Leather: Race, Gender, and Sexuality in the Colonial Contest*. New York and London: Routledge, 1995.

Phillips, Jerry. "The Mem Sahib, the Worthy, the Rajah and His Minions: Some Reflections on the Class Politics of *The Secret Garden*." *Lion and the Unicorn* 17, no. 2 (1993): 168–94.

Pratt, Mary Louise. *Imperial Eyes: Travel Writing and Transculturation*. London and New York: Routledge, 1992.

Riddle, Tohby. *The Royal Guest*. Sydney: Hodder & Stoughton, 1993.

Said, Edward. *Culture and Imperialism*. London: Vintage, 1993.

———. *Orientalism*. New York: Vintage, 1979.

Stanner, W. E. H. *After the Dreaming: Black and White Australians—An Anthropologist's View*. Sydney: ABC, 1968.

Reviews

The Key to the Treasure

Gillian Adams

Retelling Stories, Framing Culture: Traditional Story and Metanarratives in Children's Literature, by John Stephens and Robyn McCallum. Children's Literature and Culture 5. Ed. Jack Zipes. New York: Garland, 1998.

No one would quarrel, I think, with the basic premise of *Retelling Stories:* that "any particular retelling may purport to transmit elements of a culture's formative traditions and even its sustaining beliefs and assumptions, but what it always discloses is some aspect of the attitudes and ideologies pertaining at the cultural moment in which that retelling is produced" (ix). Given that premise, what John Stephens and Robyn McCallum seek to accomplish, in a series of studies of canonical texts and their retellings, is to "identify a common impulse or, better, informing metanarrative" (ix), a "global or totalizing cultural narrative schema which orders and explains knowledge and experience" (6) and which molds the process of retelling. But instead of one metanarrative, as indicated by the plural in the title of their book, they locate a series of metanarratives, "a large interlocked set which implies the existence of a less readily definable meta-meta narrative, so to speak, operating at a still more abstract level . . . the Western metaethic" (7). The authors stress that this metaethic "expresses a [European] culture-specific idea of transcendence and not a universal." For this reason, they have chosen not to examine works from non-Western, indigenous, and postcolonial cultures, whose tellings and retellings "would require a book in themselves" (7).[1]

As they explain in their initial chapter, "Pre-texts, Metanarratives,

Children's Literature 29, ed. Elizabeth Lennox Keyser and Julie Pfeiffer (Yale University Press, © 2001 Hollins University).

and the Western Metaethic," the strategy for each subsequent chapter will be to start with a canonical text or group of texts, such as the Bible, Greek myth, or the Matter of Britain, whose original target audience may have been an adult or inclusive one (the "pre-text"), and then look at retellings for children that purport to be more or less faithful to what is judged to be the original. Each chapter will conclude with an examination of some contemporary "reversions" (or revisions) that seek to question the original metanarrative by disclosing its ideologies and by introducing new or rival metanarratives.

I do not fully understand why the explanation of this project in the first chapter seems so opaque. Perhaps it is the sometimes unnecessarily pretentious critical language, a language largely abandoned, thankfully, in subsequent chapters. I have no quarrel with an initial chapter setting the stage, critically speaking, for subsequent examinations, and some of its concepts may not be easy, but it does not have to be one that the reader has to reread. In any case, the chapter warns us that because the original metanarratives may well be "androcentric, ethnocentric, and class-centric," retellings are apt to be "culturally conservative" as well, either consciously or unconsciously. But "when new metanarratives are acutely incompatible with the older metanarratives that have shaped a given story," for example, "if feminist metanarratives become socially dominant—and hence implicit and invisible—many traditional stories will be rendered unreadable and beyond recuperation" (9) as part of children's culture.

The first chapter goes on to explain that close attention will be paid to language and its register: hieratic (figurative, metaphorical, or allegorical and "implicitly grounded in transcendent significance"); epic ("exemplary, grounded in more mundane or material significances"), which may contain archaisms and other indicators of an elevated style; and demotic, everyday discourse and sometimes dialect or slang (11). The use of these registers can, in reversions, "be used to destabilize norms" and to underscore a change in focalization from the pre-text (12). The authors use the examination of language in these terms in their subsequent explorations of retellings and reversions most effectively.

Finally the initial chapter turns to the question of ideology with respect to contemporary Western humanism, a complex that "promotes tradition and the conserving of culture; imagination and its cultivation; . . . [and values] altruistically intersubjective social and personal relationships and the organic unity of texts shaped towards teleological outcomes" (18). As far as children's literature is concerned, liberal humanism emphasizes the value of the child as an individual human being and presents "transcendent truths, images of integration and transformation" (19). A prime example is provided by the "one great story," the "transcendent vision" of Joseph Campbell (15).[2]

With regard to Western literature, Stephens and McCallum locate three positions: first, that presented by conservative Christianity, whether Christian evangelical or that represented by C. S. Lewis's Narnia series: an imposed narrative outcome and "determinist and authoritarian" texts that espouse violence and are theologically reductive and religiously intolerant, racist, and hierarchical, both socially and politically (19). At the other extreme "is the conceptualization of the subject as an inscribed function of discursive and institutional structures and, incapable of agency, thereby inserted into social formations" (21), that is, a vision of the self as unable to act outside of rhetorical and institutional constraints, a self powerless and operating in a world where "consciousness is fragmentary, experience ambiguous, and truth relative." This construct of the self is generally "anathema to children's literature" (21) but sometimes appears in young adult literature. The notion that "pervades" children's literature, on the other hand, is "a romantic unitary self capable of action outside ideological systems" (20).[3] A less "naive" humanist position, according to Stephens and McCallum, is offered by Paul Smith's notion of agency, "a form of subjectivity where, by virtue of the contradictions and disturbances in and among subject-positions, the possibility (indeed the actuality) of resistance to ideological pressure is allowed for (even though that resistance too must be produced in an ideological context)" (Smith xxxv, quoted at 20). In their examination of these ideological positions as they occur in traditional narratives and their retellings, then, Stephens and McCallum are interested in revealing "what we perceive as symptoms of a long sustained trend within Western cultures" (22).

After the heavy going of the introductory chapter, it is a relief to embark on the rest of *Retelling Stories,* which falls roughly into three parts: ancient texts (the Bible and Greek myths); medieval and early modern texts (Beowulf and other epic heroes, Arthurian material, and Robin Hood tales); and folktale and the *Arabian Nights.* The concluding chapter addresses Shakespeare's *Midsummer Night's Dream, Robinson Crusoe, Treasure Island,* and *The Wind in the Willows.*

In chapter 2, "Authority, Wisdom, and Cultural Heritage: Biblical Literature as Pre-Text," we find not only the restraints generated by a biblical authority, often historical as well as theological, but also by a metanarrative that presupposes a particular moral hierarchy and a timeless and permanent reality that transcends the historical and social context and shapes human experience. In this context, how great a play will be allowed to human agency, that is, how much free will exists for the subject, varies greatly. This chapter begins with the Fall, looks at stories about biblical women and the challenges mounted by feminists on the question of gender, and ends with secular reversions of the Creation, the Fall, and the Flood (ecological disaster narratives). It is an indicator of the richness of the material explored that although this chapter intersects with part of Ruth Bottigheimer's *The Bible for Children* (1996), which must have been published after *Retelling Stories* went to press, and although McCallum, who is primarily responsible for this chapter, mentions earlier work by Bottigheimer, I do not find any repeated material or texts, with the exception of Walter de la Mare's *Stories from the Bible* (1921) and Alice Bach and Cheryl Exum's *Miriam's Well: Stories About Women in the Bible* (1991). Both Bottigheimer and McCallum reveal the ideologies behind retellings of Bible stories, but Bottigheimer takes into account controversial adult re-visioning of biblical material by such modern scholars as Elaine Pagels, demonstrating that when scholars alter the metanarrative, at least some literature for children will do the same. McCallum has chosen instead to address the recent rereadings within children's literature by differentiating "discourses that assume that meaning is predetermined and immanent, and the task of retelling is simply one of mediating authority-based significances . . . [from] discourses which construct biblical pre-texts as sites of contestation on which to argue out the grounds of human existence" (59). These latter discourses are "bricolage texts" that are "constructed intertextually from a range of generically [*sic*] linked story motifs and discursive elements" (56), for example, Peter Dickinson's *Eva* (1988).

At the end of the Bible chapter, McCallum has warned us that although in their response to and retelling of Bible stories "feminist and humanist conceptions of subjectivity and being-in-the-world . . . have often demonstrated shared objectives," the responses of feminism and humanism to classical mythology "are now sharply divergent" (59). In the third chapter, "Classical Mythology: The Mystery Underlying Everyday Things?," Stephens and McCallum rightly charge that most of the versions of Greek myths that we think of as traditional, those in Hesiod, Ovid, Homer, and the Greek tragedians, are flawed by "individualism, imperialism, masculinism, and misogyny" and "produced for an androcentric community" with "archaic social and political values" (63–64). One might add to this sorry list the prevalence of violence and heterosexual and homosexual rape. Yet the humanist belief persists that myths have value as good, even archetypal stories, that they have moral value, that they can be interpreted allegorically as part of "our" Judeo-Christian cultural heritage (68), that their existence is atemporal, and that they express spiritual insights and, as archetypes, "distill psychic truths" (64).

In the exploration of retellings, the focus is on the Icarus myth, the Prometheus myth, and the Pandora myth, and I would like to argue against the gloomy conclusions regarding feminist attempts to rework the tradition as exemplified by treatments of Pandora. Stephens and McCallum are well aware of that school of Greek historians, archaeologists, and mythographers, dating back to the nineteenth century, who argue for a pre-Hellenic matriarchal high culture transformed into a strongly patriarchal society by successive invasions of barbarian Hellenes. In terms of mythology, perhaps the most familiar works now are Robert Graves's *The White Goddess* and his scholarly two-volume collection for Penguin, *The Greek Myths* (1955), often cited in this chapter. Graves, as well as Mary Renault, has also written historical novels based on this view of Greek culture that were once popular with adolescents.

According to Graves, whereas Hesiod claims that Pandora was created to punish mankind, his account is an "anti-feminist fable, probably of his own invention" and that Pandora (all-giving) is an aspect of the earth-goddess Rhea (*Myths* 2:148). Nathaniel Hawthorne, in his influential retelling in *A Wonder Book* (1851), patronizing and sexist though it is, softens the story by making Pandora and Epimetheus orphan children and by emphasizing curiosity as the motive for opening the box; when Epimetheus comes back and finds Pandora about to do it, he says nothing and thus, according to the narrator, is equally responsible for the troubles that emerge. In the twenty-two retellings of this story included in *Children's Books on Ancient Greek and Roman Mythology: An Annotated Bibliography* (1994), the majority follow Hawthorne rather than Hesiod and some go further; Michael Dempsey's 1968 account has Epimetheus open Pandora's box instead. In Lisl Weil's 1986 *Pandora's Box*, "Pandora is made to teach the human race that good things are gifts from the gods," and after Pandora and Epimetheus open the box together, a flower rises out of it that shows that "good always accompanies bad" (Brazouski 145). Thus at least in some texts, the metanarrative is shifting away from a masculinist stance.

I do not mean to criticize Stephens and McCallum's scholarship and extensive research here, but rather to urge them not to give up on the possibility of rewritings for children of Greek myths that allow a humanist project. I was most interested in their discussion of feminist reworkings by Charlene Spretnak (1978) and Barbara Walker (1996) that revive Pandora as a pre-Hellenic goddess, and I do not think that such reworkings are "a reed against the stream" (82), in spite of the popularity of the masculinist retellings by Leon Garfield and Edward Blishen (1970) and Anthony Horowitz (1985). Thus, although "classical myth has been the area of retellings least engaged by feminist writers and critics" (88), I do not see why a return to pre-Hellenic mythology, or the construction of a bricolage text including it, as Graves and Renault have demonstrated, is incompatible with the furthering of the goals of those in children's literature who wish to "maintain traditional knowledge and a sense of the past" (88) and to transmit the cultural heritage.

Space does not permit a discussion of the fine chapters that deal with medieval material. I understand that Stephens is also a medievalist, and the breadth of his knowledge and scholarship is impressive. The fourth chapter is on heroic epic as exemplified by *Beowulf* and includes a brilliant reading of Disney's *The Lion King*, as well as a discussion of the female hero paradigm in contemporary children's fiction. The fifth covers Arthurian material, both historical and fictional (primarily Malory) and its retellings by Roger Lancelyn Green and Howard Pyle, historical novels by authors such as Rosemary Sutcliff and Henry Treece, and the "quasi-medievalism" found in novels by Tanith Lee and Tamora Pierce and in post-disaster fiction. It also includes feminist rewritings of *The Marriage of Gawain and Dame Ragnell* and contemporary realist fiction based on a Malorian pre-text (for example, Katherine Paterson's *Park's Quest*). The last chapter in this group, the sixth, deals with Robin Hood stories and the difficulties raised by their retellings, among them "a sense of hierarchy grounded in a notion of transcendent aristocracy" and a "royalist ideology" (196). Stephens, who is responsible for this chapter, remarks that "it is a curiously depressing experience to read thirty or so" of these stories, and that the texts "resoundingly confirm what we have also seen in earlier chapters, that previously told stories can be so ideologically encumbered by a deep structure metanarrative that transformations of particular details can seem in effect no more than superficial tinkering . . . Robin Hood emerges as a paradigmatic Tory voter" (198).

More encouraging, as far as reflecting the goals of modern liberal humanism in retellings and reversions is concerned, is Chapter 7, "Folktale and Metanarratives of Female Agency." Stephens looks at "how editors and writers have sought to recover and disseminate a wider range of folktales in an attempt to recuperate one of the more recalcitrant elements of folktale — gender bias and its effect on the representation of female roles" (201). Stephens is here on ground familiar to most children's literature specialists, but particularly valuable are his accounts of "more drastic processes of revision, such as parody, metafiction, or frame-breaking" (201), intertextuality, and bricolage texts such as novelizations of the "Tam Lin" story. In the next chapter, in the light of Edward Said's *Orientalism* among other theoretical constructs, Stephens addresses folk material from the Orient as filtered through Antoine Galland's 1704 French compilation, versions of "Aladdin" by Disney and others, and genie stories.

I found the last chapter of this book, "Reversions of Early Modern Classics," on the whole a disappointment. First of all, I think it tries to cover too much ground. Its goal is to "focus on the processes of reproduction and interrogation in retellings and reversions of a bundle of literary classics . . . intended for adults and children" and argues that retellings or reversions of such texts "tend to be more self-conscious about the ways they elaborate their dialogic relationship with their pre-texts and more overt about their reproductive or interrogative purposes" (253). In three sections, the chapter begins with retellings of Shakespeare's *Midsummer Night's Dream.* Although it deals with the language problem and the "overload of data" (259) that necessitates an often radical selection process, aside from an excellent discussion of solutions for the difficulties presented by the fairies, it does not address the ideologies that can prove so troubling when dealing with Shakespeare. One reason for this choice, I would guess, is space; the whole question of Shakespeare for children deserves a chapter in itself. The first section ends with a look at Terry Pratchett's bricolage text *Lords and Ladies.*

The next section looks at the relationships between Daniel Defoe's *Robinson Crusoe* (1719), R. M. Ballantyne's *The Coral Island* (1857), Robert Louis Stevenson's *Treasure Island* (1883) with Robert Leeson's *Silver's Revenge* (1978), and William Golding's *Lord of the Flies* (1954). With the exception of the connection between Stevenson and the Leeson revision, this material has received critical attention recently (which Stephens and McCallum acknowledge), and thus in spite of astute observations, I found it less interesting. The last section discusses *The Wind in the Willows* and the reversion of it by Jan Needle, *Wild Wood* (1981). Which brings me to my second disappointment with the final chapter. It provides no real sense of an ending to the book. What we have now for a conclusion is:

> In this way, the epilogue [of *Wild Wood*] constructs a dialogue between two positions: one which seeks to find a pattern and meaning (or metanarrative) in history and one which reports and comments on these theories but also disclaims them by accrediting them to someone else. This is a perspective which also neatly sums up the contradictory impulses to create reversions of classic texts which have been the subject of this chapter. (290)

This is a perfectly respectable ending for a chapter, but what about the whole book? We were promised in the preface that the authors would "identify a common impulse or, better, informing metanarrative" (ix) and in the first chapter would locate "a large interlocked set which implies the existence of a less readily definable meta-meta narrative, so to speak, operating at a still more abstract level . . . the Western metaethic" (7). And what exactly are "what we perceive as symptoms of a long sustained trend within Western cultures" (22)? Where is the trend heading? Is it, in fits and starts, heading toward a resistance to once dominant ideologies, a more general acceptance of the other, and an agency that is able to resist ideological pressure even though it resides in an ideological context (see p. 20)? If a belief in such an agency is the desired Western metaethic now, at least in terms of children's literature, are some cultures so overwhelmingly alien to it that a revisioning of their traditional stories is impossible without changing them beyond recognition?

I would urge Stephens and McCallum to take heart: there is a possibility of even the most resistant cultural contexts being revisioned for children. We don't need to burn *Babar*, as Jean Perrot has recently argued, if we more fully understand its context. But historical and cultural context is a moving target, constantly subject to revision. Recent scholarship, not only feminist, but new historicist and queer theorist, has radically revised our view of the medieval and early modern periods. Our picture of the classical world has also been overturned. As early as 1955 Graves had pointed to the Libyan origins of the goddess Athena (*Myths* 1:44–45). In 1987, Martin Bernal published *Black Athena*, which claimed that "owing to residual racism, anti-Semitism, sheer scholarly inertia, and/or exaggerated respect for authority, [classicists] have suppressed or ignored the weight of . . . overwhelming evidence for substantial Semitic and Egyptian roles in the development of Greek language and civilization" (Levine 7). Bernal's book, and a subsequent volume, set off a furor of refutations, counterclaims, and expressions of support for his thesis. Whatever one may think of his position, his work seems to have altered the paradigm for classical studies. My guess is that somewhere either a well-established children's author such as Virginia Hamilton (with one mythology collection already to her credit), or some newcomer, perhaps a classical scholar unable to find an academic position, is working on a book for children that will reflect that altered paradigm; children's writers and illustrators now usually undertake extensive research. In terms of reworkings of traditional material, even Disney movies, flawed as they still are in terms of sexism and racism, are making progress: although *Hercules* (1997) was not well received, *The Prince of Egypt* (1998), the biblical story of Moses, was extensively researched and has been given unusually good reviews.

The absence of a conclusion, then, is my only criticism of this fine book, aside from some pretentious language. *Retelling Stories* has many virtues, besides its impressive scholarship, that I have not had time to address: for example, the sophisticated approach to illustration and the close attention to movies, television, and children's videos. Besides raising our consciousness about metanarratives and the Western meta-ethic, it will provide necessary information to graduate students in children's literature and in classics and medieval studies; inspire teachers who want to build courses around traditional material; and offer researchers and critics a methodology for approaching other traditional material Stephens and McCallum did not have space for such as Homeric epic, the Reynard the Fox stories, *Gulliver's Travels,* and additional Shakespeare plays. I hope *Retelling Stories* comes out soon in paper at a lower cost—make sure it is in your library, personal and institutional.

Notes

1. The one exception might seem to be *The Arabian Nights*, but their study limits itself to earlier European translations (such as they are), retellings, and reversions of those translations.

2. The authors emphasize here and elsewhere the impact of Campbell's theories on retellers of traditional stories, whether his vision of the hero's journey is adopted or resisted and rewritten, for example, by feminists.

3. Stephens and McCallum seem to disassociate themselves from taking a position on either conservative Christianity or liberal humanism when they say, with regard to which tradition is disseminated to children: "For someone who subscribes to neither, but prefers to argue that literary canons function to uphold ideological, national, gender, and class hegemonies, the effect is the same" (22).

Works Cited

Bernal, Martin. *The Fabrication of Ancient Greece 1785–1985*. London: Free Association Press, 1987; New Brunswick, N.J.: Rutgers University Press, 1987.

Bottigheimer, Ruth B. *The Bible for Children: From the Age of Gutenberg to the Present*. New Haven: Yale University Press, 1996.

Brazouski, Antoinette, and Mary J. Klatt. *Children's Books on Ancient Greek and Roman Mythology: An Annotated Bibliography*. Westport, Conn.: Greenwood, 1994.

Dempsey, Michael W., ed. *Greek Myths and Legends*. Macdonald Junior Reference Library. London: B.P.C., 1968.

Graves, Robert. *The Greek Myths*. 2 vols. 1955. Baltimore: Penguin, 1957.

Hamilton, Virginia. *In the Beginning: Creation Stories from Around the World*. Illus. Barry Moser. New York: Harcourt Brace Jovanovich, 1988.

Levine, Molly Myerowitz. "The Challenge of *Black Athena* to Classics Today." *Arethusa* (fall 1989): 7–16.

Perrot, Jean. "The French Avant-Garde Revisited: Or, Why We Shouldn't Burn Mickey Mouse." In *Critical Perspectives on Postcolonial African Children's and Young Adult Literature*. Ed. Meena Khorana. Westport, Conn.: Greenwood, 1998. Pp. 79–85.

Smith, Paul. *Discerning the Subject*. Minneapolis: University of Minnesota Press, 1988.

Weil, Lisl. *Pandora's Box*. Illus. Lisl Weil. New York: Atheneum, 1986.

Was *the Snark a Boojum?* One Hundred Years of *Lewis Carroll Biographies*

Carolyn Sigler

Lewis Carroll: A Portrait with Background, by Donald Thomas. London: John Murray, 1996.

Lewis Carroll: A Biography, by Michael Bakewell. London: Heinemann, 1996.

Lewis Carroll and Alice, by Stephanie Lovett Stoffel. London: Thames and Hudson, 1997.

In the Shadow of the Dreamchild: A New Understanding of Lewis Carroll, by Karoline Leach. London: Peter Owen, 1999.

> *"There is nothing outside of the text."*
> —Jacques Derrida, *Of Grammatology*

> *"I only wish I had such eyes to be able to see Nobody! And at that distance too!"*
> —Lewis Carroll, *Through the Looking-Glass*

Virginia Woolf once claimed that Lewis Carroll "had no life" ("Lewis Carroll" 254). Yet Carroll—who was actually a fussy, sedentary Oxford don named Charles Dodgson—has inspired numerous "*Lives,*" making him one of the most biographied Victorian authors. In the decades following his death, popular magazines and newspapers published dozens of short recollections and reminiscences, many written by former "child-friends" such as Ethel Arnold, Ethel Rowell, and Beatrice Hatch.[1] The illustrators Henry Holiday and Harry Furniss memorialized and pilloried Carroll, respectively, in their professional memoirs.[2] Alice Liddell Hargreaves, the inspiration for Carroll's "Alice," published a short memoir in 1932, the centenary of his birth, at the urging of her son Carryl, titled "Alice's Recollections of Carrollian Days," and Carroll's niece, Violet Dodgson, one of the family mem-

Children's Literature 29, ed. Elizabeth Lennox Keyser and Julie Pfeiffer (Yale University Press, © 2001 Hollins University).

bers suspected of mutilating his diary, published her own strategically vague recollections in 1951.[3]

In addition to a plethora of short memoirs and reminiscences, nine full-length Carroll biographies were published between 1898, the year of his death, and 1995, the year of Morton Cohen's much anticipated *Lewis Carroll: A Biography*.[4] Carroll's nephew Stuart Collingwood rushed *The Life and Letters of Lewis Carroll* into print in 1898, promoted by prepublication excerpts in *The Strand Magazine*. Shortly thereafter Isa Bowman published a self-promoting memoir of her friendship with Carroll, *The Story of Lewis Carroll, Told by the Real Alice in Wonderland* (Bowman had played Alice on stage). Other early attempts both to capture and capitalize on Carroll's life include Belle Moses's biographical treacle-well, *Lewis Carroll in Wonderland and at Home: The Story of His Life* (1910), and the humorist Langford Reed's largely anecdotal and apocryphal *The Life of Lewis Carroll* (1932), both of which exemplify Robert Skideskey's characterization of much early twentieth-century biography as "a mixture of hobby and hackwork" (1). More recent and scholarly attempts to research and analyze Carroll's life include Florence Becker Lennon's psychological study, *Victoria Through the Looking-Glass* (1947), Derek Hudson's more historicized *Lewis Carroll* (1954, 1976), and Cohen's long-researched project to write a comprehensive and definitive analysis of Carroll's life and work, *Lewis Carroll: A Biography* (1995).

In his biography Cohen notes that Carroll "has provoked curiosity at all times, and literary historians and psychologists have tried to discern what made him tick. But their efforts have resulted largely in contradictory assessments. No consensus has emerged. Lewis Carroll remains an enigma, a complex human being who has so far defied comprehension" (Cohen, *Biography* xxi). Though Cohen's is to date the most successful study to "paint a total picture, . . . a portrait of the man entire" (*Biography* xv), the few years since the 1995 release of Cohen's meticulously detailed and sympathetic work have seen the publication of four new Carroll biographies: *Lewis Carroll: A Portrait with Background,* by Donald Thomas; *Lewis Carroll: A Biography,* by Michael Bakewell; *Lewis Carroll and Alice,* by Stephanie Lovett Stoffel; and *In the Shadow of the Dreamchild: A New Understanding of Lewis Carroll,* by Karoline Leach. Although these efforts no doubt anticipated the 1998 centenary of Carroll's death, the publication of five biographies of the same individual within as many years also raises an essential question: what fuels the need to keep writing and rewriting this man's life—aside from the mere fact that he is, in the final words of Cohen's biography, "a man worth writing about" (533)? If a life, as Phyllis Rose has argued, "is as much a work of fiction—of guiding narrative structures—as novels and poems," why does Carroll's life "story" still defy coherent interpretation and understanding, and the "total picture" still remain so incomplete and contradictory, despite the increasingly available abundance of critical and biographical materials (viii)?

Though Carroll left behind a vast collection of personal documentation—thirteen volumes of diaries, of which nine remain; a twenty-four-volume letter register documenting correspondence with hundreds of acquaintances, friends, and relations; and reams of other personal documents—many key pieces of the puzzle have, like the hapless Baker at the end of *The Hunting of the Snark,* mysteriously "vanished away" (Carroll 96). After Carroll's death in 1898, his brother and executor, Wilfred, arrived in Oxford to take charge of Carroll's effects and, according to Carroll's friend Thomas Vere Bayne, was "appalled at the mass of papers in his brother's rooms" (quoted in Leach 45). Working quickly—one might say ruthlessly—Wilfred put up for auction almost everything salable within four months of his brother's death. Some papers and letters were burned immediately, though it is probable that the entire diary, the letter register, and many thousands of Carroll's more than 100,000 letters all survived long enough for his nephew, Stuart Collingwood, to use them while writing the first biography of Carroll during the summer of 1898. At some point, however, after stewardship of the papers had passed on to three of Wilfred's children, many documents disappeared. Of the thirteen original manuscript volumes of the diary, four are missing or destroyed—most likely by Collingwood—and someone, most likely one of Carroll's nieces, Menella or Violet Dodgson, who had custody of Carroll's papers after 1941, used scissors, razor, and pen to mutilate large portions of what remained; a total of five and one-half years of Carroll's personal records vanished.

Ironically, Collingwood's and his cousins' censoring of Carroll's diary and other papers has only fueled a desire to compensate for the tantalizing lack of evidence and to supply the missing pieces of a challenging jigsaw. Though "diaries and letters are not necessarily true," as the biographer Ann Thwaite has observed (17), the very compulsion to fill in the missing pieces of the Carroll puzzle has perpetuated, and perhaps created, the mythos of Carroll's pedophilia and unrequited love for the child Alice Liddell. This lack "has achieved the status of a keystone" in the story of Lewis Carroll and his Dreamchild (Leach 169), a tale as often retold, and resold, as the story of *Alice's Adventures*. Ultimately, however, interpreters of these literary and biographical narratives—and their gaps—face the question of perception and perspective posed at the end of *Through the Looking-Glass:* "Which Dreamed It?" (242). Whose dream, or nightmare, are we reading?

Carroll's nonsense poem *The Hunting of the Snark* offers a useful allegory for the complex enigma of absence and presence facing all biographers, especially those of figures such as Carroll. The loss of his personal papers leaves us with a Dodgson/Carroll mythos as varied and contradictory as the Snark hunters' disparate glimpses of their elusive and inconceivable prey, which they nonetheless doggedly pursue "with forks and hope" (*Snark* 93). Indeed, Eric Homberger and John Charmley have pointed out that "[f]or every 'official' biography, and even for those written wholly without official blessing, there is a shadow or phantom story, the 'other biography,' forever unwritten of which biographers endlessly scheme to catch a furtive glimpse" (xi). Like one of the alliterative hunting party—Baker, Bellman, Bachelor—the Biographer must travel backwards "in a reverse, looking-glass procedure" (Gardiner 15), on an intertextual hunt for an unimaginable being who is in many ways like the map that guides them, "a perfect and absolute blank" (Carroll, *Snark* 56).

Though biographers have traditionally attempted to pursue and render the "fundamental coherence, unity or myth to be discovered beneath the rag-and-bone randomness of most human lives" (Frank 501), all of Carroll's biographers have grappled with the paradoxical nature of their subject. Two days after his death in January 1898, the anonymous writer of Carroll's *New York Times* obituary noted, "Mr. Dodgson's life was as grotesque in its contradictions as his most deliciously absurd conceptions" ("Rev. C. L. Dodgson"). Harry Furniss, the illustrator of the *Sylvie and Bruno* books, described Carroll as "a wit, a gentleman, a bore and an egotist . . . a spoilt child [but] not selfish" (104). Even Carroll's physical appearance suggested duality. An artist acquaintance, Edith Shute, described him in terms reminiscent of a cubist portrait, "present[ing] the peculiarity of having two very different profiles; the shape of his eyes, and the corners of the mouth did not tally" (560). "We ought to be able to grasp him whole and entire," wrote Virginia Woolf: "But we fail—once more we fail. We think we have caught Lewis Carroll; we look again and see an Oxford Clergyman. We think we have caught the Rev. C. L. Dodgson—we look again and see a fairy elf" ("Carroll" 254).

Indeed, like his fictional Alice, Carroll could seem to be "very fond of pretending to be two people" (*Wonderland* 15). He was a retiring scholar who shunned the spotlight but who was also an entrepreneurial self-promoter, ruthlessly pursuing famous subjects with his camera. He was a logician and mathematician fascinated by the illogic of nonsense. He was a photographer strictly concerned with natural realism who also penned some of the most creative and imaginative works of fantasy ever written. He was a rather snobbish political conservative who in many ways was also staunchly egalitarian. He was a man who refused to sign autographs, who claimed to "*hate* the idea of strangers being able to know me by sight," but who aggressively pursued contact with the famous and titled for their autographs and as subjects for his camera (*Letters* 446). He was a generous friend to many, characterized by one of his child friends as "infinitely kind" (Rowell 320), who could be harshly judgmental and unfeeling. He was a celibate clergyman who berated himself in agonizing diary entries for being "utterly weak, and vile, and selfish," praying for forgiveness for "all that is past" (quoted in Cohen, *Biography* 200). He was the world's most beloved children's author, and he also photographed little girls—as Carroll coyly described it in an 1879 letter to the mother of one of his subjects—"in their *perfect* simplicity" (*Letters* 348). He was the private Charles Dodgson who returned unopened mail addressed to his pseudonym but who would readily present himself as the public Lewis Carroll to children and their parents when "he was in pursuit [of a child subject for his photography] and he rightly assumed that the fame of the author of the *Alice* books would help to break the ice" (Cohen, *Biography* 191).

Morton Cohen challenges much of the earlier Dodgson/Carroll mythology, asserting firmly that his inconsistencies were human rather than pathological and that Carroll, though a complex and often contradictory individual, "did not lead a double life; . . . no Mr. Hyde lurked behind a Dr. Jekyll" (192). Three of the biographies published after Cohen's, however—Thomas's, Bakewell's and Stoffel's—accept and use the Dodgson/Carroll binary as a technique of both organization and avoidance. Thomas begins *Lewis Carroll: A Portrait with Background* by noting that he is analyzing "two personalities in one mind, the Dodgsonian and the Carrollingian. If the Reverend Dodgson had on occasion looked more carefully at what Mr. Carroll was doing or writing, he could scarcely have concealed a shudder" (xi–xii). "The assumption of this book," he goes on to say, however, "is that a man who bequeathed to the world . . . such treasures as *Alice's Adventures in Wonderland* . . . and *The Hunting of the Snark* may be forgiven anything" (xi). The result is a curiously detached biography that delves deeply into details of Victorian popular culture while managing to maintain a safe distance from issues that have long puzzled or intrigued biographers. Though we may find puzzling, for example, Morton Cohen's elaborate attempts to explain in conventional terms Carroll's "unconventional outlets" for his "differing sexual appetites" (*Biography* 530), Cohen *does* attempt to address the question of Carroll's alleged pedophilia more fully and carefully than any biographer before or since, if in highly romantic terms: "his inner springs differed from most men's; . . . his heart beat to a different drum" (*Biography* 190). Though Thomas quotes Jean Gattegno in his book's first paragraph, acknowledging that " 'Carroll's relationships with little girls undoubtedly represent the most sensitive problem his biographers have to tackle' " (1), he, like Bakewell and Stoffel, ultimately pays little attention to the issue of sexuality that animates the myth of the Dodgson/Carroll split.

Thomas—who has authored biographies of Robert Browning, Henry Fielding, and Algernon Swinburne, as well as a historically based novel featuring Carroll—does demonstrate a complex and compassionate understanding of the nineteenth century. Like Cohen's biography of the previous year—which Thomas curiously doesn't mention—*A Portrait with Background* tries to provide contexts in which Carroll's eccentricities and achievements can be understood. The density of the historical and background material, however, often serves more to divert than enlighten our understanding of Carroll and, indeed, serves as a means for Thomas to avoid some of the thornier issues presented by earlier accounts of Carroll's life.

Ultimately, Thomas's is a fairly conventional biography, with none of the originality and depth of research and analysis that characterizes Cohen's, although he does accept many of Cohen's premises. He assumes, for example, that Carroll was the child Alice Liddell's "rejected suitor" (149) without recognizing the apparent discrepancy with his later assertion that Carroll showed "no sign that he liked [Alice] as she grew up" (271), even as early as 1865, the year *Alice's Adventures in Wonderland* was published and Alice Liddell was thirteen years old. At the same time, *A Portrait with Background* is made more than just a retelling of the same Dodgson/Carroll mythos by its historical, social, and literary framework, which includes discussions of larger social issues such as Victorian educational and child-welfare reforms, publishing conventions, local demographic details about the growth and development of Eastbourne, the seaside resort town where Carroll spent the last twenty summers of his life, and a brief but interesting overview of later imitations and parodies of Carroll's work. (Thomas credits Saki's political satire *Alice in Westminster,* for instance, with creating public interest in the *Alice* books in the years immediately following Carroll's death.) Ralph Waldo Emerson once observed, "There is no History. There is only biography" (202). Both the strength and weakness of Donald Thomas's *Lewis Carroll: A Portrait with Background* lie in the reverse logic, rendering the book "a background with biography."

Beside Thomas's lively cultural detail and narrative skills, Michael Bakewell's *Lewis Carroll: A Biography* seems as dry a historical summary as the Mouse's Tale. Like Thomas, Bakewell tends to over rely on popular generalizations, many of which have been refuted, clarified, or at least complicated by the research presented in Cohen. In his acknowledgment, Bakewell notes that he read Cohen's book before publication of his own but did "not consider it necessary to revise this book in the light of Morton Cohen's invaluable biography" (viii). It is difficult to read Bakewell's *Lewis Carroll: A Biography,* however, without comparing it to Cohen's—right down to the coincidence of their titles. The greatest weakness of Bakewell's work is a tendency to repeat familiar stories or interpretations of events in Carroll's life without much questioning, development, or analysis. Whereas Bakewell characterizes Carroll, for instance, as the "scourge" of his publisher and illustrators (20), Cohen examines in detail these relationships and their important influence on Carroll's literary works. He shows, for example that, far from being a scourge, Carroll agreed to Macmillan's request and "bore the entire loss" of printing the first edition of *Alice in Wonderland* twice, after Tenniel, in his own words, " 'protested so strongly against the disgraceful printing that [Dodgson] cancelled the edition' " (quoted in Cohen, *Biography* 129, 130). Cohen also shows that Carroll's letters to Harry Furniss, a later illustrator, reveal him to have been "patient and considerate," though Furniss characterized Carroll in his own memoirs as "impossible" (quoted in Cohen, *Biography* 129). Whereas Bakewell briefly characterizes Carroll's relationship with his father as without conflict, Cohen devotes a long chapter, "The Man's Father," to analysis of what was clearly a complex and often troubled relationship, although it is difficult to resolve Cohen's characterization of Carroll's father as an exacting authoritarian with the details he provides, which portray the elder Dodgson as sympathetic, humorous, and understanding. Bakewell characterizes Carroll's juvenilia, such as the poems collected in *Useful and Instructive Poetry* (1845), as "ridiculing . . . the rules and regulations which governed the children's lives" (25). For Cohen, however, "these juvenile outpourings contain more than meets the eye," and he uncovers both the underlying pain of these early poems and their anticipation of Carroll's later work: "Behind the parodies of life at Croft [Carroll's childhood home] lurk both a keen observer and a critic, a commentator on domestic social conventions, a judge of family relationships, and, above all, an independent spirit. And beneath the banter runs a dark strain of complaint, a smarting resentment, even gratuitous violence, all of which appear more forcefully later" (*Biography* 14).[5] Bakewell consistently characterizes Carroll as having "always been an instinctive conservative" (154), but Cohen and other biographers have pointed out Carroll's curious and complex mixture of class-conscious conservatism and liberal humanism. Ultimately, Bakewell's *Lewis Carroll: A Biography* offers a much less complex portrait of Carroll, with little that is new or even distinctive to reward a reading. Whereas Thomas provides a detailed social context, Stoffel a lavish framework of images, Leach a deconstruction of long-held myths, and Cohen new connections and details, Bakewell uses a broad brush to paint a surprisingly conventional portrait of an unconventional and complex individual.

Stephanie Lovett Stoffel's *Lewis Carroll and Alice* (1987) is clearly not intended to be the detailed literary biography attempted by Bakewell and Thomas. Stoffel, a Carroll collector and scholar, offers a general, often sketchy, and always idealized overview of the life of "the man who invented Wonderland" (14), in a glossy, lavishly illustrated book that has the appealingly cheery tone and postcard dimensions of an Alice's-Shop souvenir. Instead of delving into Carroll's life and work, Stoffel places him on a pedestal; rather than defending, blaming, or analyzing Carroll for his ambiguous actions or complex inclinations, she skirts them. Like Thomas and Bakewell, Stoffel ignores the issue of Carroll's sexuality and its challenge to biographers. Disregarding evidence discussed in Cohen's biography, published two years earlier, she claims, for example, that "[w]e can never be sure if there was a sublimated sexuality mixed in with the intellectual and spiritual pleasures he derived from his friendships with young girls. But there is no evidence whatsoever that he made any sexual advances toward them" (47).[6]

An arbitrary assortment titled "Documents" is included at the end of Stoffel's text: a few letters, poems, and excerpts from other Carroll works such as *The Hunting of the Snark* and *Sylvie and Bruno*. The strength and appeal of this little book, however, lie largely in the variety and abundance of beautifully reproduced illustrations, many of the items from the Lovett-Stoffel collection, which include photographs by and of Carroll, his family, and acquaintances, illustrations from a variety of Carroll's texts and from imitations and translations of the *Alice* books, reproductions of drawings and playbills, and excerpts from letters and lesser-known Carroll texts. The illustrations, in their variety and juxtaposition, imply a far more interesting and intricate story than that told explicitly by Stoffel's text, which rarely engages directly with the richness, diversity, and complexity of the images.

Karoline Leach's *In the Shadow of the Dreamchild: A New Understanding of Lewis Carroll* (1999) is by far the most interesting of these four post-Cohen biographies because she attempts to challenge, as her subtitle suggests, traditional ways of understanding Carroll's life, and in particular "the axiom upon which the entire analysis of Carroll's life and literature depends, . . . the assumption that the girl-child was the single outlet for his emotional and creative energies, . . . that she inhabited the place in his heart occupied in more normal lives by adult friends and by lovers" (12). Carroll was not, she argues, "a lonely deviant or a victim of infantilism" (76) but a man who sought the company of, desired, and had relationships with a number of adult women, including Anne Thackeray, Gertrude Thomson, and possibly Alice's mother, Lorina Liddell. The long-perpetuated image of Carroll as a "virginal deviant," she argues, has resulted in "the sanctification and consequent dehumanization of one who was widely loved and . . . an extraordinary rewriting of personal history and individual memory" (57, 14). Her first chapter is a fascinating analysis of the development of the Carroll/Dodgson myth as a "very Victorian answer to a moral problem": "The axiom of the time was that a girl became sexualized at the age of fourteen. . . . It followed, as a result, that while a bachelor who openly consorted with girls of fourteen, sixteen, twenty or more would be suspected of sexual intent or activity, a bachelor who confined his attentions to girls below the magic age would generally be perceived as 'innocent' " (23).

Although Carroll's friendships with adult women are well documented in his own and others' private and public writings, Leach shows that Stuart Collingwood's biography ignored or altered these and other potentially scandalous aspects of his uncle's life to create the "comfortable, cosily eccentric, satisfyingly unworldly" image of Lewis Carroll that the Victorian public, and the Dodgson family, would find acceptably conventional and that would unfortunately form "the hard core for every subsequent biography for the next hundred years" (24). Even recent biographers such as Cohen, Bakewell, and Thomas, who have had access to far more documentary evidence than did earlier scholars, have been so influenced by these now-reified interpretive traditions surrounding Carroll's life, Leach argues, that they have ignored or contradicted the results of their own research. She points out that Bakewell's and Thomas's biographies come close to awareness, "repeatedly inviting consideration of how curious it was that Carroll, who was known to dislike women and society, should have spent so much time with both," but these biographers ultimately dismiss such occurrences as "uncharacteristic" (57). Leach characterizes Cohen's as both the best biography of Carroll to date and the first to "acknowledge the extent of Dodgson's adult life and adult interests"; however, she argues, "it is as if Cohen himself remained unaware of how radically his research was disassembling the conventional structure" of his subject's mythic persona (58).

Leach offers an alternative reading of Carroll's life that is both credible and revisionary, examining Carroll's personal writings alongside his literary texts from the same analytical, critical perspective. Indeed, one of the limits to the vision of Cohen's biography may be his working assumption that "[t]he task of the biographer is to look beyond the writings and into the artist [and] to bring him clearly and truthfully to life" by focusing on his personal writings, the diaries and letters, rather than his literary writings (Cohen, *Biography* xxiii). Unfortunately, Cohen does not recognize that personal writing may be no less imaginary, self-conscious, or literary than a creative work of fantasy or nonsense. Phyllis Rose has observed that "we all to some extent 'write' our own lives by creating a 'personal mythology' of meaning or significance for our experience" (viii). Whereas other biographers, particularly Cohen, have made important contributions to uncovering and analyzing the documentary details of Carroll's life, Leach has begun the critical process of uncovering and reassessing the mythologies that inform both Carroll's life and Carroll's *Lives*.

Leach also raises important questions about the extent to which Carroll and Alice have "been two parts of a bizarre and unique symbiosis": " 'Alice' is Carroll's twin in mythology. . . . In the guidebooks that tourists buy and in scholastic life stories [Carroll and Alice] walk, hand in hand, through an eternity of loosely defined golden afternoons" (15, 161). The central argument of Leach's book is ultimately that, though we have unquestioningly accepted and even "celebrated [Carroll's] aberrance," and "have rehearsed and continue to rehearse, its morals and its meanings, . . . what we have never done is test its reality" (62). She points out that Carroll's photography of young girls "is seen, both in biography and popular culture, to have only one interpretation" (61), an insight that potentially speaks to the question raised at the beginning of this essay: Why have we "bought" so many retellings of the same tangled tale? Victorian and contemporary readers of Carroll biographies have been fascinated by the narrative of a man with a "penchant for the young" (Cohen, *Biography* 152), for whom "[l]ittle girls became the air he breathed" (Bakewell xvi), whose "enthusiasm for naked girl-children sustained him until the end of his life" (Thomas 255), whose "interest in these dryads . . . contained a hidden sexual force" (Cohen, *Biography* 530), who was "in love with Alice" (Bakewell 104; Stoffel 82) but was "Alice's rejected suitor" (Thomas 149), or perhaps merely the innocent victim of *enfants fatales:* "Ah teasing. That might have had much to do with the case. Young females can bat their eyes, shake their heads, toss their locks about, feign innocence, and make outrageous suggestions, all with the intent to shock and call attention to themselves. And the three clever Liddell sisters were probably expert in these arts" (Cohen, *Biography* 102).

Simultaneously sentimental and sexual, these characterizations of Carroll and his "child-friends" suggest the extent to which Carroll has become the archetypal figure of the threatening and indefinable Other, what James Kincaid has described as "a complex image of projection and denial" (*Child-Loving* 5). Carroll's *Lives* thus may say as much about us, Carroll's biographers and readers of the last hundred or more years, and about our cultural preoccupation with eroticized images of children-in-peril and the monsters that threaten them, as about Carroll. In this light, the familiar myths of the don and his dualities, and of his idealized and eroticized Dreamchild, perform the cultural work of (re)enacting our own inconsistencies and contradictions, our complicated, often paradoxical cultural attitudes toward children and childhood, the ways in which, as Kincaid argues, "[o]ur culture has enthusiastically sexualized the child while denying just as enthusiastically that it was doing any such thing":

> We have been so busy reinventing the child as a being at risk sexually that we have allowed the happy child to wander out of our range. We have made the child we are protecting from sexual horrors into a being defined exclusively by sexual images and terms: the child is defined as the sexual lure, the one who is in danger, the one capable of attracting nothing but sexual thoughts. The laughing child has been replaced in our cultural iconography by . . . a grotesquely sexy little adult. (*Erotic Innocence* 13, 282–83)

The Dodgson/Carroll mythos thus raises questions about traditional tendencies to organize and regulate difficult-to-define categories in oppositional terms: adult and child, deviant and normal, innocent and erotic. At the same time, the complex, paradoxical aspects of Carroll's life for biographers and their readers, and the multiplicity of Carroll's *Lives,* demonstrate how these cultural categories must be perpetually constructed and performed to remain apparently normal and natural.

The problem of the Dodgson/Carroll mythos thus embodies our own tangled, often contradictory ideas about childhood, sexuality, gender, and power. It suggests as well a postmodern balancing act between the desire to recognize and celebrate multiplicity and complexity in and among ourselves and the impulse to unify a sense of self and culture. This need for individual coherence lies at the heart of biography's appeal, which Albert Camus has characterized as "[n]ostalgia for other people's lives. This is because, seen from the outside, they form a whole. While our life, seen from the inside, is all bits and pieces" (17). Indeed, Eric Homberger and John Charmley have pointed out, "Biography seeks to do what only the greatest art has ever done: to convey the feel of an individual's experience, to see the world as a single person saw it. Because it aspires to the incommunicable and the inexpressible, it is no wonder that biography is provisional. There can never be a definitive biography, merely a version, an attempt, an essay" (xi). If we accept, however, the notion of biography as an uncovering and analysis of individual "narrative structures," then understanding a life "story" as complex and paradoxical as Carroll's requires a critical biographical approach as inventive and experimental as the narrative structure of the *Alice* books and *The Hunting of the Snark:* that is, a postmodern and deconstructive rather than a unifying and reconstructive method that will question, in James Clifford's words, the "myth of personal coherence. . . and emphasize . . . openness and discontinuity" rather than "closure and progress toward individuality" (44–45). Perhaps instead of looking at, through, or around Carroll's *Looking-Glass,* we need to do as Virginia Woolf suggests and actively look for and "be prepared to admit contradictory versions of the same face" by "hanging up looking glasses at odd corners. And yet from all this diversity . . . bring out, not a riot of confusions, but a richer unity" ("Art of Biography" 226). Through these multiple looking glasses, both familiar and surprising, we can come to know and understand not only the multiple, secret, and contradictory faces of Charles Dodgson and Lewis Carroll but our own impulses to hunt indefinable and inconceivable Snarks.[7]

Notes

1. Hatch, "Lewis Carroll"; Arnold, "Reminiscences of Lewis Carroll"; Rowell, "To Me He Was Mr. Dodgson."

2. Holiday, "Snark's Significance." Furniss, "Recollections of Lewis Carroll."

3. Alice Liddell Hargreaves and Caryll Hargreaves, "Alice's Recollections of Carollinian Days"; Dodgson, "Lewis Carroll as I Knew Him." For a comprehensive selection see Cohen, *Lewis Carroll: Interviews and Recollections.*

4. Collingwood, *Life and Letters of Lewis Carroll;* Isa Bowman, *Story of Lewis Carroll;* Belle Moses, *Lewis Carroll in Wonderland and at Home;* Reed, *The Life of Lewis Carroll;* Lennon, *Lewis Carroll;* Taylor, *The White Knight;* Hudson, *Lewis Carroll;* Clark, *Lewis Carroll: A Biography.*

5. Both Cohen and Bakewell describe a juvenile poem called "My Fairy," which clearly expresses repressed pain: "I have a fairy by my side / Which says I must not sleep / When once in pain I loudly cried / It said "you must not weep." . . . / "What *may* I do?" at length I cried, / Tired of the painful task. / The fairy quietly replied, / And said "You must not ask." / *Moral:* "You mustn't" (779).

6. Cohen notes, for example, that Agnes Hull "told her son that she broke off the friendship with Charles when she felt that one of his kisses was sexual" (*Biography* 228).

7. Dodgson received shortly before his death a query about the nature of the Snark from May Barber, to which he replied: "In answer to your question, 'What did you mean the Snark was?' . . . I meant that the Snark was a Boojum. I trust that . . . you will now feel quite satisfied and happy" (*Letters* 1113).

Works Cited

Arnold, Ethel M. "Reminiscences of Lewis Carroll." *Atlantic Monthly* 143 (June 1929): 782–89.

Bakewell, Michael. *Lewis Carroll: A Biography.* London: Heinemann, 1996.

Bowman, Isa. *The Story of Lewis Carroll, Told by the Real Alice in Wonderland.* London: Dent, 1899.

Camus, Albert. *Carnets, 1942–51.* Vol. 2. Trans P. Thody. London: Hamilton, 1966.

Carroll, Lewis. [Charles Lutwidge Dodgson] *Alice's Adventures in Wonderland*. 1865. Oxford: Oxford University Press, 1989.

————. *The Hunting of the Snark: An Agony in Eight Fits*. 1876. London: Penguin, 1967.

————. *The Letters of Lewis Carroll*. Ed. Morton Cohen and Roger Lancelyn Green. 2 vols. Oxford: Oxford University Press, 1979.

————. "My Fairy." In *Complete Works of Lewis Carroll*. 1845. New York: Vintage, 1976.

————. *Through the Looking-Glass and What Alice Found There*. [1871.] Oxford: Oxford University Press: 1989.

Clark, Anne. *Lewis Carroll: A Biography*. London: Dent, 1979.

Clifford, James. " 'Hanging up Looking Glasses at Odd Corners': Ethnobiographical Prospects." In *Studies in Biography*. Ed. Daniel Aaron. Cambridge: Harvard University Press, 1978. Pp. 41–56.

Cohen, Morton. *Lewis Carroll: A Biography*. New York: Knopf, 1995.

————, ed. *Lewis Carroll: Interviews and Recollections*. Iowa City: Iowa University Press, 1989.

Collingwood, Stuart Dodgson. *The Life and Letters of Lewis Carroll*. London: Fisher Unwin, 1898.

Derrida, Jacques. *Of Grammatology*. Baltimore: Johns Hopkins University Press, 1976.

Dodgson, Violet. "Lewis Carroll as I Knew Him." *London Calling* (28 June 1951): 6–7.

Emerson, Ralph Waldo. *The Journals and Miscellaneous Notebooks of Ralph Waldo Emerson*. Ed. William H. Gilman et al. Vol. 7. Ed. A. W. Plumstead, Jr., and Harrison Hayford. Cambridge: Harvard University Press, 1969.

Frank, Katherine. "Writing Lives: Theory and Practice in Literary Biography." *Genre* 13 (winter 1980): 499–516.

Furniss, Harry. *Confessions of a Caricaturist*. London: Bradley, Agnew, 1901.

————. "Recollections of Lewis Carroll" *Strand* 35(1908): 48–52.

Gardiner, Martin. Introduction to *The Hunting of the Snark*. By Lewis Carroll. London: Penguin, 1967.

Hargreaves, Alice Liddell, and Caryll Hargreaves. "Alice's Recollections of Carollinian Days, As Told to Her Son." *Cornhill* 73 (July 1932): 1–12.

Hatch, Beatrice. "Lewis Carroll." *Strand* 15 (1898): 413–23.

Holiday, Henry. "The Snark's Significance." *Academy* (29 January 1898): 128–29. Homberger, Eric, and John Charmley, eds. *The Troubled Face of Biography*. New York: St. Martin's, 1988.

Hudson, Derek. *Lewis Carroll*. London: Constable, 1954.

Kincaid, R. James. *Child-Loving: The Erotic Child and Victorian Culture*. New York: Routledge, 1992.

————. *Erotic Innocence: The Culture of Child Molesting*. Durham, N.C.: Duke University Press, 1998.

Leach, Karoline. *In the Shadow of the Dreamchild: A New Understanding of Lewis Carroll*. London: Peter Owen, 1999.

Lennon, Florence Becker. *Lewis Carroll*. London: Cassell, 1947.

Moses, Belle. *Lewis Carroll in Wonderland and at Home: The Story of His Life* . New York: Appleton, 1910.

Reed, Langford. *The Life of Lewis Carroll*. London: Foyle, 1932.

"The Rev. C. L. Dodgson Dead." *New York Times*, 16 January 1898: 11.

Rose, Phyllis. *Woman of Letters: A Life of Virginia Woolf*. New York: Oxford University Press, 1978.

Rowell, E. M. "To Me He Was Mr. Dodgson." *Harper's*, February 1943: 319–323.

Shute, E. L. "Lewis Carroll as Artist." *Cornhill* (November 1832): 559–62.

Skidelsky, Robert. "Only Connect: Biography and Truth." In *The Troubled Face of Biography*. Ed. Eric Homberger and John Charmley. New York: St. Martin's, 1988. Pp. 1–16.

Stoffel, Stephanie Lovett. *Lewis Carroll and Alice*. London: Thames and Hudson, 1997.

Taylor, Alexander L. *The White Knight*. Edinburgh: Oliver and Boyd, 1952.
Thomas, Donald. *Lewis Carroll: A Portrait with Background*. London: John Murray, 1996.
Thwaite, Ann. "Writing Lives." In *The Troubled Face of Biography*. Ed. Eric Homberger and
  John Charmley. New York: St. Martin's, 1988. Pp. 17–32.
Woolf, Virginia. "The Art of Biography." 1942. In *Collected Essays*. London: Hogarth,
  1967. 4:221–28.
———. "Lewis Carroll." 1939. In *Collected Essays*. London: Hogarth, 1966. 1:254–55.

B Is for Battle: Children and the Civil War

Katharine Capshaw Smith

The Children's Civil War, by James Marten. Chapel Hill: University of North Carolina Press, 1998.

Lessons of War: The Civil War in Children's Magazines, ed. James Marten. Wilmington, Del.: Scholarly Resources, 1999.

Any historian of childhood faces especially daunting challenges. Not only must he or she contend with the usual erasures and elisions of historical knowledge, but in reconstructing childhood he or she confronts the absence of subjects who speak for themselves. Children usually do not write their own stories; rather, adult memoirists articulate their younger selves, often framing their accounts through nostalgic mythmaking or political, social, and aesthetic ideologies. The historian James Marten takes up the important charge of reassembling Civil War childhood, offering in *The Children's Civil War* the first comprehensive overview of the effects of the national conflict on the daily experience of northern and southern children. Marten scoured archives, manuscript collections, diaries, children's magazines and novels, memoirs, autobiographies, newspaper reports, correspondence, and interviews for evidence of the formative influence of the war on children's experience as family members and as players in the national theater. Though sometimes Marten employs his source material unreflectively by offering adult versions of childhood as historical fact, overall, the text satisfies in its outline of the war's impact on children's cultural roles and political agency.

Marten's admirable thesis argues that children were vitally engaged in the conflict, invested emotionally, morally, physically, and economically in the discord that upset their lives. Children became involved through the loss of fathers and brothers, the destruction and privation of the southern landscape, the northern practice of material sacrifice and moral exertion, and the psychological triumph and overwhelming pressures of emancipation. Their replies took various forms, from charitable participation in soldiers' aid societies and clothing drives,

Children's Literature 29, ed. Elizabeth Lennox Keyser and Julie Pfeiffer (Yale University Press, © 2001 Hollins University).

to public political assertions in demonstrations and parades, to creative response in privately published magazines and newspapers, to military action in imitative play and attempts to enlist. Actively politicized, Civil War children could not and would not stand outside the theater of war.

To set the groundwork for investigating children's political responses, Marten traces sources of information about the war that were available to children in the North and the South. He begins by acknowledging that children were consumers of mass media interpretations of the conflict. Describing the array of war-based games and toys, Marten argues for the pervasiveness of war culture even in the North, noting that young people could "imbibe the war spirit by simply browsing in their favorite shops and stores" (18). Panoramas, sanitary fairs, and the schoolhouse immersed children in public demonstrations of partisan belief, as well as information about battles, generals, and brigades. Other major sources of information about the war included correspondence from fathers and brothers. In a particularly moving chapter, Marten frames out the war's effect on definitions and responsibilities of fatherhood. Offering dozens of affecting letters to and from the battlefield, Marten argues that "[t]he overwhelming loneliness and longing of fathers and children, heartbreaking as it was, revealed the contours of the relationships between nineteenth-century children and fathers in ways that may not have been as clear if the war had not intervened" (70).

By studying Civil War correspondence, features of Victorian fatherhood come into relief, such as fathers' intense affection for their children and close involvement with their upbringing. The war also reconfigured conceptual categories by linking fatherhood with patriotism since "being a good and loyal soldier was now one of the duties of being a good father" (82). Writing "from the high moral ground they attained through patriotism and courage" (87), Civil War fathers amplified didactic and ethical concerns, instructing children (and wives) in proper ways of conducting their lives. Such instructions reveal a distressing urgency, for as Marten reminds us, many of these soldiers died shortly after writing their didactic missives. As Civil War children learned about the battlefront and the "minutiae of military life" (84) through their fathers' letters, they also absorbed their fathers' concern, affection, patriotism, and moral leadership, which may not have been articulated as clearly outside of the wartime separation. Unfortunately, Marten offers no parallel chapter describing the effects of the

war on mothers' relationships with children. Instead, he reads motherhood through the lens of fatherhood: "Mothers dutifully reported
on the comings and goings and social and academic and moral development of their offspring, hoping to bridge the distance between
soldiers and their children" (77). Certainly during the war women's
household responsibilities underwent a seismic shift; Marten might
have explored the change in definitions of motherhood during this
period, or at least investigated mothers' roles in transmitting information about the war to their children.

   In addition to public and parental communications, children's literature became another major source of knowledge about the conflict. Examining wartime magazines and novels, Marten carefully distinguishes between northern white, southern white, and southern
black children's reading materials. His description of northern white
children's literature generally lacks interpretive sophistication. As a
historian, Marten charts the general thematic course of the literature
and its connections to historical event, relying on plot summary rather
than a theoretical interpretive framework grounded in issues of class,
race, aesthetics, or politics. For example, he explains that northern literature sustained earlier decades' emphasis on "models of moral behavior" (32) but also included war material such as inspirational tales
of bravery and sacrifice. He notices a shift in theme within this body
of work: "Although the moral lessons that could be gleaned from the
war were obviously important, children's books and magazines made
the political meaning of war an even higher priority. They sought to
instill a resolute patriotism in their readers by defining northern war
aims, establishing the centrality of slavery as a cause of the war, and
recognizing the humanity of former slaves" (40). The descriptions of
war texts that follow, including works by Oliver Optic, Louisa May
Alcott, and Lydia Maria Child, fit neatly under these main categories.
However much Marten demarcates the specific ideologies of northern
and southern writing, he also repeatedly searches for commonalities,
a strategy that sometimes flattens the nuances of regional and racial
difference. Marten asserts finally that regardless of sectional variation,
northern and southern children's literatures aimed to inspire patriotism and active responses to the conflict.

   The strongest sections of the children's literature discussion contend with the southern experience, white and black. Readers familiar with northern writers during the Civil War will find in Marten's
account new material that helps offer a fuller picture of the kinds of

literature read by American children. Focusing on Confederate publishing trends, Marten notices that the South privileged pedagogical literature over creative literature, since 75 percent of the children's texts issued were revisionary schoolbooks. Responding to northern-published textbooks, which often accented the importance of national unity, Confederate schoolbooks drummed up separatist enthusiasm and regional loyalty, investing even math problems with patriotic sentiment: " 'If one Confederate soldier can whip 7 yankees, how many soldiers can whip 49 yankees?' " (57). Marten spotlights the range of didactic material published in the South, describing virulent primers, a pacifist speller, and propagandistic readers, arguing that together they "establish a Confederate tradition in pedagogical literature" (54). By opening up a dialogue about the role of didacticism in this specifically southern cultural moment, Marten implicitly raises questions that, though he does not answer them, could be taken up by future literary critics and historians. In addition to the scarcity of printing materials and the economic stresses on southern publishing houses, what ideological factors led Confederate publishers to focus their energies on schoolhouse texts? Because many southern schools were unstaffed, closed, or destroyed during the war, were Confederate textbooks used in homes? Do the books then reimagine the boundaries and possibilities of children's education in the face of wartime upheaval? What are the connections between southern pedagogy and the exigencies of nation-building? By bringing the "Confederate tradition" (54) of children's literature to the fore, Marten lays the groundwork for future critical treatment of this neglected dimension of American literary history.

Similarly, Marten probes the material available to emancipated African American children, including American Tract Society pamphlets and *The Freedman's Spelling Book, The Freedman's Primer,* and *The Freedman's Second Reader.* Marten assumes a largely descriptive approach; he lists the types of biographical and informational articles included in such texts and emphasizes the texts' construction of the emancipated reader's obligation toward white northern philanthropists. To Marten's credit, he mentions the "racist socialization" (66) advanced by the American Tract Society, as well as the condescending tone of much of the material. Marten might, however, have pushed further in his depiction of the cross-written status of "Freedman's" texts, for though the initial audience was adult, the writers also assumed that children would read " 'as a reward for diligence and good conduct' "

(63). Marten could have explored the material's patronizing tone and cross-written position in light of the period's pervasive racist configuring of black adults as childlike. (In *Lessons of War,* Marten does bring up these cultural attitudes.) The complexity of the American Tract Society materials as cross-written for both adult and child readers remains to be explored, just as the Confederate material cries out for subtle theoretical analysis by a literary critic.

When Marten turns to children's responses to war, he reasserts the formative influence of children's literature: "Magazines, novels, and schoolbooks offered children examples of how they could honorably and usefully support their country. From them they learned how to identify good and evil, Yankee and Rebel, and the right and wrong ways to act" (148–49). Marten does not offer any specific linkages between children's reading and behavior, which would be a challenging task to say the least. Instead, he regards the literature generally as the cultural milieu out of which children operated. He might have made more explicit the narratives that structured children's responses to war, for references to children's literature virtually disappear when Marten analyzes the choices children made in response to the war. Marten argues at once that the conflict "led youngsters in both sections to respond to the war in very similar ways—as participants, not as bystanders" (102) and that race and region severely affected children's wartime experience. Marten's approach is strongest when he draws explicit lines between the destruction of southern white children's domestic sphere, the relative protection of northern children's lives, and the overwhelming upheaval faced by southern African American youth. Although children in the North were touched by violence, including the 1863 draft riots, their hardships were largely emotional—bearing the loss of fathers and brothers and the distress of grieving mothers. For northern children, the war "grew in their imaginations like nightmares—or at least ripping good yarns" (118). Targets of magazine fiction and novels, sheltered northern children often understood the war through narrative. Southern children, of course, faced the bleakness and devastation of war in their everyday life, and Marten offers forceful descriptions of children's difficult lives in the war zones of Virginia and the occupied territory of New Orleans.

Marten's account of refugee African American children provides a new perspective on Civil War youth, foregrounding their struggles for economic survival and psychological freedom. Piecing together the story of emancipated black childhood, Marten describes the camps of refugee women and children centered around Union army settlements, arguing that "children bore the brunt of the hardships faced by the contrabands" (131). Marten's powerful accounts of children's specific conditions—sometimes orphaned or abandoned, laboring for food and shelter in the face of prejudice and a blighted landscape—expose the staggering challenges facing black working-class youth, a population too often ignored by American histories.

Children's active responses to the war took many forms, according to Marten. Flying in the face of deprivation and prejudice, black children in Charleston paraded alongside their elders, chanting " 'We know no caste or color' " (196). Marten describes northern white children's attempts to enlist in the army, and barring that, to learn military drills and maneuvers. Northern and southern white children played at war, and in border states such as Maryland play became bold and risky when a group of children bore Confederate flags in a protest march around a Union garrison (an account that reminds one of Faulkner's *The Unvanquished*). Children produced magazines, raised funds, picked lint, led sanitary fairs, and supported soldier and orphan homes. Marten advances a vision of children as resolutely patriotic and determined to have an effect on the conflict. Marten closes his book by examining the effects of growing up politicized on the late nineteenth-century literary and social practices of former Civil War children. At its best when examining the careers of black cultural leaders such as Frances and Archibald Grimké, this section's treatment of Reconstruction-era writers leaves much room for readings from future literary critics.

Marten relies on the memoirs and autobiographies of former Civil War children for much of the evidence in his text. He concedes, "The information memoirs and autobiographies provide may be less than emotionally truthful and may obscure the difficulties and disillusionments met by their authors. Yet these sources do provide the authors' assessments of the progression of their lives and the meanings they gleaned from their experiences" (27). But when Marten employs specific memoirs in service of his thesis, a reader might wish for more awareness that memory interprets and manufactures the past and that autobiography produces a constructed self for its reader. Similarly, Marten explains early in his book the problematic status of 1930s Works Progress Administration interviews with former enslaved people: "Although race and class inhibited completely open exchanges between the elderly former slaves and mostly white interviewers, although some questions were avoided and some answers ignored, and although age and depression and decades of racial oppression intruded on the memories of the freedmen and freedwomen, the interviews, if carefully used, remain important windows into the lives of the black children of war" (28). Marten does not uncover his strategy for carefully using the interviews, however, and when he employs the interviews, he apparently takes them at face value.

In many ways, though, Marten deserves approbation for attempting to reconstruct the experience of the black masses. Marten will not take the route of histories that view the past through the eyes of the educated elite; examining newspaper reports, correspondence, and diaries, Marten develops a compelling picture of the incredible trials facing emancipated black children. Attempting to reveal another hidden facet of Civil War experience, Marten speculates on the forms of psychological trauma experienced by children and veterans by drawing on the "modern reference points" (30) of World War II and Vietnam. Although this strategy is less effective than using excerpts from correspondence, it does point to Marten's commendable quest to excavate the buried stories of wartime life.

A teaching companion to Marten's historical volume, *Lessons of War: The Civil War in Children's Magazines* anthologizes northern and southern periodical texts written for child audiences. Marten includes a variety of texts, almost all of which were aimed at northern white children: hospital and battlefield fiction, soldier and missionary teacher correspondence, didactic editorials and declamation poetry, and moralistic tales of homefront sacrifice and piety. Many of the authors, such as Louisa May Alcott, Lydia Maria Child, and Thomas Wentworth Higginson, are familiar. Marten also includes a few playlets from Oliver Optic's *The Student and Schoolmate,* such as "The Comedy of Secession," dramas that disclose the liberating role of humor for wartime children, as well as Optic's implicit demand for youth to align themselves with the partisan plays, poems, editorials, and stories he printed. Marten uses editorial prefaces to describe moments of children's resistance to Optic's structuring of their responses to war, as when Boston schoolchildren burst into laughter after reciting what they called Optic's "'old worn-out pieces'" (62) of patriotic poetry. This kind of contextual information helps make historically grounded children's literature more alive and engaging. A reader recognizes that Marten takes much of the editorial material in *Lessons of War* directly from *The Children's Civil War,* which makes the anthology a strong teaching tool (though a repetitive read for one familiar with *The Children's Civil War*).

Marten stresses that northern children's magazines advanced a "fairly narrow look at the state of American society, from a white, middle-class, and generally small-town (although not necessarily rural) vantage point" (xvii). He effectively contextualizes patronizing depictions of African Americans in northern magazines, and he also explains that white writers within *The Freedman* magazine often imagined black youth and adults as children who "had to be coaxed, guided, and prodded into living virtuous and productive lives" (213). Though a reader might wish for more information about southern reading (Marten offers only a few nonfiction pieces and correspondence from Confederate authors), college students will discover in *Lessons of War* many opportunities to discuss the construction of gender and class roles, as well as the expectations of reader interest and investment in the war. *The Children's Civil War* and *Lessons of War* mark the beginning of inquiry into a vital field for both historians and scholars of children's literature.

"Dis house done gone crezzeh": A Consideration of Literary Blackness

Michelle H. Martin

White Supremacy in Children's Literature: Characterizations of African Americans, 1830–1900, by Donnarae MacCann. New York: Garland, 1998.

When I was in elementary school, one of my favorite TV shows was *The Three Stooges,* and the episode that made me laugh the hardest was one in which one of the stooges forgets to turn off an upstairs faucet, which results in water flooding the house. The black cook, whose very dark skin accentuates the white of his eyes and teeth, is standing in the kitchen when the light bulb above his head bursts and pours water down on him. He looks up, wide-eyed, and says, "Dis house done gone crezzeh." My favorite part of Disney's *Dumbo,* which relied on a similar type of humor, was the song of the obviously African American crows who sing: "I be done seen 'bout everythang when I see a elephant fly!" This song even made my dad laugh. Did I know, as an African American child, that these were minstrel images of black people? If I did recognize this, did it mean anything to me? Many of the issues that Donnarae MacCann's *White Supremacy in Children's Literature: Characterizations of African Americans, 1830–1900* raises caused me to think that had I been made aware of the dynamics in many of the TV shows that I saw and many of the books that I read as a child, perhaps I wouldn't have been so quick to laugh at the cook in the kitchen of the Three Stooges or the crows in *Dumbo.*

Donnarae MacCann's critical work makes a substantial addition to the body of African American children's literature scholarship. Eclectic and multidisciplinary in its critical approach and comprehensive in its treatment of antebellum and postbellum novelists who wrote for children, this contribution to the Children's Literature and Culture series, edited by Jack Zipes, provides a well-rounded discussion of the origins of "multicultural" literature in the United States. Mac-Cann's work deepens readers' understanding of the writings of well-known authors such as Mark Twain, Harriet Beecher Stowe, and Joel

Children's Literature 29, ed. Elizabeth Lennox Keyser and Julie Pfeiffer (Yale University Press, © 2001 Hollins University).

Chandler Harris, as well as those of lesser-known writers such as Matilda G. Thompson, William T. Adams, and Louise-Clark Pyrnelle. Just as accessible to classroom teachers as to scholars of children's literature, MacCann's analytical approach uses "political, biographical, institutional and literary history and theory," adding depth and breadth to the study of African American children's literature (238). Her focus on the aesthetics as well as the literary elements of the literature and her use of reader response theory, sociology, and black-child-care studies make this cultural historical study particularly effective.

In the book's introduction, MacCann defines and clarifies some important terms. In her definition of "white supremacy," MacCann distinguishes race prejudice—prejudice at an individual or localized psychological level—from institutional racism—prejudice at the level of public policy. These two kinds of racism interact with one another continuously, and MacCann's argument throughout the book illustrates this point. For instance, MacCann problematizes an idea that many scholars of anti-slavery and abolitionist texts have too long held: that "anti-slavery" also means "anti-racist." Many abolitionists and authors of antislavery texts advocated manumission of slaves while fully embracing a belief in the inferiority of people of color: in spite of their individual acts of generosity toward slaves, these abolitionists were still subject to the institutional ideology that considered those of European descent far superior to those of African descent. When emancipation became a reality, then, a noticeable shift in ideology about blacks occurred in children's literature, which reflected this belief in black inferiority. Unfortunately, these ideas remained strong in children's literature for at least the first half of the twentieth century.

In contextualizing her research within the field of children's literature and African American studies, MacCann says that because "self-definition is seen as a prerequisite of self-determination," both the stereotypical portrayal and the absence of African American characters in nineteenth-century children's literature are important to examine in puzzling out the position of black children within American literature (xvi). She argues for the importance of studying the "historically unique situation of American Blacks rather than try[ing] to conceptualize their history within the framework of worldwide political and economic oppression," as well as the importance of examining the effect that the media have had on African Americans' self image, so that correcting this "distorted cultural image" becomes possible (xvii). Throughout her study, MacCann pays special attention to the "gatekeepers" who help this literature reach its intended audience of children: the authors, publishers, editors, marketers, booksellers, review publishers, librarians, and teachers.

Part II of MacCann's work largely mirrors Part I in its content, but the first half of the book focuses on the antebellum years, the second, the postbellum years. In Part I of *White Supremacy in Children's Literature,* MacCann clearly lays out the problems inherent within both mainstream and abolitionist texts that set the stage for the disfranchisement and long-term institutional discrimination against African Americans following Reconstruction. A "sampling of narratives" illustrates the ambivalence toward blacks within abolitionist texts. In Matilda G. Thompson's *The Child's Anti-Slavery Book,* for instance, Thompson arouses sympathy for the character of Aunt Judy, a slave who is freed then enslaved again through an act of trickery, but undermines the positive message by emphasizing Judy's vulnerability and lack of intelligence and her portrayal of Judy as a "blackface" minstrel who speaks a nearly indecipherable dialect. Even committed reformers such as Lydia Maria Child, Samuel Goodrich, and Eliza Lee Follen were guilty of including mixed messages that reflected poorly on black characters. Because the antislavery theme was nearly always coupled with an underlying belief in the inferiority of blacks in the books of widely read authors such as Jacob Abbott, Harriet Beecher Stowe, and John Townsend Trowbridge, the prevailing ideology concerning black characters during the antebellum years, argues MacCann, "would have injured the self-esteem of Blacks (and inflated the egos of European Americans) in about the same degree as proslavery texts" since they all conveyed the message that "European cultural values would always be the exclusive measure of what was best" (22). Notably, MacCann does not leave room for the realistic possibility that at least some of these authors attributed the ignorance of African Americans to their lack of access to education—a fixable problem more related to social and political conditions of the time rather than to the inherent capabilities of black people.

MacCann's second chapter, which discusses the sociopolitical and artistic dimensions of abolitionist tales, shows how the political idealism found in these texts faded during the postbellum years "because it was insufficiently grounded in egalitarian principles *before* the war" (27). A particularly compelling part of this discussion is MacCann's comparison of the role of free black clergy and that of northern white clergy in abolitionism. Although some white clergy did work alongside freedmen to fight white supremacy, many others used slavery as a religious symbol, seeing themselves as rescuing slaves from their own naturally sinful, lustful, and libidinous selves and freeing them from their bondage to sin. The chief virtues for a slave, then, were humility and patience. In contrast, black clergymen—the majority of whom did not believe in black inferiority—helped to run the Underground Railroad, established night schools, and supported pragmatic programs designed both to relieve the suffering of slaves and to raise blacks' consciousness (30). Following this discussion of the religious context of the antebellum era, MacCann details major political and legal changes such as the Mexican War of 1846–48, the Fugitive Slave Law of 1850, and John Brown's 1858 raid on Harper's Ferry. In the midst of these political changes, blackface minstrelsy developed as a political art, often glamorizing slave life and thereby undermining the theme of slave emancipation. MacCann shows how these events impacted relations between the North and South and the attitude that American whites—northern and southern—held toward American blacks.

In Part II of *White Supremacy in Children's Literature,* which focuses on the postbellum period of 1866–1900, MacCann delves into the lives of postwar children's authors and certain postwar institutions that affected the literature. She also includes a discussion of relevant literary methods and conventions of this era. The "sampling" of children's literature here covers plantation stories (by authors such as Joel Chandler Harris and Thomas Nelson Page); a relatively new genre, adventure stories (by those such as George Henty and Edward Stratemeyer); and "protest" fiction (authored by Mark Twain and Martha Finley). Because Edward Stratemeyer has been so widely recognized for the volumes of boys' adventure series books that he churned out (with, of course, the aid of a band of ghost writers), and because Mark Twain's "classics" have become an important part of the American literary canon, I found MacCann's positioning of these authors' works within their social, historical, and literary contexts the most compelling aspect of the fourth chapter.

Riddled with contradictions, Stratemeyer's treatment of black characters ranges from depicting Pickles Johnsing, the protagonist of *Tour of the Zero Club, or Adventures Amid Ice and Snow* (1894–95), as a talented and noble fool to implying, through his use of blacks as drunken, disorderly thieves, that "Black culture is entirely problematic, having no redeeming characteristics" (MacCann 104, 107). Providing an excellent synthesis of existing Twain criticism dealing with race and pointing out critics' frequent dismissal of white supremacist ideology within Twain's works—particularly in *Adventures of Huckleberry Finn*—Mac-Cann argues that Twain's contribution to black literary identity is, in the end, a negative one. She counters the widely accepted argument that Jim serves as the moral center of *Adventures of Huckleberry Finn* by showing how the minstrel and muddle-headed qualities of Jim's character support the white supremacy myth, thereby making him Huck's inferior and a failure as a credible adult male. MacCann does balance this counterargument with a positive one of her own about the value of Twain's most popular novel: namely, that Jim is a catalyst for Huck in helping him "break loose from the provincial, hypocritical conditioning of his social environment" (109). This aspect of Huck's growth, however, does not, in MacCann's opinion, redeem Twain's novel from its negative portrayal of black identity. Readers who have repeatedly taught *Adventures of Huckleberry Finn,* as have I, may find themselves rethinking their perspective on the novel because of MacCann's discussion of it. I found her socio-historical contextualization of the novel within a long history of white supremacist ideology in children's literature most illuminating.

Even readers who bring to *White Supremacy in Children's Literature* a strong knowledge of the historical events surrounding Reconstruction will find MacCann's discussion of the sociopolitical context of the literature of this era useful because of the way she weaves together information on literature, politics, legal decisions, social movements, military involvement, school conditions, the work of the Freedmen's Bureau, expansionist propaganda, and changes in abolitionist ideas during the postbellum period. With this eclectic mix of information, MacCann convincingly argues that although authors of children's literature were not at the center of major social and political changes, the ideas in their books reflected the dominant ideology of racism toward African Americans and the wide dissemination of their books contributed substantially to the further propagation of these ideas:

> It was not individuals at the center of power who purchased twenty-five million copies of the George Henty books to give to children and libraries, or five million copies of Finley's "Elsie Dinsmore" novels. It was not for a specialized or elite readership that 125 American editions of *Adventures of Huckleberry Finn* were published prior to 1977. Those Reconstruction and post-

Reconstruction artifacts have had a broad base of support. (151–52)

Examining this idea from an early twenty-first-century perspective, I suspect that this "broad base of support" may, in part, explain why multicultural children's literatures that honor, respect, and celebrate nondominant cultures—rather than including merely token representations of characters of non-European descent—have taken so long to become an accepted part of the American children's literature canon.

MacCann's sixth chapter highlights important biographical details from the lives of authors who wrote after the Civil War. This wide-ranging list includes the staunch negrophobe Thomas Nelson Page, who openly supported lynching as an effective means of controlling blacks, and Martha Finley, who attacked the Ku Klux Klan in her Elsie Dinsmore series but always depicted blacks as servile. This discussion of the writers suggests that regardless of whether these authors meant good or ill by their inclusion of black characters in their texts, an examination of their lives and works reveals paradoxes through which white supremacist ideology ultimately surfaces. Even the Quakers, who established schools for slaves until the law forbade slave literacy, and who ran thirty-one postwar black schools in North Carolina by 1869, embraced segregationist, gradualist, and paternalistic policies (192–93). MacCann's discussion of postwar institutions—schools, textbooks, libraries, and periodicals—further immerses the reader in these contradictions.

In her concluding chapter, MacCann turns her attention to children, those at the receiving end of the ideas that she explores throughout the study. MacCann reemphasizes that all cultural relativism—specifically, the ability of white Americans to see their culture in relation to black culture—disappeared altogether after the Civil War, even in the writings of reformist children's authors. The end result was that all child readers, but particularly black child readers, could find nothing but overtly or implicitly negative portrayals of African Americans in children's literature. And, says MacCann, "When children internalize the concept of racial hierarchy, then the lifespan of that myth has been extended" (238). Unfortunately, this internalization continued to occur long after the close of the nineteenth century.

Although *White Supremacy in Children's Literature* caused me to think differently about both nineteenth- and twentieth-century children's literatures that feature African American characters, it also left me with several questions.

First, is MacCann perhaps too hard on nineteenth-century authors? Does she, in other words, impose late-twentieth-century expectations of race on these nineteenth-century writers? After all, how can one expect a Martha Finley, a Mark Twain, or a Thomas Nelson Page—none of whom had the benefit of living through the civil rights era—to define "antiprejudice" as do contemporary American readers? According to MacCann's analysis, the Quakers were the one group who came closest to breaking through white supremacist ideology since they believed long before mainstream Americans did that blacks were educable and worthy of being educated. But were there, I kept wondering, any non–African American groups or individuals who somehow freed themselves from the pervasive idea that blacks were inferior to whites? If so, did any of them live to write about it? If not —if what we consider antiprejudiced thought did not even *exist* within the thought patterns of whites in the South or the North—then perhaps authors who wrote on antiracist themes in the best way that they knew how for their time and place ought not to be faulted for their historically situated brand of prejudice. On the other hand, however, I find MacCann's analysis useful because many of the authors whom she discusses are still widely read by American schoolchildren, and *they* see these books through the same historical lens that MacCann does. Hence, the "filters" that she provides spark critical thinking, even if MacCann sometimes asks too much of nineteenth-century writers.

A related question also kept resurfacing in my mind as I read quotation after quotation of barely intelligible black dialect: if white authors of antebellum and postbellum children's literature went out of their way to make black speech oblique enough to suggest muddle-headedness or to create humor through the use of minstrel characters, did anyone do the anthropological work of accurately transcribing the language of uneducated blacks of this era? On recently rereading the slave narratives of Frederick Douglass and Harriet Jacobs, I was once again impressed by the complexity of their compositions and the formality of their diction. Surely, a huge educational and therefore linguistic gap exists between Frederick Douglass and Twain's Jim. MacCann's work has sparked my interest in learning more about that gap.

Finally, having studied the contribution that picture book authors and illustrators made to the "golden age of children's literature" during the late nineteenth century, I wondered about MacCann's silence on this genre. Though picture books are not the focus of this study and were likely beyond the scope of MacCann's argument, I wondered if this silence exists because of the paucity of picture books featuring African American characters during this period, or if MacCann narrowed her focus and decided to analyze only novels. Because Mac-Cann's critical work introduced me to many authors, texts, and ideas with which I was not familiar, I finished the book feeling that I'd like to read a parallel study that focuses on antebellum and postbellum picture books. Furthermore, MacCann beautifully lays the groundwork for the development of a *Part II: The Demise of White Supremacy in Children's Literature, 1900–2000*. Although I cannot tell whether MacCann has considered such an undertaking, I would be eager to digest a second volume of this fascinating work.

Works Cited

Stratemeyer, Edward. *A Tour of the Zero Club, or Adventures Amid Ice and Snow*. Philadelphia: David McKay, 1902.

Thompson, Matilda G. *The Children's Anti-Slavery Book: Containing a Few Words About American Slave Children, and Stories of Slave-Life*. New York: Carlton and Porter, 1859; reprint, Miami: Mnemosyne, 1969, 109–53.

Little Black Sambo *Revisited*

Nina Mikkelsen

Pictus Orbis Sambo: A Publishing History, Checklist, and Price Guide for THE STORY OF LITTLE BLACK SAMBO (1899–1999), by Phyllis Settecase Barton. Sun City, Calif.: Pictus Orbis Press, 1998.

The 1960s produced in America the civil rights movement, the assassinations of three political leaders, a debilitating war, baby boomers protesting that war, flower children, a new look at class consciousness and the race problem, and multicultural authenticity as a vital concept for the arts. The children's book world responded by opening the doors to writers of color and "cleansing" library shelves of racist words and pictures. One of the first books to go was Helen Bannerman's *The Story of Little Black Sambo,* originally published in 1899.

In 1959, the editors of the textbook classic *Anthology of Children's Literature* included Bannerman's story in the picture book section, asserting that the charm of this simple and dramatic story lay "in the happy choice of incidents and in the ingenious way little Sambo of India overcomes apparently impossible difficulties" (77). The problem for those just awakening to the notion of white supremacist thinking was that although the story of a small boy outwitting four large tigers was simple, dramatic, and ingenious, the pictures presented harsh caricatures of the members of a "black" family that seemed to be African rather than Indian. And her story presented a puzzling mix of foods (Indian *"ghi,"* or butter, and a recipe for Scottish hoecakes) and cultures—an Indian bazaar, Bengal tigers, and a boy called "Sambo," a name used on several continents, long before Bannerman wrote her story, to describe African, not Indian, males.

Bannerman's eclectic experiences may account for some of the mystery. Her Scottish clergyman father accepted a post on Madeira, an island off the coast of West Africa, where she lived before marrying a physician and setting off for India, where she would rear four children. But questions remained. Why would Bannerman have given an Indian child an African name? And why would she have given him and his parents large accentuated lips and rolling eyes, unless she wished

Children's Literature 29, ed. Elizabeth Lennox Keyser and Julie Pfeiffer (Yale University Press, © 2001 Hollins University).

to present this black family as the same comical curiosity that writers and illustrators often presented in that era, in Europe and America?

By the time the next edition of the *Anthology* appeared (1970), *The Story of Little Black Sambo* was no longer in sight. (Black educators had been erasing it all along.) Yet like the bad penny, it has been turning up ever since—in memorabilia of popular culture, canon wars, and new versions. In the past thirty years, six reader stances have emerged: benevolent censorship (dismissal of the book as racist), nostalgic recollections of the book, defensiveness and veiled bigotry, even-handed analysis, rehabilitation (attempts to defend and restore the original text), and revision of the book—words, pictures, or both.

Favoring the fifth stance is Phyllis Settecase Barton, who has authored a large tome, *Pictus Orbis Sambo.* The title arises from an idea of Johannes Amos Comenius, the seventeenth-century progressive educator from Bohemia, to give children lessons about the world through woodcut pictures of everyday objects, ideas, and events—or to teach them through pictures. His *Orbis Sensualium Pictus* (The Visible World) is often called the first picture book. Barton's *Pictus Orbis Sambo* is a publishing history of Bannerman's book and a catalogue of *Little Black Sambo* books published during the twentieth century. (The original book never went out of print.)

Barton is a collector of Sambo books and memorabilia and a previous owner of a children's antiquarian bookshop in California, and her mission, as expressed in *Pictus Orbis Sambo,* is to salvage Bannerman's story—as folktale—and restore it to the canon. But this may be a mission impossible, for several reasons, not the least of which is the question of genre. Is *Little Black Sambo* a picture book, as the editors of *Anthology of Children's Literature* indicate, a picture storybook, or illustrated story, as Barton identifies it in her introduction, or a folktale, as she later asserts?

Bannerman's story, in its original format, is clearly a picture book. Pictures are important for completing the early pages of text, and they are crucial for others, such as page 14: "And then wasn't Little Black Sambo grand?" At times, Bannerman even breaks her sentences between one opening—or set of facing pages—and another, in order to include more pictures: "And Black Mumbo made him a beautiful little Red coat, and a—" (page 8) "pair of beautiful little Blue Trousers" (page 10). But Bannerman's book was longer than most picture books (fifty-six pages); thus it blurs the boundaries of picture book and picture storybook. Barton emphasizes Bannerman's storytelling talents more than her artistic efforts, choosing to identify *The Story of Little Black Sambo* as a "magical, talking beast story" (86). And well she might; if Bannerman was not a bigot (and Barton takes great pains to show she was not, resorting at times to fictionalized speculation), she was at least a painfully inept artist—one who might easily have internalized the deep-seated bigotry of her era. Barton seems to see this problem; she reprints only two scenes of Bannerman's original book.

She displays the cover of the book several times, but many of the 135 black and white illustrations in Barton's book are poorly reproduced, so that what readers see are dark, fuzzy images of a spindle-legged child with an oversized head who carries a large umbrella. She also includes the title page picture of *The Story of Little Black Sambo*—the family eating the pancakes—and one small scene from *The Story of Little Black Sambo and the Twins* (Nisbet, 1937) showing the family at mealtime. But even these miniature pictures reveal the father's large, gaping, canine mouth and the mother's huge protruding lips and distorted "Neanderthal" head (theories of social Darwinism were prevalent in Bannerman's day).

Few readers have seen the pictures of Bannerman's original book, Barton says; what they remember instead are the numerous pirated editions. In other words, Bannerman's storytelling talent is what matters. But even when the story was reprinted in collections, pictures have remained important for completing the text of a story in which nearly every scene includes a human child—not usual for the talking beast story. Even when these illustrators were not merely redrawing Bannerman's pictures and even when they were better artists than Bannerman (Nelle Farnam, who illustrated the story for Olive Beaupre Miller's *My Book House* [1937] comes to mind), they produced caricatures that are unusable with children today. Barton reprints very few of these pictures—especially ironic for a book entitled *Pictus Orbis Sambo.*

Barton's book, in fact, suffers from a dearth of pictures, when pictures are crucial for supporting her contention, stated in the introduction, that these illustrators, "famous or unknown—and their artwork, good or bad—have provided a unique visual history that spans continents, and has become part of the diverse cultural heritage that defines children's literature in America" (xx). To explore this thesis, Barton sets forth a history of children's literature, a political history of *Little Black Sambo,* a biography of Bannerman, brief biographies of the illustrators of the book, a history of the different publishers of the book, a discussion of various adaptations of the book (cards, comics, dolls, films, games, music, plays, poems, puzzles, recordings, and stories), and surveys of foreign editions and series versions of the book.

But even as a thesis, Barton's contention presents certain problems, for she is actually telling two stories, one of children's literature generally and one of *Little Black Sambo*—or the story of its publishing history. There is also a chapter on the Sambo's restaurant chain that fits neither one of these "stories," but as Barton asserts at the beginning, her book is—true to the spirit of its title—an "investigation and interpretation of images" (xix). In the words of Comenius, it is a "little encyclopedia of things subject to the senses" (xvii), as she explains, or in terms of his title, it is a "view of the world [*Little Black Sambo's* world] through pictures" (xvi).

These two stories run alongside one another throughout the book rather than weaving together, as they might for a tighter focus. Is this a book about the social history of children's books, with Bannerman's book used to provide insight into this topic? If so, then Barton needed to establish at the outset how such an atypical book stands as the best exemplar of an entire field of books. Or is this a book about *The Story of Little Black Sambo,* with information about the world of children's literature woven in when necessary to produce insight about the social history of children's books? If so, then she needed to foreground her discussions of *Little Black Sambo* and move information about the field of children's literature to the background entirely.

Barton appears to be investigating the place of Bannerman's book in the world of children's books with two implied questions: How are social attitudes and changes reflected in juvenile literature, and how are they reflected in *The Story of Little Black Sambo,* in all its many editions, with all its many illustrators and its many revisions? But the answers often lie buried in all this "mix and match scholarship" (xix), if they can be discovered at all. Still, there are many interesting nuggets of information about the world of children's books—and about Bannerman's book as it has traveled through this world over the years.

Pictus Orbis Sambo certainly shows us a great deal about white supremacist thinking in artists, writers, editors, and publishers of Bannerman's day—and after. Consider that in many of the 617 different editions of the story for 100 publishers of the past century, illustrators in America and Europe continued to show an *African* child visiting an Indian bazaar and walking through an Indian jungle, filled with Indian tigers. It would seem that white readers have been most comfortable when playing the colonizer role; they have also been most comfortable, as colonizers, when the colonized person was black. And to them "black" meant African—or African American.

How else can we explain what Barton describes as the "English and French fascination with black people" as collectibles—mammy, pickaninny-golliwogg, Aunt Jemima, Rastus, and Sambo figures "that used the Negro as theme" (263)? How else can we explain Enid Blyton's continued popularity with children, despite her white supremacist feelings? Consider the plot of Blyton's *Little Black Doll,* which focuses on Matty and her black doll, Sambo, whom no other doll likes and whose face is eventually washed free of its blackness by a pixie. As Barton describes the story's ending, the pixie squeals in delight when the Sambo doll becomes the "dearest pinkest kindest face that ever I saw" (255). In the pixie's thinking, black is the opposite of dear and kind; yet books like Blyton's with their stereotypical attitudes toward race were to become the well-loved stories of many readers. Were all of the Sambo stories of this mold?

From Barton's discussion of such notable illustrators of the book as Fritz Eichenberg, Eulalie, Johnny Gruelle, Lois Lenski, Fred Marcellino, Kazuo Mori, Jerry Pinkney, Charlotte Steiner, Gustaf Tenggren, Kurt Wiese, and Milo Winter, we should learn whether, in any era, white supremacist beliefs coexisted with empathy for those of other races and ethnic groups. We should discover who resisted stereotyping people of color—and why. But except for Kazuo Mori, the artists' pictures are not here to show us what we need to know, and Barton does not tell us enough, either—for example, that Gustaf Tenggren's Sambo was a golliwogg caricature.

Jerry Pinkney's words (1996), quoted in Barton's Chapter 6, are an important addition, however. Visiting an exhibition of *Little Black Sambo* books, he found illustrated versions of the 1920s and 1930s "extremely vicious" and "really difficult to look at" (257). Studying the history of the book in the mid-1990s, he began to see that "it was frozen in a time when it was at its most negative point"; and as a black artist, he felt "a responsibility to change those stereotypes that were created by writers and artists of the past" (258). He explains that he and Julius Lester, in *Sam and the Tigers* (Dial, 1996), were trying to "thaw *Little Black Sambo* out with a new telling, bringing to it what was originally there—which was fantasy." The original story was about "a hero who overcomes an obstacle" (258), he adds. And when he held so many different versions in his hands, he knew he was doing the right thing when he joined the long line of those who took on the job of illustrating this controversial story.

Admittedly, Bannerman's story has an important theme: a child becomes a trickster to save himself; he shows courage and resourcefulness and intelligence, and he has a happy reunion with his family at the end. It has a powerful narrative pattern: four times the tigers make demands of the child; four times the child appeases them with flattery and clever gifts. They resort to self-aggrandizing behaviors, oppression, and greed, but the boy eventually regains what is rightfully his. Was Bannerman ahead of her time in dramatizing a colonial conflict (or postcolonial resolution), as the Pinkney-Lester version seems to imply, even if she did so without conscious motivation? Or was she remembering Indian folklore or Kipling's stories, as Barton implies?

Bannerman's story has musical language and cadence; it has a simplicity that has never quite been matched in revisionist versions, and it has delicious images for children to savor. On the other hand, it is so deeply embedded in its own time that the original words—and certainly the original pictures and their imitations—become impossible in our own time. To identify a child repeatedly as "little" is condescending, and to identify him and his parents specifically—and repeatedly—as "black" reveals white supremacist beliefs. As Toni Morrison explains, a white character "is white, and we know he is because nobody says so" (72). To say so is to colonize, to label, and thus decide what a particular color means, and white writers have no need or desire to colonize themselves.

To name the mother and father Mumbo and Jumbo produces a musical set of rhyming phrases, but it paints with too broad a brush what family members would be—a set of comical syllables, rather than two individuals. In short, it colonizes them. To name the boy Sambo completes the comical, colonizing triad. "Sambo" was a generic name for African—and African American—males in Bannerman's time and before. Barton would have us believe that it did not become a pejorative term until much later, yet she quotes Elizabeth Cady Stanton using the word as a negative term, denoting ignorance, simplemindedness, and inferiority, years before *Little Black Sambo* appeared.

Barton rehabilitates Bannerman's book in terms of its publishing history. Beyond this, *Little Black Sambo* is a possibility only through revision, and so far revisions have not yielded ideal solutions. Marcellino's *The Story of Little Babaji* (HarperCollins, 1996) lacks Pinkney's dynamic pictures, and Lester's storytelling lacks Bannerman's clear, simple plot. Yet Lester and Pinkney's humorous and vibrant reclaiming of the book brings Bannerman's resourceful black child back to readers and keeps alive the only picture book of a black child that Pinkney saw in childhood.

At the end of the twentieth century, one revolutionary book had produced another.

Works Cited

Bannerman, Helen. "The Story of Little Black Sambo." In *Anthology of Children's Literature,* 3d ed. Ed. Edna Johnson, Evelyn Sickels, and Frances Clarke Sayers. Boston: Houghton Mifflin, 1959.

Morrison, Toni. *Playing in the Dark: Whiteness and the Literary Imagination.* Cambridge: Harvard University Press, 1992.

Freud and Toad Are Friends

Mary Galbraith

Psychoanalytic Responses to Children's Literature, by Lucy Rollin and Mark
I. West. Jefferson, N.C.: McFarland, 1999.

Volume 18 of *Children's Literature* (1990) was devoted to a discussion of
the relation between psychoanalysis and children's literature. According to the back cover of that volume, the nine featured articles used
"psychoanalytic master narratives, as found in the writings of Freud,
Jung, Piaget[!], Bettelheim, and others" as interpretive keys to works
of children's literature. Among the featured articles were a Kleinian
interpretation of *The Velveteen Rabbit* (Daniels), a reading of William
Steig's picture books based on Bettelheim and Piaget (Wilner), and
"The Reproduction of Mothering in *Charlotte's Web,*" by Lucy Rollin,
based on Nancy Chodorow's work and reprinted in the book under
review.

Following the featured articles in volume 18 was a section labeled
"Comments," in which critics of children's literature with expertise
in psychoanalysis offered several friendly but serious criticisms of the
enterprise undertaken in the articles. These critics saw psychoanalytic interpretation of children's literature as often derivative, uncriti-
cal, and lagging in its use of psychoanalytic sources (Steig, Hogan,
and Zipes), and as therefore perpetuating many of the faults of classical psychoanalytic practice, especially its divorce from a living context and its domineering stance toward its analysand (Knoepflmacher,
Steig). Furthermore, it had not yet fully grasped its natural potential
for exposing adult defects from the point of view of childhood interests (Phillips and Wojcik-Andrews). It also lacked a philosophical articulation of its own analytic project (Hogan, Knoepflmacher, Phillips
and Wojcik-Andrews). Finally, by "denying the historical significance
of the author's psychology and fantasizing" (Zipes 141), it missed its
own deepest implications for the study of literary composition, creativity, and fantasy (Zipes, Knoepflmacher). My shorthand names for
these criticisms: scholarly weakness, universalizing, normalizing adult
defects, lacking philosophical vision, and missing the main chance.

Children's Literature 29, ed. Elizabeth Lennox Keyser and Julie Pfeiffer (Yale University
Press, © 2001 Hollins University).

My biggest disappointment with Lucy Rollin and Mark I. West's new book is that it does not substantively address any of these important criticisms. The introduction to *Psychoanalytic Approaches to Children's Literature,* a book that is avowedly aimed at introducing psychoanalysis to neophytes in the literature department, is primarily devoted to airing and revising popular perceptions about Freud as a person and as a thinker. In Rollin and West's knowledgeable but condescending portrait of Freud, the stern authority figure with burning eyes that most of us, I dare say, carry in our memory archives is replaced by a deferential fellow who can safely be invited into the literary salon and the nursery. Although they do mention several objections to classical Freudian theory, Rollin and West either remain silent or simply plead guilty to the charges raised by the Comments in volume 18 without showing how this admission has complicated their approach in the articles that follow: "The most serious, and most valid, complaint about psychoanalytic criticism is that it too often ignores historical and cultural context. It behaves, some say, as if human emotions exist in a vacuum, as if they are not affected by time or place" (Rollin and West 13). But what has been done with this insight in the articles? Here the problems of intellectual deference and vague grounding pop up— it seems that we children's literature people can't do much about this problem until some master narrative comes along to give us guidance. The introduction mentions Marxist criticism as a valid corrective to the "vacuum" problem without, however, saying how this corrective alters their own philosophy or their interpretation of children's literature. For all its avowed agreement with critics of psychoanalytic literary criticism, *Psychoanalytic Responses to Children's Literature,* like most of the articles in volume 18 of *Children's Literature,* "remains curiously unconcerned with the problematic nature of the relationship between the psychoanalytic enterprise and the interpretation of children's literature" (Phillips and Wojcik-Andrews 127).

It may be that the articles in *Psychoanalytic Responses to Children's Literature,* some dating from 1990 or earlier, predate the authors' awareness of some of the deficits of psychoanalytic literary criticism. These articles as originally published may thus be excused, but then one wonders why the authors didn't interrogate and revise their work for this new publication in light of the questions raised by their colleagues.

Consider, for example, the impact of normalizing adult defects on some of the articles in Rollin and West's collection. Mark I. West's exegesis of *James and the Giant Peach* focuses on regression as a potentially adaptive response to trauma but doesn't explore the ways in which Dahl's own childhood betrayals and his exposure to sadistic English school practices create the peculiar flavor of the book's regressive fantasies. Several of Lucy Rollin's articles normalize a failure of dialogue in families: Harriet's desperate isolation amid unhearing and unseeing adults in *Harriet the Spy* is seen as emblematic of every child's experience of home, Max's mother's isolation of Max in *Where the Wild Things Are* is an exercise of power that "mothers must invariably exert" (80), and Fern's loss of bodily contact with Wilbur in *Charlotte's Web* is labeled a "withdrawal" (55) when the story clearly shows it to be enforced by her father and uncle—Fern is ordered to put Wilbur out in the yard to sleep, then to sell him, and finally, to stay out of his pigpen. This normalizing has profound implications not only for literary interpretation but for life. If being denied access to warm human bodies and being controlled by unseeing and unhearing adults is viewed as inevitable to the process of growing up, these narratives are about universal losses that we must accept as part of being human. But if these narratives restage specific traumas brought about by the contingent and wrong practice of cultural power, then they arouse passionate indignation on behalf of the child character, the author's early predicament, and, to the extent we share this cultural heritage, ourselves.

Some of West's and Rollin's pieces do offer more edgy and historically contextualized arguments: Rollin's "Uncanny Mickey Mouse and His Domestication" traces the makeover of Mickey Mouse from a sadistic and aggressive character in the early stories to the bland "symbol of conventional adulthood" (42) we see today and speculates on the reasons for this makeover. West's "Repression and Rebellion in the Life and Works of Beatrix Potter" uses a recently published psychobiography of Potter by Alexander Grinstein along with Alice Miller's theory of creativity to argue that Beatrix Potter used her children's books to express and escape from the existential trap of her parents' expectations. Ironically, though, these more historical pieces are only weakly psychodynamic. Given the extreme shortness of all the articles (the longest is fourteen pages, and half are fewer than ten), the authors haven't given themselves enough room to fully explore their own premises.

Two other provocative essays reveal personal associations and advocate dialogue between adults and children. In "The Grotesque and the Taboo in Roald Dahl's Humorous Writings for Children," Mark I. West tells a story of giving Dahl's *The Twits* to a four-year-old friend and laughing with him at the humor of the "maggoty green cheese" and other rotting food probably lurking in Mr. Twit's beard, while the boy's mother fled the room in disgust. West defends Dahl's hostile depictions and punishments of hated adults as an imaginative leveling of the playing field between adults and children and dismisses adults' criticisms of Dahl as an underestimation of children's ability to distinguish between play and reality. I agree that Dahl's trademark hostility is emancipating insofar as it sides with the child against adults and retains a playful quality; but insofar as it perpetuates rather than plays with a sadistic stance toward both adults and children, as it often seems to me to do, it strikes me as more symptomatic than transformative.

In "Good-Enough Mother Hubbard," the longest and most complex piece in this collection, Lucy Rollin uses ambivalence about Mother's Day as an occasion to meditate on the mother-child relationship, with the aid of three famous texts: Sarah Catherine Martin's 1805 version of "Old Mother Hubbard," Freud's interpretation of the "*fort/da*" game played by his grandson, and D. W. Winnicott's considerations of the transitional object, potential space, and the "good-enough mother." Rollin's analysis and my own response to it offer different interpretations of the primal narrative of departure and reunion underlying both children's literature and psychoanalysis: who and what determines the distance between parent and child? Who controls the doorknob? And who decides what the child's experience means and what is good?

Freud observed that his eighteen-month-old grandson was seen as a "good boy" because he was obedient, didn't wake his parents at night, and didn't cry when his mother left him for a few hours. But the boy developed a habit of throwing objects away from himself and then hunting for them, saying "*o-o-o,*" which Freud and the boy's mother interpreted as meaning "gone" (*fort*). Usually, the game was inconclusive, but on some occasions the boy found the object and shouted "*da!*" Rollin sees the various objects in "Old Mother Hubbard" as functioning in this way for the dog: "She took a clean dish / To get him some tripe; / But when she came back / He was smoking a pipe." Rollin gives voice to the dog's strategy as "Since you're not here, Mom, since you've gone and left me again, I'll just find something else that pleases me" (103). In this reading, the last verse — "The dame made a curtsy, / The dog made a bow; / The dame said, Your servant, / The dog said,

Bow-wow"—shows the dog graduated to equality with Mother Hubbard and no longer needing to find substitutes for her.

The difficulty here is similar to the problem raised by Dahl's hostile "play": distinguishing a healthy release of anxiety from a dissociative defense brought about by trauma. Freud himself seemed troubled by his grandson's game: the story of the *fort/da* game comes right after his description of "war neurosis," with the note that he is leaving "the dark and dismal subject" (Freud 14) of neurosis to delve into normal development. He then describes this game as produced by the child's renunciation of crying when his mother leaves and as a "great cultural achievement" (15). But this "renunciation," and the child's separation from his mother, were not freely chosen; the boy's "great cultural achievement" was repressing his instinctual expression of grief and powerlessness at the age of one and a half. That Freud suspects that his grandson's renunciation and survival strategy may be a symptom of "unclaimed experience" (Caruth's title) rather than a healthy maturational step is supported by the tragic footnote he appends to the *fort/da* story: "When this child was five and three quarters, his mother died. Now that she was really 'gone' ('o-o-o'), the little boy showed no signs of grief" (16). In fact, the boy's mother was Freud's daughter.

From my own radical attachment perspective, the transitional object in its popular and comically perceived sense, as Linus's security blanket and Calvin's toy tiger, indicates a traumatic break in human presence. The blanket or the toy is adopted as a displaced and inferior but controllable substitute for the "real thing." But these breaks can usually be avoided in the first place by attuned parental care, and where unavoidable, they can almost always be repaired through heroic efforts at reconnection by the parent. According to this anthropologically grounded theory of attachment, when a child is ready to move away from the parent she does so readily without needing a transitional object (see Walant, Welch, Small, and Silverstein).

Rollin's reading is well-reasoned with regard to "Old Mother Hubbard," but it skates over the crucial questions of when lack of access to the mother becomes pathogenic and who decides what that access should be. In the attachment model of optimal development, it is the child who determines distance—leaves—while using the mother as a secure base to which it can return, so that the locus of control is primarily with the child. In the Winnicottian model, the good-enough parent slowly withdraws support—leaves—and the child adapts.

The key to deciding which scenario is more conducive to a child's mental health, of course, is the child's primal experience, and adults have long been arguing whether this can be ascertained with any confidence. Recent neurobiological research, increasingly elaborated theories of attachment and trauma, and radical attachment therapies that restage the bonding cycle are increasingly supporting each other's findings to such a degree that these findings can be regarded as something more than adult projections about the nature of primal experience (see, for example, Schore, Moskowitz et al., Walant, and Share). And what the evidence shows is that children may feel traumatically abandoned and discounted even in situations that to most adults in Western culture look unproblematic. But the good news is that if the child's feelings about these ruptures are fully allowed and heard by adults, the breach can almost always be repaired (Solter and Welch).

Clearly, adults have a long way to go to understand the experience of childhood. But now that more scientifically grounded and self-critical views of the adult-child relationship are being articulated, a childhood studies that includes psychoanalytic insight as well as the findings of many disciplines studying children's experience is ripe for development.

An important site of evidence, not only of children's experience but of adult strategies with respect to it, is children's literature itself. The best children's literature skillfully creates a particularized drama of primal need—deprivation, crying out, response from outside, and human consequence—and breaks through into a human connection that is honestly earned, even if this breakthrough takes place only between the fictional child self (who must be related somehow to the author) and the reader. As with any true literature, literature for children can bravely report experience from beyond the horizons of culturally accepted meanings and create fresh territory. For this and other reasons, children's literature scholars are in a unique position to help create a childhood studies that combines an intellectual and critical grasp of the issues of childhood with a sophistication about and sensitivity to issues of literature, narrative, and language.

The process of becoming a "childhood studies" critic of children's literature should include cultivation in narrative theory and aesthetics; historical grounding in ideas and practices concerning childhood and adult-child relations; wide reading in children's literature; currency in the fields of children's literature, psychoanalysis, and psychotherapy; general acquaintance with developmental neurobiology and other relevant sciences; and a commitment to admitting and addressing one's own personal stake in the issues raised by children's literature. One should also be in ongoing real dialogue, as a parent or in another primary capacity—therapist or friend—with actual children. No one I know currently meets all of these qualifications, but I see progress toward meeting them as a crucial project for a critical practice of childhood studies that will be more than derivative from other fields.

Putting aside my major disappointment about its failure to meet the challenges posed by the commentaries in *Children's Literature* 18, I find *Psychoanalytic Responses to Children's Literature* to be a refreshingly accessible book that clarifies psychoanalytic terminology through examples in children's literature. The authors' "return-to-sources" approach stimulated me to read—or reread—several original works mentioned, such as Freud's essays on the pleasure principle and the uncanny, and going one step further, E. T. A. Hoffman's amazing 1816 story "The Sandman," which underlies Freud's discussion of the uncanny and Rollin's discussion of eyes in Nancy Drew and *Harriet the Spy*. My appreciation of these original materials was in large part connected to the points raised by Rollin and West, and this book is at its best in bringing psychoanalytic texts to bear on selected motifs in children's literature, such as falling in nursery rhymes and Toad's narcissism in *Wind in the Willows*.

Children's literature is a royal road to many riches, and scholars in the field have a panoply of resources for exploring this road, including "psychoanalytic master narratives." But like a different Toad—the one waiting for mail in Arnold Lobel's story "The Letter"—we may not realize that our best support is near at hand. When his friend and colleague Frog sees Toad's longing, he writes a letter himself that reaches Toad's heart. The bonus is that, since the two are both at Toad's house when the letter finally arrives by snail, they get to read and enjoy it together.

Works Cited

Butler, Francelia, Margaret Higonnet, and Barbara Rosen, eds. *Children's Literature* 18. New Haven: Yale University Press, 1990.

Caruth, Cathy. *Unclaimed Experience: Trauma, Narrative, and History*. Baltimore: Johns Hopkins University Press, 1996.

Freud, Sigmund. *Beyond the Pleasure Principle* (1920). In vol. 18 of *The Standard Edition of the*

Complete Psychological Works of Sigmund Freud. Trans. James Strachey. 24 vols. London: Hogarth, 1955.

Hogan, Patrick. "What's Wrong with the Psychoanalysis of Literature?" In Butler. Pp. 135–40.

Knoepflmacher, U. C. "The Doubtful Marriage: A Critical Fantasy." In Butler. Pp. 131–34.

Lobel, Arnold. *Frog and Toad Are Friends*. New York: HarperCollins, 1970.

Moskowitz, Michael, Catherine Monk, and Steven Ellman, eds. *The Neurobiological and Developmental Basis for Psychotherapeutic Intervention*. Northvale, N.J.: Jason Aronson, 1997.

Phillips, Jerry, and Ian Wojcik-Andrews. "Notes Toward a Marxist Critical Practice." In Butler. Pp. 127–30.

Schore, Allan. *Affect Regulation and the Origin of the Self*. Hillsdale, N.J.: Lawrence Erlbaum, 1994.

Share, Lynda. *When Someone Speaks, It Gets Lighter: Dreams and the Reconstruction of Infant Trauma*. Hillsdale, N.J.: Analytic Press, 1994.

Silverstein, Olga. *The Courage to Raise Good Men*. New York: Penguin, 1995.

Small, Meredith. *Our Babies, Ourselves: How Biology and Culture Shape the Way We Parent*. New York: Bantam Doubleday Dell, 1998.

Solter, Aletha. *Tears and Tantrums*. Goleta, Calif.: Shining Star Press, 1998.

Steig, Michael. "Why Bettelheim? A Comment on the Use of Psychological Theories in Criticism." In Butler. Pp. 125–26.

Walant, Karen. *Creating the Capacity for Attachment: Treating Addictions and the Alienated Self*. Northvale, N.J.: Jason Aronson, 1995.

Welch, Martha. *Holding Time*. New York: Simon & Schuster, 1989.

Zipes, Jack. "Negating History and Male Fantasies Through Psychoanalytic Criticism." In Butler. Pp. 141–143.

Inside Picture Books, Outside of History

Philip Nel

Inside Picture Books, by Ellen Handler Spitz. Foreword by Robert Coles. New Haven and London: Yale University Press, 1999.

In her preface Ellen Handler Spitz explains, "This book is for mothers, fathers, grandparents, teachers, therapists, and scholars" (xiii). Though *Inside Picture Books* names scholars among its intended audiences and has been published by a university press, it does not appear to be directed at those who study children's literature. Rarely does it acknowledge any critical work on the subject and, in Jennifer K. Ruark's *Chronicle of Higher Education* profile of the author, both Spitz and Ruark convey the impression that taking picture books seriously is a new and courageous idea.[1] Indeed, Spitz's study never once mentions Barbara Bader, Perry Nodelman, or virtually any of her predecessors.

If *Inside Picture Books* has not been written for scholars, perhaps one should adopt the perspective of an imagined "general reader"—say, the parents, teachers, and therapists mentioned in the preface—and evaluate the work from that viewpoint. Acknowledging the "subjectivity of [her] criteria," Spitz says that she has chosen texts based on their "psychological richness" (13) and "staying power" (8), and a casual fan of children's picture books should enjoy her analyses of well-known works. For example, her perception of Holocaust imagery in Maurice Sendak's *In the Night Kitchen* (60–61) and discussion of gender in several works—including Russell Hoban's *Bedtime for Frances* (25, 55–56) and Dr. Seuss's *Horton Hatches the Egg* (177–80)—invite readers to think about the cultural knowledge that children absorb from what they read. Indeed, should *Inside Picture Books* encourage even a few more readers to consider children's books with the same thoughtfulness often reserved for adult books, it will have done a great service.

Most reviewers in major newspapers appear to agree. Writing in the *Times* of London, the illustrator Quentin Blake calls *Inside Picture Books* "a valuable contribution to a subject which asks for serious consideration." Though Marina Warner's *New York Times* review does note the absence of Nodelman's *Words About Pictures,* the piece concludes by

Children's Literature 29, ed. Elizabeth Lennox Keyser and Julie Pfeiffer (Yale University Press, © 2001 Hollins University).

noting that Spitz "speaks up vibrantly for the importance, complexity and place of shared reading and picture books in young lives and their future." True, the subject is important, and Spitz's decision "to advocate for the practice of reading aloud to young children" (Spitz 2) is definitely worthy of praise. Yet, I wonder if critics would rush to applaud a study of American literature (for adults)—let's call it *Inside American Literature*—in which the author does not convey a deep knowledge of the subject and who, in a breezy, anecdotal style, suggests changing the ending of a book to make it more exciting.[2] I rather doubt that an *Inside American Literature* would receive accolades merely for writing about American literature. Reviews praising the very fact that Spitz addresses picture books suggest either that studying children's literature does not require scholarly rigor or that the reviewer's praise is lukewarm.

Whichever the case, *Inside Picture Books* tries to present its indifference toward research in the guise of open inquiry, a move that only partly conceals a latent anti-intellectualism. Of Margaret Wise Brown's *Goodnight Moon* (1947), Spitz writes,

> It lies there, spine-ripped, scotch-taped and smudged, pages coming unsewn, tenderly defying all those scholars who want to historicize everything. It says: But look at me! I was made fifty years ago, before the mothers and fathers of today's young children were born, yet I am loved more than ever. Despite the changes wrought by the past half-century—McCarthyism, Sputnik, the civil rights movement, Haight-Ashbury, Vietnam, the women's movement, Watergate, gay rights, the internet, cyberspace, and the advent of a new millennium—I am still taken to bed every night by thousands of children, to whom I belong and who still need me. (37)

These sentiments are sweet, and the idea of her copy of *Goodnight Moon* delivering a monologue on its own historical transcendence is cute. But the jab at "those scholars who want to historicize everything" seems misplaced, especially given Leonard Marcus's *Margaret Wise Brown: Awakened by the Moon* (1992), an excellent and very historical biography. Though Spitz does consult a one-page article by Marcus, she might consider drawing on the biography to help place her remarks in context. At the very least, she could acknowledge that some of her insights about, say, *Goodnight Moon*'s use of color—red and green are "strong opposites that rivet the eye" (33)—have been noticed before, as when Perry Nodelman comments on the book's use of "unrelating colors in shocking combinations" (*Words About Pictures* 65).

History matters, even in a book directed more toward parents than scholars. To say of Munro Leaf's *The Story of Ferdinand* (1936, illustrated by Robert Lawson) that "[e]veryone . . . recalls it with affection" is misleading (Spitz 174). That the book was banned in Spain, burned by the Nazis as anti-Fascist, and criticized in the United States for being, alternately, pro-Fascist and pro-Communist deserves mention—even if this information were tucked away in a subordinate clause or footnote. But *Inside Picture Books* says nothing of it. Defending her decision to omit historical analysis of this work, Spitz admits, "What was going on in Spain was not insignificant. But," she continues, "I don't know that it's that helpful to a young parent bringing up a child" (Ruark A19). Perhaps not. A concerned parent who wants to prevent his child from reading a "subversive" book may want to know, however, as might a parent wishing to encourage her child to read a "radical" story. Whether *Ferdinand* truly engages with any specific political movements is beside the point. Knowing the historical background of a work enriches the reading experience, and it is condescending to assume that parents would not be interested.

If *Inside Picture Books* largely dispenses with history, it does not completely ignore critical issues in children's literature. For example, Spitz gestures toward a postcolonial reading of Sendak's *Where the Wild Things Are* (1963), linking it to the Western literary tradition "in which civilizing white-skinned male conquerors sail off to cannibal islands to tame and convert the 'savages' they find there" (132). And, at the very end of *Inside Picture Books,* Spitz relays a conversation with Hortense Spillers in which they read Helen Bannerman's *The Story of Little Black Sambo* (1899) as "an anticolonialist narrative," with the "black child as a carrier of civilization . . . in opposition to the tigers as representative of the forces of destructive nature" (213). The preceding notwithstanding, Spitz's analyses generally dwell less on race than on gender. Though she does not mention Alison Lurie's criticism of gender roles in Seuss, Spitz does discuss Horton taking on "the loving, loyal role normally given to a woman," while Mayzie "is portrayed in a derogatory way" (180). At moments such as these, *Inside Picture Books* may be at its strongest.

Unfortunately, such readings remain but moments, almost selfconscious gestures toward current trends in literary criticism. Trained in psychoanalysis, Spitz (not surprisingly) favors psychoanalytic interpretations. Indeed, the "Inside" of the title refers to her desire to get inside the psyche of the child reader and at the latent content of picture books. In Maurice Sendak's *Pierre* (1962), the lion "represents the little boy's previously disowned aggression (his dismissive 'I don't care!'), which now turns against him in the form of a hungry beast" (138–39). So, the lion swallowing Pierre indicates that the "child's own angry feelings will consume him" (140). Taking such psychological speculations a step further, the discussion of *Madeline* (1939) tells us that "evil is gendered masculine" because theft takes place "beneath the looming phallic obelisk" (185); the scene in which Madeline reveals her scar "plays on the confusions of little girls . . . about the actual location and description of their genitals" (188). Though such an approach risks treating a text as a mentally ill patient, Spitz does offer some thought-provoking close readings like these, which will be of great interest to those who share her methodology.

Though Spitz strives to get inside the unconscious of both books and readers, *Inside Picture Books* may reveal more about Spitz than about the books. For example, she argues against "books that actively confuse children" because "the overriding agenda for a picture book is to please and to comfort, as well as to instruct" (197).[3] Evaluating illustrated literature's effects on young readers is a laudable goal, but this narrow definition may well exclude such brilliantly dark works as Chris Van Allsburg's *Jumanji* (1982) or Florence Parry Heide's *The Shrinking of Treehorn* (1971).[4] This criterion could also leave out some books discussed at length in *Inside Picture Books*—such as *Where the Wild Things Are*. Likewise, one cannot presume that all children will respond in the same way to any given work. To say that Mercer Mayer's *There's a Nightmare in My Closet* (1968) "deprives children of the closure they crave and leaves them in a state of apprehension" (68) assumes that Spitz's sense of closure is identical to a child's sense of closure. Spitz conveniently trots out a three-year-old reader who happens to agree with her (a frequent tactic in *Inside Picture Books*), but she offers no justification of why this child should be considered representative of all children.

How text, images, and culture affect children is a valuable area of inquiry. And those who favor psychoanalytic approaches to children's literature may enjoy getting *Inside Picture Books*. As Julie Van Camp remarked in a review of Spitz's *Museums of the Mind* (1994), however, the author "prefers meditative, emotional responses over logic" (117).

As a result, the degree to which one's emotional responses coincide with Spitz's will, in large measure, determine any estimation of the book's critical value. And to defend *Inside Picture Books* on the ground that it tackles an important subject or has good intentions—of which this review, too, is sometimes guilty—is to risk falling into the trap of evaluating books about children's literature according to a separate set of standards. Irrespective of how well-intentioned *Inside Picture Books* might be, it's hard to give a good grade to a book that has not done its homework.

Notes

1. "Most studies of children's stories have come from literary theorists and folklorists who, like [Bruno] Bettelheim [in *The Uses of Enchantment*], have focused on the narratives. Ms. Spitz is more concerned with the aesthetic qualities of picture books," writes Ruark (A18), clearly unaware of the considerable body of scholarship on "the aesthetic qualities of picture books." Offering another version of the same error, Robert Coles's foreword to *Inside Picture Books* notes that "we have paid relatively little attention to what our sons and daughters read (or hear read), and to what moral and psychological consequence—a significant oversight now corrected by this knowing, wise book" (ix). For a concise list of other "knowing, wise book[s]" on this topic, see Perry Nodelman's "Reading About Children's Literature: A Bibliography Of Criticism" (1998) or, for more detail, see Linnea Hendrickson's *Children's Literature: A Guide to the Criticism* (1987), especially "Books of Criticism Indexed" (xvii–xxvi) and "Picture Books" (477–95).

2. Of Margaret Wise Brown's *Wait till the Moon Is Full* (1948, illustrated by Garth Williams), Spitz wonders if one might "redo the ending with the child to whom you are reading the book" (41). She suggests a "hoot-n'-holler" (41) as "a perfect way to capitalize on the book's strengths without allowing it to peter out in the end. And if a father could be involved in the moon-rumpus, so much the better" (42).

3. By way of explanation, she adds, "These books, most often read at bedtime or to calm children when they need it, should generally not introduce messages so unsettling as to belie this ulterior purpose" (197). But might these books also be read by a teacher in the classroom, at a public library's story hour, independently during the day, or for some other purpose?

4. Though she briefly discusses *Jumanji*, Spitz does not mention it as potentially troubling to children. Her book does, however, consistently misspell the two-time Caldecott Medal winner's surname as "van Allsberg" (16, 219) instead of the correct "Van Allsburg." Other consistent errors include the fact that Art Spiegelman's *MAUS* was published as a book in 1986, not 1973 (74, 224); and, in *A Midsummer Night's Dream*, the character's name is Bottom, not Bottoms (46).

Works Cited

Bader, Barbara. *American Picturebooks from Noah's Ark to the Beast Within*. New York: MacMillan, 1976.

Bannerman, Helen. *The Story of Little Black Sambo*. 1899. Bedford, Mass.: Applewood Books, 1996.

Bemelmans, Ludwig. *Madeline*. 1939. New York: Viking Press, 1958.

Blake, Quentin. "The art of making readers." *Times* (London), 23 September 1999.

Brown, Margaret Wise. *Goodnight Moon.* Illus. Clement Hurd. 1947. New York: Harper-Collins, 1991.

Heide, Florence Parry. *The Shrinking of Treehorn.* Illus. Edward Gorey. New York: Holiday House, 1971.

Hendrickson, Linnea. *Children's Literature: A Guide to the Criticism.* Boston: G. K. Hall, 1987.

Hoban, Russell. *Bedtime for Frances.* Illus. Garth Williams. 1960. New York: Harper-Trophy, 1995.

Leaf, Munro. *The Story of Ferdinand.* Illus. Robert Lawson. 1936. New York: Viking Press, 1977.

Lurie, Alison. "The Cabinet of Dr. Seuss." *New York Review of Books,* 20 December 1990: 50–52.

Marcus, Leonard. *Margaret Wise Brown: Awakened by the Moon.* 1992. New York: Quill, 1999.

Mayer, Mercer. *There's a Nightmare in My Closet.* 1968. New York: E. P. Dutton, 1992.

Nodelman, Perry. "Reading About Children's Literature: A Bibliography Of Criticism" <http://www.uwinnipeg.ca/~nodelman/criticism.htm> 15 Nov. 1998.

——. *Words About Pictures: The Narrative Art of Children's Books.* Athens: University of Georgia Press, 1988.

Ruark, Jennifer K. "Scary and Soothing: How Picture Books Shape the Mind of a Child." *Chronicle of Higher Education,* 14 May 1999: A18–A19.

Sendak, Maurice. *In the Night Kitchen.* 1970. New York: HarperCollins, 1995.

——. *Pierre.* 1962. New York: HarperTrophy, 1991.

——. *Where the Wild Things Are.* 1963. New York: HarperCollins, 1988.

Seuss, Dr. *Horton Hatches the Egg.* 1940. New York: Random House, 1966.

Van Allsburg, Chris. *Jumanji.* Boston: Houghton Mifflin, 1981.

Van Camp, Julie. Review of *Museums of the Mind. Journal of Aesthetic Education* 31.1 (spring 1997): 117–20.

Warner, Marina. "Gods and Monsters." *New York Times Book Review,* 15 Aug. 1999: 10.

Dissertations of Note

Compiled by Rachel Fordyce and Elizabeth Mayfield

Anderson, Cheri Louise. "Children's Interpretations of Illustrations and Written Language in Picture Books." Ph.D. diss. University of Arizona, 1998. 270 pp. DAI 59: 4085A.

Anderson's dissertation documents children's responses to picture books through language and art, using qualitative research methods. Her findings are organized within two major areas: meaning-making within a picture book and meaning-making within an artwork. Anderson concludes that the students' responses were "extremely sophisticated and showed that they were capable of complex understandings of art and literature."

Anderson, Diane Downer. "Casting Gender: The Constitution of Social Identities Through Literacy Practices Among Third and Fourth Graders." Ph.D. diss. University of Pennsylvania, 1998. 488 pp. DAI 59:4096A.

Anderson's study looks at the "social and academic worlds of third and fourth graders to ascertain how literary practices [are] used to constitute gendered social identities." She finds that children define gender variously: by naming and renaming characters, selves, and peers; intertextually, through genre structures, metaphors, anthropomorphism, and personification; through bodycasts such as clothing, voice, hair, and other physical characteristics; and through interactions, especially verbal interactions. Anderson supports understanding literacy as a continuous view of social, personal, and academic learning.

Ayala-Schueneman, Maria de Jesus. "A Study of Library Services Provided to Students in Bilingual Education Programs by Elementary School Library Media Centers in South Texas." Ed.D. diss. Texas A&M University at Kingsville, 1998. 137 pp. DAI 59:2308A.

Ayala-Schueneman surveyed librarians and media to determine whether the Bilingual Education Act of 1968, which stipulates that financial assistance will be provided to develop and carry out new and imaginative programs to meet the educational needs of limited-English-speaking children, has been completely implemented. In addition to problems with funding, her survey reveals problems with the number and quality of Spanish titles available, as well as a lack of cooperation between teachers and librarians.

Backman, Nelina Esther. "Evangelism Embarrassed: Christian Literature in a Post-Christian Culture." Ph.D. diss. Brown University, 1999. 282 pp. DAI 60:1570A.

Backman's dissertation explores the "rhetorical situation of the avowedly Christian literary artist in the post-Christian twentieth century" as it relates to the work of C. S. Lewis. She argues that Christian literary discourse, both in its articulation and in its reception, occupies a "crucial site of lay interpolation of what it means to be religious in a modern secular world" and illustrates how the "complex and changing boundaries of religion and culture are negotiated."

Blanchard, Walter Louis. "The Organizational Storyteller and the Social Construction of Meaning." Ph.D. diss. Fielding Institute, 1999. 225 pp. DAI 60:899A.

Blanchard identifies the role of organizational storytellers who facilitate and add to "the construction of meaning constituted by social experiences in organizations." Ten organizational storytellers were identified and interviewed, along with nine associates, to shed additional light on the role of the organizational storyteller.

Children's Literature 29, ed. Elizabeth Lennox Keyser and Julie Pfeiffer (Yale University Press, © 2001 Hollins University).

The interviews were analyzed using research methods influenced by ethnomethod-
ology, social construction, and discourse analysis to illustrate how organizational
storytellers account for their roles. He concludes that their credibility, as well as
a large part of their sense of corporate identity, stems from the storytelling role
"performed within a communal sense of meaning as negotiated between teller and
listener."

Boettcher, Cynthia Ann Elizabeth King. "How and Why Gender-Conscious Teachers
Select Female Literature for the Intermediate Grade Classrooms." Ph.D. diss. Texas
A&M University, 1998. 223 pp. DAI 59:4347A.

Using a qualitative multicase research design, Boettcher discovered that
gender-conscious teachers are aware of the differences between girls' and boys' experiences and their academic requirements, as well as the "gender and ethnic diversity of their students." The findings are influenced by studies of literature-based
instruction, diversity in children's literature, adolescent girls, feminist theory and
pedagogy, and teacher education and philosophy.

Bouzoukis, Carol Elaine. "Fairy Tales in the Treatment of Chronically Ill Children."
Ph.D. diss. New York University, 1999. 383 pp. DAI 60:1833A.

Bouzoukis' study seeks to determine the effectiveness of dramatizing fairy tales
for chronically ill children in order to reduce stress. Five patients participated in ten
individual drama therapy sessions conducted by the Researcher/Drama Therapist.
The three major sources of stress in chronically ill children (separation anxiety, loss
of control, and fear of bodily harm) are explored as they directly relate to specific
characters in each fairy tale and as each patient enacted them. Results indicated
that the use of fairy tales is an effective means of stress reduction with selected
chronically ill children.

Boza, Linda Anne. "Cultural and Adolescent Issues of Multicultural Adolescent Literature." Ed.D. diss. University of Central Florida, 1998. 135 pp. DAI 59:4086A.

Boza examines the extent to which cultural and adolescent issues are presented in selected multicultural adolescent literature to determine whether there
are any similarities or dissimilarities in issues among Hispanic, African American,
and Asian cultures. Her results are intended to expose educators to twenty-four
multicultural adolescent novels that can be used in the classroom as alternatives to
novels currently in use. Findings indicated that adolescent issues are more visible
than cultural issues in multicultural adolescent settings, with a primary focus on
parent-adolescent issues.

Braboy, Beth Ann. "Values in Children's Literature: A Descriptive Content Analysis of
Beatrix Potter's *23 Tales for Children*." Ed.D. diss. University of Central Florida, 1998.
159 pp. DAI 59:4041A.

This descriptive study investigated which of the eighteen instrumental values
found in the Rokeach Value Survey can be found in Beatrix Potter's *23 Tales for Children*. Braboy rates each of the tales, and five of the *Tales* are analyzed by a group
of volunteer teachers. Data collected provide information concerning the values in
all twenty-three of the tales.

Broughton, Mary Ariail. "Early Adolescent Girls and Their Reading Practices: Reflection and Transformation of Subjectivities Through Experiences with Literature."
Ph.D. diss. University of Georgia, 1998. 216 pp. DAI 59:1948A.

This qualitative study examines four sixth-grade girls as they read and discussed a novel about two adolescent Mexicans seeking a new life in America. Results
indicate that the girls' identities and subjectivities were reflected and transformed
through discussions of literature. The girls demonstrated their subjectivities as they
constructed virtual texts from the actual text, and they also used literature as a way
to understand their cultural links to Hispanicism. The study indicates that, "by reading about others who have coped with difficult situations and by discussing their

responses and interpretations with their peers, the girls could discover new ways of dealing with the vicissitudes of their own lives."

Buczkowski, Paul James. "The Theatrical Strategies of James Robinson Planché." Ph.D. diss. Wayne State University, 1999. 573 pp. DAI 60:2036A.

Buczkowski argues that examining Planché's work yields a wealth of insight into the social, theatrical, and literary atmosphere of his time, as well as into his particular creative processes. Attention is given to the context of his "pieces," and typical topical references are identified. The importance of Planché's involvement in "pictorial theatre" is also examined.

Church, Gladdys Westbrook. "The Significance of Louise Rosenblatt on the Field of Teaching Literature." Ph.D. diss. State University of New York at Buffalo, 1998. 523 pp. DAI 59:110A.

Church's bibliographic research study examines the influence of Rosenblatt's writings on the community of English education writers, especially those associated with reader response. Church attempts to determine the nature and scope of Rosenblatt's influence and quantitatively determines why she was a significant contributor to this field.

Coats, Karen S. "Performing the Subject of Children's Literature." Ph.D. diss. George Washington University, 1998. 201 pp. DAI 59:1157A.

Coats attempts to articulate, through a close reading of children's books and Lacanian theory, how children's texts become vehicles through which the child performs his or her own subjectivity. She argues that a modern reader, "while aware of his or her split between conscious and unconscious processes, nevertheless strives toward closure and stability, largely because the narratives that she encounters move in that direction," and that certain postmodern trends in literature for children undermine these values and therefore "have the possibility to radically alter subjectivity as we currently understand it."

Cotter, Janet Elaine. "Stance and Lens: A Reading of Sociohistorical Fantasy Time Warp Novels for Middle School Students." Ed.D. diss. University of Georgia, 1998. 223 pp. DAI 59:3395A.

In her study, Cotter examines how a reader makes meaning while she analyzes a sample of sociohistoric fantasy time warp novels for middle school readers. Results show that there are two major influences on a reader's life: literary critical theory and critical social theory. The novels included were found to offer "powerful and moving experiences with history that students may not be exposed to in school or in history texts."

Davis, Brook Marie. "Constance D'Arcy Mackay: Playwright, Director, and Educator, Inspiring Women, Children, and Communities Through Amateur Theatre." Ph.D. diss. University of Maryland at College Park, 1999. 297 pp. DAI 60:941A.

Davis, by examining the different types of works by Constance D'Arcy Mackay, explores her theatrical career in order to chronicle her accomplishments. This study "increases our understanding of the confluence of the several strands of amateur theatre" of the early 1900s and the intersection of Mackay's life and work with gender issues.

Dawes, James Roger. "Language in Violence: Mortality and Ethics in the Literature of War." Ph.D. diss. Harvard University, 1998. 343 pp. DAI 59:3817A.

Dawes's dissertation deals with cultural responses to massive, organized violence and focuses on the way war trauma is narrated, organized, and reproduced through the "work of memory and representation." He examines the causal link between "certain modes of verbalization and the release of violence" associated with the Civil War, World War I, and World War II, while exploring a wide range of texts. He then shows how "pressures of violence in each historical moment give rise to urgent new aesthetic forms and cultural discourses" while he traces the effects of these wars on public representation and also examines how these representations affect war itself. One of the authors he discusses is Alcott.

De Rosa, Deborah Carolina. "Into the Mouths of Babes: Nineteenth-Century Abolitionists' Literary Subversions." Ph.D. diss. University of North Carolina at Chapel Hill, 1998. 287 pp. DAI 59:2498A.

This study analyzes the convergence of discourses about slavery, gender, and children in juvenile literature from 1830 to 1865. De Rosa argues that by choosing to write abolitionist juvenile literature, domestic abolitionists maintained their identities as "exemplary mother-educators and preserved their claims to 'femininity' while entering the public arena." The recovered texts suggest that women used abolitionist juvenile literature as a means to express their views about childhood, family, religion, and government in the public realm during times when society condemned such expression.

Duggan, Anne Elizabeth. "Narrative Strategies and Political Allegory in the Works of Madeleine de Scudery and Marie-Catherine D'Aulnoy." Ph.D. diss. University of Minnesota, 1998. 242 pp. DAI 59:3013A.

Duggan explores the various narrative strategies that de Scudery and d'Aulony employ as a reaction to the breakdown of "traditional" sociopolitical order in early modern French society. She argues that the narrative strategies of the *histoire*, the "anecdote" (chronicle and gazette), and the *conte de fée* are part of an "overall historical or historicizing project" since both authors rewrite and revise earlier historical narratives to redefine gender relations and subjectivity, as well as to "legitimate specific socio-political orders." Duggan hopes to resituate these two prolific women writers of seventeenth-century France within the literary canon and to open the critical paradigm by which women writers are currently being studied.

Gagnon, Monika Kin. "Race-ing Disney: Race and Culture in the Disney Universe." Ph.D. diss. Simon Fraser University, 1998. 175 pp. DAI 60:1803A.

Gagnon links textual analyses of the Disney theme parks and films to an interdisciplinary body of work that deals theoretically with issues of race and cultural difference. Then she argues that the Disney films must be examined in relation to broader cultural contexts in order to be properly understood. She considers the ways in which racial and cultural meaning "circulate within the Disney universe" and suggests that there is a fundamental and problematic reinforcement of racial difference in Disney's seeming celebration of multicultural themes in movies and attractions. She stresses that her examination has urgent value, because Disney's "inescapable domination of children's culture across multiple media combined with the company's global cultural expansion represents a trans-cultural power with profound influence."

Gilabert Juan, Jesus. "Literature for Children and Young People: The Spanish Historical Novel Set in the Middle Ages." Ph.D. diss. Universitat de Valencia, 1998. 417 pp. DAI 59:829C. (In Spanish)

This dissertation analyzes historical Spanish fiction for children and young people and focuses on novels set in the Middle Ages and those published in the second half of the twentieth century. The twenty-two works published between 1961 and 1993 fit into two classifications: one marks the end of the Spanish dictatorship, the other, the establishment of democracy. The works are evaluated in terms of narrator, main character, degree of integration of history and fiction, structural patterns, theme, and the use of the imaginary and the miraculous.

Gill, S. David. "Aiden Chambers: A Critical Biography." Ed.D. diss. University of Tennessee, 1998. 94 pp. DAI 59:3000A.

This dissertation explores Aiden Chambers as a novelist, critic, and editor, and evaluates the strengths and weaknesses of his work. Gill divides Chambers's novels into two groups, based on their audience, and examines the overall stylistic merits of his work.

Gordy, Linda Mary. "Stepping Outside the Usual: Teachers Interacting with Multicultural Literature." Ph.D. diss. University of Wisconsin at Madison, 1998. 381 pp. DAI 59:2309A.

Gordy's qualitative study follows the experiences of six teachers who participated in a ten-month literature discussion group. The white, female, middle-class, monolingual teachers examined unfamiliar texts that expressed the "diverse voices and perspectives that speak within and through children's multicultural literature." Gordy concludes that, as society becomes increasingly diverse, teachers must re-examine their curricula and teaching methods to ensure that they are meeting the needs of all children.

Graham, Deborah Denise. "Family Life and Reading Achievement of Inner-City African American First and Fourth Graders." Ph.D. diss. University of Akron, 1998. 164 pp. DAI 59:727A.

Graham addresses reading failures among low-income African American students by examining the relations among the students' family literacy, their socialization experiences, and their reading outcomes. She argues that a consideration of literacy development across ages seems urgent given the widening achievement gap between white and black students in late elementary grades, beginning with fourth grade. The findings suggest that there is no overall difference in the family literacy and socialization practices for proficient and nonproficient readers in first and fourth grade and that the differences in group proficiencies for first and fourth graders can not be explained on the basis of significant family variations.

Gray, Janet Sinclair. "Race and Time: American Women's Poetics from Antislavery to Racial Modernity." Ph.D. diss. Princeton University, 1999. 312 pp. DAI 60:1558A.

In a dissertation that deals with American women poets and "the relationship between poetry and social power," Gray concludes her dissertation with a discussion of poetry for children: "The Three Little Kittens," "Mary's Lamb," and poems by Mary Mapes Dodge, as well as poetry Dodge published in *St. Nicholas*, specifically poetry in which "stereotypical black figures," functioning as nonsense, "mask contradictions in the construction of white childhood."

Griffin, Sean Patrick. "Tinker Belles and Evil Queens: Consuming Disney Queerly." Ph.D. diss. University of Southern California, 1998. 250 pp. DAI 59:2760A.

Griffin chronicles the history of the Disney company's attitude toward homosexual consumers and toward sexuality in general. Using close textual analysis of a large number of Disney artifacts, he analyzes the importance of popular culture in the "power dynamics of defining and controlling sexual identity" and examines the advantages and disadvantages of reading Disney queerly.

Hines, Maude Elizabeth. "Making Americans: National Fairy Tales and Fantasies of Transformation, 1865–1900." Ph.D. diss. Duke University, 1998. 251 pp. DAI 59:2980A.

This project traces the popularity of European fairy tales in the United States by focusing on four late nineteenth-century novels as sites of fantasies about the creation of American citizens. Hines's argument centers on the idea that the novels use scenes of transformation that are structurally similar to those in fairy tales to "work out complicated fantasies about immigration, race, gender, and nation."

Hock, Beverly Vaughn. "The Labyrinth of Story: Narrative as Creative Construction. A Participatory Study." Ed.D. diss. University of San Francisco, 1999. 259 pp. DAI 60:2015A.

Hock's dissertation "examines the effect of a defining story upon the lives of authors of children's literature [and] explores the connection between early remembered narrative on life patterns and creative endeavor, using the metaphor of the labyrinth to describe the circling journey of subject and theme that continually carries one back to a *defining narrative* from childhood." Authors she focuses on are Jack Zipes, Betsy Hearne, Marina Warner, Joseph Campbell, Lauren Artress, Gianni Rodari, Alan Dundes, Carl Jung, Alma Flor Ada, and Iona and Peter Opie.

Hu, Mi. "An Analytical Study of Selected Newbery Award–Winning Novels: Young Adult Protagonists and the Development of Essential Capacities." Ph.D. diss. University of Tennessee, 1998. 200 pp. DAI 59:2892A.

Hu examines eleven Newbery Award–winning novels to determine whether the essential capacities of autonomy and self-respect, as suggested by Attfield, are found in outstanding literature for children and young adults. He concludes that changes in values and attitudes are consistently related to the development of autonomy and that "the sense of responsibility for one's beliefs, attitudes, and actions comes from an awareness of consequences and a readiness to handle those consequences."

Huang, Jui-Yi. "An Artist of Tai Chi: A Critical Study of the Life, Art, and Cultural Philosophy of the Children's Literature Artist Ed Young." Ph.D. diss. Ohio State University, 1998. 191 pp. DAI 59:3758A.

Huang studies the relation of the theory and pedagogy to the interplay of the visual and the verbal in picture books, specifically in the life, work, and cultural philosophy of the Chinese American children's literature artist Ed Young. He also notes the paucity of studies about the historical, cultural, and educational value of the works of picture book author-artists.

Jacob, Hella R. "Twins in German Prose." Ph.D. diss. State University of New York at Buffalo, 1999. 313 pp. DAI 60:1579A.

Jacob examines twin relationships in German prose, including the tales collected by the Brothers Grimm, and expands previously "inadequate" studies of nineteenth- and twentieth-century prose. She focuses on clearly introduced biological twins while separating her examples by whether they are opposite-sex or same-sex twins, rather than fraternal or identical. She links the twin theme to frequently repeated motifs and argues that the theme of "special birth" has intrigued authors because of the archetypal significance of the twinning phenomenon, although scientific information has also shaped twin literature.

Jenkins, Emily Lockhart. "The Reading Public and the Illustrated Novel, 1890–1914." Ph.D. diss. Columbia University, 1998. 355 pp. DAI 59:3830A.

This study brings together documented reader responses, and the physical objects to which readers respond, to examine reading practices related to illustrated novels in England from 1890 to 1914. Each chapter deals with one novel and posits a relation between the book as a physical object and the uses to which the fiction it contained was put. Jenkins finds that often responses are tightly connected to the novel's illustrations and that "very often both the illustrations and the revisionary responses anchored a scandalous or problematic text so as to bring its meaning in line with cultural norms." Works by Conan Doyle and Lewis Carroll are considered.

Johnson, Holly Harrison. "Sand, Soul, and Psyche: A Study of Fairy Tale and the Healing Imagination in the Clinical Practice of Psychoanalysis." Ph.D. diss. Union Institute, 1998. 231 pp. DAI 59:3696A.

In a Jungian study, Johnson uses the Grimm's fairy tales, as well as clinical cases from analytic practice, to develop the thesis that "imagery is the language of the psyche, and the human imagination the primordial field in which the seemingly mutually exclusive aspects of mind and matter interpenetrate." Her study demonstrates how projective techniques are expressed through sandplay, drawing, and dreams.

Johnson, Judith Ann. "Passive Perfection: Images of Women in Nineteenth Century English Art and Children's Book Illustration." Ph.D. diss. University of Minnesota, 1999. 201 pp. DAI 60:1808A.

Johnson analyzes the way females are frequently depicted in Victorian (Pre-Raphaelite) art and children's book illustration to determine whether "visual icons reinforced the literature and social philosophy of the time." She examines the reasons for a repressive style of portrayal and concludes that women were purposefully depicted in a passive manner and subject to contemporary conventions.

Judd, Judithann T. "Intercultural Children's Literature: A Critical Analysis of Picture Books Published Between 1983 and 1998." Ed.D. diss. University of San Francisco, 1999. 103 pp. DAI 60:1551A.

Judd puts the content of multicultural children's literature into three categories: books that are culturally specific, books that promote global understanding, and books that show cultures interacting with each other. She found very few books in the final category, and she concludes by encouraging authors and publishers to produce more picture books of an intercultural nature.

Junker, M. Sue Christian. "Searching for the Moral: Moral Talk in Children's Literature Study Groups." Ph.D. diss. Arizona State University, 1998. 243 pp. DAI 59:4062A.

Junker examines the moral meanings that young children create when they talk about books. Her data reveal four primary types of moral discussions, and she believes that "significant moral observations seem to result from children making metaphorical connections between the texts and their lives or society." Judd also notes that books that foster moral responses are not didactic in nature but allow room for reader interpretation and concludes that "literature study as an instructional venue encourages moral meaning making and, therefore, holds promise for helping children develop as moral beings."

Kaser, Sandra E. "Exploring Identity Through Responses to Literature." Ph.D. diss. University of Arizona, 1999. 347 pp. DAI 60:1019A.

This teacher research study focuses on "reflection and literature response as a way to explore the identity development of children" in a fourth- and fifth-grade multi-age classroom. Kaser examines drama, literature, discussion, written responses, and visual images to explore how students construct their own identities (within a school context), and she concludes that learning experiences are open-ended and allow for collaboration, reflection, dialogue, and personal response.

Kim, Keumhee. "The Portrayal of the Child in Korean Folk Stories Written in English for Children." Ph.D. diss. Texas A&M University, 1999. 108 pp. DAI 60:1947A.

Kim describes how child characters are portrayed in Korean folk stories written in English for children and published in the United States and Korea. The study provides demographic information about the characteristics of the child characters, as well as a look at traditional Korean values, and evaluates the authenticity of the pictorial presentation of children in Korean folk stories.

Kim, Yun-Tae. "History of Children's Theatre in Korea: From the Beginning to the Present Time, 1920–1998." Ph.D. diss. New York University, 1999. 257 pp. DAI 60:1835A.

Kim examines the development of children's theatre in Korea from the time of its introduction, through Western culture at the end of the nineteenth century, to the present. His survey begins with religious plays that primarily served propagandistic purposes and concludes with a discussion of the educationally important children's theater at the end of the 1980s.

Kwiatek, Deirdre Marisa. "Playing Indian: A Consideration of Children's Books by Native Americans, 1900–1940." Ph.D. diss. University of Toronto, 1998. 193 pp. DAI 60:130A.

Kwiatek explores previously overlooked children's books written by Native North Americans and concludes that by writing children's stories, the Native American authors studied were able to "make the foundational stories of their cultures available to a wide audience [who] needed to know them."

Lang, Linda Louise. "Teaching with Drama: A Collaborative Study in Innovation." Ph.D. diss. University of Alberta, 1998. 182 pp. DAI 59:4351A.

The author worked with two elementary school classroom teachers, "who [had] participated in a summer school class in educational drama pedagogy," to develop and sustain "educational drama strategies" (based on children's literature) after they returned to the classroom. She discusses seven themes related to drama in the classroom: accountability, constraint, authority, creativity, concern, connections, and praxis.

Larison, Isaac Willis. "Seeing with the Heart: Learning and Teaching About Homelessness." Ph.D. diss. Ohio State University, 1998. 258 pp. DAI 59:2844A.

Larison uses ethnographic research and service learning projects to study "cognitive and moral development in young children and the whole language and literature-based instructional practices employed by the classroom teacher." He then develops a curriculum that focuses on homelessness, while analyzing the children, teachers, and social service workers who are intended to work with and learn from his curriculum.

Lee-Harris, Stephanie. "Every Family Has a Story: An Overview of Early Childhood Children's Literature on Contemporary Families." Ph.D. diss. Union Institute, 1998. 246 pp. DAI 59:720A.

Lee-Harris' premise is that "providing young children with literature that depicts their own world is beneficial to their social and emotional development," and her dissertation focuses on contemporary realistic picture books for young children. She also includes a "resource guide of developmentally appropriate literature" that illustrates different family lifestyles. She believes that "using picture books as a teaching tool" teaches young children to deal with "the meaning of life around them," to be more understanding of other people, and to develop self-esteem while exploring their emotions and feelings.

Liu, Li. "Images of Chinese People, Chinese-Americans, and Chinese Culture in Children's and Adolescents' Fiction (1980–1997)." Ed.D. diss. University of Massachusetts, 1998. 247 pp. DAI 59:2310A.

In an effort to eliminate Chinese and Chinese American stereotypes in children's and adolescents' literature, Liu analyzed children's books to determine the ways in which Chinese people are portrayed and the ways Chinese culture is represented. She determined that most non–Chinese American authors and illustrators make inaccurate representations. She intends her study to be useful to authors, illustrators, book reviewers, curriculum specialists, and others who work with written materials about China, Chinese, and Chinese Americans, as well as scholars of children's literature who "wish to analyze other cultures well."

Lowery, Ruth McKoy. "A Critical Sociology of Literature: Representations of Immigrants in Literature for Children." Ph.D. diss. Pennsylvania State University, 1998. 271 pp. DAI 59:2984A.

Lowery examines the portrayal of immigrants to the United States from 1820 to the 1990s, focusing on how issues of race and class affect or influence their representation. Using a critical sociology of literature to analyze her historical review of immigration in the United States, she demonstrates that racial and class representations of immigrants in the novels are generally negative and suggests that literature should not be used in isolation to present the experiences of immigrants.

Lyke, Patrice Phelan. "A Rhetorical Critique of Oscar Wilde's Fairy Tales." Ph.D. diss. Texas Woman's College, 1998. 253 pp. DAI 59:2523A.

Lyke regrets the lack of critical attention to Oscar Wilde's fairy tales in the century since their publication. Using an Aristotelian approach, which comprehensively considers the multiple causes of a work, she asserts that Wilde used the fairy tale to "argue for the role of beauty in promoting compassion and empathy in man's daily existence."

Malone, Charles Proctor. "Ordering Childhood: Figures of Children, Pedagogical Address, Love of the World, and the Mis-Education of Desire." Ph.D. diss. University of California at Berkeley, 1998. 152 pp. DAI 59:2899A.

Malone explores "how childhood and childhood sexuality are figured in the intersections between political, psychoanalytical, and educational discourses." She argues that the figure of the child is pieced together into an ideal that establishes a "normative trajectory of human development." She also replaces theories of education, those that assume a stable cultural legacy or a naïve developmental idealism, with an account of "education as seduction," advancing the theory that the child is an "inauthentic other" because of its "immaturity," someone who is "both open to and in need of the world of adult desire, and capable of transforming different regimens of pleasure, knowledge and identity."

McCabe, Colleen Therese. "Multicultural Children's Literature: Its Effect on the Cultural Attitude of Fifth-Grade Students." Ph.D. diss. Virginia Commonwealth University, 1998. 312 pp. DAI 59:2401A.

In an examination of the effect of multicultural children's literature on the cultural attitudes of fifth-grade students, McCabe concludes that her findings do not support previous research which found that reading multicultural children's literature had a positive effect on the cultural attitudes of students toward other cultures as well as their own. She supports the studies of Nieto (1992) and Banks (1993), asserting that multicultural children's literature must be part of a total multicultural curriculum if it is to be effective.

Mello, Robin Ann. "Narrating Gender: Children's Responses to Gender Roles Depicted in Orally Told Folk Tales and Other Traditional Stories." Ph.D. diss. Lesley College, 1999. 331 pp. DAI 60:1947A.

Using a feminist methodology, Mello examines the reactions of ten fourth-grade students to the gender roles depicted in orally told folktales. The study finds that storytelling has "a profound impact on students' perceptions of their own gender roles" and that "stories told aloud cause participants to build meaningful relationships to both text and teller."

Mitchell, Deirdre Ruth. "Reading Character in the Caldecotts: Adult and Child Perceptions of Character Traits in Children's Picture Books." Ph.D. diss. Ohio University, 1999. 220 pp. DAI 60:1500A.

Mitchell examines the texts and pictures of Caldecott medal books for character traits, as perceived by both adults and children. Several differences between adult and child readings of the books appear, but most significant is that, in contrast to adults', children's readings are more visually based than text-based as they perceive character traits. Mitchell suggests that "character trait analysis of picture books should be a flexible framework to assist children to discern and discuss perceived messages in texts and illustrations" and that participating in this process may help adults better understand how children construct meaning in picture books.

Monhardt, Leigh Christopher. "The Effect of Teaching Strategies Focusing on Student Ideas, Parent Partnerships, and Children's Literature on Elementary Students' Perception About and Attitudes Toward Science." Ph.D. diss. University of Iowa, 1998. 189 pp. DAI 59:3395A.

Monhardt's study examines whether elementary school students can perceive changes in their science education when both teachers and parents participate in the Science: Parents, Activities and Literature (Science PALs) program. Few significant differences in student attitudes or perceptions between participating and nonparticipating science classes were noted at lower grade levels, although more significant differences were observed in the upper grade levels.

Mullen, Paul J. "The Grinch, Lorax, Yertle the Turtle, and Others as Advocates in a Literature-Based Collaborative Group Approach to Social Skills Building in a Therapeutic Day School: A New Use for Seuss." Psy.D. diss. Chicago School of Professional Psychology, 1999. 89 pp. DAI 60:1012A.

Mullen investigates "the use of juvenile literature as part of a collaborative group intervention to facilitate the development of social skills." Focusing on a practical framework for collaborative bibliotherapy described by Pardeck and Pardeck (1990), he states that the study results should be "approached with caution," owing to a number of different and contradictory variables, but suggests that "bibliotherapeutic interventions may have positive impacts upon children when used to help develop social skills."

Neemann, Harold Peter. "Piercing the Magic Veil: Toward a Theory of the *Conte*." Ph.D. diss. University of Colorado at Boulder, 1998. 272 pp. DAI 59:840A.

In this multidisciplinary study, Neemann examines the ways seventeenth-century authors of literary fairy tales shaped the definition and reception of the genre and argues that the "complex issues concerning the production and reception of the *contes* clearly demonstrate that the tales are neither timeless nor universal and indeed have a history." This study includes a critical discussion of several interpretative approaches to the genre.

O'Kelly, James B. "Children's Learning of Science Through Literature." Ed.D. diss. Rutgers, The State University of New Jersey at New Brunswick, 1999. 172 pp. DAI 60:694A.

O'Kelly examines the effect of picture books from different literary genres on how primary grade students learn science. He discovers that, contrary to expectations, children who encounter nonfiction literature produce significantly more creative ideas than students who read fiction or modern fantasy do. He concludes that nonfiction has the strongest impact on the learning of science when students have little knowledge of the subject.

Ostry, Elaine Margaret. "Social Dreaming: Dickens and the Fairy Tale." Ph.D. diss. University of Toronto, 1998. 300 pp. DAI 60:141A.

Ostry believes that "Dickens played a key role in establishing the fairy tale as an important literary form for the Victorian middle class." To support her thesis, she traces "the heritage to which Dickens was exposed" and shows how he used tales to promote his own social views and why be believed that fairy tales could add "a high cultural value" to readers oppressed by "the mechanical age." The second part of her dissertation discusses "Dickens's role in the [early nineteenth-century] cultural dispute . . . over the value of the fairy tale for children, when writers battled for access to children's minds [to] perpetuate their belief systems."

Pereida-Beihl, Barbara. "Female Elder as Culture Bearer in Multicultural Children's Literature." Ed.D. diss. University of San Francisco, 1998. 148 pp. DAI 59: 2402A.

Pereida-Beihl explores the role of the female elder in multicultural children's literature as she conveys wisdom to children through stories and domestic arts. She argues that "respect for story in its varied forms and domestic arts as a binding fabric [yields] a vehicle for understanding one's own history and culture," which leads to self-esteem and an understanding of all cultures.

Pitts, Paul Douglas. "Weaving Words: A Synthesis of Navajo World View Made Pivotal in Fiction for Young Girls." Ed.D. diss. Brigham Young University, 1998. 282 pp. DAI 59:4035A.

Pitts identifies the basic tenets of the Navajo worldview and its important cultural traditions. These tenets are then used to develop characters, setting, and plot for a young adult novel. "The processes of preparing to produce such a work of fiction, exploring Navajo culture, and writing the story are also analyzed."

Raynard, Sophie Gabrielle. "Preciosity and Representations of the Feminine in Fairy Tales from Charles Perault to Mme LePrince de Beaumont." Ph.D. diss. Columbia University, 1999. 619 pp. DAI 60:1589A. (In French)

Raynard attempts "to rediscover" French feminine fairy tales of the late seventeenth and early eighteenth centuries. She argues that their female authors, like the *précieuses*, wrote from a "feminocentric" point of view that can be viewed as feminist because the authors used the marvelous to emphasize feminine heroism. Raynard distinguishes tales written by women from those of Perrault and places them in the context of feminist discourse alongside the canonical *précieux* authors.

Riddell, Kim Ann. "The Meaning Movers: An Exploration of the Thinking (Discourse) of Three Teachers Teaching a Methods Course in Creative Drama." Ph.D. diss. University of Pittsburgh, 1998. 165 pp. DAI 60:394A.

Examining how "teachers at various points in their apprenticeships think, plan, enact, reflect, and devise revisions" in a creative dramatics methods course, Riddell proposes a theoretical frame based on the proposition that teaching teachers involves the acquisition of a pedagogical discourse. She proposes a definition of a "metapedagogy" that builds from the idea that "planning for teaching takes place in the imagination and includes aspects of working with multiple pedagogical discourses." She also suggests a four-phase process of authoring, reading, researching, and transforming texts on teaching to move teachers beyond their existing ways of imagining teaching.

Roberts, Catherine Elizabeth. "Telling 'Truth Truly': The Startling Self of Adolescent Girls in Nineteenth-Century New England Diaries." Ed.D. diss. Harvard University, 1999. 262 pp. DAI 60:1944A.

Roberts explores how adolescent girl diarists "reveal, over time, their understanding of education and their relationships within families and communities, including evaluations of their own growth and character," by examining the development of three girls in early nineteenth-century Massachusetts as revealed through their diaries. She argues that the learning experiences of these girls challenges the historical definitions of adolescence. She finds that these girls do not fit neatly into the traditional paths that current scholarship suggests were available to them.

Robin, Regina Spires. "Science for Children and the Untutored in Eighteenth-Century England." Ph.D. diss. City University of New York, 1998. 255 pp. DAI 59:3622A.

This study attempts to bridge the gap between children's literature and the popular tracts on science by examining books written for children and the untutored in eighteenth-century England. Robin examines five authors who "enjoyed recognition in the world of adult literature and who sought to simplify scientific material while conserving sophisticated language and complex ideas." She argues that these authors used their literary and scientific knowledge to further the cause of home schooling and to stress industry, honesty, self-reliance, and hard work as necessary corollaries to scientific exploration. She also addresses a number of social issues, including the place of women in science.

Rosa, Kathy Susanne. "Gendered Technologies: Gender in Electronic Children's Literature." Ed.D. diss. University of Houston, 1999. 90 pp. DAI 60:1523A.

Rosa examines the issue of gender bias in electronic forms of children's literature (ECL) and addresses the question of whether ECL contains gender-stereotyped settings, behaviors, and activities similar to those found in the traditional canon of children's literature. Results confirm that the pattern of gender bias found in schools, children's literature, and curricular materials is being perpetuated in ECL.

Ruumet, Marika. "Values in the Best-Selling Children's Books in the United States, 1990–1997." Ed.D. diss. University of San Francisco, 1998. 166 pp. DAI 60:2031A.

Ruumet analyzes values embedded in the best-selling fiction and picture books for children and young adults in the United States from 1990 to 1997. She identifies four common themes that "reflect prosocial behaviors": "despondent independence"; unconditional love and friendship; tolerance of difference; and the assumption that with every challenge there may not be resolution, but there is hope in the future.

Schlichting, Kathleen Ann. "The Story Within: A Qualitative Inquiry into the Power and Potential of Children's Literature on Young Children's Learning and the Sociocultural Context of the Classroom." Ph.D. diss. University of South Carolina, 1998. 406 pp. DAI 59:2426A.

Inquiring into the impact of children's literature on young children's speech and learning, and on the sociocultural context of the classroom, Schlichting identifies three major themes, each consisting of a variety of patterns: (1) children's cognitive abilities are enhanced through literature, (2) demonstrations built on engagements with children's literature "promoted social growth and consequently built a genuine classroom community," and (3) children begin to believe in themselves and have "expectations of themselves" through transaction with literature.

Stephanides, Adam Louis. "Tomorrow's Women and Yesterday's Men: Junior Novels and Social Change, 1946–1964." Ph.D. diss. University of Illinois at Urbana-Champaign, 1999. 284 pp. DAI 60:863A.

Stephanides examines critically recommended novels for adolescents published in the United States between 1946 and 1964, arguing that the values expressed in these novels were much more progressive than the novels written for adolescents in the 1950s would lead one to expect, particularly in regard to gender and racial and ethnic minorities.

Stevenson, Deborah Jane. " 'For All Our Children's Fate': Children's Literature and Contemporary Culture." Ph.D. diss. University of Chicago, 1999. 236 pp. DAI 60:2023A.

Stevenson focuses on the work of Jon Scieszka, Maurice Sendak, and Beverly Cleary, drawing on "research and practice in library science, education, history, sociology, and art" to create a synthesis of scholarship. She is particularly interested in the polarized responses provoked by these authors, as well as "artistic innovation in the postmodern picture book, arousal and control of emotion in neosensational texts, the pervasive underestimation of the everyday-life story, the cultural position of children's literature classics, and the non academic nature of literature's dominant canon."

Stringam, Jean. "Canadian Short Adventure Fiction in Periodicals for Adolescents: Canada, England, the United States, 1847–1914." Ph.D. diss. University of Alberta, 1998. 324 pp. DAI 60:120A.

Stringam analyzes Canadian-content short adventure fiction in eight periodicals from Britain, Canada, and the United States published from the nineteenth century to the outbreak of World War I. Her study includes discussions of colonial class, race, and gender issues, while she investigates concepts of manliness and the imperial boy-hero, locating the stories within the "social and historical matrix of Canada and her powerful neighbors."

Swerdfeger, Steven E. "Because They Think They Can." Ph.D. diss. Union Institute, 1998. 621 pp. DAI 59:4430A.

Swerdfeger's study traces the history and development of children's literature through five adolescent problem novels. He then draws on the twelve stages of the archetypal Hero's Journey to construct a fictional adolescent novel "founded on research in education, learning theory, critical thinking, psychology, hypnosis, and guided imagery."

Timmons, Daniel Patrick. "Mirror on Middle-Earth: J. R. R. Tolkien and the Critical Perspectives." Ph.D. diss. University of Toronto, 1998. 271 pp. DAI 60:143A.

Timmons evaluates the criticism of the works of J. R. R. Tolkien, including the author's self-criticism. He argues that the commonly held views of Tolkien's negative critical reception are misinformed, and he provides an assessment of the current state of the extensive and diverse commentary on Tolkien. He begins with criticism of *The Hobbit*, in 1937, and concludes with reviews of the second edition of *The Lord of the Rings*, in 1965, and *The Silmarillion* in 1976.

Tolson, Nancy Deborah. "Black Children's Literature Got the Blues: The Aesthetic Creativity of Black Writers and Illustrators of Black Children's Literature." Ph.D. diss. University of Iowa, 1998. 177 pp. DAI 59:1576A.

This dissertation examines black children's literature from the perspective of the blues aesthetic and includes a history of black children's literature and of the scholars who have defined the blues aesthetic in black culture. Tolson concludes by arguing that the blues aesthetic can provide a "powerful lens for seeing the value of Black children's literature and for tracing its connections to the roots of Black literature and Black culture," and that black children's literature, too long overlooked, can assist children in understanding cultural differences and similarities.

Torres, Mychelle Marie. "Understanding the Multiracial Experience Through Children's Literature: A Protocol." Psy.D. diss. California School of Professional Psychology at Berkeley/Alameda, 1998. 149 pp. DAI 59:3126B.

Torres "examines common psychological dynamics that have been established in research literature" and uses the findings to create a children's book that conveys the intricacies of being multiracial. She intends for the book to be helpful to teachers, psychologists, parents, and children, and for it to generate conversations that examine issues of race and ethnicity.

Turner-Bowker, Diane Marie. "Picture Images of Girls and Women in Children's Literature." Ph.D. diss. University of Rhode Island, 1998. 130 pp. DAI 59:4544B.

Turner-Bowker examines characters and the content of illustrations in award-winning children's books from two time periods, 1967–1976 and 1987–1996, to determine whether sexism exists in books for preschool children. Findings confirm that male and female characters are not represented equally in illustrations and that girls and women are presented in "subordinate and degrading images" more often than boys and men are. However the books published from 1987 to 1996 contain fewer of these images than do those published from 1967 to 1976.

Voorhees, Susan C. "An Investigation of Children's Re-Enactments During Episodes of Storybook Reading as a Reflection of Parents' Mediating Styles." Ed.D. diss. Hofstra University, 1998. 159 pp. DAI 59:1511A.

The purpose of Voorhees' study is to examine whether young children's re-enactments of shared storybook reading with parents reflects the parent's mediating styles during storybook reading. Results suggest that the instructional history of preschool children prior to formal schooling needs to be included as a component of reading models. Parents should be guided to reflect on their beliefs about reading and instructed concerning the reading process and effective storybook mediating strategies.

Webster, Jerry Wayne. "The Effects of Ninth Graders' Culture-Specific Schemata on Their Responses to Multicultural Literature." Ph.D. diss. University of Maryland at College Park, 1999. 510 pp. DAI 60:1004A.

Webster compares students' reports of their multicultural awareness to a test sample of multiracial students who have been exposed to a range of multicultural literature. Results confirm the students' high self-ratings in terms of their cultural development.

Williams, Amanda Jane. "Providers' Perceptions of Public Library Storytime: A Naturalistic Inquiry." Ph.D. diss. University of Texas at Austin, 1998. 342 pp. DAI 59:1818A.

Williams examines how individuals who provide storytime in public libraries perceive what happens during the reading. Data indicate that readers find pleasure in their work and that they recognize that storytime is an important social experience for young children and that it facilitates learning. From these results, Williams conceptualizes a preschool storytime model for large groups and suggests areas for further research.

Wolfenbarger, Carol Driggs. "Gifted Middle School Students' Response to Nonfiction/ Informational Books Illustrated with Photographs." Ph.D. diss. Ohio State University, 1999. 307 pp. DAI 60:1487A.

Wolfenbarger explores how gifted middle school students respond to nonfiction or informational books illustrated with photographs, then groups the observable responses into categories. Students were asked to use text and graphic design, as well as their understanding of other characteristics of the genre, to create their own nonfiction or informational books.

Woodson, Stephani Etheridge. "Mapping the Cultural Geography of Childhood or Constructing the Child in Child Drama: 1950 to the Present." Ph.D. diss. Arizona State University, 1999. 202 pp. DAI 60:596A.

Woodson's study "unpacks and explores" the ways in which American culture, and specifically American child drama, shapes the child. She investigates the "metaphorical topography of childhood constructs found under the surface of the American child drama field's dramatic literature, practices, texts, and educational and promotional materials" by contrasting them with mainstream American culture. She argues that mixing child drama narratives with stories drawn from popular culture and the media allows her to "link and to explore a wide variety of discourses constituting and reconstituting childhood."

Ylonen, Hilkka. "The World of the Golden Cap and Silver Shoes: How Kindergarten Children Listen to, View, and Experience Fairy Tales." Dre.D. diss. Jyvaskylan Yliopisto, 1998. 189 pp. DAI 60:669C. (In Finnish)

Ylonen concludes that kindergarten children can "cope with and handle" their real-life experiences via the metaphors offered by a fairy tale and that they can find solutions to some of their problems and, possibly, "enrich and enhance" their personal lives. She uses *The Wizard of Oz* as her text.

Also of Note

Al-Jafar, Ali Ashour. " 'Not Like Now': The Dialogic Narrative in the Educational Act." Ph.D. diss. Indiana University, 1998. 202 pp. DAI 59:1441A.

Part of Al-Jafar's dissertation focuses on storytelling with sixth-graders and tales from *1001 Nights.*

Arshad, Mahzan Bin. "Malaysian Student Teachers' Responses to Multicultural Literature." Ph.D. diss. University of Pittsburgh, 1998. 190 pp. DAI 60:367A.

Arshad believes that student teachers should be "introduced" to multicultural literature and that teachers should use "literary texts" that reflect their students' cultural and linguistic backgrounds.

Asplund, Carlsson, Maj. "The Doorkeeper and the Beast: The Experience of Literary Narratives in Educational Contexts." Fil.Dr. diss. Goteborgs Universitet, 1998. 106 pp. DAI 60: 222C. (In Swedish)

In an examination of reader response theory, Asplund studies "recall of narratives [in] a more qualitative way" than has been done in the past "to compare schools, children in different age groups and different educational cultures."

Bell, Michelle Anne. "Shared Book Reading in Kindergarten: Nature and Outcomes." Ph.D. diss. University of Guelph, 1999. 179 pp. DAI 60:376A.

"The purpose of this study was to examine qualitative aspects of shared book reading interactions between kindergarten children who are just beginning to read and their parents."

Bianchi, Lisa Lenz. "Finding a Voice: Poetry and Performance with First Graders." Ph.D. diss. University of New Hampshire, 1999. 304 pp. DAI 60:993A.

Bianchi develops a "ten week immersion unit in reading, writing, and performance of poetry" informed by the work of Bakhtin, Dewey, Louise Rosenblatt, Erving Goffman, and Anne Haas Dyson.

Cary, Stephen. "The Effectiveness of a Contextualized Storytelling Approach for Second Language Acquisitions." Ed.D. diss. University of San Francisco, 1998. 208 pp. DAI 59:758A.

Cary concludes that CLA (Contextualized Storytelling Approach) is a "potentially highly effective approach for second language acquisition."

Copenhaver, Jeane Fullmore. "Children's Responses to Read-Alouds and Group-Shared Writing in a Multi-Ethnic, Multi-Age Primary Grade Classroom." Ph.D. diss. University of Florida, 1998. 291 pp. DAI 60:339A.

Copenhaver describes the "possible relationships between children's ethnicities and their responses to read-alouds" in a multi-age primary classroom and finds that some teachers have a "hidden curriculum" when they work with poor, ethnic minority students.

Desachy-Godoy, Elvira. "Cri-Cri: El Mundo Creativo de Francisco Jose Gabilondo Soler." Ph.D. diss. University of New Mexico, 1998. 215 pp. DAI 59:2531A. (In Spanish)

Desachy-Godoy discusses Soler's short stories and songs for children and his contributions to Mexican radio broadcasting from 1930 to 1960.

Downey, Glenn Robert. "The Truth About Pawn Promotion: The Development of the Chess Motif in Victorian Fiction." Ph.D. diss. University of Victoria, 1998. 282 pp. DAI 59:4435A.

Downey analyzes Anne Brontë's *The Tenant of Wildfell Hall*, Thomas Hardy's "A Pair of Blue Eyes," and Carroll's *Through the Looking Glass.*

Duncan, Carolyn. "Ladies of Misrule: A Re-Vision of Nineteenth- and Early Twentieth-Century Women Writers' Double-Voiced Carnivalesque Texts with a Special Focus on the Works of Elizabeth Stuart Phelps." Ph.D. diss. University of Toledo, 1998. 166 pp. DAI 59:2499A.

Among other "Ladies of Misrule," Duncan discusses Louisa May Alcott in the context of Balkhtin's theory of carnival.

Ferguson, Christine Jeandheur. "A Descriptive Analysis of Children's Literacy Behaviors During Sociodramatic Play in One Kindergarten Classroom." Ph.D. diss. University of South Carolina, 1999. 257 pp. DAI 60:1006A.

Ferguson believes that her study "offers educators explicit means to initiate child-centered learning strategies that support, enhance, and foster children's literary learning."

Forbes, Benjamin Channing. "La Oficina: An Ethnographic Study of Language and Power in Second Grade Peer Play." Ed.D. diss. University of Massachusetts, 1999. 300 pp. DAI 60:340A.

Forbes concludes that "social theories of discourse" are inadequate to describe children at play.

Freitag, Robert Wayne. "A Content Analysis of American and German Bibliotherapeutic Literature About Divorce Using Allport's Descriptive Statistics: Emic and Etic Multicultural Themes." Ed.D. diss. Northern Illinois University, 1998. 353 pp. DAI 59:1470A.

Freitag concludes that "content analysis of children's bibliotherapeutic literature is a viable method of uncovering non-stereotypic emic and etic cultural traits."

Ginsberg, Lesley Ellen. "The Romance of Dependency: Childhood and the Ideology of Love in American Literature, 1825–1870." Ph.D. diss. Stanford University, 1998. 357 pp. DAI 59:2023A.

Ginsberg explores "how representations of childhood and/or dependency in the fictions of Poe, Hawthorne, Stowe, and Alcott both reify and challenge the period's dominant ideologies of love."

Guedet, Gabrielle Marie. "Beauty in the Beast: A Study of a Woman's Journey to Meet with the Animus." Ph.D. diss. Pacifica Graduate Institute, 1998. 190 pp. DAI 60:829B.

This dissertation in clinical psychology and women's studies demonstrates an eight-stage developmental progression based on the Beauty and the Beast motif.

Haegert, Sheila Ann. "How Does Love Grow? Attachment Processes in Older Adoptees and Foster Children as Illustrated by Fictional Stories." Ph.D. diss. University of Victoria, 1999. 269 pp. DAI 60:1903A.

Haegert's dissertation in educational psychology shows "how children in the context of new relationships with healthy attachment figures who do not abandon or hurt them modify their inferred internal constructions of attachment figures."

Hansen, Cory Cooper. "Getting the Picture: Talk About Story in a Kindergarten Classroom." Ph.D. diss. Arizona State University, 1998. 260 pp. DAI 59:719A.

Hansen shows how to use classical works for children while working with kindergarten students as they develop an ability to talk about literature.

Hermansson, Casie Elizabeth. "Feminist Intertextuality and the Bluebeard Story." Ph.D. diss. University of Toronto, 1998. 286 pp. DAI 60:139A.

Hermansson believes that the "Bluebeard story metafictively illustrates two types of intertextuality: monologic . . . and dialogic."

Kelleher, Mary Alice. "Laboring Under a Misconception: Writing About Work and Writing as Work in Four Antebellum New England Authors." Ph.D. diss. New York University, 1999. 246 pp. DAI 60:1559A.

Kelleher concludes that Alcott found work "exhausting and health breaking. Yet work is the reason for existence [and] the reward for hard work is not leisure but more work."

Koplitz Harty, Stephanie Jane. "Home Literacy Background and School Literacy Expectations: Observations of First Graders' Responses to a Story." Ph.D. diss. University of Minnesota, 1998. 174 pp. DAI 59:2424A.

Koplitz Harty finds that children with high "Home Literacy" scores have better "aesthetic response" and reading-with-writing comprehension than children with low scores, but they are not better at "identifying story elements [and] using literary devices."

Laird, Julie Ann. "Young Children's Explorations of Written Language During Free Choice." Ph.D. diss. University of Arizona, 1998. 519 pp. DAI 59:4087A.

Laird defends her thesis that "allowing young children time for free choice engagements and play" is both appropriate and necessary for them to develop written literacy.

Lim, Young Sook. "Facilitating Young Korean Children's Language Development Through Parent Training Picture Book Interaction." Ph.D. diss. University of Washington, 1999. 98 pp. DAI 60:1053A.

Lim found that training parents was a low-cost and efficient way of improving literacy skills for typical young children and those who are language-delayed.

Logan Hastings, Mary Eileen. "Zemlinsky, Wilde: Values and Illusions." DMA. diss. University of Maryland College Park, 1998. 57 pp. DAI 59:1828A.

Logan examines the deliberate change in the character of the *Infanta in Der Zwerg,* Alexander Zemlinsky's opera adaptation of Oscar Wilde's "The Birthday of the Infanta," and addresses "what may be a typical 1920's modernist perception of women on the part of Zemlinsky."

Loudin, Maureen F. "The Role of the Family in the Literacy Development of Four First Graders from Low-Income Homes Who Are Succeeding in Early Literacy." Ph.D. diss. Kent State University, 1998. 220 pp. DAI 60:378A.

If the family and the community support literacy, both cognitively and emotionally, Loudin believes, then low-income children become successful readers.

Marchant, Jamie Laree. "Novel Resolutions: Revising the Romance Plot, the Woman's Movement, and American Women Novelists, 1870–1930." Ph.D. diss. Claremont Graduate University, 1998. 232 pp. DAI 59:172A.

Marchant begins her dissertation with a discussion of Lousia May Alcott.

Marsh, Prudence. "The Role of Children's Literature in the Family Context: In-Depth Interviews with Parents." Ph.D. diss. University of Massachusetts, 1999. 233 pp. DAI 60:1486A.

Marsh examines the significance of current research into family literacy practices and the relation between the social and the academic lives of children and concludes that the subject needs further exploration.

McLellan, Janet Elizabeth. "Storybook Interactions of African-American Mothers and Their Children: A Longitudinal Study." Ph.D. diss. University of North Carolina at Chapel Hill, 1998. 133 pp. DAI 59:2908A.

McLellan examines the "quality of mother-child storybook interactions and later language and literacy learning," particularly with two- and three-year-old children.

Pyrczak, Richard Matthews. "Growing Pains: Figures of Growth and Childhood in Nineteenth-Century France." Ph.D. diss. New York University, 1999. 284 pp. DAI 60:1589A.

Among other authors, Pyrczak discusses Rousseau *(Emile)*, Balzac, Sand, Hugo, Daudet, Verne, and Alain-Fournier "in terms of [the child figure's] proper evolution and the debate around the meaning and value of childhood."

Ramirez, Anne West. "Sisters in Search: Emily Dickinson's Affinities with the Tradition of Christlike Women in Literature." Ph.D. diss. Indiana University of Pennsylvania, 1999. 382 pp. DAI 60:2030A.

The "female prototype" for Ramirez's Christlike women "is the folktale figure of the sister who seeks and saves her brothers." Among other authors, Ramirez discusses the Brothers Grimm, Charlotte Brontë, George MacDonald, and Ursula K. Le Guin.

Rodgers, Adrian R. "Teacher and Teacher-Researcher Classroom Collaboration: Planning and Teaching in a Secondary English Classroom Using Process-Oriented Drama Approaches." Ph.D. diss. Ohio State University, 1999. 228 pp. DAI 60:385A.

Rodgers believes that "collaborative professional development is a powerful way of accomplishing educational reform."

Rodriguez, Richard J. "Representations of Childhood in Twain, Crane, and James." Ph.D. diss. New York University, 1998. 225 pp. DAI 59:3458A.

Rodriguez challenges Aries' contention that pre-modern children were "small scale adults." He believes that "there have been at least three major paradigms of childhood in the course of American history" and that these are reflected in the works of Twain, Crane, and Henry James.

Roe, Mileta. "Talking Books: Storytelling in New World Narratives." Ph.D. diss. Brandeis University, 1999. 160 pp. DAI 60:1122A.

Roe demonstrates how the art of storytelling affects the fabric of novels and film.

Romano, Stephanie Anne. "The Effects of Three Presentation Methods (Read-Aloud, Small Group, and Independent) of Interacting with Literature on the Quality of the Students' Written Responses to Their Literature Logs." Ed.D. diss. Lehigh University, 1998. 115 pp. DAI 60:91A.

Using a quasi-experimental format, Romano investigates the three presentation methods and their effect on the quality of written responses in fifth-grade students' literature logs. "The most significant differences were found in the quality of written responses between read-aloud and small-group methods."

Scott, Jonathan Paul. "The Blood of Others: Class Struggle and Popular Culture in the Writing of Langston Hughes." Ph.D. diss. State University of New York at Stony Brook, 1998. 354 pp. DAI 59:2988A.

Scott questions why Hughes turned "to children's literature at the very moment when children's literature was being attacked by the anticommunist right" if he was "scared away" from radical politics in the late forties.

Sili, Surya. "An Exploration of the Implementation of Literature-Based Instruction in Three Fourth-Grade Indonesian Classrooms: Promises and Challenges." Ph.D. diss. Ohio State University, 1999. 236 pp. DAI 60:369A.

Sili demonstrates how to model literature-based instruction.

Smith, Cynthia Rose. " 'Click' and Turn the Page: A Case Study of a Young Child Developing Multiple Storybook Literacy." Ph.D. diss. Ohio State University, 1998. 178 pp. DAI 59:3761A.

Smith chronicles how a young child "interacts with and explores traditional, Language-Experience Approach (LEA), and CD-ROM storybooks" and concludes that technology is a significant factor in learning.

Winters, Paul Edward. "Ending Well: The Ideology of Selected Endings in the Novels of Dickens, Eliot, and Forster." Ph.D. diss. Lehigh University, 1999. 221 pp. DAI 60:2044A.

Winters discusses *Dr. Jekyll and Mr. Hyde* and *Pickwick Papers,* among other works.

Yang, Shih-Mei. "A Case Study: An Examination of Literary Transactions of Four Elementary Chinese-American Male Children Responding to Selected Children's Books." Ed.D. diss. University of Northern Colorado, 1998. 367 pp. DAI 59:2862A.

Yang studies Chinese American students as they read realistic fiction involving Chinese-American cultures and "mainstream U.S.-American culture."

Contributors and Editors

GILLIAN ADAMS has recently retired as the editor of *Children's Literature Abstracts* and associate editor of the *ChLA Quarterly*. She plans to continue research and publication on ancient and medieval children's literature.

SANDRA BECKETT is professor of French at Brock University and the president of the International Research Society for Children's Literature. She is the author of several books on contemporary French literature and the editor of *Reflections of Change: Children's Literature Since 1945* (1997) and *Transcending Boundaries: Writing for a Dual Audience of Children and Adults* (1999). She is currently completing a book on contemporary retellings of *Little Red Riding Hood*.

JENNIFER BOLTON is a graduate student at Virginia Tech and Hollins University. Her research interests include English, children's literature, and gender studies. She hopes to earn her doctorate in the next ten years.

CLARE BRADFORD is an associate professor of literary studies at Deakin University in Melbourne, Australia. She is the editor of the journal *Papers: Explorations into Children's Literature*, and has published widely on picture books and colonial and postcolonial literature for children. Her most recent book, *Reading Race*, a study of representations of Aborigines in Australian children's literature, will be published by Melbourne University Press in 2001.

RUTH CARVER CAPASSO is associate professor of French at Kent State University. She has published on the fairy tales of Mme D'Aulnoy and the tales for children written by George Sand. Her current research focuses on the *Bibliothèque Rose Illustrée* and children's formation, including messages concerning the social order, gender roles, and relations with the Other such as the poor or the colonized.

LAURA B. COMOLETTI received her bachelor's degree in English from Wheaton College in 1999. She is the winner of Wheaton's Anne Louise Knowles '55 Prize in English and is currently preparing to enter graduate school in English.

CHRISTINE DOYLE is an associate professor of English at Central Connecticut State University, where she teaches courses in children's literature, storytelling, American literature, and women writers. She is the author of *Louisa May Alcott and Charlotte Brontë: Transatlantic Translations* (2000).

MICHAEL D. C. DROUT is assistant professor of English at Wheaton College, where he teaches medieval literature and Anglo-Saxon as well as fantasy literature and science fiction. He recently completed an edition of *Beowulf and the Critics*, a previously unpublished manuscript of *Beowulf* criticism written by J. R. R. Tolkien in the 1930s. His publications include articles on *Piers Plowman*, Ken Kesey, Susan Cooper, and the Old English poem "The Fortunes of Men." Drout is currently completing a book on tradition and cultural transmission during the tenth-century English Benedictine reform.

RACHEL FORDYCE is the vice chancellor for academic affairs at the University of Hawai'i, Hilo and a former executive secretary of the Children's Literature Association. She is the author of five books—on late Renaissance literature, children's theater and creative dramatics, and Lewis Carroll.

MARY GALBRAITH teaches children's literature at San Diego State University. Her research interests include the psychohistory of classic picture books, the attachment dynamics of intense scenes in children's literature, and the need for a multidisciplinary childhood studies program.

ELIZABETH LENNOX KEYSER is an associate professor of English at Hollins University, where she teaches children's literature and American literature. She is the author of *Whispers in the Dark: The Fiction of Louisa May Alcott* (1993) and Little Women: *A Family Romance* (1999) as well as the editor of *The Portable Alcott.*

FERN KORY is a professor of English at Eastern Illinois University, where she teaches courses in children's literature and early twentieth-century American literature, among others. Her current projects include a book-length study of the folk and fairy tales in the *Brownies' Book.*

KATE LAWSON is an assistant professor of English at the University of Northern British Columbia, where she teaches Victorian and children's literature.

MICHELLE H. MARTIN is an assistant professor of English at Clemson University, where she teaches children's and young adult literature and, most recently, women's studies. Her latest publication, "Postmodern Periods: Menstruation Media in the 1990s," appeared in the September 1999 issue *of The Lion and the Unicorn.*

ELIZABETH MAYFIELD teaches in the Department of English at Montclair State University in New Jersey and is a collector of American, British, and German children's books. Her current research focuses on Lord Byron and his treatment of the Bluestocking Circle, as well as on Native American fiction and mythology.

NINA MIKKELSEN is the author of *Virginia Hamilton* (1994), *Susan Cooper* (1998), *Words and Pictures: Lessons in Children's Literature and Literacies* (1999), and many essays in the area of children's multiethnic literature, including most recently "Insiders, Outsiders, and the Question of Authenticity: Who Shall Write for African-American Children?" (1998) and "Strange Pilgrimages: Cinderella Was a Trickster and Other Unorthodoxies of American and African American Heroic Figures" in *The Heroic Figure in Popular Culture* (2000).

PHILIP NEL is an assistant professor of English at Kansas State University, where he teaches courses in children's literature and in contemporary American literature. His articles have appeared in *Children's Literature, Modern Fiction Studies,* and *The Dictionary of Literary Biography.* He is working on a biography of Crockett Johnson.

CLAUDIA NELSON is an associate professor of English at Southwest Texas State University, where she teaches children's literature and Victorian studies. She is currently at work on her fifth book, a study of representations of adoption and foster care in American texts between 1851 and 1929.

KEN PARILLE is completing his Ph.D. at the University of Virginia. His essay on Laurie and *Little Women* comes from his dissertation, which focuses on boyhood in the United States from 1835 until 1870. He has recently contributed to the *Louisa May Alcott Encyclopedia.*

JULIE PFEIFFER is an assistant professor of English at Hollins University, where she teaches English and women's studies. Her work focuses on gender and children's and women's literatures.

DONELLE RUWE is an assistant professor of English at Fitchburg State College, Massachusetts, where she teaches British literature, romanticism, and poetry. She has published articles on Charlotte Smith, Felicia Hemans, Sara Coleridge, Mary Lamb, and Charles Lamb. She is on the governing board of the Eighteenth- and Nineteenth-Century British Women Writer's Association and is co-editing a collection of essays titled *Re-Presenting Power: British Women Writers, 1780–1900.*

CAROLYN SIGLER is an assistant professor at San José State University, where she teaches Victorian and children's literatures.

KATHARINE CAPSHAW SMITH is an assistant professor of English at Florida International University. She is working on a book about Harlem Renaissance children's literature and an edition of Bessie Woodson Yancey's poetry and political writings.

Award Applications

The Children's Literature Association (ChLA) is a nonprofit organization devoted to promoting serious scholarship and high standards of criticism in children's literature. To encourage these goals, the Association offers various awards and fellowships annually.

ChLA Research Fellowships and Scholarships have a combined fund of $1,000 per year, and individual awards may range from $250 to $1,000, based on the number and needs of the winning applicants. The fellowships are awarded for proposals dealing with criticism or original scholarship with the expectation that the undertaking will lead to publication and significantly contribute to the field of children's literature. In honor of the achievement and dedication of Dr. Margaret P. Esmonde, proposals that deal with critical or original work in the areas of fantasy or science fiction for children or adolescents will be awarded the Margaret P. Esmonde Memorial Scholarship. The awards may be used only for research-related expenses, such as travel to special collections or materials and supplies. The annual deadline for applications is February 1. For further information and application guidelines, contact the Scholarship Chair (see address below).

In addition to fellowships and scholarships, ChLA recognizes outstanding works in children's literature annually through the following awards. The ChLA Article Award is presented for the article deemed the most noteworthy literary criticism article published in English on the topic of children's literature within a given year. The ChLA Book Award is presented for the most outstanding book of criticism, history, or scholarship in the field of children's literature in a given year.

The Phoenix Award is given to the author, or estate of the author, of a book for children published twenty years earlier that did not win a major award at the time of publication but that, from the perspective of time, is deemed worthy of special recognition for its high literary quality.

The Carol Gay Award is presented for the best undergraduate paper written about some aspect of children's literature. The annual deadline for applications is January 20.

For further information or to send nominations for any of the awards, contact the Children's Literature Association, P.O. Box 138, Battle Creek, MI 49016-0138, phone 616 965-8180; fax 616 965-3568; or by e-mail chla@mlc.lib.mi.us. This information is also at our Web site, address http://ebbs.english.vt.edu/chla.

Order Form   Yale University Press
P.O. Box 209040, New Haven, CT 06520-9040
Phone orders 1-800-YUP-READ (U.S. and Canada)

Customers in the United States and Canada may photocopy this form and use it for ordering all volumes of **Children's Literature** available from Yale University Press. Individuals are asked to pay in advance. All payments must be made in U.S. dollars. We honor both MasterCard and VISA. Checks should be made payable to Yale University Press.

Prices given are 2001 list prices for the United States and are subject to change without notice. A shipping charge of $3.50 for the U.S. and $5.00 for Canada is to be added to each order, and Connecticut residents must pay a sales tax of 6 percent.

Qty.	Volume	Price	Total amount	Qty.	Volume	Price	Total amount
___	10 (cloth)	$45.00	_____	___	23 (paper)	$19.00	_____
___	11 (cloth)	$45.00	_____	___	24 (cloth)	$45.00	_____
___	12 (cloth)	$45.00	_____	___	24 (paper)	$19.00	_____
___	13 (cloth)	$45.00	_____	___	25 (cloth)	$45.00	_____
___	14 (cloth)	$45.00	_____	___	25 (paper)	$19.00	_____
___	15 (cloth)	$45.00	_____	___	26 (cloth)	$45.00	_____
___	15 (paper)	$19.00	_____	___	26 (paper)	$19.00	_____
___	16 (paper)	$19.00	_____	___	27 (cloth)	$50.00	_____
___	17 (cloth)	$45.00	_____	___	27 (paper)	$18.00	_____
___	17 (paper)	$19.00	_____	___	28 (cloth)	$50.00	_____
___	20 (cloth)	$50.00	_____	___	28 (paper)	$18.00	_____
___	21 (cloth)	$45.00	_____	___	29 (cloth)	$49.00	_____
___	22 (paper)	$19.00	_____	___	29 (paper)	$19.00	_____
___	23 (cloth)	$45.00	_____				

Payment of $_____ is enclosed (including sales tax if applicable).

MasterCard no. _____

4-digit bank no. _____ Expiration date _____

VISA no. _____ Expiration date _____

Signature _____

SHIP TO: _____

_____

_____

See the next page for ordering issues from Yale University Press, London. Volumes out of stock in New Haven may be available from the London office.

Volumes 1–7 of **Children's Literature** can be obtained directly from Susan Wandell, The Children's Literature Foundation, P.O. Box 94, Windham Center, Conn. 06280.

Order Form Yale University Press, 23 Pond Street, Hampstead, London NW3 2PN, England

Customers in the United Kingdom, Europe, and the British Commonwealth may photocopy this form and use it for ordering all volumes of **Children's Literature** available from Yale University Press. Individuals are asked to pay in advance. We honour Access, VISA, and American Express accounts. Cheques should be made payable to Yale University Press.

The prices given are 2001 list prices for the United Kingdom and are subject to change. A post and packing charge of £1.95 is to be added to each order.

Qty.	Volume	Price	Total amount	Qty.	Volume	Price	Total amount
——	8 (cloth)	£40.00	——————	——	17 (paper)	£14.95	——————
——	8 (paper)	£14.95	——————	——	22 (paper)	£14.95	——————
——	9 (cloth)	£40.00	——————	——	23 (cloth)	£40.00	——————
——	9 (paper)	£14.95	——————	——	23 (paper)	£14.95	——————
——	10 (cloth)	£40.00	——————	——	24 (cloth)	£40.00	——————
——	11 (cloth)	£40.00	——————	——	24 (paper)	£14.95	——————
——	11 (paper)	£14.95	——————	——	25 (cloth)	£40.00	——————
——	12 (cloth)	£40.00	——————	——	25 (paper)	£14.95	——————
——	12 (paper)	£14.95	——————	——	26 (cloth)	£40.00	——————
——	13 (cloth)	£40.00	——————	——	26 (paper)	£14.95	——————
——	13 (paper)	£14.95	——————	——	27 (cloth)	£40.00	——————
——	14 (cloth)	£40.00	——————	——	27 (paper)	£14.95	——————
——	14 (paper)	£14.95	——————	——	28 (cloth)	£40.00	——————
——	15 (cloth)	£40.00	——————	——	28 (paper)	£14.95	——————
——	15 (paper)	£14.95	——————	——	29 (cloth)	£35.00	——————
——	16 (paper)	£14.95	——————	——	29 (paper)	£14.95	——————
——	17 (cloth)	£40.00	——————				

Payment of £ _____ is enclosed.

Please debit my Access/VISA/American Express account no. _____

Expiry date _____

Signature _____ Name _____

Address _____

See the previous page for ordering issues from Yale University Press, New Haven.

Volumes 1–7 of **Children's Literature** can be obtained directly from Susan Wandell, The Children's Literature Foundation, Box 94, Windham Center, Conn. 06280.